D1416323

THE VIET-NAM READER

*Articles and Documents on American Foreign Policy
and the Viet-Nam Crisis*

THE
VIET-NAM
READER

Articles and Documents
on American Foreign Policy
and the Viet-Nam Crisis

EDITED BY

Marcus G. Raskin
and
Bernard B. Fall

REVISED EDITION

RANDOM HOUSE · NEW YORK

FOR

Nicole Françoise Fall	Age 7
Erika Bay Raskin	Age 6
Elisabeth Anne Fall	Age 5
Jamin Ben Raskin	Age 2

in the hope of a better world for all children

In Memoriam

1926-1967

As this book goes to press we have learned of the death of Bernard Fall, killed by a mine in South Viet-Nam. I cannot describe the sadness which has gripped me. Fall was full of life. He was brilliant, boisterous, a gourmet who loved life, blessed with a beautiful artist wife and three children.

God, he could talk and work. He would sit in his basement library office in Washington, writing, thinking and planning his next projects. He would be on the telephone this time to the White House, next time to a young student or to a Communist diplomat, or another time to a wounded army friend he met in Viet-Nam. He was able to see through the farce of ideology; that people were people whatever their pretension, rhetoric or aspiration. He was a great teacher at Howard University, and he taught anyone who cared to see, what the effects of high policy were in the real world.

Bernard Fall loved America perhaps as only a Frenchman can love and he intended upon his return from Viet-Nam to become an American citizen even though in his last few years he became increasingly a critic of American foreign policy. It was a criticism which stemmed from an innate disgust at murder and pillage for empire. He had seen his own native France lose too much in the jungles of Viet-Nam, lose a generation of young in colonial wars, lose its purpose and part of its humanity. He saw this happening to the United States and he was appalled. Yet Bernard Fall loved that camaraderie which war creates among soldiers; a sense of common purpose and shared meanings which are felt among those who live together under the pain of death. For him, bonds of amity were created in a war situation which lesser men deprecate. Indeed, although he returned to Viet-Nam so that he could learn and write about the NLF through first-hand experience I am sure that one reason was to recapture that sense of camaraderie and seeming clarity which is felt among men at the front. He would invariably chastise me and insist that I come "visit" with him so that I would understand the meaning of civil war and the ties which develop.

The last time my wife and I saw Bernard Fall was at his home a few days before he left for Viet-Nam. Another couple also had come to say goodbye to Bernard. The man had been an AID Director of a province in Viet-Nam whom Fall had met during his last visit there. That man had been seriously wounded by a mine. The result of his injury was that he lost six inches of height. When that man left, a man whom Fall visited many times during his recovery period, they embraced. It was the kind of affection and caring which passes between those who know the meaning of suffering. Fall himself knew the absurdity of physical pain. A few years ago a kidney of his was removed as a result of a medical misdiagnosis.

It was in the last several years that Bernard Fall thought more deeply about the consequences and meanings of military policy. Perhaps I am saying that only because it was in the last several years that he and I came to agree on the direction that American policy was taking and the course which we thought it should take. Indeed, people in establishment Washington could not understand how we could collaborate together on a book supposedly because our perspectives were so different. As the reader will see in the revised edition our views continued to change, but as a team. More than ever our views reflected our wonderment at the absurdity of it all, the Caligula-like casualness with which the United States exercised its "restrained" policy of genocide in the name of what? and the desperate measures of the NLF.

Bernard Fall did what he had to do. He died recklessly, but he lived carefully with skill and understanding. He believed that his scholarship and empathy could only be expressed through the reckless participation of his whole being in that which he needed to understand and effect. So, my friend is dead. We are left with his books, our memories of him, and our responsibility to bring the American—Viet-Nam slaughter to an end.

Marcus G. Raskin

Washington, D.C.
February 28, 1967

ACKNOWLEDGMENTS

We wish to thank the contributors who wrote especially for this volume and those who gave permission to use their articles. This book could not have been written and collated without the aid of Jacqueline Lushin, and we acknowledge our debt to her.

Contents

Part Three   The Second Indochina War

A.   As Seen from Washington

B.   The Other Side

Introduction
to Second Edition

THE ISSUES AT STAKE

This revised edition was compiled by the editors in the summer of 1966, approximately a year after the first edition. In that period of time the Viet-Nam war escalated to the point where over one and a half billion dollars a month was spent by the United States specifically for the support of the war in Viet-Nam. Demonstrations against the war occurred in cities and major American universities. The Johnson Administration found itself faced with the Buddhists, the National Liberation Front and the military Junta of General Ky in Viet-Nam, the various effects of further escalation on the relations between the Administration and its public at home, and its allies and friends abroad. In actual fact, it heeded only its own counsel.

Since the volume was first issued in mid-1965, the expanding Vietnamese war, from being the central issue of American foreign policy, has become the central issue of American society. For those of draft age, an increasing number, it is the central issue of their lives. Considering its "ripple effect" on American society in the economic, political and social sphere, this is the first war which will affect the American society radically since the American Civil War a hundred years ago.

In the field of foreign policy for those who hoped that the

United States would act as a supporter of reconstructive rather than status quo power, the war in Viet-Nam has clouded the real interests of the United States. Our ability to work toward resolution with other nations on major political issues—such as the arms race and the economic development of poor countries—is contingent on the course of the war in Viet-Nam.

Escalation of the war in Viet-Nam, in the name of a new "globalism" has become the compulsive means to what is viewed in Washington as the best way to stop revolutionary movements from becoming Communist success stories—not only in Viet-Nam but in all of Asia and, by extension, elsewhere. This view has hardened into a policy that is committing us to a growing number of military interventions as well as an open-ended war on the Asian mainland.

But in the United States remarkably few people know anything about Viet-Nam or the character of the American involvement there. Although it can be argued that war is not the time to debate an already-made commitment, we believe it to be the obligation of a democratic nation to hold public dialogue based on facts and careful analysis, on historical evaluation and critical regard for truth, and on awareness that policies are not abstractions but realities that translate themselves into concrete actions and consequences, ultimate success or failure, possible tragedy and destruction. Thus, such discussions must be based, as President Johnson says, not only on "informed opinion" but must also take place in a moral context. Otherwise, too often the argument descends to the irrelevant technicality or the inhuman abstraction. It is our earnest hope that the reader will be able to guard against the ideological or rhetorical in analyzing the Viet-Nam crisis, since it is only in the comprehension of the political, that is, the highly particular, that the problem of Viet-Nam is capable of solution.

In this book we have attempted to present the war in Viet-Nam as a problem per se and to indicate its relationship to the continuing crisis in American foreign policy. Our purpose has been to offer the reader a sufficiently wide-ranging selection of documents and articles to provide the basis for coherent national discussion.

The fears expressed by the editors in the first edition as to the ultimate effects of an expanding Viet-Nam war—"the United

States will have become the most heavily involved nation in
the world, and yet its most isolated"—already have materialized.
Room for political military maneuvering in the context of the
old assumptions has disappeared in the shambles of the clashes
between the Saigon military and various other non-Communist
factions. More than ever before official expressions of "guarded
optimism"—though constantly recurring in official statements—
have been disproved within hours by the harsh events in Viet-
Nam itself.

The Editors have written articles and spoken out about present
policy critically but we hope constructively, advancing possible
solutions or new directions American foreign policy could take.
We believe that our view of international politics is pragmatic—
pragmatic in the philosophical sense. We are not unaware of the
importance of power in international politics. (One editor saw
its use in four guerrilla wars and one world war, the other on the
Special Staff of the National Security Council at the White
House.) But, more important, we recognize that power in a time
of great change takes on many guises. Between Martin Luther
King and Birmingham Police Commissioner "Bull" Connor,
power as it is usually measured would appear to have rested
with Connor, who had the sources of organized violence on his
side. Or, as we look at the military situation in Southeast Asia,
is there any reason to believe that power does not rest with the
United States? Yet there are many cases on record in which
those who relied on naked power have lost to the seemingly
powerless, or have destroyed themselves because they had too
narrow a view of what moves or persuades men.

In broad terms, therefore, we believe that without the context
of law and morality for the use of power, we are reduced to the
law of the jungle—or sandbox. Power, where it is used without
wisdom and only in the name of one nation, will result in the
ultimate corruption of the good ends that that nation originally
might have wished to achieve—and in the corruption of that
nation itself. In the world of nuclear weapons, irrational men,
frightened nations, rampant technology, and permanent revolution, it is the foolish nation indeed which attempts to arrogate
to itself the role of world policeman or moral arbiter without
recourse to what others think, do, want or need.

Thus, American foreign policy should be based on the premise that we are the rich citizen in the world community, and should pay heavy taxes to it and perform responsibility within it. As events in NATO, the Dominican Republic and Viet-Nam show, the United States should not act like a corporation running a company town.

The editors regretfully admit their overoptimism expressed in the earlier edition when they hoped that American ability to come to terms with pressing internal problems could be applied with the same empathy to the values and opinions of other nations and cultures. It is still inconceivable that the possibilities of greatness and tranquillity in our own society must be sacrificed on the altar of a foreign policy whose goals no longer are understood by its very framers, nor shared by many of their fellow-citizens and public opinion abroad.

THE VIET-NAM READER

*Articles and Documents on American Foreign Policy
and the Viet-Nam Crisis*

PART ONE

The Crisis of American Foreign Policy

INTRODUCTION

Since the Second World War it has been generally assumed by American statesmen and scholars that the United States has "world responsibilities." What "world responsibilities" have actually involved operationally has depended on who was doing the analysis. For some, the phrase was just another term for empire, in that the United States undertook benignly—as all empires invariably begin—to spread its gospel by words, aid, ideology, and, most of all, military presence. For others, the idea of world responsibility developed from the fear that if the United States did not "lead," others judged inimical to United States interests would do so. Proponents of this form of *noblesse oblige* —Dean Acheson, John Foster Dulles, McGeorge Bundy, Thomas Dodd—feared power vacuums. Thus it became a cardinal principle of American foreign policy to fill all political power vacuums, whether real or imagined, with an American presence wherever possible. In the Cold War, American presence was visualized primarily in military terms. Although economic and political methods were also used, diplomats and the military in the American government since 1945 have believed military power to be both the final arbiter and our trump card in international politics.

While this is the dominant strain in American foreign policy, voices have been raised from time to time against its root assumptions and operations. In the early days of the Cold War such disparate figures as Robert Taft and Henry Wallace argued that the United States was undercutting the possibilities for the United Nations and for working out normal relationships with the Soviet Union. The Korean War, which was a central issue in the 1952 Presidential campaign, seemed to strengthen the position of those in the nation who argued that the United States would not commit its troops to a land war in Asia. Leaders from President Eisenhower to Robert Taft to Wayne Morse tended to agree on that issue.

While our involvements in Latin America, the Middle East, Europe, and Asia intensified, the voices of dissatisfaction grew among those who had once favored American foreign policy and shaped its contours. Their fears were legion. They feared a land war in Asia, or a nuclear war over Europe. Others were disturbed by a blurring of judgment on the part of our leaders, who, it was thought, could not distinguish the important from the marginal. Still others feared that the United States was assuming a new arrogance, willing to go to any lengths, to break any international rules, in order to obtain ends that it had not carefully defined. Former architects of the U.N. thought we had overthrown all pretense of respect for the United Nations. Other critics of American foreign policy, like Richard J. Barnet, felt that the United States turned from being the reluctant but virtuous unwed mother in international politics who had "responsibility" thrust upon her, to a self-appointed custodian with a vision of world order which could be promoted only by military intervention.

One may ask whether, inherent in the origins of American Cold War policy, there were the seeds of the present policy, with which even the intellectual leaders of the power school like Hans J. Morgenthau, or the senior architect of intelligent containment, George F. Kennan, or the leaders of the internationalist school like Quincy Wright now find themselves in such disagreement.

For our present purposes the important question is how it happened that the United States found it relatively easy for those so inclined to pursue under President Johnson a "forward" foreign policy. The reason rested in part in the fact that nuclear deterrence failed. Until 1962 most people believed that there was a balance of terror in which the Great Powers contested for the world, but were deterred from armed conflict because of nuclear weapons. However, the Cuban missile crisis of 1962 taught American diplomatic and military leadership that the Soviet Union is inherently conservative when it comes to a confrontation of either a nuclear or large-scale military nature. The Soviets did not intend to defy the U.S. where it felt its vital national interests were not involved.

The United States had already learned that it had a vast nuclear superiority over the Soviet Union, that although the Soviet Union could grievously harm the United States in a nuclear war, the United States could destroy the Soviet Union with greater efficiency and ease. Further, we could mount a type of first strike on the Soviet Union which could substantially destroy its strategic delivery capability. But more important than the arithmetical nuclear superiority, the United States had brandished its nuclear capability with seeming alacrity and skill over the situations in Berlin and Cuba. It appeared that the American leadership was more willing to offer its society as hostage in the nuclear "brinkmanship" game than were the Russians. Second, the United States, under President Kennedy, Secretary of Defense McNamara and General Maxwell Taylor, had adopted the "brushfire"- or counterinsurgency-war concept which meant that the American armed forces were now prepared to intervene directly (and not through local proxies) in small wars in local situations of revolution and instability. This new "ability" intensified the illusion that the United States could solve inherently socio-political, economic, and diplomatic problems in the underdeveloped world by military means. The rise of the brushfire-war concept also coincided with the Sino-Soviet declarations of support for wars of national liberation. Both policies found themselves pitted against each other in Viet-Nam, and the unfortunate Vietnamese people became unwilling hosts and their country the test bed of this dubious experiment. Many observers, who are enamored with what the Editors believe to be an oversimplified historical parallel, tend to view Viet-Nam as a test of wills comparable to the confrontation between nazism and democracy at Munich in 1938. But very few seem inclined to find a more appropriate parallel between Viet-Nam in 1965 and Spain in 1936. There, what had started out as a social reordering was attacked on the one hand by right-wing totalitarians. On the other hand, when the democracies failed to come to the rescue of the moderates, the left-wing totalitarians took over the Loyalist side. And both sides rode roughshod over the bodies and feelings of the people whom they were supposedly "saving," in their frenzy to field-test not only their competing ideologies, but also their newest antitank guns, dive-bombers, and armored vehicles.

Some observers, such as Kennan, Raskin, and Wright, also feel that present American foreign policy may well become a test case for American democracy. Is it still possible for the United States to curb its recent penchant for military solutions to complex foreign policy problems in favor of the more conventional tools of international law, negotiation, conciliation, international organization, and effective multilateral consultation (to replace our present policy of advising our allies at the last minute of about-to-be-accomplished facts)? The sheer fact that the proponents of military intervention, like Senator Thomas Dodd, now consider themselves as true "internationalists"—and are taxed with "globalism" by such critics as Walter Lippmann—and in turn accuse their opponents of "neo-isolationism," clearly shows that a reordering of policy priorities as well as of policy methods is badly needed.

The only logical alternative to law, negotiation, and conciliation would be for the United States to get on the lonely treadmill of world-wide empire in which the measure of politics is raw power, and ever present and ever committed military force becomes the arbiter of national greatness and, eventually, of national survival in a universe divided, in Camus' terms, into victims or executioners.

QUINCY WRIGHT

Principles of Foreign Policy*

It seems particularly important to clarify in legal terms the meanings of the [United Nations] Charter principles: no use or threat of force in international relations against the territorial integrity or political independence of other states, and non-intervention in their domestic jurisdiction. The first of these seems to prohibit military attacks upon other states (either their territory or their ships at sea), thus barring the use of military force in international relations, except as provided in the Charter, in individual or collective self-defense against armed attack (Article 51) or in collective security operations under the authority of the United Nations (Article 39). Acts of so-called "indirect aggression," such as subversion, infiltration, economic assistance to guerrillas, etc., should be regarded, not as aggressions justifying military action in defense, but rather as interventions which should be dealt with by different methods.

It is difficult to draw the line between such illegitimate interventions in the domestic jurisdiction of another state and proper exertions of influence through diplomatic communication, debate in United Nations organs, and the maintenance of information agencies. It is important that states be free to develop their own models of government and economy for domestic progress without interference, but it is also important that they should be able to communicate the results of their efforts to other states in order that human progress may be promoted according to the Jeffersonian thesis that the best ideas will prevail in a free market of opinion. The problem of distinguishing proper exertions of influence from improper interventions is, however, frequently difficult to solve.

It is to be expected that the United States will seek to promote its conceptions of human dignity based on democracy and respect for civil liberties, and that the Soviet Union will seek to promote

* Excerpt from *Worldview* (publication of the Council on Religion and International Affairs), February, 1965.

its conception of human dignity through centralized planning and the development of social and economic rights of individuals. The debate on the universal declaration of human rights in the United Nations, and on covenants to implement this declaration, indicates the diversity of views on what is essential for human dignity at various stages of economic development. But the debate also indicates the possibility of gradual accommodation, if each becomes aware of the meaning of other conceptions and adapts creatively rather than insisting dogmatically on the superiority of its own traditions for everyone.

A policy directed toward the domestic realization of American values and respecting the equal rights of other countries to pursue within their territories their own values is a desirable policy; in fact, one could say that it is necessary for a stable world. In pursuing such a policy it should be realized, as it was in the early stages of American history, that every state as a matter of domestic jurisdiction enjoys the "right of revolution" and that, therefore, intervention at the request either of the recognized government or of the insurgents is not permissible when domestic strife exists in a foreign country. The theory that such intervention on request of the recognized government is permissible denies the right of revolution and encourages intervention in behalf of the insurgents, thus escalating internal to international war. On the other hand, intervention at the request of the insurgents denies the right of the government to govern and also invites counterintervention by other states. Nonintervention on either side in domestic strife, required by inter-American conventions and accepted by most of the powers during the Spanish civil war of the 1930's, is the only proper policy.

To pursue this policy, it is necessary sharply to distinguish civil strife from foreign aggression. Collective self-defense or intervention for collective security at the request of the United Nations in cases of aggression is, of course, permissible under the Charter. Furthermore, if in a particular situation there is danger that civil strife may, through foreign interventions and counterinterventions, develop into international war it is permissible and may be necessary for the United Nations, but not for countries individually, to intervene. Its explicit power to deal with "threats" to international peace and security permits the United Nations to take action to stop civil strife which threatens international peace as it did in the Congo, but such intervention by the United Nations is in a wholly different category from interventions by nations individually.

This outline of United States policy is based on four assumptions which many have questioned and may continue to question.

First, that policy should seek to prevent nuclear war by co-operating for the development of a world reasonably satisfactory to all, rather than by building superior power to deter others from initiating such a war. The policy of building armaments as a support of diplomatic policy, whether by a state or an alliance, leads to rivalry, because opponents will not regard such arms as intended solely for deterrence or defense. Threats to use such arms must be credible if they are to serve as instruments of mutual deterrence. A threat cannot be both credible and incredible at the same time. The problem of war concerns the whole world, not just one part of it, and it is primarily a psychological, not a technological problem.

Second, the world must be treated as a moral order rather than a natural order. In the nuclear age, states can survive only through creating a moral and legal order reasonably satisfactory to all, and thus serving the self-interest of all, rather than by conviction that survival depends on individual superiority in a struggle for existence certain to eventuate in nuclear war. Each state, in a shrinking world, must seek its security by subordinating some of its immediate interests to the long-run interest of all in a stable and peaceful world.

Third, at the present time only a world based upon the concepts of internationalism, in which sovereign states peacefully coexist and co-operate, is feasible. These concepts must take priority over concepts of isolationism, of interventionism, and even of a cosmopolitanism, whether of religion or ideology, which conceives of a human order in which state boundaries are insignificant and the human race operates as a single unit to protect the rights of man. It is possible that in a remote future such a world community, whether sustained by conscience or world government, will become feasible, but at the present time with wide diversity of cultures, conditions, and ideals in the world, efforts to make any one of these conceptions universal militates against the only possible peaceful order.

Finally, this conception of an international order rests upon a sharp distinction between domestic and international questions, it accords each state self-determination and freedom to deal with its domestic problems, including revolutionary movements, in its own way, and it defines domestic problems as those which impose upon the state no international obligations. If international obligations exist, their maintenance through diplomacy, the United Nations, or adjudication should be accepted by all states and not considered encroachments upon their domestic jurisdictions.

While situations, such as those in Viet-Nam and Santo Domingo, are complex, the policy for dealing with them, which would flow from these assumptions, is fairly clear. In both of these areas the basic situation is that of civil strife and the United States should not have intervened with armed force or otherwise unless there were very strong reasons for doing so.

The only such reasons recognized by the United Nations Charter are (1) authorization by the United Nations, or (2) collective self-defense, if an outside state is supporting one side in the civil strife by armed force. The Charter, based on the principle of sovereign equality of states and nonintervention in their domestic jurisdictions, permits each to adopt whatever form of government or ideology it wants and to change that form by constitutional process or revolution. Civil strife is to be settled by each state in the exercise of its sovereignty, and other states are not permitted to intervene.

In neither Viet-Nam nor Santo Domingo has the United States been authorized to intervene by the United Nations, as it was in the case of Korea. In the Santo Domingo case a resolution proposed by the United States in the Security Council which would have left the matter to the Organization of American States (OAS) was rejected. The OAS as a regional organization is forbidden by the Charter (Article 53) to initiate "enforcement measures" without authorization of the Security Council but it has assumed mediatorial functions in Santo Domingo and has proposed to substitute an OAS force for the American Marines for policing purposes. Several OAS conventions, including those of Havana (1928) and Bogotá (1948), expressly prohibit intervention of any kind by one American state in another, especially in cases of civil strife, and the Rio treaty of 1947 forbids unilateral action of forcible character except for defense against *armed attack.* The latter convention does permit the Organ of Consultation of the OAS to authorize the use of armed force against lesser action "endangering the peace of America." A resolution of the Caracas Conference of 1954 declared that penetration of the Communist movement in an American state would endanger the peace of America, but reaffirmed that this "did not impair the inalienable right of each American state freely to choose its own form of government and economic system and to live its own social and cultural life," and did not permit "intervention on the part of any state or group of states, either directly or indirectly, in its domestic or external affairs." It has been suggested that these resolutions permit the OAS to take "preventative," if not "enforcement," measures against Communist penetration even without United Nations authorization. It seems clear, however, that the United States invasion of Santo Domingo, prior to any authorization by either the U.N. or the OAS, violated its legal obligations.

The United States has contended that South Viet-Nam is the victim of armed attack by North Viet-Nam, and that the United States is therefore justified under Article 51 of the U.N. Charter to engage in "collective self-defense" at the invitation of the government of South Viet-Nam. This argument assumes that the two Viet-Nams are independent states and they have actually functioned as such since 1954. The Geneva Conference of that date, however, recognized Viet-Nam as one state, referred to the two zones into which it was temporarily divided by the cease-fire line, and provided for an election in 1956 to effect the union. North Viet-Nam sought to arrange for this election for three years, but was frustrated by the refusal of the government of South Viet-Nam to concur, and finally sought to effect union by supporting the Viet-Cong, which included migrants from North Viet-Nam and which in 1960 began to oppose the government in Saigon by guerrilla operations. The Diem government of South Viet-Nam in Saigon took this obstructive attitude toward the election because under United States advice it had not ratified the Geneva Accord. The United States had given this advice because, as President Eisenhower said in his memoirs, it was clear that in an election, 80 per cent of the people of Viet-Nam would vote to unite under Ho Chi Minh, the President of North Viet-Nam and for years the leader of Vietnamese nationalism, although he was a Communist. Other states in the Geneva Conference—France and Great Britain—had urged, along with India, that the elections be held, and the United States, while not ratifying the Geneva Agreements, had made a unilateral statement that it favored the principle of self-determination. In view of this history, it would appear that the hostilities against the South Viet-Nam government, whether by the Viet-Cong or by North Viet-Nam, constitute civil strife, and that outside intervention is forbidden. Furthermore, the United States' contention that it has a legal commitment to defend the independence of South Viet-Nam appears to have no basis. No commitment was made except to the Diem government, which ceased to exist in 1963, and in any case the Geneva Agreements contemplated a union of the two Viet-Nams.

While presenting dubious legal justifications for its interventions, the United States seems actually to be pursuing the political policy of containing communism, which it believed might take over South Viet-Nam and Santo Domingo. The United States is, therefore, putting its policy of containment ahead of the United Nations principle of self-determination of peoples and its international obligation to refrain from aggression and from intervention in the domestic affairs of other states.

The American policy of intervening in support of anti-Communist groups in foreign states resembles the Communist policy of intervening in support of Communist groups in other states in order to win what the Communists call "wars of liberation." The Soviet Union has repudiated this policy since the death of Stalin, and has adopted a policy of "peaceful coexistence," and "non-export of revolution or counterrevolution." China, while asserting that it will not engage in armed aggression to help "wars of liberation," has indicated that it will give other forms of assistance. The United States and Communist China appear, therefore, to be the main supporters of the policy of intervention in civil strife to forward an ideology which either one favors.

DEAN ACHESON

Ethics in International Relations Today*

Is it moral to deny ourselves the use of force in all circumstances, when our adversaries employ it, under handy excuses,
whenever it seems useful to tip the scales of power against every
value we think of as moral and as making life worth living? It
seems to me not only a bad bargain, but a stupid one. I would
almost say an immoral one. For the very conception of morality
seems to me to involve a duty to preserve values outside the con-
tour of our own skins, and at the expense of foregoing much
that is desired and pleasant, including—it may be—our own
fortunes and lives.

But, however that may be, those involved in the Cuban crisis
of October, 1962, will remember the irrelevance of the supposed
moral considerations brought out in the discussions. Judgment
centered about the appraisal of dangers and risks, the weighing
of the need for decisive and effective action against considerations of prudence; the need to do enough, against the consequences of doing too much. Moral talk did not bear on the
problem. Nor did it bear upon the decision of those called upon
to advise the President in 1949 whether and with what degree
of urgency to press the attempt to produce a thermonuclear
weapon. A respected colleague advised me that it would be better
that our whole nation and people should perish rather than be
party to a course so evil as producing that weapon. I told him
that on the Day of Judgment his view might be confirmed and
that he was free to go forth and preach the necessity for salvation. It was not, however, a view which I could entertain as a
public servant.

What, then, is the sound approach to questions of foreign
policy? I suggest that it is what we might call the strategic approach—to consider various courses of action from the point of
view of their bearing upon major objectives. On August 22,

---

* Excerpts from an address at Amherst College, December 9, 1964.

1862, President Lincoln wrote to Horace Greeley in response to the latter's question as to how the President viewed the question of slavery in relation to the war then in progress, "my paramount object in this struggle is to save the Union, and is not either to save or destroy slavery. If I could save the Union without freeing any slave, I would do it; and if I could save it by freeing all the slaves, I would do it; and if I could do it by freeing some and leaving others alone, I would also do that. What I do about slavery and the colored race, I do because I believe it helps to save this Union; and what I forbear, I forbear because I do not believe it would help to save the Union. I shall do less whenever I shall believe what I am doing hurts the cause, and I shall do more whenever I shall believe doing more will help the cause."

This is what I mean by the strategic approach. If you object that is no different from saying that the end justifies the means, I must answer that in foreign affairs only the end can justify the means; that this is not to say that the end justifies any means, or that some ends can justify anything. The shifting *combinazioni,* sought by the weak Italian city states of the Renaissance to plunder one another, not only failed to justify the means they used, but gave their diplomacy and its expounder, Niccolò Machiavelli, the bad name they have today.

The end sought by our foreign policy, the purpose for which we carry on relations with foreign states, is, as I have said, to preserve and foster an environment in which free societies may exist and flourish. Our policies and actions must be tested by whether they contribute to or detract from achievement of this end. They need no other justification or moral or ethical embellishment. To oppose powerful and brutal states which threaten the independence of others is not less admirable because it helps secure our own as well; nor is it less good to help others improve their lot because it is necessary to keep the free world free and to strengthen it.

In conducting our foreign affairs we can use any amount of intelligence, perseverance, nerve, and luck. But if we have an excess of moral or ethical enthusiasm or idealism, let us not try to find an outlet for it in the formulation of foreign policies. Rather in how we carry them out. In this country we have an unfortunate tendency to do fine and noble things in a thoroughly

churlish way. Let us remember that often what we do
less important than how we do it. "What one lives for i
uncertain," writes Lord Robert Cecil. "How one lives is not
can be faulted far less in what we do, than in how we do

GEORGE F. KENNAN

*American Involvement**

MR. HAMILTON: You conclude with this paragraph, and I
would like to quote it:

I can think of nothing we need more, at this stage, than a readiness to relax; not to worry so much about these remote countries
scattered across the southern crescent, to let them go their own way,
not to regard their fate as our exclusive responsibility, to wait for
them to come to us rather than our fussing continually over them.
The more we exert ourselves to protect them from communism, the
less the exertion they are going to undertake themselves.

The members of this subcommittee spent a good part of the
morning listening to the Defense Secretary tell us how crucial
Viet-Nam is to our interest. The question I would like to direct
to you as well as the other members of the panel is: Just how
important is Viet-Nam to the national interest of the United
States in light of this paragraph?

MR. KENNAN: In itself, if you could segregate this Viet-Nam
situation from the repercussions that it radiates in all directions,
from the factors of prestige that now became associated with it,
in itself I would not think that Viet-Nam was an area of vital
importance to this country. I can well realize that a situation has
been created there today where we could not afford simply to get
out and to turn it over to the Chinese Communists. But it is my
belief that we are seriously overextended in this world, that we

* In Report of the Subcommittee on the Far East and the Pacific, of the
Committee on Foreign Affairs, House of Representatives, released May
14, 1965.

are trying to do too much, that we are involved in too many places, that in many instances if we would only simply do what people ask and get out we would be better off and it would not be very long before others would wish we were back there again. When I read these summons for "Yankee go home" in these places, I often wish these people could be punished by having their wishes acceded to promptly and rapidly; because I don't think they really mean it, in half the instances. I think this is the only way to call their bluff. I must say: when people speak about us, about our aid and about our efforts on their behalf, in the words that we have heard from the governmental leaders in Indonesia and in Cambodia and Egypt within this last year, I think there is only one proper response on our side, and that is to say that: you people will be left so strictly alone that you will be surprised, and then really get out and leave them alone.

This is what I had in mind in writing these words. I might, if it would be permissible, read the passage just before that one ... the paragraph that came before that in the complete address, because I think it is relevant to your query here. I had said that with regard to Viet-Nam:

I would be the last to generalize about such situations, or to suggest that a hands-off policy is everywhere possible and desirable. But there is one thing we might usefully bear in mind. The surest way to invite a strong and effective Communist involvement in situations of this nature is to involve ourselves heavily, particularly in a military way.

Where we lay off, the road may be open, ostensibly, to Communist intrigue and penetration (it is usually open, no matter what we do) and there may well be take-overs by political forces that make a pretense of Marxist conviction and look to Moscow or Peiping for economic aid and political support. But this is not always so intolerable to our interests as we commonly suppose.

The less we are in the picture, the less is there any excuse for actual military intervention on the part of the Communist powers and the greater are the chances for rivalry between Moscow and Peiping for political predominance in the region concerned. But in the absence of a Communist military presence, and where this Chinese-Soviet rivalry exists, the local regimes, whether nominally Communist or otherwise, are almost bound to begin to act independently in many ways—to develop, in other words, Titoist tendencies.

And this is not always the worst solution, from our standpoint. It is harder for either Moscow or Peiping to interfere extensively with a regime that calls itself Communist than with one that does not. And since we have not engaged our prestige extensively, the situation affords to the Communist powers no such opportunities for political gains at our expense as those the Chinese and North Vietnamese Communists are now reaping in Viet-Nam.

Let me add one word to that. I would emphasize I do not mean we can just clear out everywhere in the world. I think there are situations, places, and times where we have to continue our effort. But I doubt that we will solve our world problems unless we make use of the device of laying off as well as of the device of committing ourselves. In other words, there are some places where I think we would do better to get out and let things take their course.

MR. HAMILTON: I think I understand your general view. I don't understand how you apply it to Viet-Nam, specifically now that we are as far committed as we are.

MR. KENNAN: I don't apply it to Viet-Nam in this sense: that I think we could just walk out of there today. On the other hand I think the best we can hope in this situation is that we will be able to get out with reasonable protection of the security of surrounding countries and protection of our own prestige. If any of our friends feel that they can be helpful to us in that respect through their own diplomatic efforts, I think we should not rebuff them.

MR. GALLAGHER: Ambassador Kennan, with regard to your statement and the concluding paragraph, is not our involvement in these remote areas, remote countries, small countries, a hangover we suffer from a policy that was a national policy of our country called containment?

MR. KENNAN: It is a question of how you define that policy. The definition of it which people most frequently think of is the Truman Doctrine statement, at the time of our intervention in Greece. I personally objected—I think I can safely say this now; enough time has gone by—to the wording of that statement, considered that it was too sweeping, and amounted to a promise to intervene everywhere in the world where people were threatened by communism, quite regardless of their own efforts to defend themselves and quite regardless of the prospects for success of any efforts that we may make on their behalf.

This is where I differ from this sweeping statement. I do feel very strongly, you know, that the only people really worth helping in this world are the people who say: "We propose to survive whether you help us or not, but it will be a little easier for us if you help." The ones who come along and say to us: "If you don't help us, we are going to go Communist, and then where would you be"? I think by definition are beyond helping.

MR. GALLAGHER: Our present involvement in some of these remote areas where we have troops and where we have very heavy financial commitments, such as Viet-Nam, these people are accepting very high casualties; in Korea, where the Koreans accepted very high casualties.

MR. KENNAN: But there is not just the military encounter. Unless the people are willing to give us full support in the sense of making a success of a government within their own sphere, they make it very difficult for us. . . .

MR. MC VICKER: You stated that you felt that America was heavily overextended. I presume you mean overextended in the free world, in the emerging countries, in the areas to which we have given economic and military assistance?

MR. KENNAN: Yes.

MR. MC VICKER: I am somewhat puzzled, sir, to think that America could ever be overextended when anyone needed and wanted help to gain their own liberty, their own freedom. Surely that is also the American way, isn't it?

MR. KENNAN: If this is what they really want and if they are willing to do their share and if what they want from us is within reason, I see no objection in trying to do it. I had a bit to do with the origins of the Marshall Plan and probably feel as . . . as responsible as anyone else was among the advisers at that time for this measure. I must say that I think anything we can do for other people can never be more than marginal to what they do for themselves. Unless they are willing to shoulder the overwhelming preponderance of the load, why, no good is going to come from it.

MR. MC VICKER: Where, Mr. Ambassador, is it not true? Can you add some examples where we have been asked to leave and haven't; or where we are doing a major part of the country's own work?

MR. KENNAN: Well, it seems to me that we shouldn't have had

to wait to be asked to get out in places like Cambodia and Indonesia, that we should have been out before they came along and suggested it.

MR. MC VICKER: But, sir, were we not withdrawing and cutting down on our aid extensively already in Indonesia?

MR. KENNAN: It seems to me that we were, very belatedly. I would say the greatest misgivings I have about the Viet-Nam situation is the people themselves. It seems to me that an awful lot of people there are sitting on their hands and saying "We are going to look and see who wins between the Americans and the North Vietnamese, and we will come down on the winning side when it is advantageous for us to do so."

This isn't a satisfactory attitude. I think you find that in other areas too.

MR. ZABLOCKI: Wasn't the same sort of accusation made about Yugoslavia? That is, if there were a war in Europe, Yugoslavia would sit it out, yet you did not advocate, Mr. Ambassador, that we discontinue aid to Yugoslavia?

MR. KENNAN: I am sorry. I did not favor aid programs to Yugoslavia. I was against withdrawing the most-favored-nation treaty from them. But I cannot remember pleading for any aid programs.

In fact, I folded the aid mission while I was there as Ambassador. I considered aid wasn't generally sound. I did feel we ought to be prepared to give developmental loans on satisfactory terms for dollar repayment.

MR. ZABLOCKI: There was, as I recall, quite a controversy about the sale of certain planes.

MR. KENNAN: This was not aid. These were things for which the Yugoslavs were prepared to pay in cash and there was no question of aid from our Government.

MR. ZABLOCKI: The pilots would have been trained here and the planes sold at a rather reasonable cost.

MR. KENNAN: The alternative was to scrap these planes. The planes had been purchased and paid for before I ever came there. The training of pilots was incidental to the purchase of the planes. The planes were not given to these people on an aid program. The military aid program had terminated in 1957, had been terminated at actually Yugoslav initiative, not ours.

MR. ZABLOCKI: They didn't want to meet certain requirements

that the legislation set down for the aid program, such as the supervision of end use of the items that we were giving to them. When they refused to abide by the requirements of the law, aid was discontinued.

MR. KENNAN: They came to us and they said "We don't want the aid program."

MR. ZABLOCKI: Yes, because of the conditions imposed by the law.

MR. KENNAN: It was perfectly all right. They were willing to pay after this in cash, which they did. The issue at the time I was there was whether we should sell them the supplementary equipment that went with these planes and without which the planes, for which they had already paid a couple of million dollars, were practically inoperable.

I would call your attention to this: Up to that time for some nearly fifteen years since the break with the Soviet Union they had to my knowledge purchased no military equipment from the East, only from the West. When we denied them this equipment, they began for the first time to purchase there. Personally I didn't think this was in our interest.

These planes were surplus, obsolete, and ancient. I don't think they were the ones that we had ever used since the Korean War or would ever use again. I think it was important to us to see that one of the three largest armies in Europe outside of Soviet control remained in the hands of an authority relatively independent of the Soviet Union. This is what was involved.

MR. ZABLOCKI: I didn't mean to take the gentleman's time, but I thought that Yugoslavia might possibly parallel the situation in Indonesia. Where, when we discontinue aid, they will have to obtain their assistance elsewhere.

MR. KENNAN: This is the difference between normal purchasing and aid programs. It is one thing to say to the Indonesians that "We are not going to aid you in any way. You are on your own now. What you get from us you will pay for." It is another thing to go to them with an aid program and say "You can have this for free." This is where I would draw the distinction.

MR. MC VICKER: Would it be a fair thing to say, Mr. Ambassador, that in a new program such as the Peace Corps which no country asked for because we didn't have it, once we developed the concept and the actual functioning of the Peace Corps, do

you feel this would fit into the same theory that you are ex-
pounding?

MR. KENNAN: No; I think the Peace Corps is quite different
from the thing that I had in mind. I don't think, in the first place,
that to make the Peace Corps available in another country represents a political commitment. This is my understanding that is
what it is not supposed to represent.

This is a form of assistance given for purposes quite ulterior
to the present political—

MR. MC VICKER: Are you saying that our aid program is a political program?

MR. KENNAN: It does seem to me most of these aid programs
are linked, in the manner that they are presented here on the
Hill, to our conflict with world communism.

MR. MC VICKER: I take it then that it is your position that in
most of the emerging countries of the world we sit back and wait
to see how the dynamics of the forces are going, and if they bend
in our direction and the governments decide they are going to put
in with the West, we can be friendly with them and assist them
where they wish us to and ask us to. Otherwise it might be to
our advantage to let them go in whatever direction the country
decides to go, is that right?

MR. KENNAN: I would feel this: In most instances they need us
more than we need them. If we don't show ourselves too over-
eager and press them, eventually they will come to us and we can
discuss with them perhaps in a favorable atmosphere what we
could and could not do for them. I am rather against pressing
aid programs on anyone. I don't think we can expect by our own
efforts to determine the development of political life in every one
of these countries.

I think we are going to have to recognize some of this is out of
our hands.

MR. MC VICKER: I would be interested to know, sir, if you think
this is the concept that Soviet Russia has in its aid program?

MR. KENNAN: No; I think that the Russians have fallen prey
to some of the same confusions that we have. I would, happily in
some instances, leave them to sweat with that problem just the
way that we have to.

MR. GALLAGHER: I think left hanging in the air, Ambassador,
was a statement that you made that in Viet-Nam there are many

people sitting on their hands waiting to see the outcome before they make a commitment. And that certainly is true. But I think it is also worth noting that the Vietnamese are sustaining a fatality rate in their war for independence higher than has ever been encountered by the United States.

MR. KENNAN: That certainly is a factor that involves our respect and serious consideration. . . .

MR. FRELINGHUYSEN: Mr. Ambassador, I would like very briefly to ask about your theory—and you really should be in front of the full committee which is discussing foreign aid, as you know—that perhaps we are heavily overextended in certain areas and that we should certainly avoid overcommitment.

We had, interestingly enough, the Secretary of Defense before our committee this morning. I think his testimony has been released. He talked about the indissoluble relationship between our national security and regional alliances for collective security into which we have entered. Is it your feeling that there are specific areas where we should cut back, where we are overcommitted, where there are not indissoluble relationships which require a continuation of ties?

In other words, where are we engaged in a relationship where there isn't enough effort on the part of the recipient nation, where there isn't a direct enough tie to our own national interest to justify continued aid?

MR. KENNAN: I have found it difficult to follow our involvements in various African countries, including the Congo, in recent years and I wonder really how much good we have done with all the attention and effort we have given there. In these countries in east Africa, which now seem to be making themselves vulnerable to Chinese Communist influence, it seems to me if I may put it very bluntly—and I hope this isn't too blunt—that people who take that view, who make the statements they do with regard to ourselves, who accept the sort of aid they do from the Chinese Communists, it seems to me they deserve exactly what they are going to get through an intimacy with the Chinese Communists and the Chinese Communists deserve them.

MR. FRELINGHUYSEN: That is a very facile argument, Mr. Ambassador. The trouble is that this approach may well result in a lot of Communist governments being set up. It is easy to minimize the effect of a Tito government, and perhaps there is even something admirable about it. Yet, if there is competition and there is some possibility of keeping some of these newly emerging countries at least reasonably free of these ties, as you tried to keep Yugoslavia reasonably free from unnecessary ties with the East, I don't think we should laugh it off and say this is not our responsibility.

I don't assume that is what you are trying to do.

MR. KENNAN: I wouldn't say that, either. I must say unless they know that we are capable of leaving them alone and not helping them as well as of giving them this help, I don't think we can deal effectively with these people. We are going to have to use at some point the weapon of our withdrawal and our noninvolvement as well as of a heightened involvement.

You have to use the carrot and the stick.

MR. FRELINGHUYSEN: I wouldn't want to argue about the generalities, but I am still not sure specifically what you mean. You seem to be clearly implying that perhaps we should be reappraising or should have reappraised our situation in Viet-Nam—we are back to that familiar subject again—before we got ourselves into the predicament we are now in. You also suggested, by a reference to Cambodia and Indonesia, that our withdrawal is often belated, and you have indicated that perhaps we are belated in some way in Viet-Nam.

I am not sure just what you mean with respect either to Viet-Nam or other countries. Specifically, what other countries would you apply this generality to?

MR. KENNAN: If the question with regard to Viet-Nam is whether we should have gotten involved in this way in the first place, my answer is "No." If the question is whether we can cut this involvement today without disruption, that is another question.

MR. FRELINGHUYSEN: It is easy to say we couldn't cut it abruptly. You are suggesting that we should be doing something to minimize and reduce sharply as soon as possible, with help from allies, and so on, our commitment there; are you not?

MR. KENNAN: That is correct. I think it ought to be our purpose to not be committed in that area as soon as this can be done without damage to our international position and the prospects of world peace. . . .

MR. WHALLEY: Mr. Kennan, Red China and Soviet Russia

are Communist partners. Russia would like to have coexistence, and China wants a hot war. Since China and the United States are the two principal rivals of Russia, do you think Russia would like to see us get involved in a hot war, pretty much destroying each other?

MR. KENNAN: If you had asked me that about the Chinese and whether they felt that way about the Russians and ourselves, I would be inclined to say "Yes." In the case of the Soviet Government I think that they are now experienced enough to realize that any shock to the international situation as great as that of a full-fledged state of hostilities between the Chinese and ourselves would be a very dangerous thing to all countries and particularly to the Soviet Union, and would create great embarrassment for them, because they would inevitably be confronted with the question as to what extent they should help the Chinese. Personally, I do not think they want to see hostilities between the United States and China.

MR. WHALLEY: Even though Russia would use its regular system of just supplying material and arms and not getting involved in the way of men?

MR. KENNAN: Even then it would be my view that they would not like to see it. My colleagues at this table would have views probably better founded than my own on this question, but mine is that the Russians would not want it. . . .

MR. ZABLOCKI: Ambassador Kennan, do you agree the Soviet Union has reached the state of maturity so that it will continue to turn the other cheek?

MR. KENNAN: I don't see what else it can do. I do not think that the sort of unified control over the world Communist movement that existed in Stalin's time can ever be restored within our lifetimes here. There would have to be some entirely new world situation.

This movement . . . has broken up and nobody can reassert this kind of control over it. It seems to me likely as far as influence goes, ideological influence, the Chinese are in a better position with relation to those Communist Parties which are not yet in power, outside of Europe—leave aside for a moment Europe —whereas those that are in power will tend rather to look to the Russians.

In addition to this I think the great European Communist

Parties, the Italian and the French, will probably continue to look to the Russians, because they must realize very well that they face a unique problem now in Western Europe. The old idea of revolution, as Lenin conceived it coming in Western Europe, has really gone.

Yet that is what the Chinese have in mind. The Communist movement in Europe as a revolutionary movement of a Leninist type is really today a matter of history. It just won't happen. I don't think this is satisfactory to the Russians. In fact it is a great blow to them. They don't like it.

But I don't see what they can do about it, and I don't think they see what they can do. I certainly agree it would not be worth their while at all to try to settle this problem by force of arms. To do so would be merely to split what remains of the façade of unity in this world Communist movement in I don't know how many different ways. They are simply caught. . . .

I think the Chinese figure their prospects are pretty good for taking leadership, at least in that great section of the Communist movement which consists of parties not yet arrived in power— parties that are struggling for power. There has always been a great premium in the Communist movement in being the fellow furthest to the Left. The Soviet leaders, for the first time now, are in the uncomfortable position of not being able to occupy that spot due to their own physical commitments as a going regime. This is a situation that I am sure they hate.

The Chinese have occupied it. The Chinese have outflanked them to the Left. In all these little struggling groups of people who make up the Communist Parties in various countries around the world, which are still competing for power, there are usually fanatics, soreheads, extremists of one sort or another, and the most strongly inflammatory and leftist view always has pulling power.

The Chinese have this advantage today. The Russians are aware of it and are worried about it. They see no escape from the situation.

I am sure the Chinese feel this way, and I think that by and large the Chinese will come out with greater influence or at least wider influence geographically, probably, in the world Communist movement than will the Russians, which they realize.

On the other hand, so extreme, so unreal, in terms of this

world today, is the ideological nature of the Chinese influence that I think they are going to condemn a great many of their Communist Party protégés to a lack of political success, just the way that Stalin condemned a great many of the Communist Parties in the old days to a lack of political success by insisting that they follow very unreal and inflammatory programs that didn't have great pulling power.

MR. MC DOWELL: That is true, but fundamentally the Russians, in building their real satellite countries, have never let go. They have been willing in the final analysis to throw all ideologies aside and move in with blunt, brute military force to see that they didn't lose countries that were essential to them.

MR. KENNAN: It is a question of what you mean by "lose them." It is a question of which one. They didn't move in with military force in the case of Yugoslavia. They permitted the Finns, who at one time had a Communist Ministry of the Interior, Communist control of their police, to get rid of this and to begin to behave in many respects as an independent country again.

MR. MC DOWELL: Is not their economy fully related to Russia today?

MR. KENNAN: I would not think so. I think the Finns have a good deal of their trade with the West. It is my belief that the Russians will let these Eastern European countries go very far along independent paths provided they do not do one of two things: One is to declare themselves no longer Socialist governments, in other words to get rid of the whole Marxist ideology, and the second is to cut the ties with the Warsaw Pact. That is, if any of them come up and say: "We want to leave the Warsaw Pact"—holding open the possibility that they might associate themselves with the Atlantic Pact—this would be too much for the Russians, and this in my opinion would provoke, as of today, a military intervention in any of these countries.

Outside of that, they can do, as you see today with the Rumanians and with the Hungarians, pretty much as they like.

MR. MC DOWELL: We always seem to come back to Viet-Nam. If, as you suggest, that not now, of course, but if we could have had our ifs at one time, if we had disengaged ourselves there, is there any doubt in your mind that the country would today be under the domination of the Communist Chinese regime?

MR. KENNAN: It would be under the domination of its own local Communists. I doubt there would be Chinese troops there. Perhaps if there is one generalization you can make about people in Asia, it is that they are extremely flexible and inventive politically. I dare say these local Communists would have found ways to manifest a very considerable independence of policy just in the way that the Eastern European countries are doing today. Probably not to the point of associating themselves in a military alliance with ourselves, or anything like that, but probably following the line not identical with that of the Chinese Communists.

I think this is the way of the world. I think it is very difficult for any one country to control any other great country unless it occupies it in permanence. Human nature is ornery and obstinate everywhere. This is true with Communists. Unless you sit on them with actual military or police power, the tendency is going to be for national traditions, national deviations of psychology, national interests, national pride, to assert themselves, and they will begin to act as independent governments at some point.

MR. MC DOWELL: Mr. Ambassador, I quite agree with you. But I can't get away from experiences—the hard experiences we have had in the past—that when any type of aggression was allowed to run wild, in the final analysis it had to come back to a military confrontation and we become involved in it.

MR. KENNAN: Mr. McDowell, we face, when we think back to the experiences that we had in the Stalin area, two dangers: One is to ignore those experiences entirely and forget them and behave naïvely toward these people. The other is to overrate the relevance of these experiences to the present. This is a moving situation in the Soviet Union, and the personality of this government is a great deal different today from what it was twenty years ago. There is, furthermore, a difference that is often ignored in this country—and the fact that it is ignored troubles me very much—between the sort of aggression that we were confronted with in the case of Hitler and the sort of aggression that we have faced in the case of the Soviet Union. This is the question of whether you regard all-out war, straight military attack, as your favored method of increasing your power, or whether you do it by other methods.

I have never felt that the Soviet government had intentions of embarking on an aggressive path by the same methods that Hitler used. For this reason I felt our responses, too, had to be different ones. I think this has been proven correct over the course of the years. And so far as the Soviet government is concerned, if we can get through with this present crisis over Viet-Nam in some way that does not entirely destroy our relations with the Soviet Union, we need not despair of an evolution of their policy, an evolution of the nature of Soviet power, of its attitude toward its world relationships, which would permit an improving relationship with ourselves. That is my feeling.

Since that possibility exists and since it is the only hopeful one that I can see in a world where you have loose such things as nuclear weapons, I think we should be very, very careful not to damage it.

MR. WHALLEY: Mr. Ambassador, some people in the Western world feel the United States should be more friendly with Red China, that we should trade with them, permit them to join the U.N., and this is pretty much on the theory that you catch more flies with sugar than with vinegar. What do you think?

MR. KENNAN: I don't think it would do us much good in this instance because I think we have, even over and above Viet-Nam, we have by virtue of Taiwan and Korea real political issues between ourselves and the Chinese Communist government that are so bitter, so difficult of solution today, that efforts to achieve a good relationship, ignoring them, would not appear to be very successful.

This is my own view. I do agree there are other situations where you do catch more with sugar than you do with vinegar. . . .

I see, myself, no possibility today of moving toward an improvement of our relations with the Chinese. I think their attitude does not permit it and that the conflicts we have over these areas that I have mentioned are too bitter. The point I was making here is that our present relationship with mainland China is obviously abnormal. The Chinese people are a great people, people of many wonderful qualities, and one of the great civilizing forces in the world in the past. It is not natural, and we must not assume it to be a permanent state of affairs, that so negative a relationship should exist between the American people and the

Chinese people. We have to hold in mind, therefore, the fact that some day this miserable conflict in which we are involved with these people will have to be brought to an end. Some day we will have to negotiate and arrange our affairs with the people on the Chinese mainland.

MR. ZABLOCKI: If we continue to remain firm, as has been advocated by everyone we have heard here today, how can a way then be found, unless the Chinese take the initiative?

MR. KENNAN: I think they will have to take some initiative and their views will have to change. On the other hand, I think we will have to make some changes, too. I think this will have to be eventually a compromise, an accommodation, as all settlements are in international affairs. My point in this lecture was that when we come to the day when we really try in earnest, when there may be a possibility of sitting down at a table and talking about our mutual problems with the Chinese, it will be advisable that we have a tolerable and decent relationship at that time with the Soviet Union, and that the Soviet Union not be pushed entirely over to the Chinese Communist side. In other words, I think we will find it easier to deal with the Chinese in the long run if the Russians remain in a reasonably close and intimate relationship with the West.

If this relationship is destroyed and the Russians have no choice then but to hold closely to the Chinese, our prospects for ever reaching any sort of a satisfactory accommodation with China will be much worse.

MR. ZABLOCKI: Mr. Ambassador, in your earlier statement you say that we are overextended, and now you say that we ought to make some accommodations. I gather and read into it that there would have to be some concession made to Red China, possibly trade, and how can that be justified when we hear you say that we are already overextended?

MR. KENNAN: Mr. Chairman, I am talking, in the first place, about things that would presumably happen in the far future, when a good deal more water has flowed over the dam, and when presumably their views are different, when the world situation is different. But in addition to this, the very point of such an accommodation would be to get us out of some of these extensive involvements. I would certainly hope if we ever had an accommodation with the Chinese, one effect of it would be that we not be in the sort of situation in Viet-Nam that we are in today, that this would not be necessary. I would hope the same would be true of Korea. Because I don't regard an involvement of this sort in Korea as natural and right as a permanent fixture of American policy.

MR. ZABLOCKI: Mr. Ambassador, there is no doubt in my mind that both Russia and Communist China—as a matter of fact, all Communist countries—want the United States influence to be removed from Asia? Would this be the type of accommodation that you would endorse?

MR. KENNAN: No; of course not.

MR. ZABLOCKI: If we follow your suggestion, if we reduce our Asian role and find some way out of Viet-Nam, we are in effect abdicating our role and our position in Asia and doing exactly what the Communists were hoping for many years they could accomplish.

MR. KENNAN: I hope there is no misunderstanding about it. I am not advocating we should pick up and leave Viet-Nam. But I agree with the view that has been expressed by one of our distinguished columnists in the press, that there is a lot of difference between an involvement like this one on the Asian mainland, where our whole naval power is less effective, and American involvement in the islands and off the Asian mainland. I do regard the security of the Pacific Ocean as vital to our own security, and for this reason I think we have a very vital interest in the security of the Japanese archipelago, of Taiwan and of the Philippine archipelago. It would be nice too to have in Viet-Nam a fine liberal democratic government along Western lines. But in the first place I don't see the likelihood of that, even if the Chinese Communists were not in the picture. Secondly, I don't think we are the sort of people who can supply such a government even with our military efforts. It is a question of what you have to build on. This makes a lot of difference. In Japan we have people used to independence, people with a political tradition of their own, people with enormous abilities in many ways, organizational and otherwise. This is a different proposition.

MR. MC DOWELL: All I was going to ask, Mr. Ambassador, was, and I agree with you, this is the structure, but can we afford to withdraw, can we afford to adopt, not necessarily in

South Viet-Nam, can we afford to withdraw even in our foreign-aid programs because at the moment we may not have won a popularity contest? Can we afford to show as a national posture weakness and then expect these people in this whole periphery around Asia to be reinforced in their views that they can sustain themselves without assistance?

MR. KENNAN: It is a question of the terms on which we would withdraw. I have never advocated that we do this unilaterally and without concessions on the other side. This is the same issue that exists in Europe. For years I have been known as a partisan of what is called disengagement. I think some of those countries would manage to maintain their independence even if we were not there in a military sense. I dread the assumption that we cannot maintain the type of world that is consistent with our security unless we are militarily present in every place where there may be a Communist influence. This carries very, very far and will land us in endless confusion.

MR. MC DOWELL: They still choose the point of contact. It is not by our choice. We are not confronted in South Viet-Nam militarily any more than we were confronted in Korea by our choice.

MR. KENNAN: That is true. I think there are areas where we would probably be better off not to try to contest it by our military presence.

THOMAS J. DODD

The New Isolationism*

There has been developing in this country in recent years a brand of thinking about foreign affairs which, I believe, can aptly be described as "the new isolationism." This internal phenomenon is, in my opinion, potentially more disastrous in terms of its

---

* From a speech in the Senate of the United States, February 23, 1965. See also page 164.

consequence than the major external problems that confront us.

Its background is a growing national weariness with Cold War burdens we have been so long carrying, a rising frustration with situations that are going against us in many places, a long-simmering indignation over the fact that our generosity and sacrifice have too often been met abroad, not just with indifference and ingratitude, but even with hostility and contempt.

Its political base seems to be to the Left of center, although it forms as yet a distinct minority there.

Its scareword is "escalation"; its cure-all is "neutralization."

Its prophets include some of my colleagues in the Congress, influential spokesmen in the press, and leading figures in the academic world. Some are new volunteers in this cause of retrenchment; they regard themselves as pragmatists. Others are old hands at Pollyanna-ism, those unshakable romantics who were disillusioned by Moscow at the time of the Hitler-Stalin pact, disillusioned by Mao when they discovered that he was not really an agrarian reformer, disillusioned by Castro when they learned that he was not a cross between Thomas Jefferson and Robin Hood—and who, having again dusted themselves off, now look for new vistas of adventure.

If I may digress, let me say that I have always admired their durability. The manner in which they have survived, unchastened, a whole series of intellectual Dunkirks is, if nothing else, a tribute to man's invincible confidence in himself; and their adeptness in avoiding discreditation, in the face of repeated catastrophes and evacuations, must be acknowledged as one of the marvels of modern history—a triumph of self-rectitude over reason.

The basic premise of the new isolationism is that the United States is overextended in its attempt to resist Communist aggression around the world, overcommitted to the defense of distant outposts, and overinvolved in the murky and unintelligible affairs of remote areas.

The corollaries of the new isolationism are many. It is contended that we should de-emphasize the Cold War and reverse our national priorities in favor of domestic improvements; that we should withdraw from South Viet-Nam; that we should cease involvement in the Congo; that we should relax the so-called rigidity of our Berlin policy; that foreign aid has outlived its usefulness and should be severely cut back; that our Military Establishment and our C.I.A. organizations that seem particularly suspect because they are symbols of world-wide involvement, should be humbled and "cut down to size" and stripped of their influence in foreign policy questions.

In my judgment all of these propositions have one thing in common. Each of them would strike at the heart of our national effort to preserve our freedom and our security; and collectively they add up to a policy which I can describe by no other name than "appeasement," subtle appeasement, unintentional appeasement, to be sure, but appeasement nonetheless.

My purpose, this afternoon then, is to oppose these propositions and to enlist Senators' opposition against them—for the new isolationism is as bankrupt as the old.

First of all—to tackle the main premise—I reject the assumption that the United States is overextended, or overcommitted, or overinvolved.

We are enjoying a spectacular growth in every index of national strength. Our population, our wealth, our industrial capacity, our scientific potential, our agricultural output, all are enjoying great upward surges. We were informed that our Gross National Product was again up in January, and the trend seems ever upward.

Far from overextending ourselves in the Cold War, we are actually in a period of declining defense budgets, of steadily lowered draft calls, of sharply reduced foreign aid, of one tax cut after another.

Let me emphasize this: In every basic resource, we have greater capacity today than during the past five years; by every military or economic standard, we are stronger; and by every physical measurement, the percentage of our resources going into the Cold War is lower. Why then should we talk of weariness or overcommitment?

We are not even straining ourselves. We are actually pursuing today a policy not only of both guns and butter, but of less guns and more butter.

So far as our resources go, we are capable of indefinite continuation and even intensification of our present efforts, if need be. It is only our mental, and perhaps our moral, resources which seem to be feeling the strain.

We would, of course, prefer to live in a world in which it were possible for us to have no commitments, a world in which we could devote all of our energies to the task of perfecting our society at home and enriching the lives of our people.

But we must face the world as it is. And the basic fact of our world is that Western civilization, itself terribly rent and divided, both politically and philosophically, has been forced into a twilight war of survival by a relentless and remorseless enemy.

It is incontestable, in terms of peoples enslaved and nations gobbled up over the past twenty years, that we have not been holding our own. And each year, the world Communist movement is committing more and more of its resources to the task of subjugating our allies, all around the perimeter of freedom.

Against this background it is preposterous to maintain that we should reduce our effort and lessen our commitment to the great struggle of our century.

Yet, according to *Time* magazine, it is the widespread sentiment of the academic world that we have overreached ourselves and ought to pull back. Walter Lippmann, the well-known columnist, for whom I have great respect, says that "the American tide will have to recede."

It has been argued that we would be in a "precarious situation" if we were attacked on several fronts. Of course we would, but does anyone believe that we can solve the problem by abandoning our commitments and defensive alliances? Would the loss of these countries be any the less disastrous because they were given up undefended?

On the contrary, if we are not strong enough to honor our commitments today, then we should solve the problem, not by reducing our commitments, but by becoming stronger, and by aiding our allies to become stronger.

The defense of the free world rests on a very delicate balance. The key elements in that balance are American power and American determination. If we lack the power to maintain that balance, then certainly all is lost. If we reveal that we lack the determination, if we, for instance, allow ourselves to be pushed out of Viet-Nam, such a humiliation may indeed be the second shot heard around the world; and a dozen nations might soon throw in the sponge and make whatever accommodation they could with an enemy that would then seem assured of victory.

Fortunately, at the present time we do not lack the power to carry on the defense of freedom. Our power is at its peak and we have the capacity to increase it vastly if necessary. It is our spirit, apparently, that needs shoring up.

Four years ago, after a visit to Southeast Asia, I said on the floor of the Senate:

If the United States, with its unrivaled might, with its unparalleled wealth, with its dominion over sea and air, with its heritage as the champion of freedom—if this United States and its free-world allies have so diminished in spirit that they can be laid in the dust by a few thousand primitive guerrillas, then we are far down the road from which there is no return.

In right and in might, we are able to work our will on this question. Southeast Asia cannot be lost unless we will it to be lost; it cannot be saved unless we will it to be saved.

This problem, seemingly so remote and distant, will in fact be resolved here in the United States, in the Congress, in the administration, and in the minds and hearts of the American people.

The passage of four years has not diminished my belief in this course.

If the main premise of the new isolationism is erroneous, then surely the lesser premises are fraught with terrible danger.

It is argued that we should de-emphasize the Cold War and turn more of our resources to domestic welfare.

The annual congressional revolt against the foreign aid bill grows more violent and successful each year, and the administration, forced to yield, now sends foreign aid requests 40 per cent below what it solemnly declared two years ago to be the minimum figure tolerable for free world survival.

And a small but growing band of Senators have begun offering each year amendments making across-the-board percentage cuts in our defense budget, cuts not directed to any specific economy, but rather to a principle—the principle that we should be spending less on defense and more on welfare.

Here, in my judgment, are sure-fire formulas for defeat.

Where are the victories in the Cold War that would justify such a reversal of priorities? In what global trouble spots are there lessened tensions or improved postures that would make this plausible? I can see a lot of Cold War areas where things are looking worse—but very few where things are getting better.

More effort, more sacrifice—not less—is the need of our time. And I speak as one who does not disparage the need or the importance of domestic improvements. As a credential of this I recommend to Senators my score card, compiled last year by the ultraconservative Americans for Constitutional Action, which asserts that I voted right only 13 per cent of the time— one of the worst records, alas, in the Congress.

But I say to you that if our foreign affairs are going badly, no aspect of internal welfare is secure or stable. And if we cope successfully with the great problem, the Cold War, no internal problem can long defy solution.

Our first national priority is and must ever be the survival of our country and our freedom—and if the twentieth century has taught men anything, it is that survival and freedom cannot be purchased on the cheap, in a discount store or a bargain basement.

But our situation is such that we can meet our needs both at home and abroad—not as handsomely as we would prefer, but well enough. This I take to be the objective of the Johnson Administration. The war on poverty and the struggle against tyranny can go hand in hand, if our vision be broad.

Twenty-five years ago, our country, comparatively new and untried among the great nations of the earth, through passage of the Lend-Lease Act, described by Winston Churchill as "the most unsordid act of recorded history," embarked irrevocably upon the path that has brought us to our present posture in history. Through that act, we affirmed the preservation and expansion of liberty as our highest goal; we acknowledged that freedom was insecure everywhere so long as tyranny existed anywhere; and we assumed the burden, and the glory, of being the champion and defender of man's highest aspirations.

Since that embattled hour, when the light of freedom was but a flicker in the dark, our journey across the pages of history has been fantastic and unprecedented: tragic, to be sure, in its mistakes and naïveties, but heroic in its innovations and commitments, prodigious in its energy and power, gigantic in its generosity and good will, noble in its restraint and patience, and sublime in its purpose and in its historic role.

We have not realized the high goals we set for ourselves in World War II.

But we have preserved freedom and national independence in more than half the earth; we have prevented the nuclear holocaust; we have restored Western Europe; we have helped friend and foe to achieve prosperity, freedom and stability; we have launched a world-peace organization and have kept it alive; we have offered the hand of friendship and help to the impoverished and backward peoples of the world if they will but take it.

It may be said of our country today, as of no other in history, that wherever people are willing to stand up in defense of their liberty, Americans stand with them.

We cannot know at this hour whether our journey has just begun or is nearing its climax; whether the task ahead is the work of a generation, or of a century. President Kennedy said, in his Inaugural Address, that the conflict would not be resolved in our lifetime.

The Chief of Staff of the Army recently told the Congress that it might well take ten years to decide the issue in Viet-Nam alone. And Viet-Nam is only one symptom of the disease, the epidemic, we are resisting.

Against this somber background, how foolish it is to talk of de-emphasizing the Cold War, of pulling out of Viet-Nam, of abandoning the Congo to Communist intrigue, of slashing the defense budget by 10 per cent, or of any of the other irresponsibilities of the new isolationism.

HANS J. MORGENTHAU

- We Are Deluding Ourselves in Viet-Nam*

We are militarily engaged in Viet-Nam by virtue of a basic principle of our foreign policy that was implicit in the Truman Doctrine of 1947 and was put into practice by John Foster Dulles from 1954 onward. This principle is the military containment

* From the *New York Times Magazine,* April 18, 1965. © 1965 by The New York Times Company. Reprinted by permission.

of communism. Containment had its origins in Europe; Dulles applied it to the Middle East and Asia through a series of bilateral and multilateral alliances. Yet what was an outstanding success in Europe turned out to be a dismal failure elsewhere. The reasons for that failure are twofold.

First, the threat that faced the nations of Western Europe in the aftermath of the Second World War was primarily military. It was the threat of the Red Army marching westward. Behind the line of military demarcation of 1945 which the policy of containment declared to be the western-most limit of the Soviet empire, there was an ancient civilization, only temporarily weak and able to maintain itself against the threat of Communist subversion.

The situation is different in the Middle East and Asia. The threat there is not primarily military but political in nature. Weak governments and societies provide opportunities for Communist subversion. Military containment is irrelevant to that threat and may even be counterproductive. Thus the Baghdad Pact did not protect Egypt from Soviet influence and SEATO has had no bearing on Chinese influence in Indonesia and Pakistan.

Second, and more important, even if China were threatening her neighbors primarily by military means, it would be impossible to contain her by erecting a military wall at the periphery of her empire. For China is, even in her present underdeveloped state, the dominant power in Asia. She is this by virtue of the quality and quantity of her population, her geographic position, her civilization, her past power remembered and her future power anticipated. Anybody who has traveled in Asia with his eyes and ears open must have been impressed by the enormous impact which the resurgence of China has made upon all manner of men, regardless of class and political conviction, from Japan to Pakistan.

The issue China poses is political and cultural predominance. The United States can no more contain Chinese influence in Asia by arming South Viet-Nam and Thailand than China could contain American influence in the Western Hemisphere by arming, say, Nicaragua and Costa Rica.

If we are convinced that we cannot live with a China predominant on the mainland of Asia, then we must strike at the heart of Chinese power—that is, rather than try to contain the power of China, we must try to destroy that power itself. Thus there is logic on the side of that small group of Americans who are convinced that war between the United States and China is inevitable and that the earlier that war comes, the better will be the chances for the United States to win it.

Yet, while logic is on their side, practical judgment is against them. For while China is obviously no match for the United States in over-all power, China is largely immune to the specific types of power in which the superiority of the United States consists—that is, nuclear, air and naval power. Certainly, the United States has the power to destroy the nuclear installations and the major industrial and population centers of China, but this destruction would not defeat China; it would only set her development back. To be defeated, China has to be conquered.

Physical conquest would require the deployment of millions of American soldiers on the mainland of Asia. No American military leader has ever advocated a course of action so fraught with incalculable risks, so uncertain of outcome, requiring sacrifices so out of proportion to the interests at stake and the benefits to be expected. President Eisenhower declared on February 10, 1954, that he "could conceive of no greater tragedy than for the United States to become involved in an all-out war in Indochina." General MacArthur, in the Congressional hearings concerning his dismissal and in personal conversation with President Kennedy, emphatically warned against sending American foot soldiers to the Asian mainland to fight China.

If we do not want to set ourselves goals which cannot be attained with the means we are willing to employ, we must learn to accommodate ourselves to the predominance of China on the Asian mainland. It is instructive to note that those Asian nations which have done so—such as Burma and Cambodia—live peacefully in the shadow of the Chinese giant.

This *modus vivendi*, composed of legal independence and various degrees of actual dependence, has indeed been for more than a millennium the persistent pattern of Chinese predominance on the mainland of Asia. The military conquest of Tibet is the sole exception to that pattern. The military operations at the Indian border do not diverge from it, since their purpose was the establishment of a frontier disputed by both sides.

On the other hand, those Asian nations which have allowed themselves to be transformed into outposts of American military power—such as Laos a few years ago, South Viet-Nam, and Thailand—have become the actual or prospective victims of Communist aggression and subversion. Thus it appears that peripheral military containment is counterproductive. Challenged at its periphery by American military power at its weakest—that is, by the proxy of client-states—China or its proxies respond with locally superior military and political power.

In specific terms, accommodation means four things: (1) recognition of the political and cultural predominance of China on the mainland of Asia as a fact of life; (2) liquidation of the peripheral military containment of China; (3) strengthening of the uncommitted nations of Asia by nonmilitary means; (4) assessment of Communist governments in Asia in terms not of Communist doctrine but of their relation to the interests and power of the United States.

In the light of these principles, the alternative to our present policies in Viet-Nam would be this: a face-saving agreement which would allow us to disengage ourselves militarily in stages spaced in time; restoration of the status quo of the Geneva Agreement of 1954, with special emphasis upon all-Vietnamese elections; co-operation with the Soviet Union in support of a Titoist all-Vietnamese Government, which would be likely to emerge from such elections.

This last point is crucial, for our present policies not only drive Hanoi into the waiting arms of Peking, but also make it very difficult for Moscow to pursue an independent policy. Our interests in Southeast Asia are identical with those of the Soviet Union: to prevent the expansion of the *military* power of China. But while our present policies invite that expansion, so do they make it impossible for the Soviet Union to join us in preventing it. If we were to reconcile ourselves to the establishment of a Titoist government in all of Viet-Nam, the Soviet Union could successfully compete with China in claiming credit for it and surreptitiously cooperate with us in maintaining it.

Testing the President's proposals by these standards, one realizes how far they go in meeting them. These proposals do not preclude a return to the Geneva Agreement and even assume the existence of a Titoist government in North Viet-Nam. Nor do they preclude the establishment of a Titoist government for all of Viet-Nam, provided the people of South Viet-Nam have freely agreed to it. They also envision the active participation of the Soviet Union in establishing and maintaining a new balance of power in Southeast Asia. On the other hand, the President has flatly rejected a withdrawal "under the cloak of a meaningless agreement." The controlling word is obviously "meaningless," and only the future can tell whether we shall consider any face-saving agreement as "meaningless" regardless of its political context.

However, we are under a psychological compulsion to continue our military presence in South Viet-Nam as part of the peripheral military containment of China. We have been emboldened in this course of action by the identification of the enemy as "Communist," seeing in every Communist party and regime an extension of hostile Russian or Chinese power. This identification was justified twenty or fifteen years ago when communism still had a monolithic character. Here, as elsewhere, our modes of thought and action have been rendered obsolete by new developments.

It is ironic that this simple juxtaposition of "communism" and "free world" was erected by John Foster Dulles's crusading moralism into the guiding principle of American foreign policy at a time when the national communism of Yugoslavia, the neutralism of the third world, and the incipient split between the Soviet Union and China were rendering that juxtaposition invalid.

Today, it is belaboring the obvious to say that we are faced not with one monolithic communism whose uniform hostility must be countered with equally uniform hostility, but with a number of different communisms whose hostilities, determined by different national interests, vary. In fact, the United States encounters today less hostility from Tito, who is a Communist, than from de Gaulle, who is not.

We can today distinguish four different types of communism in view of the kind and degree of hostility to the United States they represent: a communism identified with the Soviet Union —e.g., Poland; a communism identified with China—e.g., Albania; a communism that straddles the fence between the Soviet

Union and China—e.g., Rumania; and independent communism —e.g., Yugoslavia. Each of these communisms must be dealt with in terms of the bearing its foreign policy has upon the interests of the United States in a concrete instance.

It would, of course, be absurd to suggest that the officials responsible for the conduct of American foreign policy are unaware of these distinctions and of the demands they make for discriminating subtlety. Yet it is an obvious fact of experience that these officials are incapable of living up to these demands when they deal with Viet-Nam.

Thus they maneuver themselves into a position which is antirevolutionary *per se* and which requires military opposition to revolution wherever it is found in Asia, regardless of how it affects the interests—and how susceptible it is to the power— of the United States. There is a historic precedent for this kind of policy: Metternich's military opposition to liberalism after the Napoleonic Wars, which collapsed in 1848. For better or for worse, we live again in an age of revolution. It is the task of statesmanship not to oppose what cannot be opposed with a chance of success, but to bend it to one's own interests. This is what the President is trying to do with his proposal for the economic development of Southeast Asia.

Why do we support the Saigon government in the civil war against the Viet-Cong? Because the Saigon government is "free" and the Viet-Cong are "Communist." By containing Vietnamese communism, we assume that we are really containing the communism of China.

Yet this assumption is at odds with the historic experience of a millennium and is unsupported by contemporary evidence. China is the hereditary enemy of Viet-Nam, and Ho Chi Minh will become the leader of a Chinese satellite only if the United States forces him to become one.

Furthermore, Ho Chi Minh, like Tito and unlike the Communist governments of the other states of Eastern Europe, came to power not by courtesy of another Communist nation's victorious army but at the head of a victorious army of his own. He is, then, a natural candidate to become an Asian Tito, and the question we must answer is: How adversely would a Titoist Ho Chi Minh, governing all of Viet-Nam, affect the interests of the United States? The answer can only be: not at all. One can even maintain the proposition that, far from affecting adversely the interests of the United States, it would be in the interest of the United States if the western periphery of China were ringed by a chain of independent states, though they would, of course, in their policies take due account of the predominance of their powerful neighbor. . . .

Until the end of last February, the government of the United States started from the assumption that the war in South Viet-Nam was a civil war, aided and abetted—but not created—from abroad, and spokesmen for the government have made time and again the point that the key to winning the war was political and not military and was to be found in South Viet-Nam itself. It was supposed to lie in transforming the indifference or hostility of the great mass of the South Vietnamese people into positive loyalty to the government.

To that end, a new theory of warfare called "counterinsurgency" was put into practice. Strategic hamlets were established, massive propaganda campaigns were embarked upon, social and economic measures were at least sporadically taken. But all was to no avail. The mass of the population remained indifferent, if not hostile, and large units of the army ran away or went over to the enemy.

The reasons for this failure are of general significance, for they stem from a deeply ingrained habit of the American mind. We like to think of social problems as technically self-sufficient and susceptible of simple, clear-cut solutions. We tend to think of foreign aid as a kind of self-sufficient, technical economic enterprise subject to the laws of economics and divorced from politics, and of war as a similarly self-sufficient, technical enterprise, to be won as quickly, as cheaply, as thoroughly as possible and divorced from the foreign policy that preceded and is to follow it. Thus our military theoreticians and practitioners conceive of counterinsurgency as though it were just another branch of warfare like artillery or chemical warfare, to be taught in special schools and applied with technical proficiency wherever the occasion arises.

This view derives of course from a complete misconception of the nature of civil war. People fight and die in civil wars because they have a faith which appears to them worth fighting and dying for, and they can be opposed with a chance of success only by people who have at least as strong a faith.

Magsaysay could subdue the Huk rebellion in the Philippines because his charisma, proven in action, aroused a faith superior to that of his opponents. In South Viet-Nam there is nothing to oppose the faith of the Viet-Cong and, in consequence, the Saigon government and we are losing the civil war.

A guerrilla war cannot be won without the active support of the indigenous population, short of the physical extermination of that population. Germany was at least consistent when, during the Second World War, faced with unmanageable guerrilla warfare throughout occupied Europe, she tried to master the situation through a deliberate policy of extermination. The French tried "counterinsurgency" in Algeria and failed; 400,000 French troops fought the guerrillas in Indochina for nine years and failed.

The United States has recognized that it is failing in South Viet-Nam. But it has drawn from this recognition of failure a most astounding conclusion.

The United States has decided to change the character of the war by unilateral declaration from a South Vietnamese civil war to a war of "foreign aggression." "Aggression from the North: The Record of North Viet-Nam's Campaign to Conquer South Viet-Nam" is the title of a White Paper published by the Department of State on the last day of February, 1965. [See page 143 below.] While normally foreign and military policy is based upon intelligence—that is, the objective assessment of facts—the process is here reversed: a new policy has been decided upon, and intelligence must provide the facts to justify it.

The United States, stymied in South Viet-Nam and on the verge of defeat, decided to carry the war to North Viet-Nam not so much in order to retrieve the fortunes of war as to lay the groundwork for "negotiations from strength." In order to justify that new policy, it was necessary to prove that North Viet-Nam is the real enemy. It is the White Paper's purpose to present that proof. . . .

There is an ominous similarity between this technique and that applied to the expedition in the Bay of Pigs. We wanted to overthrow Castro, but for reasons of public relations we did not want to do it ourselves. So it was not done at all, and our prestige was damaged far beyond what it would have suffered had we worked openly and single-mindedly for the goal we had set ourselves.

Our very presence in Viet-Nam is in a sense dictated by considerations of public relations; we are afraid lest our prestige would suffer were we to retreat from an untenable position.

One may ask whether we have gained prestige by being involved in a civil war on the mainland of Asia and by being unable to win it. Would we gain more by being unable to extricate ourselves from it, and by expanding it unilaterally into an international war? Is French prestige lower today than it was eleven years ago when France was fighting in Indochina, or five years ago when she was fighting in Algeria? Does not a great power gain prestige by mustering the wisdom and courage necessary to liquidate a losing enterprise? In other words, is it not the mark of greatness, in circumstances such as these, to be able to afford to be indifferent to one's prestige?

The peripheral military containment of China, the indiscriminate crusade against communism, counterinsurgency as a technically self-sufficient new branch of warfare, the conception of foreign and military policy as a branch of public relations— they are all misconceptions that conjure up terrible dangers for those who base their policies on them.

RICHARD J. BARNET

The American Responsibility

The U.S. decision to rely on its own power and judgment rather than on international law and the U.N. Charter as a guide for coping with the political problems of Cold War and revolution rests on a rationalization something like this: There is a better chance of creating the possibility of a peaceful world if the U.S. uses military power when it chooses than if it takes a chance on using the machinery of international institutions to try to build a legal and moral order within which the aggressive ambitions of nations might be contained and social change might be carried out peacefully. If the exploiters of unrest: the Russians, the Chinese, Communists everywhere, could once be taught that their intervention in the new societies will not work, then the U.S., with other co-operative countries, could begin a world-wide effort of political reconstruction and reform. In the meantime, no price is too high to contain communism.

The purpose of law in any social system is to provide a framework for the fulfillment of politics. The essence of politics is that members of a society do not act to the limit of their physical power. They derive security from the presence of limits —on themselves as well as on others. Nowhere are such limits needed more than in the international society, which has always been in a state of varying degrees of disorder, but which now faces the prospect of unprecedented anarchy. Much of the world is in the process of revolution, violent and nonviolent. Two world powers, and soon three, each with the capacity to incinerate a substantial proportion of humanity, seem to be committed to dominating this revolution. Many new powers are about to obtain nuclear weapons. The very changes in international relations that have convinced U.S. leaders that international law is a luxury actually make the rebuilding of a system of legal limits a necessity for survival. We need to observe legal restraints for classic moral and social reasons: to encourage others to behave in the same way. If, as is more than likely, Russia and China see the U.S. as the principal threat to the peace, rather than its defender, they too may feel free to "pay any price" to stop us. The likely consequences of two powers claiming the role of policeman is the ruin of both.

But we also need to submit to legal limits on our power for our own health. It would appear that there is a connection between lawlessness abroad and lawlessness at home, although this is difficult to document. But what is much clearer is that in a "no-holds-barred" world the judgment of leadership is taxed beyond human capability. There are no reference points by which to judge specific decisions. Without some outside limits, the number of "options" for a powerful government is almost infinite. When everything is permitted, there is an overreach and self-destruction.

True, there is much to be said for the argument that the classic rules of international law are not adequate to the problems of the modern world. The system of international law which developed in the last 350 years was based on some premises which no longer apply. It was assumed that political relations would be carried on exclusively by princes, each representing a geographical and political unit, the nation. What happened within the boundaries of each nation was of no proper concern to any outsider. Exceptions grew up. The rules against intervention were often violated. But they were felt to be the foundation of the nation-state system, for each prince felt that his throne was safe so long as he did not interfere with what his brother princes did at home.

However, the simple formulation of nonintervention is no longer a sufficient guide to action. Within states, many groups which formerly had no influence on foreign relations now have interests in the internal affairs of other countries which their own governments cannot disregard. In the modern state, business corporations, ethnic and religious groups, humanitarian organizations, and scientific and technical groups all have a direct concern with events in the domestic life of other countries. National governments themselves are deeply involved in economic and technical assistance in many other countries for the express purpose of bringing about internal change. All countries feel free to condemn the way in which other countries treat their own minorities. The Soviet Union attacks the U.S. for segregation. The U.S. chides the U.S.S.R. for its treatment of Jews. The U.N. condemns South Africa for *apartheid*. The economic and technical interdependence of the present world means that we are involved in the affairs of others. Isolationism, or withdrawing from the world, is not a possibility. Nor is it an issue.

The truism of the shrunken planet is not an excuse for abandoning international law or the efforts to develop it. International law has evolved slowly to take account of new political realities. The U.N. Charter was a major, although inadequate, effort to cope with the requirements of the modern world. It is clear that we need new law. One often hears the argument that the great lack in the international system is some means of enforcement. We need an international law with teeth, Bernard Baruch argued in 1946. But a prior need is a set of appropriate rules to guide the behavior of states in a rapidly changing world.

The modern nation needs to know what it must do and what it must not do to fulfill its responsibility before it is in a position to police others. A policeman is just a man with a gun unless he is enforcing some legitimate law. He cannot be the source of the law himself. The U.S., either acting alone or with the proxy of others, cannot be the source of law in the modern world. Yet when we reject the old distinction between civil war and international war, and do not seek the acceptance of a rule to take its place, we are saying that we refuse to accept limitations on our actions other than what our own discretion or our weakness may dictate. This is arrogating to ourselves the role of world legislator.

As the richest nation in the world, the U.S. has the most to gain in promoting a system of law which can provide a framework for peaceful change. As the most powerful nation, our example to others is of paramount importance in shaping the future direction of international politics. In working toward a more adequate legal framework, the U.S. should build on the rules and institutions we already have. For example, in Viet-Nam the U.S. might have asked the Secretary General to investigate the situation before it became a major crisis. He could have reported to the United Nations and the international body could have proposed a specific solution or called for a conference. The Secretary General might have been asked to use his good offices to clarify the negotiating positions of the various sides which have remained obscure, or to take the initiative in arranging discussions of a possible settlement when none of the belligerents wished to be the first to make a conciliatory move. Instead, his early efforts in this direction were dismissed.

International machinery could have been used to untangle the issues and to deal with them separately. Instead of using a series of indictments of the Viet-Cong and the Hanoi government as justification for conducting an undeclared war, it might have been possible to deal with these charges as separate problems for political resolution. If the Viet-Cong are systematically killing village leaders and the local government is incapable of coping with the problem, then the U.N. should have been invited to investigate and propose solutions. The chances for finding political solutions would have been far greater if the situation in Viet-Nam had been viewed as a group of concrete issues in need of resolution rather than as a test of will. At the very least, the remedies provided by law should have been exhausted before the U.S. acted to take the law into its own hands. In neither the Dominican Republic nor Viet-Nam has the U.S. gained by its haste.

To press for political solutions to bitter conflicts, however, implies a willingness to take a chance on the outcome. When a nation supports a system for the peaceful resolution of conflict, it implicitly agrees that the system is more important than the outcome of any particular dispute. But this is pecisely the judgment the U.S. refuses to make when it defines the American Responsibility as a global mission against communism.

To accept an order based on law rather than on power, it is necessary to believe in the reality of concrete cases, i.e., that a particular set of issues can be settled in a number of conceivable ways without the world's ending. But if the U.S. regards each conflict primarily as a symbol of a global struggle, and sees the issue of ultimate victory or defeat in each crisis, whatever its cause and whatever its dimension, it can believe in no system of order other than what it can impose on others.

This concept of the American Responsibility is of course a recipe for permanent American military involvement around the world. There are no geographical limitations. Nor are there clear limitations on the amount of military power to be used. The U.S. has already hinted that it is prepared to use nuclear weapons if the war in Viet-Nam escalates. The policy is defended as a tragic choice imposed by others. It is acknowledged to be a dangerous policy, but it is justified as the only available way of "buying time."

But when the U.S. acts unilaterally in defiance of international law it does not buy time. It sets the clock back. After the crisis has passed, it cannot expect again to take up its rhetorical commitment to world order, as if nothing had happened. As the most powerful nation in the world, the U.S. creates standards of conduct by its acts. That others disregard international law is undeniable. The important question, however, is not whether the Viet-Cong or North Viet-Nam have also violated the law, but whether the United States by its acts encourages them and the rest of the world to build a system of legal limits or to throw off the few restraints that remain.

When America behaves so as to suggest the futility of building an international legal order, it must expect that the less powerful will take the hint. The Turks bomb Cyprus or the Israelis cross the border into Jordan because they are convinced that they cannot realize what they think are vital interests by peaceful means. This is not a surprising reaction when the mightiest nation on earth demonstrates that it relies on its power, rather than law or diplomacy, to achieve its will.

President Kennedy once said:

We must face the fact that the United States is neither omnipotent nor omniscient, that we cannot always impose our will on the other 94 per cent of mankind, that we cannot right every wrong or reverse each adversity, and that therefore there cannot be an American solution for every world problem.

Such an attitude is today often characterized as isolationism, but it is in fact the intellectual and moral basis for building a true internationalism. It is based on a recognition that the United States government is responsible to only 6 per cent of the world's population. Although it commands more than 50 per cent of the world's consumable resources and vastly greater power than any other nation, it cannot act for the other 94 per cent on its own initiative without taking the path of empire. A nation is a peculiarly poor instrument for securing freedom or justice for others, since national leaders scarcely understand the meaning of these terms within the context of radically different societies. A nation is not interested in good works. If it acts generously toward others, as the United States has often done, it is to promote its own defense or to extend its power. The motive for giving foreign aid to other countries has been to keep them on our side. We have believed that the world must be made safe for democracy so that democracy can flourish safely in the United States. But the irony is that a campaign to make the world safe for democracy through war strains our own democracy.

During the Cold War we have assumed realistically that we could not impose democracy, but that if we combatted and defeated communism wherever it sought to come to power in the underdeveloped world, we would at least create the possibility of democracy, or, as the current State Department formula puts it, the possibility of "a world of diversity." In practice, however, we have almost invariably fought for feudal regimes which have resisted the radical reforms which their populations have increasingly demanded. The result has been that the United States has often taken over the management of client governments. Difficult as it is to find competent officials to help run the United States, the President now must spend his time passing on the qualifications for premier, chief of state, or provincial governor in various Asian and Latin American societies in which the United States has become involved militarily. When a President conceives of the American Responsibility as converting "the moment of decision" into "the moment of action," statecraft degenerates into nothing more than permanent crisis management.

The American Responsibility must be defined differently. It should be our major task to help create a framework for tempering the violence which accompanies the modernization of ancient societies, while at the same time supporting that process. The goals of "stability" and "order" cannot be achieved by alliances with the groups in those societies whom the people wish to overthrow. If we need a slogan, it should be, "Let us make the world safe for revolution." Revolutions will occur. The challenge is to develop policies that will help to keep them from becoming pawns or battlefields for the great powers. It is strongly in our interests to develop an international climate in which nations do not engage in spasm responses to internal disorder in other countries. It is far more important to the long-run security of the United States to build an international system in which nations have the incentive to observe legitimate rules of conduct than to try to resolve each revolutionary crisis according to its preferred solution. What is needed is time to find ways to ease the world into the next century, in which familiar ideologies and the familiar patterns of nationhood will almost surely be profoundly altered.

Another aspect of the American Responsibility is the obligation to try to find out what is happening to us and to the three billion people who share the planet with us. We often defend our policy in pedagogical terms. We are teaching the Communists that aggression does not pay. We are teaching Mao Tse-tung that Wars of National Liberation are not the wave of the future. But it may be more important for us to learn than to teach. We need answers to the problem of internal violence in developing societies because such wars do threaten world peace. But fighting wars on their soil is not the answer. We need to develop a framework under which great nations can assist revolutions without taking them over. We need to find ways for international institutions to play a role both in encouraging and assisting internal change and in settling internal conflicts. We need to learn how to anticipate political and social situations which threaten to involve international violence and to cope with the causes of revolutionary war. Perhaps most difficult, we need to be able to coexist with disorder; to try to deal with it, but to recognize that many new countries may not be able to make the transition they wish without revolutionary violence.

PART TWO

The Rise of the
Viet-Nam Problem

INTRODUCTION

America's present commitment in Viet-Nam began with the collapse of the Nationalist Chinese regime on the mainland in 1949 and the North Korean attack against South Korea in June, 1950. Contrary to earlier optimistic expectations, the Chinese warlords in the western Chinese provinces of Yünnan, Ninghsia, and Tsinghai offered little resistance to the Chinese Communist forces, with the result that the latter arrived in strength at the northern rim of Southeast Asia early in 1950.

There, particularly in Viet-Nam and Laos, the French were engaged in a colonial holding operation against Ho Chi Minh and his Viet-Minh movement. Although a Communist since 1920, Ho had gathered around himself many Vietnamese nationalists who had found the French in opposition to their aspirations for nationhood. After some initial support by the Chinese Nationalists and local American missions in 1945–46, Ho Chi Minh had attempted to come to an understanding with France. His efforts had met with good will in Paris, but the French authorities in Indochina itself successfully sidetracked the intentions of their home government. There is also some evidence that Ho may have been overtaken by his own radical elements. After a series of increasingly serious incidents, the Indochina War broke out on

December 19, 1946. Cut off from the outside world—Communist as well as non-Communist—the Viet-Minh fought on in total isolation.

The arrival of the Chinese Communists on the Vietnamese border radically changed the dimensions of the problem—for both sides. On the Viet-Minh side, outside Communist support was now available, and with it the gradual "communization" of the Ho Chi Minh regime became quasi-mandatory. On the French side, the outbreak of the Korean War and the openly Communist character of the enemy served to overcome initial American reluctance to help a colonial power engaged in military operations against its own subjects: the Indochina War now became a "Crusade against Communism" and an integral part of the international power struggle. The compromise that ended the Korean War increased pressure in France for a similar compromise in Indochina—but in this case, Washington took a different view. In Korea the war ended substantially where it had begun: on the 38th Parallel; but in Viet-Nam, the thinking went, a ceasefire based on a division of the country (and no other solution seemed readily in sight) would be tantamount to handing world communism another "victory" and giving it an entrée into the "soft underbelly" of the whole Asian continent.

Hence the decision was made to provide France with vastly increased financial support, large stores of war matériel, and more military advisers and technicians (two hundred Air Force mechanics were based at Da Nang early in 1954 to service French combat aircraft) for the purpose of pursuing the war to its victorious conclusion. That policy was laid down in the Navarre Plan—named after the French commander in chief at the time, General Henri-Eugène Navarre—which was designed, in the words of the late Secretary of State John Foster Dulles, to "break the organized body of Communist aggression by the end of the 1955 fighting season." But at the onset of the 1954 "fighting season," the French already were hard-pressed by Ho Chi Minh's guerrillas and jungle-wise regulars. In the hopes of drawing the Viet-Minh forces into a set-piece battle, the French had gambled 15,000 of their best troops at a jungle valley called Dien Bien Phu, more than 220 miles behind enemy lines.

The battle began on March 13, 1954, and was to last fifty-six days, but as early as mid-April it was deemed hopeless unless the French received immediate American aid—not equipment or technicians this time, but actual combat support. At first that support was meant to consist of aerial bombardment only, but some highly placed Americans as well as some members of the French government also expected it to include combat troops on the ground, if necessary. Only a last-minute Congressional revolt, coupled with a British refusal to join, and the high reluctance of American ground-forces commanders to see their troops again drawn into an extensive land war in Asia, strengthened President Eisenhower's resolve not to commit the United States to such a course of action—as Chalmers Roberts explains.

Bernard Fall points out that while the United States did not sign the Geneva Accords of 1954, it did commit itself to respect the provisions of the accords; and so did the South Vietnamese government of Ngo Dinh Diem, whose country emerged from the proceedings divided but free of French influence. It now became Washington's decision to step into the vacuum created in Southeast Asia. In September, 1954, the Southeast Asia Treaty Organization (SEATO) was created, which included only three Asian states (Thailand, the Philippines, and Pakistan) but also the United States, Australia, New Zealand, Britain and France. A special protocol of the SEATO treaty covered the protection of the Indochina states from Communist-led "internal aggression." But the American commitment to Viet-Nam itself took on a far more specific character. On October 23, 1954, President Eisenhower sent a letter to President Ngo Dinh Diem in which he outlined certain conditional procedures under which the United States would help South Viet-Nam. Since this letter has in recent times been made a cornerstone of American policy in Viet-Nam, the study by Don and Arthur Larson on the subject adds a great deal of clarity to that important point.

Inside South Viet-Nam, however, the early bright promises of the Ngo Dinh Diem regime fell short of the mark. Far from developing into even a rudimentary democracy or, as Senator Mike Mansfield once ably put it, into a responsive, if not responsible government, the Diem regime turned increasingly oppressive. Contrary to later mythology, it was opposed not only by the guerrilla Left and the pro-colonialist Right, but also by the Catholic and Buddhist middle class from which it should logically have drawn its most important support. Eighteen of its most respectable representatives issued in April, 1960, a manifesto in Saigon (see page 98), which poignantly warned the Diem regime (and, hence, its American supporters) of the impending catastrophe. The fact that the signers included many of the men who in 1964–65 led South Viet-Nam adds to the significance of the document.

In the countryside of Viet-Nam, on the other hand, the time for respectful petitioning of the government was long past. Buddhist religious elements, disgruntled peasants, and Communist guerrillas left over from the French-Indochina War now were joined by elements who infiltrated from North Viet-Nam and who helped to shape the loosely formed opposition into the National Liberation Front of South Viet-Nam (NLFSV), known to the West by the pejorative term "Viet-Cong" (Vietnamese Communists). A new type of warfare then emerged, which at first was totally ignored in Saigon and Washington since it did not fit the preconceived notions of Communist aggression of the open Korea type. When it finally was recognized, the official view—represented here by W. W. Rostow—still tended to dismiss the socio-political components in favor of the military aspects of what now became known as "counterinsurgency."

With the implementation of the Taylor Plan late in 1961— devised by the then Military Adviser to the President and later Ambassador to South Viet-Nam, General Maxwell D. Taylor— which provided for the increased commitment of American forces to the war, a public rationale had to be found for such an expanded effort. That was supplied in two White Papers issued by the State Department, which were to prove that the deteriorating situation in South Viet-Nam was due to a concerted "aggression" from North Viet-Nam, and to that aggression only. The differences of evaluation between the two papers as to whether the war was an insurgency or an invasion reveal the contradictory attitude of United States officials toward the Viet-Nam situation. The relative thinness of the cases as then presented—the North Vietnamese commitment of men and some materials was to become more open later, as the United States commitment became more overt—was pointed up by numerous observers. But the question of who supported whom became irrelevant as the limited counterinsurgency operation in South Viet-Nam blossomed out into a full-fledged second edition of the Indochina War.

CHALMERS M. ROBERTS

The Day We Didn't Go to War *

Saturday, April 3, 1954 was a raw, windy day in Washington, but the weather didn't prevent a hundred thousand Americans from milling around the Jefferson Memorial to see the cherry blossoms—or twenty thousand of them from watching the crowning of the Cherry Blossom Queen.

President Eisenhower drove off to his Maryland mountain retreat called Camp David. There he worked on an upcoming Monday speech, designed, so the White House said, to quiet America's fears of Russia, the H bomb, domestic Communists, a depression. But that Saturday morning eight members of Congress, five Senators and three Representatives, got the scare of their lives. They had been called to a secret conference with John Foster Dulles. They entered one of the State Department's fifth-floor conference rooms to find not only Dulles but Admiral Arthur W. Radford, chairman of the Joint Chiefs of Staff, Undersecretary of Defense Roger Kyes, Navy Secretary Robert B. Anderson, and Thruston B. Morton, Dulles's assistant for Congressional Relations. A large map of the world hung behind Dulles's seat, and Radford stood by with several others. "The President has asked me to call this meeting," Dulles began.

Urgency and a Plan

The atmosphere became serious at once. What was wanted, Dulles said, was a joint resolution by Congress to permit the President to use air and naval power in Indochina. Dulles hinted that perhaps the mere passage of such a resolution would in itself make its use unnecessary. But the President had asked for its consideration, and, Dulles added, Mr. Eisenhower felt that it was indispensable at this juncture that the leaders of Congress feel as the Administration did on the Indochina crisis.

---

* From *The Reporter,* September 14, 1954. Copyright 1954 by Fortnightly Publishing Company.

Then Radford took over. He said the Administration was deeply concerned over the rapidly deteriorating situation. He used a map of the Pacific to point out the importance of Indochina. He spoke about the French Union forces then already under siege for three weeks in the fortress of Dien Bien Phu.

The admiral explained the urgency of American action by declaring that he was not even sure, because of poor communications, whether, in fact, Dien Bien Phu was still holding out. (The fortress held out for five weeks more.)

Dulles backed up Radford. If Indochina fell and if its fall led to the loss of all of Southeast Asia, he declared, then the United States might eventually be forced back to Hawaii, as it was before the Second World War. And Dulles was not complimentary about the French. He said he feared they might use some disguised means of getting out of Indochina if they did not receive help soon.

The eight legislators were silent: Senate Majority Leader Knowland and his G.O.P. colleague Eugene Millikin, Senate Minority Leader Lyndon B. Johnson and his Democratic colleagues Richard B. Russell and Earle C. Clements, House G.O.P. Speaker Joseph Martin and two Democratic House leaders, John W. McCormack and J. Percy Priest.

What to do? Radford offered the plan he had in mind once Congress passed the joint resolution.

Some two hundred planes from the thirty-one-thousand-ton U.S. Navy carriers *Essex* and *Boxer,* then in the South China Sea ostensibly for "training," plus land-based U.S. Air Force planes from bases a thousand miles away in the Philippines, would be used for a single strike to save Dien Bien Phu.

The legislators stirred, and the questions began.

Radford was asked whether such action would be war. He replied that we would be in the war.

If the strike did not succeed in relieving the fortress, would we follow up? "Yes," said the chairman of the Joint Chiefs of Staff.

Would land forces then also have to be used? Radford did not give a definite answer.

In the early part of the questioning, Knowland showed enthusiasm for the venture, consistent with his public statements that something must be done or Southeast Asia would be lost.

But as the questions kept flowing, largely from Democrats, Knowland lapsed into silence.

Clements asked Radford the first of the two key questions: "Does this plan have the approval of the other members of the Joint Chiefs of Staff?"

"No," replied Radford.

"How many of the three agree with you?"

"None."

"How do you account for that?"

"I have spent more time in the Far East than any of them and I understand the situation better."

Lyndon Johnson put the other key question in the form of a little speech. He said that Knowland had been saying publicly that in Korea up to 90 per cent of the men and the money came from the United States. The United States had become sold on the idea that that was bad. Hence in any operation in Indochina we ought to know first who would put up the men. And so he asked Dulles whether he had consulted nations who might be our allies in intervention.

Dulles said he had not.

The Secretary was asked why he didn't go to the United Nations as in the Korean case. He replied that it would take too long, that this was an immediate problem.

There were other questions. Would Red China and the Soviet Union come into the war if the United States took military action? The China question appears to have been side-stepped, though Dulles said he felt the Soviets could handle the Chinese and the United States did not think that Moscow wanted a general war now. Further, he added, if the Communists feel that we mean business, they won't go "any further down there," pointing to the map of Southeast Asia.

John W. McCormack, the House Minority Leader, couldn't resist temptation. He was surprised, he said, that Dulles would look to the "party of treason," as the Democrats had been called by Joe McCarthy in his Lincoln's Birthday speech under G.O.P. auspices, to take the lead in a situation that might end up in a general shooting war. Dulles did not reply.

In the end, all eight members of Congress, Republicans and Democrats alike, were agreed that Dulles had better first go shopping for allies. Some people who should know say that

Dulles was carrying, but did not produce, a draft of the joint resolution the President wanted Congress to consider.

The whole meeting had lasted two hours and ten minutes. As they left, the Hill delegation told waiting reporters they had been briefed on Indochina. Nothing more.

This approach to Congress by Dulles and Radford on behalf of the President was the beginning of three weeks of intensive effort by the Administration to head off disaster in Indochina. Some of those at the meeting came away with the feeling that if they had agreed that Saturday to the resolution, planes would have been winging toward Dien Bien Phu without waiting for a vote of Congress—or without a word in advance to the American people.

For some months now, I have tried to put together the bits and pieces of the American part in the Indochina debacle. But before relating the sequel, it is necessary here to go back to two events that underlay the meeting just described—though neither of them was mentioned at that meeting.

On March 20, just two weeks earlier, General Paul Ely, then French Chief of Staff and later commander in Indochina, had arrived in Washington from the Far East to tell the President, Dulles, Radford, and others that unless the United States intervened, Indochina would be lost. This was a shock of earthquake proportions to leaders who had been taken in by their own talk of the Navarre Plan to win the war.

In his meetings at the Pentagon, Ely was flabbergasted to find that Radford proposed American intervention without being asked. Ely said he would have to consult his government. He carried back to Paris the word that when France gave the signal, the United States would respond.

The second event of importance is the most difficult to determine accurately. But it is clear that Ely's remarks started a mighty struggle within the National Security Council, that inner core of the government where our most vital decisions are worked out for the President's final O.K. The argument advanced by Radford and supported by Vice President Nixon and by Dulles was that Indochina must not be allowed to fall into Communist hands lest such a fate set in motion a falling row of dominoes.

Eisenhower himself used the "row-of-dominoes" phrase at a press conference on April 7. On April 15, Radford said in a speech that Indochina's loss "would be the prelude to the loss of all Southeast Asia and a threat to a far wider area." On April 16, Nixon, in his well-publicized "off-the-record" talk to the newspaper editors' convention, said that if the United States could not otherwise prevent the loss of Indochina, then the Administration must face the situation and dispatch troops. And the President in his press conference of March 24 had declared that Southeast Asia was of the "most transcendent importance." All these remarks reflected a basic policy decision.

It is my understanding, although I cannot produce the top-secret NSC paper to prove it, that some time between Ely's arrival on March 20 and the Dulles-Radford approach to the Congressional leaders on April 3, the NSC had taken a firm position that the United States could not afford the loss of Indochina to the Communists, and that if it were necessary to prevent that loss, the United States would intervene in the war—*provided* the intervention was an allied venture and *provided* the French would give Indochina a real grant of independence so as to eliminate the colonialism issue. The decision may have been taken at the March 25 meeting. It is also my understanding that this NSC paper has on it the approving initials "D.D.E."

On March 29, Dulles, in a New York speech, had called for "united action" even though it might involve "serious risks," and declared that Red China was backing aggression in Indochina with the goal of controlling all of Southeast Asia. He had added that the United States felt that "that possibility should not be passively accepted but should be met by united action."

The newspapers were still full of reactions to this speech when the Congressional leaders, at the April 3 secret meeting with Dulles and Radford, insisted that Dulles should line up allies for "united action" before trying to get a joint resolution of Congress that would commit the nation to war.

The Secretary lost no time. Within a week Dulles talked with diplomatic representatives in Washington of Britain, France, Australia, New Zealand, the Philippines, Thailand, and the three Associated States of Indochina—Viet-Nam, Laos, and Cambodia.

There was no doubt in the minds of many of these diplomats that Dulles was discussing military action involving carriers and planes. Dulles was seeking a statement or declaration of intent designed to be issued by all the nations at the time of the U.S. military action, to explain to the world what we were doing and why, and to warn the Chinese Communists against entering the war as they had done in Korea.

In these talks Dulles ran into one rock of opposition—Britain. Messages flashing back and forth between Washington and London failed to crack the rock. Finally Dulles offered to come and talk the plan over personally with Prime Minister Churchill and Foreign Secretary Anthony Eden. On April 10, just a week after the Congressional meeting, Dulles flew off to London and later went on to Paris.

Whether Dulles told the British about either the NSC decision or about his talks with the Congressional leaders I do not know. But he didn't need to. The British had learned of the Congressional meeting within a couple of days after it happened. When Dulles reached London they were fully aware of the seriousness of his mission.

The London talks had two effects. Dulles had to shelve the idea of immediate intervention. He came up instead with a proposal for creating a Southeast Asia Treaty Organization (SEATO). Dulles felt this was the "united front" he wanted and that it would lead to "united action." He thought that some sort of *ad hoc* organization should be set up at once without waiting for formal treaty organization, and to this, he seems to have felt, Churchill and Eden agreed.

Just what the British did agree to is not clear, apparently not even to them. Dulles, it appears, had no formal SEATO proposal down on paper, while the British did have some ideas in writing. Eden feels that he made it plain that nothing could be done until after the Geneva Conference, which was due to begin in two weeks. But he apparently made some remark about "going on thinking about it" in the meantime.

At any rate, on his return to Washington Dulles immediately called a SEATO drafting meeting for April 20. The British Ambassador (who at this point had just read the Nixon off-the-record speech in the newspapers) cabled London for instructions and was told not to attend any such meeting. To cover up, the meeting was turned into one on Korea, the other topic for the Geneva Conference. Out of this confusion grew a thinly veiled hostility between Dulles and Eden that exists to this day. Dulles felt that Eden had switched his position and suspects that Eden did so after strong words reached London from Prime Minister Nehru in New Delhi.

Eden at the Bridge

A few days later, Dulles flew back to Paris, ostensibly for the NATO meeting with Eden, France's Georges Bidault, and others during the weekend just before the Geneva Conference opened.

On Friday, April 23, Bidault showed Dulles a telegram from General Henri-Eugène Navarre, then the Indochina commander, saying that only a massive air attack could save Dien Bien Phu, by now under siege for six weeks. Dulles said the United States could not intervene.

But on Saturday Admiral Radford arrived and met with Dulles. Then Dulles and Radford saw Eden. Dulles told Eden that the French were asking for military help at once. An allied air strike at the Viet-Minh positions around Dien Bien Phu was discussed. The discussion centered on using the same two U.S. Navy carriers and Philippine-based Air Force planes Radford had talked about to the Congressional leaders.

Radford, it appears, did most of the talking. But Dulles said that if the allies agreed, the President was prepared to go to Congress on the following Monday, April 26 (the day the Geneva Conference was to open) and ask for a joint resolution authorizing such action. Assuming quick passage by Congress, the strike could take place on April 28. Undersecretary of State Walter Bedell Smith, an advocate of intervention, gave the same proposal to French Ambassador Henri Bonnet in Washington the same day.

The State Department had prepared a declaration of intentions, an outgrowth of the earlier proposal in Washington, to be signed on Monday or Tuesday by the Washington ambassadors of the allied nations willing to back the venture in words. As it happened, there were no available British or Australian carriers and the French already were fully occupied. Hence the strike would be by American planes alone, presented to the world as a "united action" by means of the declaration of intentions.

Eden, on hearing all these details from Dulles and Radford, said that this was a most serious proposition, amounting to war, and that he wanted to hear it direct from the French. Eden and Dulles thereupon conferred with Bidault, who confirmed the fact that France was indeed calling desperately for help—though no formal French request was ever put forward in writing.

Eden began to feel like Horatius at the bridge. Here, on the eve of a conference that might lead to a negotiated end of the seven-year-old Indochina war, the United States, at the highly informal request of a weak and panicky French government, was proposing military action that might very well lead to a general war in Asia if not to a third world war.

Dulles's Retreat

Eden said forcefully that he could not agree to any such scheme of intervention, that he personally opposed it. He added his conviction that within forty-eight hours after an air strike, ground troops would be called for, as had been the case at the beginning of the Korean War.

But, added Eden, he alone could not make any such formal decision on behalf of Her Majesty's Government. He would fly to London at once and put the matter before a Cabinet meeting. So far as I can determine, neither Dulles nor Bidault tried to prevent this step.

Shortly after Eden flew off that Saturday afternoon, Dulles sat down in the American Embassy in Paris with his chief advisers, Messrs. MacArthur, Merchant, Bowie, and McCardle, and Ambassador Dillon. They composed a letter to Bidault.

In this letter, Dulles told Bidault the United States could not intervene without action by Congress because to do so was beyond the President's Constitutional powers and because we had made it plain that any action we might take could only be part of a "united action." Further, Dulles added, the American military leaders felt it was too late to save Dien Bien Phu.

American intervention collapsed on that Saturday, April 24. On Sunday Eden arrived in Geneva with word of the "No" from the specially convened British Cabinet meeting. And on Monday, the day the Geneva Conference began, Eisenhower said in a speech that what was being sought at Geneva was a *modus vivendi* with the Communists.

All these events were unknown to the general public at the time. However, on Sunday, the *New York Times* printed a story (written in Paris under a Geneva dateline) that the U.S. had turned down a French request for intervention on the two grounds Dulles had cited to Bidault. And on Tuesday Churchill announced to a cheering House of Commons that the British government was "not prepared to give any undertakings about United Kingdom military action in Indochina in advance of the results of Geneva" and that "we have not entered into any new political or military commitments."

Thus the Geneva Conference opened in a mood of deepest American gloom. Eden felt that he had warded off disaster and that now there was a chance to negotiate a peace. The Communists, whatever they may have learned of the behind-the-scenes details here recounted, knew that Britain had turned down some sort of American plan of intervention. And with the military tide in Indochina flowing so rapidly in their favor, they proceeded to stall.

In the end, of course, a kind of peace was made. On June 23, nearly four weeks before the peace, Eden said in the House of Commons that the British Government had "been reproached in some unofficial quarters for their failure to support armed intervention to try to save Dien Bien Phu. It is quite true that we were at no time willing to support such action . . ."

This mixture of improvisation and panic is the story of how close the United States came to entering the Indochina war. Would Congress have approved intervention if the President had dared to ask it? This point is worth a final word.

On returning from Geneva in mid-May, I asked that question of numerous Senators and Representatives. Their replies made clear that Congress would, in the end, have done what Eisenhower asked, provided he had asked for it forcefully and explained the facts and their relation to the national interest of the United States.

Whether action or inaction better served the American interest at that late stage of the Indochina war is for the historian, not for the reporter, to say. But the fact emerges that President Eisenhower never did lay the intervention question on the line. In spite of the NSC decision, April 3, 1954, was the day we *didn't* go to war.

ROBERT SCHEER and WARREN HINCKLE

The Viet-Nam Lobby*

Among the stacks of wood-based engravings filed in dusty pyramids in the *New Leader's* editorial offices is a generously-sized, full-faced reproduction of the late Ngo Dinh Diem.

The typed label on the back that used to identify Diem as "Viet-Nam's Democratic Alternative" has been torn off. The steel plate is worn from rubbing, face down, against the shellacked surface of the public school surplus-type furniture in the magazine's quarters in the old social democratic Rand School Building on New York's still-cobblestoned Fifteenth Street.

The *New Leader's* cut file is a strange place to begin the story of the "Viet-Nam Lobby," but then it is a strange story. It is the history of a small and enthusiastic group of people—including a Cardinal, an ex-Austrian Socialist leader, and a C.I.A. agent—who maneuvered the Eisenhower Administration and the American press into supporting the rootless, unpopular and hopeless regime of a despot and believed it actually was all an exercise in democracy. That this group was able to accomplish this against the better thoughts of Eisenhower and over the traditional wariness of the press is testimony to its power and its persuasiveness. Another chapter of the history of the "Viet-Nam Lobby" is how its thesis came to be accepted by a broad consensus of liberals and intellectuals in America—a consensus that only recently has begun to splinter and is still largely intact.

The thesis is based on an overriding belief in the beauty of the American way of life—and in the nefarious nature of communism. It is the belief that the only reason a nation might vote

* From *Ramparts*, July, 1965

communistic is because it hasn't been properly exposed to the democratic way of life: If a people know democracy, they will vote democratic. And if it becomes necessary on occasion to tolerate undemocratic means to achieve the ultimate democratic goal—well, it is all for the people's own good.

For the *New Leader,* a liberal, militantly anti-Communist biweekly with a strong belief in social reform, this theory was naturally applicable to the case of Diem, a firm anti-Communist. The *New Leader* in 1959 hailed Diem's "Democratic One Man Rule." To the school of liberalism where anti-communism is the *sine qua non,* the idea of a "Democratic One Man Rule" is not an anomaly.

The story of the "Viet-Nam Lobby" is a case study in American politics from the mid-1950's to the early 1960's, and the role of the *New Leader* in that period is worth singling out for special attention because the magazine played a smaller but similar role in spreading the thesis of the nation's most famous pressure group—the China Lobby. The disillusioned idealists and ex-radicals that C. Wright Mills once dubbed "The NATO intellectuals" were prominent in both lobbies. Like the *New Leader,* they were willing to believe the best about anything or anyone anti-Communist.

The history of the "Viet-Nam Lobby" dates from a meeting in a Tokyo tea room in 1950. There Wesley Fishel, a young Michigan State University political scientist, had a serious conversation with Ngo Dinh Diem. Diem was in the seventeenth year of a self-imposed exile. A sort of Catholic mandarin, he was by family background, personal inclination and training, a member of Viet-Nam's feudal aristocracy. The mandarin sense of survival called for co-operation with the French, and Diem had risen to the rank of Governor of Phat Diem Province* in the French colonial civil service. A militant anti-Communist, in 1933 he helped the French fight the Communists who were then leading the Vietnamese anti-colonial revolt. But Diem decided that France and Viet-Nam were incompatible, and went into exile. It is illustrative of his character that he chose voluntary exile rather than remain in his country and fight with the "masses" (which

---

* Official Vietnamese records show this to have been Phan Thiet Province instead.—Eds.

included the Communists) against the French. Diem was a firm believer in the ways of God dictating the acts of men. He would wait for some Hegelian force to sweep him back onto the center-stage of his country's history. Providence, in 1950, took the form of Wesley Fishel.

The young professor was impressed by Diem's long wait to rule his country and his views on independent nationalism, anti-communism and social reform. Fishel urged Diem to come to the United States to seek this government's support. When Diem agreed, Fishel arranged for Michigan State to sponsor the trip. On the Michigan State campus, Diem found kinship and support among both faculty and administration—a relationship which later developed into the university's extensive aid project to Diem's government, where a team of some twenty professors did everything from drafting his budgets to training his secret police. Outside the academic world, Diem found support in the hierarchy of the Catholic Church. Diem's brother, Bishop Can, arranged for the Vietnamese exile to stay in Maryknoll seminaries in New Jersey and New York. This was Cardinal Spellman's territory, and the Cardinal and the Vietnamese mandarin soon developed a close relationship. And no wonder. Diem was an anti-Communist *and* he was a Catholic. His brother was even a Bishop. One could not approach the Cardinal with better credentials.

In addition to the academicians and the clerics, Diem found to his surprise that he had a strong appeal with American liberals and intellectuals. When Diem was in the United States, from 1950 to 1953, Senator Joseph McCarthy was on the loose and liberals felt it mandatory to show their anti-communism. The liberal-intellectual world was still quaking from the shocks of the loss of China, the Korean War, and the conviction of Alger Hiss. To suggest dealing with Communists—*any* Communists—on any terms was unthinkable in this climate. Yet Communist forces in Asia had monopolized the undeniably popular twin battle cries: nationalism and social reform. The liberals searched for a "third way." They thought they found it in the anti-Communist Diem as the leader of a "free" Vietnam. To think that the Vietnamese people would suddenly give to an absentee aristocrat the credit and gratitude for the fruits of the twenty-year anti-colonial war the Communists had been leading against the

French was, to say the least, naïvely optimistic. It also ignored Vietnamese history. It proved disastrous. The same tragic results were to occur a decade later when, again ignoring recent history, the Kennedy-Johnson Administrations followed the same fruitless military path of the French before them.

One of the first liberals to openly champion Diem was inveterate traveler, Supreme Court Justice William O. Douglas. Justice Douglas had just returned, discouraged, from a visit to Viet-Nam. An influx of American military aid hadn't helped the French in their losing war against Ho Chi Minh's Viet-Minh forces. The Viet-Minh clearly had the support of the people; but the Viet-Minh were Communist-led, and thus clearly unacceptable as leaders of Viet-Nam. Then Douglas met Diem in Washington, and became enthusiastic. The Justice arranged a breakfast with Senators Mike Mansfield and John F. Kennedy and introduced them to Diem. Both men were taken with him. And during the next few years, before Dien Bien Phu, both Mansfield and Kennedy were extremely critical of the French presence in Viet-Nam and of the Eisenhower Administration's support of them. They called for an "independent nationalist alternative," a phrase which later was to become a cliché. Kennedy, in a major speech immediately before the Geneva Conference in April of 1954, warned against any negotiated solution that would allow participation in the Vietnamese government by Ho Chi Minh. The Communists, he said, would then eventually take over because they were so popular. Instead, he called for an independent—i.e., a democratic and anti-Communist—Viet-Nam, supported by the United States. This Viet-Nam, Diem was to lead.

The Geneva Conference, of course, called for no such thing. It affirmed the independence of the colonial government of Viet-Nam and called for an end to hostilities. A sort of interim trustee arrangement was agreed upon whereby the French would preside in the South and the Viet-Minh in the North for two years, ending in national elections in 1956 when the Vietnamese people would choose their own government. Those elections were never held because the "Viet-Nam Lobby" didn't want them. Clearly, Ho Chi Minh would have won a popular vote—and that would have been the end of the "independent nationalistic alternative."

Thus men as diverse in their backgrounds as Spellman, Douglas, and Kennedy—not to mention John Foster Dulles—came to support an aggressive policy against a popular adversary in the name of freedom and to believe in it.

The telephone operator in the Chancery was used to such things, but even she blinked a little when Cardinal Spellman picked up the telephone and said: "Get me Joe Kennedy." When these two powerful men got on the line together, one winter afternoon in 1955, they settled quickly, as men of decision do, the steps that had to be taken to swing the wavering Eisenhower Administration solidly behind the young regime of Premier Ngo Dinh Diem. The report of this extraordinary conversation comes from Joseph Buttinger, an official of the International Rescue Committee, who was sitting in Spellman's office. Buttinger had just returned from Saigon, and he brought bad news. Diem's administration was in trouble. Buttinger thought Diem was the only hope of Viet-Nam, but needed to consolidate his power. There was opposition from the Vietnamese, from the French, and from some key Americans. Diem could not survive without increased United States support, yet the present United States commitment appeared in danger of waning. Eisenhower's special Ambassador to Viet-Nam, General Lawton Collins, was openly skeptical of Diem's ability to establish a viable regime. The journalist Joseph Alsop felt Diem's base of support was too narrow to effectively rival the popular Viet-Minh. Eisenhower himself was not particularly sympathetic to Diem. The General recognized Ho Chi Minh's popularity, and was opposed to the effort to install an "alternative" as both undemocratic and of dubious success, as he later remarked in his book *Mandate for Change*.

But the Eisenhower Administration, not noted for its rigidity of purpose, was vulnerable to the political pressures marshaled by Cardinal Spellman and the elder Kennedy. Kennedy arranged for Buttinger to meet with Senator Mansfield and some key State Department personnel in Washington. His son, Senator John F. Kennedy, was in California, but Buttinger had a long conversation with the Senator's assistant, Ted Sorensen. Spellman took care of the press. He set up meetings for Buttinger with editors of the *New York Times,* the editorial board of the *Herald-Tribune,* and key editors of both *Time* and *Life.* Two days later the *Times* printed an editorial containing the Buttinger thesis.

Buttinger himself took pen in hand and wrote an article for the *Reporter* praising Diem as democracy's "alternative" in Southeast Asia.

To fully appreciate Buttinger's role in the "Viet-Nam Lobby" it is necessary to go back to Diem's ascendance to the premiership in July, 1954. The new premier from his first day in office began to crush all opposition and concentrate power within a small, nepotistic group. Diem's targets included the private armies of the religious sects, anti-Communist Vietnamese leaders who made the mistake of also being anti-Diem, and the identifiable Viet-Minh partisans remaining in South Viet-Nam. This did not make for popular acclaim but Diem wasn't looking for popularity. He knew that his base of support was minuscule, that he would have trouble with the majority of the population who had been supporting the Viet-Minh in the long war against the French. So force was the only way he could effectively ready his people for the "democratic alternative." His authoritarian tactics were not widely reported in the American press until eight years later, when he fell from favor.

Diem's strong-man rule in South Viet-Nam gave the United States two policy choices. It could keep the Viet-Minh from power, block the scheduled 1956 national elections, prevent unification of the country, hang on and trust for the best. Or it could follow the new French policy of flexibility in a hopeless situation, allow the elections, learn to live with an unquestionably greater Communist influence in Viet-Nam, and accept the necessary parallel of a lessening of Western power there.

There were arguments for both positions within the Eisenhower Administration. Helpful in pushing the United States into a "hard line" of support for the authoritarian Diem was an unusual array of visitors to Saigon in the early days of the new premier's rule.

Cardinal Spellman, who told an American Legion Convention that the Geneva agreements meant "taps" for freedom in Southeast Asia, flew to Viet-Nam to hand-deliver the first check of Catholic Relief Agency aid. Wesley Fishel, the Michigan State University professor, took up residence in the Presidential Palace and became one of Diem's chief advisers. Also bedding down in the palace was Wolf Ladejinsky, a New Dealer who had stayed on in the Agriculture Department only to be plowed under in the

McCarthy period. Diem hired Ladejinsky to study land reform, which convinced many American liberals that Diem was serious about social reforms. (These reforms proved later to be not only inefficient but laughable. Diem tried to restore the colonial property balance by returning to absentee landlords land that the bewildered peasants thought they owned—land the Communists had given them during the revolutionary period.)

Another important visitor to Diem was Leo Cherne, the president of the International Rescue Committee. Founded to help refugees from Germany in the Hitler period, the Committee turned during the Cold War to aiding refugees from Communist countries. Cherne spent two and a half weeks in Viet-Nam and came away convinced that Diem had great potential as an anti-Communist leader. He then sent his assistant, Joseph Buttinger, to set up a Viet-Nam operation for the Committee. There Buttinger met Colonel (now General) Edward Lansdale, the C.I.A.'s Man in Saigon, hero of Eugene Burdick's *The Ugly American* and villain of Graham Greene's *The Quiet American*. Lansdale, a gregarious former San Francisco advertising man who believes in "selling" the American way abroad, is given sole credit in the recent book on the C.I.A., *The Invisible Government,* for the United States support of Diem. That is not quite fair. It ignores the hard work of Cardinal Spellman and Buttinger. It was the unlikely triumvirate of the C.I.A. man, the Cardinal and Buttinger, an ex-Austrian Socialist leader, that was responsible for forming United States policy behind Diem.

Lansdale went through channels. He convinced C.I.A. Director Allen Dulles of Diem's worth. Dulles talked to his brother, the Secretary of State. And John Foster Dulles brought the word to Eisenhower.

Spellman's influence was important in certifying Diem as a solid anti-Communist, no small thing in the McCarthy era.

Buttinger made the contacts in the ex-radical and the liberal circles which were to eventually support the consensus of the "Viet-Nam Lobby" for the next six years.

Buttinger's background is important in understanding the eagerness with which he accepted Diem as the "alternative." A disillusioned Socialist, Buttinger saw in the stocky, five-foot-five premier the nationalist answer to communism that he had himself attempted to provide as an Austrian Socialist leader in the

1930's. Buttinger was then one Gustav Richter, the provincial youth leader of the Social-Democratic party which had been forced underground by the waves of victorious fascism. Buttinger fought back, but it was an embittering experience. His one accomplishment, he relates in his memoirs, *In the Twilight of Socialism,* was to halt the spread of the Communists. But just when Buttinger had reorganized his party, the Nazis goose-stepped in. He fled to Paris and then to New York, and in flight the certainty of his world of Socialist politics vanished, and so did his ideology. Buttinger did not join the Socialist Party in America, though in a continuing search for new ideas to replace his fallen Marxist certainty he dabbled in Socialist politics as an editor of *Dissent* magazine.

He took to Diem with the enthusiasm that can only be mustered by an ex-radical who, once again, has something to believe in. He had been in Viet-Nam only four days when, at Lansdale's request, he met Diem. He was to meet with him frequently during the ensuing three months. Lansdale took Buttinger under his wing and introduced him to the top security people in Diem's government and the Vietnamese Army. This convinced Buttinger that Diem had the strength to remain in power, if only the United States would give him complete support.

Before Buttinger left for the United States in December, 1954, he had several five and six hour conversations with Diem. He returned a man with a mission: to settle for nothing less than a total commitment to Diem by the United States.

With the aid of Lansdale and Cardinal Spellman, he succeeded, and the "Viet-Nam Lobby" was born.

The "Viet-Nam Lobby" was an unusual alliance of ex-Left intellectuals, conservative generals and liberal politicians. Its primary goal was to convince the public that "free Viet-Nam" was accomplishing miracles and could withstand the Red onslaught if the United States would continue its support. One year after Buttinger's return from Viet-Nam, in the fall of 1955, the "lobby" achieved a measure of formal organization with the establishment of the American Friends of Viet-Nam. The Friends, for the next six years, were in the forefront of the fight to maintain Diem's regime as a "showcase of democracy."

Like all such organizations, the American Friends of Viet-

Nam had a letterhead with a string of impressive names running in small print down the side. But the Friends' list was unusual because it was virtually a rollcall of the liberal center: Senators John F. Kennedy and Richard Neuberger, intellectuals Max Lerner and Arthur Schlesinger, Jr., Representatives Emmanuel Celler and Edna Kelly, diplomat Angier Biddle Duke. For balance, there was Socialist Norman Thomas (who has since changed his position radically) and ultraconservative J. Bracken Lee. Two famous generals, "Wild Bill" Donovan and "Iron Mike" O'Daniel, were co-chairmen.

The Friends was run by its fourteen-member executive committee. An analysis of the committee reveals a curious relationship between the Friends, the International Rescue Committee, and a New York fund raiser and public relations man named Harold Oram. The relationship is extraordinary because the executive committee of the International Rescue Committee, the executive committee of the American Friends of Viet-Nam, and Harold Oram's executive personnel were all pretty much the same people.

It was Oram, then public relations man for the International Rescue Committee and a former promoter of '30's Leftist causes, who later became associated with anti-Communist and liberal center groups, whom Buttinger first approached for help when he returned from Viet-Nam in late 1954. Oram arranged through a friend at the Catholic Relief Agency in Washington for Buttinger to meet with Cardinal Spellman.

Two months before the organization of the American Friends of Viet-Nam was announced, Oram's public relations firm signed a contract to represent the Vietnamese government for $3,000 a month plus expenses. They stayed on the job until 1961. Oram was a member of the executive committee of the American Friends of Viet-Nam. So was Elliot Newcomb, his partner at the time the contract was signed with the Diem regime. Newcomb left the firm a year later, but remained on the executive committee and was subsequently treasurer. The Executive Secretary, and later Corporation Secretary and Assistant Treasurer of the American Friends of Viet-Nam, was a young man named Gilbert Jonas—Oram's account executive and "campaign director" on the Viet-Nam account. Oram and Jonas were registered as foreign agents acting for the Republic of Viet-Nam during the same period they held key executive positions on the Friends, a seemingly independent committee dedicated to the blameless purpose of working "to extend more broadly a mutual understanding of Vietnamese and American history, cultural customs and democratic institutions."

The interlocking directorates of the International Rescue Committee and the Friends was more to be expected than the strange connection between the Republic of Viet-Nam and the Friends of Viet-Nam. Nine of the fourteen directors of the Friends were also members of the Board of Directors of the International Rescue Committee, or were its employees. Both Leo Cherne and Joseph Buttinger were on the Friends' board. Cardinal Spellman was represented by Msgr. Hartnett, a key official of the Catholic Relief Agency. Two writers for the *New Leader,* Norbert Muhlen and Sol Sanders, were also on the executive committee of the Friends. The anti-communism and quest for social reform that characterized the *New Leader* was typical of the philosophies of men on these two groups: New Deal liberals like Leo Cherne and ex-radicals like Buttinger, Oram and Jonas. Jonas later became public affairs director of the International Rescue Committee, and served on Kennedy's Presidential campaign staff in 1960 as an adviser on minority group problems.

Oram earned his $3,000 a month. Diem was not always an easy man to keep popular. His consolidation of power in Viet-Nam had authoritarian overtones, and his off-the-cuff remarks were often blatantly undemocratic. The first task of the "Viet-Nam Lobby" was to package Diem as a commodity palatable to the American public. The packaging operation assumed grand-scale proportions during Diem's triumphal "official visit" to the United States in 1957. Diem landed aboard President Eisenhower's personal plane, addressed a joint session of Congress, then took off for New York and breakfast with Cardinal Spellman. Mayor Wagner hailed him as the man "to whom freedom is the very breath of life itself." At a dinner jointly sponsored by the International Rescue Committee and the American Friends of Viet-Nam, Angier Biddle Duke presented Diem with the Admiral Richard E. Byrd Award for "inspired leadership in the cause of the free world."

Diem's American advisers took care that his speeches were liberally salted with democratic clichés. Many of Diem's speeches were written by Buttinger, others by Sol Sanders. Sanders, a Friends' director who was writing articles on Southeast Asia for the *New Leader,* had been close to Diem when the Vietnamese leader was in exile in America during the early 1950's. They enjoyed a poignant reunion, recalling those more difficult times when both were low on funds and Diem would come into New York by train from the Maryknoll seminary in Ossining and have tea with Sanders in a Greenwich Village café. (Sanders, now an Asia correspondent for *U. S. News and World Report,* was one of Diem's few friends who remained loyal to the end—even when he fell from U.S. favor. To Sanders' credit, he resigned from the American Friends of Viet-Nam when the executive committee fired off a congratulatory telegram to the generals who had deposed and murdered Diem. The telegram arrived while Diem's body was still, literally, warm.) But in 1957 Diem was the certified President of South Viet-Nam, and during three years in office had managed to crush rival religious sects and independent politicians and surround himself with a court of American advisers—Michigan State University professors, military advisers, A.I.D. officials, Catholic Welfare aides.

Diem, however, had achieved little else in three years in office. But during his visit to America the "lobby" promoted the "miracle" myth. Everything that Diem did, or attempted, was described as a miracle. Articles appeared in magazines, from the *Reporter* to *Look,* hailing the "miracles" of political stability, land reform, refugee settlement and economic development allegedly achieved by the Diem regime. But the "miracle" was actually only a miracle of public relations.

The "Viet-Nam Lobby" also perpetuated a second myth—that free elections for all Viet-Nam, which would include the Communists, and called for in the Geneva Agreements, were simply a means of enslaving the free people of Viet-Nam. Since the Communist-backed Viet-Minh would almost certainly win, because they had "duped" the populace, the United States was actually striking a blow for freedom by keeping the people of Viet-Nam from holding a national election. We were "saving" them from themselves, and at the same time teaching them the golden way of American democracy through Diem's "showcase" government. This type of rationale Kipling used to write poems about.

In many ways the most important of the myths promoted by the "Viet-Nam Lobby" was the refugee myth. The dramatic story of one million refugees fleeing to the South from the Communist North supported the theory of the North Viet-Nam leaders as "devils" and Diem's regime as the sanctuary of freedom. Naïve, well-meaning publicists like Dr. Tom Dooley projected this view with extraordinary success in the United States (*Ramparts,* January, 1965). What Americans were not told was that the refugees were almost all Catholics, many of whom had fought with the French against the Communist Viet-Minh, and who realized they could get better treatment under the Catholic Diem. These refugees were settled and well cared for through extensive American aid, becoming a privileged minority in South Viet-Nam. But Diem had to use repressive police measures to keep in line the remainder of the population (thirteen million) which did not share the Catholics' visceral hatred of communism, and in fact were sympathetic toward the Viet-Minh. It took an equally dramatic event—the protest of self-immolation by a Buddhist monk —to center attention on Diem's preferential treatment of the Catholic minority.

The "lobby" had a myth for almost every occasion. When things began to go badly for Diem in 1961, the Kennedy Administration rationalized the radical increase in this nation's military involvement in Viet-Nam by adhering to the myth that aggression by the Communists had wrecked Diem's progressive programs, and even forced him to adopt some totalitarian means —temporarily, because of the crisis, of course. So persuasive and pervasive were the myths postulated by the "Viet-Nam Lobby" that few people were willing to believe that the source of the trouble might lie with Diem himself.

The crowd in Madison Square Garden was dressed like it was a coming-out party instead of a political rally. But the tweeds and swept-back coiffures were proper because the Young Americans for Freedom's big "Tshombe Freedom Rally" in October of 1962 was something of a coronation ceremony: the right-wing college group was presenting awards to its heroes. John Wayne got an award. So did John Dos Passos and Strom Thurmond. And so did Marvin Liebman.

Marvin Liebman is a forty-one-year-old ex-Communist-turned-publicist for right-wing causes—apparently a good publicist, judging from the way the Y.A.F. chose to honor him. Liebman provides an interesting link between the activities of the two great Cold War pressure groups: the China Lobby and the "Viet-Nam Lobby." A late-blooming member of the China Lobby, Liebman quit the Communist Party in 1945 but it was not until 1957, while working with the International Rescue Committee, that his politics took a sharp curve to the Right. Liebman, working for Harold Oram's public relations firm (his name appeared on Oram's stationery alongside that of Gilbert Jonas during the middle '50's), was instrumental in setting up the Committee of One Million Against the Admission of Communist China to the U.N.

Liebman became a sort of right-wing establishment man. He was Secretary of the Committee of One Million, an adviser to the Young Americans for Freedom, a collaborator with *National Review* editor William F. Buckley, Jr., in setting up the Committee for Freedom of All Peoples—which was outdone in its protest over Khrushchev's visit to the United States only by the *National Review*'s black-bordered cover.

The China Lobby, like the "Viet-Nam Lobby," fused liberal and right-wing elements in the impassioned promotion of an anti-Communist leader (for Diem, read Chiang Kai-shek), whose prime and perhaps sole qualification for leadership was his anti-communism. Ross Y. Koen, in his book *The China Lobby in American Politics* (remarkably unavailable since shortly after its 1960 publication), names among the prime outlets for pro-Chiang propaganda, *Life,* the *Reader's Digest*—and the *New Leader.*

The *New Leader*'s role in the China Lobby became a *cause célèbre* in 1963 when Senator William Fulbright's Foreign Relations Committee released testimony stating that Chiang Kai-shek's New York publicity firm had paid the *New Leader* $3000, in 1958, to publish a pro-Chiang article. There are two conflicting accounts. One was given to Senator Fulbright's Committee by Mr. Hamilton Wright, Jr., a principal in the publicity firm then working for Chiang.

. . . as I recall, they [*New Leader* editors] approached me and said, "Look, you are representing the Republic of China. We have this wonderful article that has been written, and we are going to put this out as a special supplement. Now, it is going to go; you know our circulation is to the intellectual group and, gee, we just don't have enough money to get this into print all the way. We can certainly use a contribution."[1]

The other version is the *New Leader's*. It is even more interesting because it blames the whole thing on Marvin Liebman. S. M. Levitas, the *New Leader's* longtime editor and a bitter anti-Communist out of the East European Socialist tradition, died in 1961. The magazine's new editor, Myron Kolatch, wrote Fulbright and said that a check of the files revealed no such payoff. Kolatch said that the $3000 came to the *New Leader* from the American-Asia Education Exchange in connection with an article "Communist China: Power and Prospects," by Dr. Richard L. Walker. The article was to appear in a special issue of the magazine and Levitas asked the Exchange to purchase 10,000 reprints for $3000 to help finance the issue. Levitas was a member of the Exchange. The author, Dr. Walker, was on its Board of Directors and Marvin Liebman, whom the *New York Times* described as "a publicist connected with Nationalist Chinese causes," was the Secretary-Treasurer. The Exchange, in fact, operated out of Liebman's publicity office. Kolatch said that he subsequently learned that the Exchange got the $3000 from Liebman who got it, in turn, from Chiang's publicity firm. The *New Leader*, Kolatch said, had not been aware that the funds originated in the Nationalist China camp.

The China-Lobby/"Viet-Nam Lobby" syndrome came full circle in the spring of 1964 when Liebman was revealed as the promoter of an advertisement in the Washington *Star*, signed by the parents of American soldiers killed in Viet-Nam, which called for an extension of the war.

The *New Leader*, in recent years, has lost much of the blind anti-communism which allowed it to accept too readily the positions of the China Lobby and the "Viet-Nam Lobby," according to author Paul Jacobs:

The *New Leader* today is much different than it was under Levitas. For Levitas, the primary role of the magazine was fighting the

---

[1] *Activities of Nondiplomatic Representatives of Foreign Principals in the United States,* Part 7, Page 725, Government Printing Office, Washington, 1963.

Communists and very often he subordinated all else to it. Considering the bitter experience the non-Communist Left had with the Communists, Levitas' position was understandable. But the tragedy was that it led not only to an obsession but to an inability to accept the fact that changes were taking place inside the Communist world. Today the *New Leader* does have a better understanding of the problems the world faces and an article is no longer measured only by how anti-Communist it may be.

But the *New Leader* school of anti-communism—shared in the '50's by the *Reporter* and other liberal publications and such groups as the International Rescue Committee and the Congress for Cultural Freedom—is important because it helped to shape the Cold War as we live it today. When World War II ended, the State Department and the Pentagon had to formulate policies for a world where the Communists were now the enemy—but where splinter socialist movements, both "democratic" and "undemocratic," were emerging all over Europe and Asia. It was obvious that we couldn't be against *everybody*. Instrumental in helping decide where to draw the line was the circle of ex-radicals and disillusioned intellectuals, and social democrats such as Levitas, whose principled anti-communism dated from the creation of the Third International. Where a State Department career man might be insensitive to the crimes of the Third International against the intellectuals, old Bolsheviks, and the Jews, a former East European Socialist like Levitas could speak with passion about who were the good guys and who were the bad guys— and which side the United States should support in the name of anti-communism.

The same liberals who backed Diem fought Senator Joseph McCarthy, but they fought McCarthy on his own battleground of anti-communism. This was the only ground acceptable in the hate climate of the '50's and the anti-communism of the ex-radical turned "liberal" had paramount influence in the hard line of America's postwar politics.

The "Viet-Nam Lobby" was the ultimate product of this school of liberal Cold War anti-communism. Unlike the businessmen, missionaries, and military politicians that joined the China Lobby for self-seeking reasons, the members of the "Viet-Nam Lobby" were True Believers. They were on a Crusade for Democracy. Looking at the world through anti-Red glasses, they convinced themselves that a Diem could be a democrat. They had trouble convincing Eisenhower, so they pressured his Administration into line. Then they set out to convince the country. They succeeded, and the myths that they created—that we were "asked" to step in by the Vietnamese people, that we are protecting "democracy" by blocking elections—remain long after Diem to haunt the State Department White Paper, and President Johnson's speeches.

Senator Fulbright, in a recent speech on ideology and foreign policy, cited a thought of William Makepeace Thackeray that applies with extraordinary precision to the "Viet-Nam Lobby": "The wicked are wicked, no doubt," wrote Thackeray, "and they go astray and they fall, and they come by their deserts; but who can tell the mischief which the very virtuous do?"

BERNARD B. FALL

How the French Got Out of Viet-Nam*

The war in Viet-Nam continues to escalate. Yet, above the sound of mortar fire and jet bombers, one repeatedly hears the phrase: "the essentials of the Geneva Agreements of 1954." These accords, reached almost eleven years ago on the shore of a Swiss lake, have been cited in recent days by men as far apart as President Johnson in Baltimore, Senate Majority Leader Mike Mansfield on Capitol Hill, and Communist spokesmen in Moscow and Hanoi. If there is to be an end to the Vietnamese conflict, it seems, it must be on the basis of the Geneva Agreements. But just what were they?

There are many interpretations of what the agreements meant. What exactly was signed by whom? There is even a question whether some nations signed anything at all, though they were physically present and listed as full participants. Lastly, there exists the major question, hotly disputed by both sides, as to who violated the agreements first—and how, therefore, a future

---

* From the *New York Times Magazine,* May 2, 1965. © 1965 by Bernard B. Fall.

similar agreement could produce a more adequate machinery to deal with such violations. In order to understand these problems it will be necessary to return briefly to the background of what brought about the Geneva Agreements.

Soon after the cease-fire in Korea, in July, 1953, Communist equipment and advisers began to flow more plentifully to Ho Chi Minh's Viet-Minh forces fighting the French in Indochina. Pressure began to build up in France for a negotiated settlement along Korean lines. At the Bermuda Conference of December, 1953, President Eisenhower, Prime Minister Churchill, and Premier Joseph Laniel of France decided to discuss the Indochina problem with the Soviet Union at the Foreign Minister level.

The Foreign Ministers, meeting in Berlin, in February, 1954, agreed to a conference of interested powers to discuss both Korea and Indochina, to be held at Geneva toward the end of April, 1954. That was the signal for General Vo Nguyen Giap, Ho's Commander in Chief, to deliver a stunning blow to the French in Indochina, so as to strengthen his side's negotiating position to the utmost.

When the conference began at Geneva on April 27 the ghastly news of the agony of Dien Bien Phu completely overshadowed the Korean part of the negotiation, which soon quagmired into a stalemate. By the time the delegates turned to Indochina on May 8, 1954, Dien Bien Phu had fallen a few hours earlier, and France's Foreign Minister, Georges Bidault, his voice choked with tears, could do little else but to begin the discussion with a eulogy to his country's fallen heroes.

But in areas other than Dien Bien Phu, the war was not going well for France, either. Indeed, only in South Viet-Nam proper was the situation at all encouraging. Terrorism in Saigon had been brought to an almost total standstill, and the Buddhist Cao-Dai and Hoa-Hao sects and Roman Catholic militia units had cleared extensive sections of the Mekong Delta of Viet-Minh control. But the determining factor was the deteriorating situation in the North: Vietnamese morale fell rapidly as the situation worsened.

The Vietnamese National Army, created by France in 1948, counted about 200,000 regulars and 50,000 village militiamen by February, 1954, while another 30,000 Vietnamese served within the 178,000-man French Expeditionary Force in Indochina and another 50,000 Cambodians and Laotians served in the armies of their own countries in the struggle against the Viet-Minh.

On the Communist side, Ho Chi Minh's forces had come a long way from the badly armed guerrilla bands of the mid-forties. The Viet-Nam People's Army now comprised seven hard-core divisions abundantly equipped with modern American weapons captured by the Chinese in Korea and passed along. The Communist forces, with fewer than 100,000 regulars, 50,000 regional semiregulars and about 225,000 local guerrillas, were numerically inferior to the French Union troops, but in a type of war where experts believe that the defending force must hold a 10-to-1 superiority in order to win (in 1965 the South Vietnamese and American forces hold a 5-to-1 lead over the Viet-Cong), the French 1.2-to-1 edge made the military contest—all other factors aside—well-nigh hopeless.

The French felt that the only way to tip the scales in their favor—or at least to prevent an outright military disaster—would be an open military commitment by the United States on their behalf. An American Military Assistance Advisory Group (M.A.A.G.) to the French forces in Indochina had been set up as early as July, 1950, and American financial and matériel aid to Indochina had totaled an actual expenditure of $1 billion by the time the fighting stopped.

But the United States was reluctant, so soon after the Korean War, to become embroiled again in an Asian conflict—and one in support of a colonial power, at that. Britain was eager not to jeopardize the chances of a *détente* between East and West over what seemed a marginal issue at best, and a lost cause at worst.

Besides the Western Big Three, the other participants in the talks were the French-sponsored State of Viet-Nam, Laos, and Cambodia on the one hand and, on the other, the Viet-Minh's Democratic Republic of Viet-Nam, Russia, and Communist China. Britain and Russia, in the persons of Foreign Secretary Anthony Eden and Foreign Minister Vyacheslav Molotov, were co-chairmen.

At first, the Saigon delegation insisted on territorial unity for all of Viet-Nam and national elections under U.N. supervision. Considering the progress of the war, the Western powers felt that partition would be unavoidable. The Viet-Minh delegation, like Saigon, at first opted for nation-wide elections, but after a hurried meeting between China's Premier Chou En-lai and Ho, it agreed to accept partition into "temporary regroupment areas."

What followed then was merely a "battle of the parallels"— attempts by both sides to enlarge the zones allotted them and to fill in the details of the armistice supervisory machinery—all punctuated by further bad news for the French and Vietnamese as their military efforts failed and Saigon's administrative machinery slowly disintegrated.

The American delegation, under pressure from home not to give the impression of "approving" a "surrender to communism," had for all practical purposes ceased to influence events. Secretary Dulles had left Geneva on May 4, even before the Indochina conference began. In President Eisenhower's words, the "American delegation [was] downgraded to an 'observer' mission." This attempt at saving face at home was to have important consequences as the negotiations reached their climax.

It must be remembered that the Geneva Agreements were *military cease-fire* agreements, though negotiated at the highest political and diplomatic level. The actual signature of the agreements and their ultimate execution were to be reserved to *military* authorities on both sides.

On July 20, agreement was reached on Viet-Nam when the hitherto intractable Molotov relented and made the Viet-Minh accept the 17th Parallel as the cease-fire line (though it meant relinquishing territory they held in the south). Separate agreements on Laos and Cambodia remained to be worked out, but by about two o'clock the next morning the package was completed.

Brigadier General Henri Delteil, representing the French Army High Command in Indochina, signed first. Brigadier General Ta Quang Buu, Oxford-educated and a former leader of the French-sponsored Vietnamese Boy Scout movement, signed for the Viet-Minh and invited Delteil to share a glass of champagne with him. Delteil quietly said: "I am sure that you understand that this is not possible." At 3:43 A.M. of July 21, 1954, the first Indochina war was over.

The document signed by the two generals was officially known as an "Agreement on the Cessation of Hostilities in Viet-Nam,"

covering 47 articles and a brief annex on the geographic delinea-
tion of the regroupment areas. Chapter I of the agreement deals
with the establishment of a demarcation line and a demilitarized
zone on the 17th Parallel, and Chapter II with the technicalities
of moving troops and equipment through each other's area. In
that section, one important article, No. 14, has a bearing on present events:

a—Pending the general elections which will bring about the unification of Viet-Nam, the conduct of civil administration in each regrouping zone shall be in the hands of the party whose forces are to
be regrouped there in virtue of the present agreement. . . .

c—Each party undertakes to refrain from any reprisals or discrimination against persons or organizations on account of their
activities during the hostilities and to guarantee their democratic
liberties.

d—. . . until the movement of troops is completed, any civilians
residing in a district controlled by one party who wish to go and
live in the zone assigned to the other party shall be permitted and
helped to do so by the authorities in that district.

It is Chapter III, however, which constitutes the heart of the
agreement, with its ban on the introduction of new troops and
weapons and of new military bases. Article 17 bans "reinforcements" (that is, increases above replacement of equipment already there) "in the form of all types of . . . war matériel, such
as combat aircraft, naval craft, jet engines and jet weapons, and
armored vehicles." Article 18 prohibits "the establishment of
new military bases . . . throughout Viet-Nam territory" and
Article 19 makes the following important points:

. . . no military base under the control of a foreign state may be
established in the regrouping zone of either party; the two parties
shall ensure that the zones assigned to them do not adhere to any
military alliance and are not used for the resumption of hostilities
or to further an aggressive policy.

Article 24 contains a potentially potent clause in its quiet re-
minder that both sides are to respect the "territory under control
of the other party and shall not engage in blockade of any kind
in Viet-Nam."

The final section of the agreement deals with the establishment
of an International Commission for Supervision and Control.
The I.C.S.C. was to be composed (and still is) of Canadian,

Indian, and Polish members, with India presiding, and was to set up fixed and mobile teams to supervise the execution of the cease-fire provisions. Its decisions on procedural matters were to be decided by majority vote, but all decisions dealing with substantive violations must be taken unanimously. And that is, of course, where the system failed.

An important adjunct to the I.C.S.C. was to be a system of Joint Commissions (J.C.) composed of representatives of the two opposing armies and operating in small teams. Their role was particularly important when it came to extricating the various irregular units infiltrated in remote areas and in settling dangerous incidents on the spot. (As will be seen, they were abolished later at South Viet-Nam's request.)

The agreement left the political arrangements for Viet-Nam unresolved. They were settled at Geneva later in the day on July 21, in the course of the final meeting of the conferees, presided over by Anthony Eden. One by one, he read off the list of documents that were part of the conference record, adding: "Finally, gentlemen, there is a Draft Declaration by the Conference which takes note of all these documents."

In turn, every conference member spoke his approval of the draft declaration: Britain, France, Laos, Red China, the Soviet Union, Cambodia, the Democratic Republic of Viet-Nam—there were no disclaimers so far.

Then it was the turn of Undersecretary of State Walter Bedell Smith of the United States. Smith stated that "my government is not prepared to join in a declaration by the conference such as is submitted." Instead, he submitted a separate declaration in which the United States affirmed that it would "refrain from the threat or the use of force to disturb" the agreements but would view "any renewal of the aggression in violation of the aforesaid agreements with grave concern and as seriously threatening international peace and security."

Smith added that, in the "case of nations divided against their will," the United States supported efforts "to achieve unity through free elections, supervised by the United Nations. . . ."

This left the delegation from the State of Viet-Nam to be heard from. The nominal head of state, former Emperor Bao Dai, had just named the courageous nationalist Ngo Dinh Diem to be Premier. Diem's Foreign Minister and delegate at Geneva was

Dr. Tran Van Do, a former chief of the Vietnamese Army's medical service and a man with a reputation of towering integrity. (He was to break with Diem a few months later over the latter's growing authoritarianism; he was imprisoned by Diem; now he is again South Viet-Nam's Foreign Minister.) Cold-shouldered by everyone, Dr. Do had fought a lonely battle, trying to save his country from partition and what then seemed imminent domination by Ho Chi Minh.

Dr. Do now rose to make a final plea, but the matter was obviously considered settled by everyone else. All that he could obtain was that the other conferees "take note" of the State of Viet-Nam's promise "not to use force to resist the procedures for carrying the cease-fire into effect." A few minutes later, he informed Diem in Saigon by cable of the failure of his mission: "Absolutely impossible to surmount the hostility of our enemies and the perfidy of false friends. . . ." But the Final Declaration stood.

Articles 6 and 7 of the Final Declaration were to be of deep significance for Viet-Nam:

The essential purpose of the agreement relating to Viet-Nam is to settle military questions with a view to ending hostilities. . . . The military demarcation line is provisional and should not in any way be considered as constituting a political or territorial boundary. . . .

So far as Viet-Nam is concerned, the settlement of political problems, effected on the basis of respect for the principles of independence, unity and territorial integrity, shall permit the Vietnamese people to enjoy fundamental freedoms, guaranteed by democratic institutions established as a result of free general elections by secret ballot. . . . General elections shall be held in July, 1956, under the supervision of an international commission composed of the Member States of the International Supervisory Commission. . . .

There is no question as to the language of that declaration: It fully prescribes the mechanism of general elections for all Viet-Nam, to be held two years hence. But there is some question as to the declaration's form—for it was an *unsigned document*.

This fact has not entirely escaped astute observers, and surely was not an oversight on the part of the negotiators in either camp. Two authoritative French writers, Jean Lacouture and Philippe Devillers, in a book on the Geneva negotiations, have noted that this absence of a signature "would permit [the participants] to act as if the organization of elections in Viet-Nam within two years had been a simple project" rather than a formal commitment. They added:

> The Geneva Conference will thus have invented a new form of peaceful coexistence—that which results from the tacit consent of the negotiators—as well as a new form of legal obligation between states: the unsigned treaty.

The question of why the Communists accepted a document whose legal force was so questionable has never been satisfactorily resolved. Some authorities say that, since South Viet-Nam was expected to collapse anyway, the two-year provision was a mere face-saver for the West (just like the clause in the 1962 transfer of West Irian from the Netherlands to Indonesia, which provides for "free elections" for the hapless Papuans in 1969). Others hold that, on the contrary, Hanoi accepted the final declaration, knowing that it would never be implemented, in preference to a continuation of the war and the always possible chance of American intervention on the French side—even at that late date. In view of the situation then prevailing in Viet-Nam, the first of the two hypotheses seems the more convincing.

In Viet-Nam itself, the state of affairs which resulted from the Geneva settlement was grim: 860,000 refugees—more than 500,-000 of them Catholics—began to pour into what was now rapidly becoming "South Viet-Nam"—i.e., Viet-Nam south of the new demarcation line at the 17th Parallel. North of the line, stolid-faced Viet-Minh regulars began to occupy the cities and towns left behind by withdrawing French troops.

Some 190,000 Franco-Vietnamese troops moved south of the demarcation line, although many of the Vietnamese whose home villages were in the North preferred to desert in order not to be separated from their families. In the South, it is now admitted (though it was carefully hushed up at the time), perhaps as many as 80,000 local guerrillas and regulars and their dependents, including almost 10,000 mountain tribesmen, went northward.

Perhaps another 5,000 to 6,000 local hard-core guerrillas—probably the élite of the Viet-Minh's military and political operators in the South—simply went underground. They hid their weapons and radio equipment and became anonymous villagers—at least for a while. In the cities, others, such as the Viet-

Cong's present leader, Nguyen Huu Tho, created "legal struggle" organizations with the aim of propagating the new catch-phrase of "peace and reunification in two years." They, however, were soon disbanded or arrested by the Saigon police.

In Saigon, the fledgling Diem regime was trying to cope both with the administrative chaos resulting from partition and the influx of refugees, and with the challenges against its survival from various political and religious groups and sects. The government's chances of surviving even as long as the two-year election deadline were rated as poor. President Eisenhower summed up the situation in his memoirs:

I have never talked or corresponded with a person knowledgeable in Indochinese affairs who did not agree that had elections been held as of the time of the fighting, possibly 80 per cent of the population would have voted for the Communist Ho Chi Minh as their leader rather than Chief of State Bao Dai.

Since the North controlled a population of more than 15 million and the South fewer than 12 million, and since the North could be trusted to "deliver" its electorate in overwhelming numbers, such an election would beyond a doubt have resulted in a peaceful take-over of all of Viet-Nam by Ho Chi Minh in July, 1956. (It is worth noting that Diem disposed of Bao Dai by a rigged plebiscite, held in 1955. Diem got 98.8 per cent of the vote. Diem was overthrown and assassinated in a coup in 1963; Bao Dai is now living in France.)

Little wonder, then, that the Diem Government almost immediately took the position that the Geneva Agreements, signed by a foreign military command (i.e., the French) "in contempt of Vietnamese national interests," were not binding upon it. It not only refused to consult with its northern counterpart about elections, but it also turned down repeated proposals by North Viet-Nam to normalize economic and postal relations, arguing that "we cannot entertain any Communist proposal as long as we do not have evidence that they place the interests of the Fatherland above those of communism."

That attitude amounted in fact to an economic blockade— which hurt, for North Viet-Nam had until then received an average of more than 200,000 tons a year of southern rice to cover its internal food deficit.

The French, already embroiled in the beginnings of a new colonial war in Algeria, offered little argument when the Diem regime requested in February, 1956 (that is, before the July deadline on elections), that they withdraw their troops. The French high command in Indochina, which had been the formal signer of the 1954 Geneva Agreements, was dissolved on April 26, 1956. Some hotheads in Saigon toyed with the idea of declaring the Geneva Accords nil. Indeed, carefully coached mobs ransacked the Saigon offices and billets of the International Commission for Supervision and Control on the first anniversary of the Geneva cease-fire.

But cooler counsel prevailed (some say, at American behest) and a few days before the July, 1956, deadline for national elections, the South Vietnamese Foreign Secretary, while denouncing the validity of the agreements, established what he called "de facto co-operation" with the I.C.S.C. The Joint Commissions, however, were soon abolished; Saigon argued that the North Vietnamese members stationed in Saigon were engaging in subversive activities and obtained their recall in 1957.

As for the elections, the deadline passed without either a ballot or undue incident. Both North Viet-Nam and the Soviet Union made protests against this apparent violation of the Geneva Agreements, but both South Viet-Nam and the United States— the latter in a statement by Walter S. Robertson, then Assistant Secretary of State, on June 1, 1956—argued that North Viet-Nam already had violated the cease-fire provisions with regard to increases in troops and equipment, as well as with regard to the freedom-of-movement provisions. Indeed, in a diplomatic note sent in April, 1956, by Britain to the Soviet Government, as co-chairman of the Geneva Conference, London pointed out that North Vietnamese regular units had increased from seven to twenty divisions.

In the South, difficulties arose over such matters as the entry and departure of military equipment and American advisers, about whose exact numbers there were disagreements from the start. The I.C.S.C. complained, in its January, 1957, report, that "While the commission has experienced difficulties in North Viet-Nam, the major part of its difficulties has arisen in South Viet-Nam."

As for the North Vietnamese, the passage of the July, 1956, election deadline was the signal that South Viet-Nam would not come to terms willingly. As long as there was even a remote chance of peaceful reunification, Hanoi—as well as the guerrilla stay-behinds inside South Viet-Nam—had presented to the outside world a picture of sweet reasonableness: After all, there was hardly any point in risking international good will, as well as valuable cadres, to hasten what was assumed to be an orderly take-over.

But within a few months after the deadline had passed in 1956, the killing of village chiefs in South Viet-Nam began—by stay-behind guerrillas, not the "outside aggressors" of 1959-60 cited by the recent State Department white paper. By the time the South Viet-Nam problem had become a military challenge to the United States late in 1961, the second Indochina war had been under way for almost five years.

In all this turmoil, the I.C.S.C. led an increasingly shadowy and ineffectual life. If the North Vietnamese interfered with the freedom-of-movement provisions of the cease-fire, the South Vietnamese interfered with the section dealing with reprisals against former enemy combatants. They finally informed the commission that they would no longer provide it with information in the matter. An order issued by Diem in January, 1956, providing for indefinite detention in concentration camps of all those "who are considered dangerous for national defense and public security," gave an inkling of what was going on, however.

Soon, both sides were openly violating the armament provisions of the cease-fire. Personal observations in both zones have provided me with my own stock of ludicrous stories about nonenforcement, such as that of U.S. warplanes being landed by an aircraft carrier in sight of Saigon's main thoroughfare, while a handsomely turbaned Indian I.C.S.C. officer said: "Yes—but *officially* we have not been informed of the presence of the aircraft carrier."

Or there is the response given to the I.C.S.C. by the Hanoi Government, when the commission wanted to inspect the largest airfield in North Viet-Nam, Haiphong's Cat-Bi airport:

"But you cannot visit that airport."

"Why not?" asked the I.C.S.C. representative.

"Because it belongs to a private flying club—and private property is exempted from commission control."

Not that the commission did not try to do its job. In June, 1962, its Legal committee, by a 2-to-1 vote (Poland dissenting), found that "there is evidence to show that the P.A.V.N. [People's Army of Viet-Nam] has allowed the zone in the North to be used for inciting, encouraging and supporting hostile activities in the Zone in the South, aimed at the overthrow of the Administration in the South . . . in violation of Articles 19, 24 and 27 of the agreement. . . ." That part of the report, pleasant to Western ears, finds itself widely reported to this day.

What is somewhat less prominently displayed is Paragraph 20 of the same report, in which the commission, by the same majority, concludes that "the Republic of Viet-Nam [i.e., South Viet-Nam] has violated Articles 16 and 17 of the Geneva Agreement in receiving increased military aid from the United States," and that the "establishment of a U.S. Military Assistance Command in South Viet-Nam, as well as the introduction of a large number of U.S. military personnel . . . amounts to a factual military alliance, which is prohibited under Article 19 of the Geneva agreement."

The recent American air raids on North Viet-Nam gave rise to another split report—this time with India and Poland voting in the majority. Last February 13, both nations addressed to the British and Soviet co-chairmen a note pointing to the "seriousness of the situation and indicat[ing] violations of the Geneva Agreement," while the Canadian member argued that the American raids could not be taken out of the wider context of being "the direct result of the intensification of the aggressive policy of the government of North Viet-Nam." The two co-chairmen failed to act on either report.

Within South Viet-Nam, I.C.S.C. teams have found it increasingly difficult to move about, the Saigon government arguing that it cannot guarantee their security. In North Viet-Nam, the Hanoi government has demanded their recall—on the grounds that their lives were being endangered by American air raids. There matters stand.

Where did the old agreements fail, and how could new (or renovated) agreements do better?

(1) The original 1954 agreements failed politically and economically before they even failed militarily. There can be no doubt but that the Diem regime's total intransigence in the field of trade relations—whose existence (as in the case of the two Germanys) could have eased the situation considerably—contributed to a rapid exacerbation of the conflict. It is a documented fact that until 1958 Hanoi made repeated overtures for low-level agreements with the South, all of which were turned down by Saigon.

(2) The constant drumfire of the Saigon government against the 1954 agreements did not enhance respect for the agreements on either side of the demarcation line. The fact that the other Western participants in the 1954 conference did not, at least publicly, reaffirm their support of the "essentials" of the agreements must have given considerable encouragement to the activists in Hanoi who saw in the Geneva cease-fire a mere way-station to ultimate domination of all of Viet-Nam—if not all of Indochina.

(3) The sudden development of respect for the I.C.S.C. by South Viet-Nam and the United States as the situation inside South Viet-Nam worsened in the early sixties added ammunition to Hanoi's contention that the I.C.S.C. had come down on the side of the West. From a tone of polite solicitousness toward the I.C.S.C., the Ho regime became increasingly vituperative. After the June, 1962, I.C.S.C. report, Hanoi (this writer was there at the time) was treated to the spectacle of a "public demonstration" against the commission.

(4) On the Western side, the obvious ineffectualness of the I.C.S.C. in dealing with guerrilla depredations as distinct from overt invasion (contrast this record with those of truce commissions in Korea, Palestine, the Sinai or Cyprus) augurs ill for yet another such experiment. In Laos, the commission neither stops the Pathet-Lao and its North Vietnamese sponsors from attacking in the Plain of Jars or from using staging areas, nor does it stop American jets from operating all over the country at will.

A new, or "renovated," Geneva conference would have to embody conditions and an enforcement mechanism stronger than now exist. There are some encouraging signs that the West and, perhaps to a lesser degree, Moscow (though probably not yet Hanoi, and certainly not Peking) would be willing to accept a somewhat more realistic attitude toward the problem than prevailed under John Foster Dulles and Diem in 1954.

Relations with the other side, far from being considered a mortal sin, may now include, as President Johnson has indicated, some sort of economic "carrot"—of which direct aid may perhaps be less important to Hanoi than the removal of the *de facto* economic blockade with which it has been surrounded since 1954.

President Johnson's affirmation at Baltimore that South Viet-Nam shall be free to "shape its relationships to all others" constitutes a definite return to the spirit of the Geneva Agreements of 1954, just as did the late President Kennedy's phrase of March 23, 1961, about Laos: "And if in the past there has been any possible ground for misunderstanding of our desire for a truly neutral Laos, there should be none now."

All this leaves open the potentially most explosive of all the "essentials" of Geneva: that of reunification. Diplomats and scholars will debate for decades as to whether an unsigned declaration was a binding diplomatic document, or whether the whole promise of general elections in Viet-Nam was a mere sop thrown to the North Vietnamese for their surrender, under Sino-Russian pressure, of vast tracts of territory south of the 17th Parallel.

There is a larger dimension to the problem: One cannot be for reunification for Germany and Korea (where the non-Communist population vastly exceeds that in the Communist-held areas) and deny the same right to the Vietnamese (whose northern zone is more populous).

The official American view on this issue seems to be that expressed by McGeorge Bundy in a public interview last month: "I don't think we ever felt that there was any bar in the long run to working out a future of Viet-Nam which would not necessarily be divided." Or, as another White House aide expressed it more colorfully, but privately: "When the subject [of eventual reunification] came up, nobody fell over the table and vomited."

Obviously, no one has in mind handing over South Viet-Nam to any Vietnamese regime that is, in the American view, a mere

Communist Chinese proxy, but some sort of progressive co-operation between the two zones seems not excluded.

There still remains the issue of policing whatever new arrangements might be made, but perhaps here the difficulties are less real than apparent. First of all, the violations against which there must be a guarantee are no longer of the kind which were important in 1954. It is more important to keep down, say, the number of battalion-size Viet-Cong attacks *inside* South Viet-Nam than to watch whether either the United States or China sends jets into Viet-Nam. Joint North-South Vietnamese cease-fire teams under the control of an international supervisory body (as in the case in Palestine) could be useful.

Yet, all the discussions about an international settlement of the Vietnamese problem must not hide the fact that in one essential item the situation may well have changed radically since 1954:

During the First Indochina War there was no question that Ho Chi Minh was the uncontested master of all guerrilla operation throughout Indochina. General Giap's People's Army could enforce a cease-fire and a withdrawal of Viet-Minh forces from south of the 17th Parallel without much difficulty.

Whether the Viet-Cong, after eight years of fighting on its own account and after taking tremendous losses, would be willing to give up all that it has gained through fighting and subversion, simply to please the dictates of Hanoi—just as Hanoi gave up the south in 1954 to comply with the long-range policies of its outside backers—is not certain.

After all, it must be remembered, in 1954 both Russia and Red China were putting pressure on Ho to comply with such a pull-out. Today, Peking might well put its pressure on Hanoi in the opposite sense. Or—failing this—Peking might even leap-frog Hanoi in order to help the Viet-Cong sabotage any agreement that Hanoi might subscribe to at the southern guerrillas' expense.

All these considerations must weigh heavily in the balance as policy-makers survey the broken hopes left from the first Geneva Agreement on Viet-Nam, and as the dim outlines of yet another negotiated settlement of the same problem begin to appear on the horizon.

FINAL DECLARATION OF GENEVA CONFERENCE, July 21, 1954*

Final declaration, dated July 21, 1954, of the Geneva Conference on the problem of restoring peace in Indochina, in which the representatives of Cambodia, the Democratic Republic of Viet-Nam, France, Laos, the People's Republic of China, the State of Viet-Nam, the Union of Soviet Socialist Republics, the United Kingdom, and the United States of America took part.

1. The Conference takes note of the agreements ending hostilities in Cambodia, Laos, and Viet-Nam and organizing international control and the supervision of the execution of the provisions of these agreements.

2. The Conference expresses satisfaction at the ending of hostilities in Cambodia, Laos, and Viet-Nam; the Conference expresses its conviction that the execution of the provisions set out in the present declaration and in the agreements on the cessation of hostilities will permit Cambodia, Laos, and Viet-Nam henceforth to play their part, in full independence and sovereignty, in the peaceful community of nations.

3. The Conference takes note of the declarations made by the governments of Cambodia and of Laos of their intention to adopt measures permitting all citizens to take their place in the national community, in particular by participating in the next general elections, which, in conformity with the constitution of each of these countries, shall take place in the course of the year 1955, by secret ballot and in conditions of respect for fundamental freedoms.

4. The Conference takes note of the clauses in the agreement on the cessation of hostilities in Viet-Nam prohibiting the intro-

---

* Cmd. 9239, Miscellaneous No. 20 (1954), Her Majesty's Stationery Office, London, 1954.

duction into Viet-Nam of foreign troops and military personnel as well as of all kinds of arms and munitions. The Conference also takes note of the declarations made by the governments of Cambodia and Laos of their resolution not to request foreign aid, whether in war material, in personnel or in instructors except for the purpose of the effective defence of their territory and, in the case of Laos, to the extent defined by the agreements on the cessation of hostilities in Laos.

5. The Conference takes note of the clauses in the agreement on the cessation of hostilities in Viet-Nam to the effect that no military base under the control of a foreign state may be established in the regrouping zones of the two parties, the latter having the obligation to see that the zones allotted to them shall not constitute part of any military alliance and shall not be utilized for the resumption of hostilities or in the service of an aggressive policy. The Conference also takes note of the declarations of the governments of Cambodia and Laos to the effect that they will not join in any agreement with other states if this agreement includes the obligation to participate in a military alliance not in conformity with the principles of the Charter of the United Nations or, in the case of Laos, with the principles of the agreement on the cessation of hostilities in Laos or, so long as their security is not threatened, the obligation to establish bases on Cambodian or Laotian territory for the military forces of foreign Powers.

6. The Conference recognizes that the essential purpose of the agreement relating to Viet-Nam is to settle military questions with a view to ending hostilities and that the military demarcation line is provisional and should not in any way be interpreted as constituting a political or territorial boundary. The Conference expresses its conviction that the execution of the provisions set out in the present declaration and in the agreement on the cessation of hostilities creates the necessary basis for the achievement in the near future of a political settlement in Viet-Nam.

7. The Conference declares that, so far as Viet-Nam is concerned, the settlement of political problems, effected on the basis of respect for the principles of independence, unity and territorial integrity, shall permit the Vietnamese people to enjoy the fundamental freedoms, guaranteed by democratic institutions established as a result of free general elections by secret ballot.

The Viet-Nam Reader

In order to ensure that sufficient progress in the restoration of peace has been made, and that all the necessary conditions obtain for free expression of the national will, general elections shall be held in July, 1956, under the supervision of an international commission composed of representatives of the Member States of the International Supervisory Commission, referred to in the agreement on the cessation of hostilities. Consultations will be held on this subject between the competent representative authorities of the two zones from 20 July 1955 onwards.

8. The provisions of the agreements on the cessation of hostilities intended to ensure the protection of individuals and of property must be most strictly applied and must, in particular, allow everyone in Viet-Nam to decide freely in which zone he wishes to live.

9. The competent representative authorities of the Northern and Southern zones of Viet-Nam, as well as the authorities of Laos and Cambodia, must not permit any individual or collective reprisals against persons who have collaborated in any way with one of the parties during the war, or against members of such persons' families.

10. The Conference takes note of the declaration of the government of the French Republic to the effect that it is ready to withdraw its troops from the territory of Cambodia, Laos, and Viet-Nam, at the request of the governments concerned and within periods which shall be fixed by agreement between the parties except in the cases where, by agreement between the two parties, a certain number of French troops shall remain at specified points and for a specified time.

11. The Conference takes note of the declaration of the French government to the effect that for the settlement of all the problems connected with the re-establishment and consolidation of peace in Cambodia, Laos, and Viet-Nam, the French government will proceed from the principle of respect for the independence and sovereignty, unity and territorial integrity of Cambodia, Laos, and Viet-Nam.

12. In their relations with Cambodia, Laos, and Viet-Nam, each member of the Geneva Conference undertakes to respect the sovereignty, the independence, the unity, and the territorial integrity of the above-mentioned states, and to refrain from any interference in their internal affairs.

13. The members of the Conference agree to consult one another on any question which may be referred to them by the International Supervisory Commission in order to study such measures as may prove necessary to ensure that the agreements on the cessation of hostilities in Cambodia, Laos, and Viet-Nam are respected.

DON R. and ARTHUR LARSON

What Is Our "Commitment" in Viet-Nam?*

The point of no return is rapidly being approached in Viet-Nam. The Marines have landed. Our planes and our men are engaged in almost daily bombing of a foreign land and people. The sending of ground forces in division strength is hinted at by the Army Chief of Staff. The committing of as many as 250,000 American troops is in the short-range contingency planning. The prospect of thousands of American men laying down their lives in a war on the Asiatic mainland looms larger with every day that passes.

Why?

Every time President Johnson is asked this question—and he now says that he has answered it over fifty times—the first reason he gives is always the same: We must do what we are doing to honor the commitments we have made to the Vietnamese people ever since 1954.

President Johnson bases his statement on two documents: the letter of President Eisenhower to President Diem of October 23, 1954, and the Southeast Asia Collective Defense treaty and protocol ratified in February 1955.

To understand the purpose of the Eisenhower letter, one must recall that it followed directly upon an agreement with France that "economic aid, budgetary support, and other assistance" would thereafter be furnished direct to Laos, to Viet-Nam, and

---

* From *Vietnam and Beyond,* by Don R. and Arthur Larson. Durham, N.C.: Rule of Law Research Center, Duke University, 1965.

Cambodia, rather than through France. Pursuant to this understanding, President Eisenhower wrote to President Diem to open
discussion of this possibility. After a brief introduction and reference to our aid with the refugee problem, he said:

We have been exploring ways and means to permit our aid to
Viet-Nam to be more effective and to make a greater contribution
to the welfare and stability of the Government of Viet-Nam. I am,
accordingly, instructing the American Ambassador to Viet-Nam to
examine with you in your capacity as Chief of Government, how an
intelligent program of American aid given directly to your Government, can serve to assist Viet-Nam in its present hour of trial, provided that your Government is prepared to give assurances as to the
standards of performance it would be able to maintain in the event
such aid were supplied.

The purpose of this offer is to assist the Government of Viet-Nam
in developing and maintaining a strong, viable state, capable of
resisting attempted subversion or aggression through military means.
The Government of the United States expects that this aid will be
met by performance on the part of the Government of Viet-Nam
in undertaking needed reforms. It hopes that such aid, combined
with your own continuing efforts, will contribute effectively toward
an independent Viet-Nam endowed with a strong government. Such
a government would, I hope, be so responsive to the nationalist
aspirations of its people, so enlightened in purpose and effective in
performance, that it will be respected both at home and abroad and
discourage anyone who might wish to impose a foreign ideology on
your free people.

That is all.

Since this letter has been invoked many times as the beginning
point of a policy supposedly unchanged during three presi-
dencies, a policy which now calls for using our own planes and
men to fight a foreign nation on foreign soil, it is well worth
a few moments to analyze what President Eisenhower really said.

There are six sentences. The first says that we have been
"exploring" ways and means. The second relates that our Ambassador is being instructed to "examine" a program with Diem,
subject to a condition relating to Vietnamese performance. The
third states the purpose of "this offer," which can only refer to
the offer to "examine" the assistance program; that purpose is to
help build a viable state, which in turn would be capable of re-

sisting subversion and aggression. The fourth sentence is another condition, the making of needed reforms. The fifth sentence expresses a hope, and so does the sixth—hopes for a strong, enlightened, effective, and respected government—hopes that seem poignant indeed today in view of the sordid story that began with the assassination of Diem.

Where in this highly tentative, highly conditional opening of negotiations and statement of hopes is the "commitment," the "obligation," the pledging of our word? Even if we seem to have indicated a willingness to do something to help, what is that something—beyond aid in developing a strong, viable state?

The actual assistance program during the Eisenhower Administration confirms this concept. Of total aid from 1953 to 1961, less than one-fourth was classified as military, and more than three-fourths economic. Some idea of the relatively small size of the military side may be seen from the announcement on May 5, 1960, that the Military Assistance and Advisory Group would be increased by the end of the year from 327 to 685.

In short, the nearest thing to a commitment at this stage was an indicated willingness, subject to some stiff (and as yet unsatisfied) conditions and understandings, to provide economic and technical assistance, including military advisers, material, and training.

The other document allegedly imposing an obligation on us to fight to defend South Viet-Nam is a legal instrument, the SEATO treaty, signed in September, 1954, and ratified in February, 1955. Since this is indeed a "solemn obligation," it is even more important in this instance to take the time to find out precisely what we have agreed to, before we contemplate the wholesale sacrifice of American lives in its name.

The treaty was signed by Australia, France, New Zealand, Pakistan, the Philippines, Thailand, the United Kingdom, and the United States. South Viet-Nam was not a party to the treaty, but it was by protocol added to the area covered by the defense and economic provisions of the treaty, along with Cambodia and Laos.

The true fact is that the United States has had no obligation to South Viet-Nam or anyone else under the SEATO treaty to use its own armed forces in the defense of South Viet-Nam.

The following three reasons are offered in support of this statement.

1. *The specified events calling for direct action have not occurred.*

The two operative defense provisions of the SEATO treaty occur in Article IV. They are set in motion by two different kinds of events, and call for two entirely different kinds of action by the parties.

Paragraph 1 comes into play when there is "aggression by armed attack." The obligation on each party is "to meet the common danger in accordance with its constitutional processes."

Paragraph 2 applies when "the territory or the sovereignty or political independence of any (covered area) . . . is threatened in any way other than by armed attack or is affected or threatened by any fact or situation which might endanger the peace of the area." In this event, the only obligation is that "the Parties shall consult immediately in order to agree on the measures which should be taken for the common defense."

It is clear from all the discussions and occurrences leading to this treaty that the type of situation in Viet-Nam has been considered by the parties to fall under Paragraph 2, not under Paragraph 1.

The guide to interpretation is the intention of the parties, and this is found in the *travaux préparatoires,* which include the discussions leading up to the treaty.

The reason that this document had two different defense provisions rather than merely one inclusive obligation was that the parties had in mind the two different types of Communist threat in the area. The first was the Korea-type aggression, in which there is an old-fashioned overt armed invasion across a boundary. The second was the Indochina-type situation, in which there are internal uprisings supported by outside Communist aid. The parties recognized that the first kind of invasion could be met head-on by countervailing armed force of the same kind, as in Korea. They also realized that the second kind of problem could not be so met, but would require a much more complex solution.

This was all spelled out in detail by Secretary of State John Foster Dulles in an address on June 11, 1954, just a few months before the treaty was signed. The first type of threat he identified as that of "open military aggression by the Chinese Communist regime." The second he described as "disturbances fomented from Communist China but where there is no open invasion by Communist China."

The actions that these events would call for are then described by Dulles in terms that closely parallel the language of the SEATO treaty. (It must be remembered that Dulles was the author of the SEATO treaty, and had been urging it for a long time.)

If the first type of "overt military aggression" occurred, Dulles said:

The United States would of course invoke the processes of the United Nations and consult with its allies. But we could not escape ultimate responsibility for decisions closely touching our own security and self-defense.

But as to the second type of situation he said:

The situation in Indochina is not that of open military aggression by the Chinese Communist regime. Thus, in Indochina, the problem is one of restoring tranquility in an area where disturbances are fomented from Communist China, but where there is no open invasion from Communist China.

And now note the pointblank statement of how *not* to deal with this problem:

This task of pacification, in our opinion, cannot be successfully met merely by unilateral armed intervention.

Which is precisely what we are attempting today.

He goes on to say:

Some other conditions need to be established. Throughout these Indochina developments, the United States has held to a stable and consistent course and has made clear the conditions which, in its opinion, might justify intervention. These conditions were and are (1) an invitation from the present lawful authorities; (2) clear assurance of complete independence to Laos, Cambodia, and Viet-Nam; (3) evidence of concern by the United Nations; (4) a joining in the collective effort of some of the other nations in the area; and (5) assurance that France will not itself withdraw from the battle until it is won.

Only if these conditions were realized could the President and the Congress be justified in asking the American people to make the sacrifices incident to commiting our Nation, with others, to using force to help to restore peace in the area. (Italics supplied.)

There, in plainest terms, was the real policy of the United States in 1954. It bears little resemblance to the present policy, which claims to have continued unchanged from that time to this.

Present policy ignores the peacekeeping role of the United Nations, tries to achieve pacification by unilateral armed intervention, and disregards all of Dulles' five conditions except the first, that of invitation—and there are even those who would disregard the first. Most conspicuously, there has been no significant joining in the collective effort by other nations of the area, and as for France staying in the battle until it is won—the less said about that the better.

This, then, was what the signers of the treaty, including France, knew to be the intent of the agreement. It is written into the language of the treaty, which begins both its Preamble and its first Article by invoking the principles and procedures of the United Nations, then sets forth the two kinds of threat and action, and adds the absolute condition that there must be invitation by the government concerned.

2. No measures have been agreed upon by the SEATO powers.
Since the parties in the past considered this type of situation covered, not by Paragraph 1, but by Paragraph 2, the main obligation was to consult with the other parties in order to agree on measures for the common defense. We have indeed consulted several times, notably on October 1, 1961, April 8 to 10, 1963, and April 13 to 14, 1964. There was no lack of talk at these meetings about what a serious threat to the peace the Viet-Nam situation presented and how important it was to defeat the Viet-Cong, but when it came to action, the communiqués were eloquently noncommittal. The most they could muster even in 1964 was an agreement that "the members of SEATO should remain prepared, if neccessary, to take further concrete steps within their respective capabilities of fulfillment of their obligations under the treaty." Even this weak statement did not receive unanimous agreement; France (specifically singled out by Dulles as having to stay in the battle to the end, as we have

seen) refused to go even this far in carrying out its pledge under the treaty.

3. *Any SEATO obligation to defend South Viet-Nam is inoperative as long as the other signers fail to recognize such an obligation.*

The heart of international law is reciprocity. No matter what the SEATO treaty might have said—indeed even if it in plain terms said that each party must dispatch a stipulated amount of armed force to defend South Viet-Nam—that obligation would not at this time bind the United States. The reason is that other SEATO signers have done virtually nothing under the treaty to help defend South Viet-Nam.

It must be remembered that our obligation under this treaty does not run to South Viet-Nam. South Viet-Nam is not a party, and indeed has on its part agreed to nothing. The commitment of the treaty runs to the other signers. As long as the other signers acknowledge no obligation to us to send troops in the present circumstances we have no such obligation to them.

Another way to view the matter would be this. The obligation of Paragraph 1 is couched in vague terms: "to meet the common danger in accordance with its constitutional processes." Does this mean to make war on a foreign nation, to send in ground forces, and to engage air and sea units? The only way to know is to see how the parties interpret the clause in practice. According to the current practice of the other parties, there is as of now no such obligation.

For the rest of the Eisenhower Administration, there can be found statements of the seriousness of the danger and of our willingness to continue to increase our assistance program, but no more.

As for President John F. Kennedy, the most revealing personal statement he made was in a CBS interview with Walter Cronkite on September 2, 1963, shortly before the assassination. He said:

I don't think that unless a greater effort is made by the government to win popular support that the war can be won out there. In the final analysis, it is their war. They are the ones who have to win it or lose it. We can help them, we can give them equipment, we can send our men out there as advisers, but they have to win it—the people of Viet-Nam—against the Communists. We are prepared to continue to assist them, but I don't think that the war can be won unless the people support the effort, and, in my opinion, in the last two months the government has gotten out of touch with the people.

That was President Kennedy's conception of our "commitment." When this is coupled with the fact that subsequent violent internal dissensions and a succession of coups have resulted in even less support by the people for the effort, and in the government's being even more out of touch with the people, President Kennedy's statement would indicate no unqualified commitment to fight a war against the Viet-Cong and North Vietnamese on behalf of the South Vietnamese regime.

If one examines the major documents, speeches, press conferences, and communiqués bearing on this subject since 1950, it is a curious fact that one cannot find the words "commitment," "obligation," or "pledge" used to describe our relation to South Viet-Nam until the Johnson Administration. The word "commitment" does appear in a statement by McGeorge Bundy on September 30, 1963, a fact which is of no significance in itself as a commitment, since a Special Assistant to the President has no authority to commit anybody in his own right. With the advent of the Johnson Administration, "commitment," "obligation," and "pledge" begin to blossom with increasing profusion in public statements, especially those of Secretary McNamara and of President Johnson himself. But the significant thing is that the "pledges" are usually referred to as having been made in the past, with the now-familiar refrain that the whole policy has come down unchanged since 1954. It has been the concern of the present analysis to show that those supposed pledges did not exist. It is one thing to announce that one is willing or prepared to give assistance, or that it is one's policy to provide such assistance, or that our own security requires that we help another country militarily. It is quite another thing to say that we have pledged our word and our honor to go on doing it at all costs and forever, if asked to do so.

What President Johnson has done is to convert imperceptibly a diplomatic statement of policy based ultimately on considerations of American security, into an unconditional moral obligation to another country, suffused with overtones of national integrity and honor. On April 20, 1964, he said in New York that to fail to respond to the need to defeat the Communists in the area "would reflect on our honor as a nation, would under-mine world-wide confidence in our courage. . . ." On June 2, 1964, he said:

It may be helpful to outline four basic themes that govern our policy in Southeast Asia.
First, America keeps her word.

He adds:

On the point that America keeps her word, we are steadfast in a policy which has been followed for ten years in three administrations. . . .
In the case of Viet-Nam, our commitment today is just the same as the commitment made by President Eisenhower in 1954. . . .

And so on. The word "commitment" had by this time become so habitual that it turns up five times in three successive sentences.

Warming to this theme, President Johnson on August 12, 1964, allowed himself to say that to do other than we are doing would be "morally unthinkable." On April 7, 1965, this be-comes an "unforgivable wrong."

The trouble with all this is that if we keep saying over and over that we would "dishonor" ourselves by doing anything except plunge deeper into Asiatic war, eventually the world may believe us, and we will have needlessly destroyed that prime essential of international relations—flexibility in choice of future courses.

The more sophisticated members of the world community would not consider us dishonored or lacking in courage if, at any given moment, we took the line dictated by cold-blooded national interest—which is, after all, what every other nation is doing. That is—not unless we build up the moral case against such a course so eloquently in advance that we would look foolish doing precisely what both President Eisenhower and President Kennedy carefully left themselves room to do if neces-sary.

There *is* one obligation in Viet-Nam. It is supreme, because we have expressly agreed in the United Nations Charter that Charter obligations take precedence over all others. Article 37 of the Charter states in unqualified terms that when other means of dealing with a threat to the peace have failed, the matter *"shall"* be referred to the Security Council. We have been making a vigorous stand for years on Article 19, stating that a delinquent member "shall have no vote." But the "shall" in Article 37 is the same "shall" as that in Article 19, and a hundred times more important. The prime point here is that if we are worried about our honor and our pledged word, we should start by honoring this most important obligation we have ever assumed, an obligation which is unconditional, overriding, peremptory—and real.

W. W. ROSTOW

*Guerrilla Warfare in Underdeveloped Areas**

It does not require much imagination to understand why President Kennedy has taken the problem of guerrilla warfare seriously. When this Administration came to responsibility it faced four major crises: Cuba, the Congo, Laos, and Viet-Nam. Each represented a successful Communist breaching—over the previous two years—of the Cold War truce lines which had emerged from the Second World War and its aftermath. In different ways each had arisen from the efforts of the international Communist movement to exploit the inherent instabilities of the underdeveloped areas of the non-Communist world, and each had a guerrilla warfare component.

Cuba, of course, differed from the other cases. The Cuban revolution against Batista was a broad-based national insurrection. But that revolution was tragically captured from within by the Communist apparatus; and now Latin America faces the danger of Cuba's being used as the base for training, supply, and direction of guerrilla warfare in the hemisphere.

More than that, Mr. Khrushchev, in his report to the Moscow conference of Communist parties (published January 6, 1961), had explained at great length that the Communists fully support

---

* Address to the graduating class at the U.S. Army Special Warfare School, Fort Bragg, June, 1961.

what he called wars of national liberation and would march in the front rank with the peoples waging such struggles. The military arm of Mr. Khrushchev's January, 1961, doctrine is, clearly, guerrilla warfare.

Faced with these four crises, pressing in on the President from day to day, and faced with the candidly stated position of Mr. Khrushchev, we have, indeed, begun to take the problem of guerrilla warfare seriously.

To understand this problem, however, one must begin with the great revolutionary process that is going forward in the southern half of the world; for the guerrilla warfare problem in these regions is a product of that revolutionary process and the Communist effort and intent to exploit it.

What is happening throughout Latin America, Africa, the Middle East, and Asia is this: Old societies are changing their ways in order to create and maintain a national personality on the world scene and to bring to their peoples the benefits modern technology can offer. This process is truly revolutionary. It touches every aspect of the traditional life—economic, social, and political. The introduction of modern technology brings about not merely new methods of production but a new style of family life, new links between the villages and the cities, the beginnings of national politics, and a new relationship to the world outside.

Like all revolutions, the revolution of modernization is disturbing. Individual men are torn between the commitment to the old familiar way of life and the attractions of a modern way of life. The power of old social groups—notably the landlord, who usually dominates the traditional society—is reduced. Power moves toward those who command the tools of modern technology, including modern weapons. Men and women in the villages and the cities, feeling that the old ways of life are shaken and that new possibilities are open to them, express old resentments and new hopes.

This is the grand arena of revolutionary change which the Communists are exploiting with great energy. They believe that their techniques of organization—based on small disciplined cadres of conspirators—are ideally suited to grasp and to hold power in these turbulent settings. They believe that the weak transitional governments that one is likely to find during this modernization process are highly vulnerable to subversion and to guerrilla warfare. And whatever Communist doctrines of historical inevitability may be, Communists know that their time to seize power in the underdeveloped areas is limited. They know that, as momentum takes hold in an underdeveloped area—and the fundamental social problems inherited from the traditional society are solved—their chances to seize power decline.

It is on the weakest nations, facing their most difficult transitional moments, that the Communists concentrate their attention. They are the scavengers of the modernization process. They believe that the techniques of political centralization under dictatorial control—and the projected image of Soviet and Chinese Communist economic progress—will persuade hesitant men, faced by great transitional problems, that the Communist model should be adopted for modernization, even at the cost of surrendering human liberty. They believe that they can exploit effectively the resentments built up in many of these areas against colonial rule and that they can associate themselves effectively with the desire of the emerging nations for independence, for status on the world scene, and for material progress.

This is a formidable program; for the history of this century teaches us that communism is not the long-run wave of the future toward which societies are naturally drawn. But, on the contrary it is one particular form of modern society to which a nation may fall prey during the transitional process. Communism is best understood as a disease of the transition to modernization.

What is our reply to this historical conception and strategy? What is the American purpose and the American strategy? We, too, recognize that a revolutionary process is under way. We are dedicated to the proposition that this revolutionary process of modernization shall be permitted to go forward in independence, with increasing degrees of human freedom. We seek two results: first, that truly independent nations shall emerge on the world scene; and, second, that each nation will be permitted to fashion, out of its own culture and its own ambitions, the kind of modern society it wants. The same religious and philosophical beliefs which decree that we respect the uniqueness of each individual make it natural that we respect the uniqueness of each national society. Moreover, we Americans are confident that, if the independence of this process can be maintained over the coming years and decades, these societies will choose their own version of what we would recognize as a democratic, open society. These are our commitments of policy and of faith. The United States has no interest in political satellites. Where we have military pacts we have them because governments feel directly endangered by outside military action and we are prepared to help protect their independence against such military action. But, to use Mao Tse-tung's famous phrase, we do not seek nations which "lean to one side." We seek nations which shall stand up straight. And we do so for a reason: because we are deeply confident that nations which stand up straight will protect their independence and move in their own ways and in their own time toward human freedom and political democracy.

Thus our central task in the underdeveloped areas, as we see it, is to protect the independence of the revolutionary process now going forward. This is our mission, and it is our ultimate strength. For this is not—and cannot be—the mission of communism. And in time, through the fog of propaganda and the honest confusions of men caught up in the business of making new nations, this fundamental difference will become increasingly clear in the southern half of the world. The American interest will be served if our children live in an environment of strong, assertive, independent nations, capable, because they are strong, of assuming collective responsibility for the peace.

The diffusion of power is the basis for freedom within our own society, and we have no reason to fear it on the world scene. But this outcome would be a defeat for communism—not for Russia as a national state, but for communism. Despite all the Communist talk of aiding movements of national independence, they are driven in the end, by the nature of their system, to violate the independence of nations. Despite all the Communist talk of American imperialism, we are committed, by the nature of our system, to support the cause of national independence. And the truth will out.

The victory we seek will see no ticker-tape parades down Broadway, no climactic battles, nor great American celebrations of victory. It is a victory which will take many years and decades of hard work and dedication—by many peoples—to bring about. This will not be a victory of the United States over the Soviet

Union. It will not be a victory of capitalism over socialism. It will be a victory of men and nations which aim to stand up straight, over the forces which wish to entrap and to exploit their revolutionary aspirations of modernization. What this victory involves, in the end, is the assertion by nations of their right to freedom as they understand it. And we deeply believe this victory will come—on both sides of the Iron Curtain.

If Americans do not seek victory in the usual sense, what do we seek? What is the national interest of the United States? Why do we Americans expend our treasure and assume the risks of modern war in this global struggle? For Americans the reward of victory will be, simply, this: It will permit American society to continue to develop along the old humane lines which go back to our birth as a nation—and which reach deeper into history than that—back to the Mediterranean roots of Western life. We are struggling to maintain an environment on the world scene which will permit our open society to survive and to flourish.

To make this vision come true places a great burden on the United States at this phase of history. The preservation of independence has many dimensions.

The United States has the primary responsibility for deterring the use of nuclear weapons in the pursuit of Communist ambitions. The United States has a major responsibility to deter the kind of overt aggression with conventional forces which was launched in June, 1950, in Korea.

The United States has the primary responsibility for assisting the economies of those hard-pressed states on the periphery of the Communist bloc, which are under acute military or quasi-military pressure which they cannot bear from their own resources; for example, South Korea, Viet-Nam, Taiwan, Pakistan, Iran. The United States has a special responsibility of leadership in bringing not merely its own resources but the resources of all the free world to bear in aiding the long-run development of those nations which are serious about modernizing their economy and their social life. And, as President Kennedy has made clear, he regards no program of his Administration as more important than his program for long-term economic development, dramatized, for example, by the Alliance for Progress in Latin America. Independence cannot be maintained by military measures alone.

Modern societies must be built, and we are prepared to help build them.

Finally, the United States has a role to play—symbolized by your presence here and by mine—in learning to deter guerrilla warfare, if possible, and to deal with it, if necessary.

I do not need to tell you that the primary responsibility for dealing with guerrilla warfare in the underdeveloped areas cannot be American. There are many ways in which we can help—and we are searching our minds and our imaginations to learn better how to help; but a guerrilla war must be fought primarily by those on the spot. This is so for a quite particular reason. A guerrilla war is an intimate affair, fought not merely with weapons but fought in the minds of the men who live in the villages and in the hills, fought by the spirit and policy of those who run the local government. An outsider cannot, by himself, win a guerrilla war. He can help create conditions in which it can be won, and he can directly assist those prepared to fight for their independence. We are determined to help destroy this international disease; that is, guerrilla war designed, initiated, supplied, and led from outside an independent nation.

Although as leader of the free world the United States has special responsibilities which it accepts in this common venture of deterrence, it is important that the whole international community begin to accept its responsibility for dealing with this form of aggression. It is important that the world become clear in mind, for example, that the operation run from Hanoi against Viet-Nam is as clear a form of aggression as the violation of the 38th Parallel by the North Korean armies in June, 1950.

In my conversations with representatives of foreign governments, I am sometimes lectured that this or that government within the free world is not popular; they tell me that guerrilla warfare cannot be won unless the peoples are dissatisfied. These are, at best, half-truths. The truth is that guerrilla warfare, mounted from external bases—with rights of sanctuary—is a terrible burden to carry for any government in a society making its way toward modernization. As you know, it takes anywhere between ten and twenty soldiers to control one guerrilla in an organized operation. Moreover, the guerrilla force has this advantage: its task is merely to destroy, while the government must build and protect what it is building. A guerrilla war mounted from outside a transitional nation is a crude act of international vandalism. There will be no peace in the world if the international community accepts the outcome of a guerrilla war, mounted from outside a nation, as tantamount to a free election.

The sending of men and arms across international boundaries and the direction of guerrilla war from outside a sovereign nation is aggression; and this is a fact which the whole international community must confront and whose consequent responsibilities it must accept. Without such international action those against whom aggression is mounted will be driven inevitably to seek out and engage the ultimate source of the aggression they confront.

I suspect that in the end the real meaning of the conference on Laos at Geneva will hinge on this question: It will depend on whether or not the international community is prepared to mount an International Control Commission which has the will and the capacity to control the borders it was designed to control.

In facing the problem of guerrilla war, I have one observation to make as a historian. It is now fashionable—and I daresay for you it was compulsory—to read the learned works of Mao Tse-tung and Che Guevara on guerrilla warfare. This is, indeed, proper. One should read with care and without passion into the minds of one's enemies. But it is historically inaccurate and psychologically dangerous to think that these men created the strategy and tactics of guerrilla war to which we are now responding. Guerrilla warfare is not a form of military and psychological magic created by the Communists. There is no rule or parable in the Communist texts which was not known at an earlier time in history. The operation of Marion's men in relation to the Battle of Cowpens in the American Revolution was, for example, governed by rules which Mao merely echoes. Che Guevara knows nothing of this business that T. E. Lawrence did not know or was not practiced, for example, in the Peninsular Campaign during the Napoleonic wars, a century earlier. The orchestration of professional troops, militia and guerrilla fighters is an old game whose rules can be studied and learned.

My point is that we are up against a form of warfare which is powerful and effective only when we do not put our minds clearly to work on how to deal with it. I, for one, believe that with purposeful efforts most nations which might now be susceptible to guerrilla warfare could handle their border areas in wars which would make them very unattractive to the initiation of this ugly game. We can learn to prevent the emergence of the famous sea in which Mao Tse-tung taught his men to swim. This requires, of course, not merely a proper military program of deterrence but programs of village development, communications, and indoctrination. The best way to fight a guerrilla war is to prevent it from happening. And this can be done.

Similarly, I am confident that we can deal with the kind of operation now under way in Viet-Nam. It is an extremely dangerous operation, and it could overwhelm Viet-Nam if the Vietnamese—aided by the free world—do not deal with it. But it is an unsubtle operation by the book, based more on murder than on political or psychological appeal.

When Communists speak of wars of national liberation and of their support for "progressive forces," I think of the systematic program of assassination now going forward in which the principal victims are health, agriculture, and education officers in the Viet-Nam villages. The Viet-Cong are not trying to persuade the peasants of Viet-Nam that communism is good; they are trying to persuade them that their lives are insecure unless they co-operate with them. With resolution and confidence on all sides and with the assumption of international responsibility for the frontier problem, I believe we are going to bring this threat to the independence of Viet-Nam under control.

My view is, then, that we confront in guerrilla warfare in the underdeveloped areas a systematic attempt by the Communists to impose a serious disease on those societies attempting the transition to modernization. This attempt is a present danger in Southeast Asia. It could quickly become a major danger in Africa and Latin America. I salute in particular those among you whose duty it is—along with others—to prevent that disease, if possible, and to eliminate it where it is imposed.

As I understand the course you are now completing, it is designed to impress on you this truth: You are not merely soldiers in the old sense. Your job is not merely to accept the risks of war and to master its skills. Your job is to work with understanding with your fellow citizens in the whole creative process of modernization. From our perspective in Washington you take your place side by side with those others who are committed to help fashion independent, modern societies out of the revolutionary process now going forward. I salute you as I would a group of doctors, teachers, economic planners, agricultural experts, civil servants, or those others who are now leading the way in the whole southern half of the globe in fashioning new nations and societies that will stand up straight and assume in time their rightful place of dignity and responsibility in the world community; for this is our common mission.

Each of us must carry into his day-to-day work an equal understanding of the military and the creative dimensions of the job. I can tell you that those with whom I have the privilege to work are dedicated to that mission with every resource of mind and spirit at our command.

MANIFESTO OF THE EIGHTEEN*

The President of the Republic of Viet-Nam
Saigon

MR. PRESIDENT:

We the undersigned, representing a group of eminent citizens and personalities, intellectuals of all tendencies, and men of good will, recognize in the face of the gravity of the present political situation that we can no longer remain indifferent to the realities of life in our country.

Therefore, we officially address to you today an appeal with the aim of exposing to you the whole truth in the hope that the government will accord it all the attention necessary so as to urgently modify its policies, so as to remedy the present situation and lead the people out of danger.

Let us look toward the past, at the time when you were

* April 26, 1960. English text from B. B. Fall, *The Two Viet-Nams,* New York, 1963, reprinted by permission of Frederic A. Praeger, Inc.

abroad. For eight or nine years, the Vietnamese people suffered many trials due to the war: They passed from French domination to Japanese occupation, from revolution to resistance, from the nationalist imposture behind which hid communism to a pseudo-independence covering up for colonialism; from terror to terror, from sacrifice to sacrifice—in short, from promise to promise, until finally hope ended in bitter disillusion.

Thus, when you were on the point of returning to the country, the people as a whole entertained the hope that it would find again under your guidance the peace that is necessary to give meaning to existence, to reconstruct the destroyed homes, put to the plow again the abandoned lands. The people hoped no longer to be compelled to pay homage to one regime in the morning and to another at night, not to be the prey of the cruelties and oppression of one faction; no longer to be treated as coolies; no longer to be at the mercy of the monopolies; no longer to have to endure the depredations of corrupt and despotic civil servants. In one word, the people hoped to live in security at last, under a regime which would give them a little bit of justice and liberty. The whole people thought that you would be the man of the situation and that you would implement its hopes.

That is the way it was when you returned. The Geneva Accords of 1954 put an end to combat and to the devastations of war. The French Expeditionary Corps was progressively withdrawn, and total independence of South Viet-Nam had become a reality. Furthermore, the country had benefited from moral encouragement and a substantial increase of foreign aid from the free world. With so many favorable political factors, in addition to the blessed geographic conditions of a fertile and rich soil yielding agricultural, forestry, and fishing surpluses, South Viet-Nam should have been able to begin a definitive victory in the historical competition with the North, so as to carry out the will of the people and to lead the country on the way to hope, liberty, and happiness. Today, six years later, having benefited from so many undeniable advantages, what has the government been able to do? Where has it led South Viet-Nam? What parts of the popular aspirations have been implemented?

Let us try to draw an objective balance of the situation, without flattery or false accusations, strictly following a constructive line which you yourself have so often indicated, in the hope that the government shall modify its policies so as to extricate itself from a situation that is extremely dangerous to the very existence of the nation.

Policies

In spite of the fact that the bastard regime created and protected by colonialism has been overthrown and that many of the feudal organizations of factions and parties which oppress the population were destroyed, the people do not know a better life or more freedom under the republican regime which you have created. A constitution has been established in form only; a National Assembly exists whose deliberations always fall into line with the government; antidemocratic elections—all those are methods and "comedies" copied from the dictatorial Communist regimes, which obviously cannot serve as terms of comparison with North Viet-Nam.

Continuous arrests fill the jails and prisons to the rafters, as at this precise moment; public opinion and the press are reduced to silence. The same applies to the popular will as translated in certain open elections, in which it is insulted and trampled (as was the case, for example, during the recent elections for the Second Legislature). All these have provoked the discouragement and resentment of the people.

Political parties and religious sects have been eliminated. "Groups" or "movements" have replaced them. But this substitution has only brought about new oppressions against the population without protecting it for that matter against Communist enterprises. Here is one example: the fiefs of religious sects, which hitherto were deadly for the Communists, now not only provide no security whatever but have become favored highways for Viet-Minh guerrillas, as is, by the way, the case of the rest of the country.

This is proof that the religious sects, though futile, nevertheless constitute effective anti-Communist elements. Their elimination has opened the way to the Viet-Cong and unintentionally has prepared the way for the enemy, whereas a more realistic and more flexible policy could have amalgamated them all with a view to reinforcing the anti-Communist front.

Today the people want freedom. You should, Mr. President,

liberalize the regime, promote democracy, guarantee minimum civil rights, recognize the opposition so as to permit the citizens to express themselves without fear, thus removing grievances and resentments, opposition to which now constitutes for the people their sole reason for existence. When this occurs, the people of South Viet-Nam, in comparing their position with that of the North, will appreciate the value of true liberty and of authentic democracy. It is only at that time that the people will make all the necessary efforts and sacrifices to defend that liberty and democracy.

Administration

The size of the territory has shrunk, but the number of civil servants has increased, and still the work doesn't get done. This is because the government, like the Communists, lets the political parties control the population, separate the elite from the lower echelons, and sow distrust between those individuals who are "affiliated with the movement" and those who are "outside the group." Effective power, no longer in the hands of those who are usually responsible, is concentrated in fact in the hands of an irresponsible member of the "family," from whom emanates all orders; this slows down the administrative machinery, paralyzes all initiative, discourages good will. At the same time, not a month goes by without the press being full of stories about graft impossible to hide; this becomes an endless parade of illegal transactions involving millions of piastres.

The administrative machinery, already slowed down, is about to become completely paralyzed. It is in urgent need of reorganization. Competent people should be put back in the proper jobs; discipline must be re-established from the top to the bottom of the hierarchy; authority must go hand in hand with responsibility; efficiency, initiative, honesty, and the economy should be the criteria for promotion; professional qualifications should be respected. Favoritism based on family or party connections should be banished; the selling of influence, corruption, and abuse of power must be punished.

Thus, everything still can be saved, human dignity can be re-established; faith in an honest and just government can be restored.

Army

The French Expeditionary Corps has left the country, and a republican army has been constituted, thanks to American aid, which has equipped it with modern matériel. Nevertheless, even in a group of the proud elite of the youth such as the Vietnamese Army—where the sense of honor should be cultivated, whose blood and arms should be devoted to the defense of the country, where there should be no place for clannishness and factions—the spirit of the "national revolutionary movement" or of the "personalist body" divides the men of one and the same unit, sows distrust between friends of the same rank, and uses as a criterion for promotion fidelity toward the party in blind submission to its leaders. This creates extremely dangerous situations, such as the recent incident of Tay-Ninh.[1]

The purpose of the army, pillar of the defense of the country, is to stop foreign invasions and to eliminate rebel movements. It is at the service of the country only and should not lend itself to the exploitation of any faction or party. Its total reorganization is necessary. Clannishness and party obedience should be eliminated; its moral base strengthened; a noble tradition of national pride created; and fighting spirit, professional conscience, and bravery should become criteria for promotion. The troops should be encouraged to respect their officers, and the officers should be encouraged to love their men. Distrust, jealousy, rancor among colleagues of the same rank should be eliminated.

Then in case of danger, the nation will have at its disposal a valiant army animated by a single spirit and a single aspiration: to defend the most precious possession—our country, Viet-Nam.

Economic and Social Affairs

A rich and fertile country enjoying food surpluses; a budget which does not have to face military expenditures;[2] important

---

[1] This refers to the destruction of a complete Vietnamese Army Battalion in February, 1960, when Communist forces slipped into their camp through treachery and captured several hundred weapons.—B.B.F.

[2] The military expenditures of the Vietnamese budget are paid out of U.S. economic and military aid.—B.B.F.

war reparations; substantial profits from Treasury bonds; a colossal foreign-aid program; a developing market capable of receiving foreign capital investments—those are the many favorable conditions which could make Viet-Nam a productive and prosperous nation. However, at the present time many people are out of work, have no roof over their heads, and no money. Rice is abundant but does not sell; shop windows are well-stocked but the goods do not move. Sources of revenue are in the hands of speculators who use the [government] party and group to mask monopolies operating for certain private interests. At the same time, thousands of persons are mobilized for exhausting work, compelled to leave their own jobs, homes, and families, to participate in the construction of magnificent but useless "agrovilles" which weary them and provoke their disaffection, thus aggravating popular resentment and creating an ideal terrain for enemy propaganda.

The economy is the very foundation of society, and public opinion ensures the survival of the regime. The government must destroy all the obstacles standing in the way of economic development; must abolish all forms of monopoly and speculation; must create a favorable environment for investments coming from foreign friends as well as from our own citizens; must encourage commercial enterprises, develop industry, and create jobs to reduce unemployment. At the same time, it should put an end to all forms of human exploitation in the work camps of the agrovilles.

Then only the economy will flourish again; the citizen will find again a peaceful life and will enjoy his condition; society will be reconstructed in an atmosphere of freedom and democracy.

Mr. President, this is perhaps the first time that you have heard such severe and disagreeable criticism—so contrary to your own desires. Nevertheless, sir, these words are strictly the truth, a truth that is bitter and hard, that you have never been able to know because, whether this is intended or not, a void has been created around you, and by the very fact of your high position, no one permits you to perceive the critical point at which truth shall burst forth in irresistible waves of hatred on the part of a people subjected for a long time to terrible suffering and a people who shall rise to break the bonds which hold it

122 •   *The Viet-Nam Reader*

down. It shall sweep away the ignominy and all the injustices
which surround and oppress it.

As we do not wish, in all sincerity, that our Fatherland should
have to live through these perilous days, we—without taking
into consideration the consequences which our attitude may bring
upon us—are ringing today the alarm bell in view of the imminent danger which threatens the government.

Until now, we have kept silent and preferred to let the Executive act as it wished. But now time is of the essence; we feel that
it is our duty—and in the case of a nation in turmoil even the
most humble people have their share of responsibility—to speak
the truth, to awaken public opinion, to alert the people, and to
unify the opposition so as to point the way. We beseech the government to urgently modify its policies so as to remedy the situation, to defend the republican regime, and to safeguard the
existence of the nation. We hold firm hope that the Vietnamese
people shall know a brilliant future in which it will enjoy peace
and prosperity in freedom and progress.

Yours respectfully,

1. TRAN VAN VAN, *Diploma of Higher Commercial Studies, former
   Minister of Economy and Planning*
2. PHAN KHAC SUU, *Agricultural Engineer, former Minister of
   Agriculture, former Minister of Labor*
3. TRAN VAN HUONG, *Professor of Secondary Education, former
   Prefect of Saigon-Cholon*
4. NGUYEN LUU VIEN, *M.D., former Professor at the Medical
   School, former High Commissioner of Refugees*
5. HUYNH KIM HUU, *M.D., former Minister of Public Health*
6. PHAN HUY QUAT, *M.D., former Minister of National Education,
   former Minister of Defense*
7. TRAN VAN LY, *former Governor of Central Viet-Nam*
8. NGUYEN TIEN HY, *M.D.*
9. TRAN VAN DO, *M.D., former Minister of Foreign Affairs, Chairman of Vietnamese Delegation to the 1954 Geneva Conference*
10. LE NGOC CHAN, *Attorney at Law, former Secretary of State for
    National Defense*
11. LE QUANG LUAT, *Attorney at Law, former Government Dele-
    gate for North Viet-Nam, former Minister of Information and
    Propaganda*
12. LUONG TRONG TUONG, *Public Works Engineer, former Secre-
    tary of State for National Economy*

13. NGUYEN TANG NGUYEN, *M.D., former Minister of Labor and Youth*
14. PHAM HUU CHUONG, *M.D., former Minister of Public Health and Social Action*
15. TRAN VAN TUYEN, *Attorney at Law, former Secretary of State for Information and Propaganda*
16. TA CHUONG PHUNG, *former Provincial Governor for Binh-Dinh*
17. TRAN LE CHAT, *Laureate of the Triennial Mandarin Competition of 1903*
18. HO VAN VUI, *Reverend, former Parish Priest of Saigon, at present Parish Priest of Tha-La, Province of Tay-Ninh*

DEPARTMENT OF STATE

*A Comparison—Two Statements on
North Viet-Nam's Effort to Conquer
South Viet-Nam*

*White Paper, 1961**

On September 25, 1961, in an address to the United Nations, President Kennedy warned that body and the people of the world of the dangers of "the smoldering coals of war in Southeast Asia." Nowhere do those coals glare more ominously than in South Viet-Nam. While attention is diverted elsewhere—to Berlin, to negotiations over Laos, to turmoil in the Congo, to the United Nations itself, as well as to dozens of other problems—the Communist program to seize South Viet-Nam moves ahead relentlessly.

It is a program that relies on every available technique for spreading disorder and confusion in a peaceful society. Today it may call for the murder of a village chief known to be unfriendly to the Communists; tomorrow it may produce an attack in battalion strength against an outpost of the Army of the Republic of Viet-Nam. No tactic, whether of brutal terror, armed

---

* From Department of State Publication 7308, released December, 1961.

action, or persuasion, is ignored. If mining a road will stop all transport, who cares that a school bus may be the first vehicle to pass? If halting rice shipments means that many people go hungry, perhaps they will blame it on the government. If people object to paying taxes to both the Communists and to the government in Saigon, they are urged to refuse the latter.

The basic pattern of Viet-Cong (Vietnamese Communist) activity is not new, of course. It operated, with minor variations, in China, and Mao Tse-tung's theories on the conduct of guerrilla warfare are known to every Viet-Cong agent and cadre. Most of the same methods were used in Malaya, in Greece, in the Philippines, in Cuba, and in Laos. If there is anything peculiar to the Viet-Nam situation, it is that the country is divided and one-half provides a safe sanctuary from which subversion in the other half is directed and supported with both personnel and matériel.

What follows is a study of Viet-Cong activities in South Viet-Nam and of the elaborate organization in the North that supports those activities. The Communists have made the most elaborate efforts to conceal their role and to prevent any discoveries that would point an accusing finger at them for causing what is happening. But their efforts have not been totally successful.

In such a large-scale operation there are always some failures. There are defections. There are human frailties and some misjudgment. In major military operations prisoners are taken and documents are seized. All these and more have occurred in Viet-Nam. Over the years the authorities in Saigon have accumulated a mass of material exposing the activities of the Viet-Cong.

This report is based on an extensive study of much of that material. It relies on documentary and physical evidence and on the confessions of many captured Viet-Cong personnel. Officials of the government of the Republic of Viet-Nam gave unselfishly of their time and their expert advice in connection with this investigation. Countless individuals and agencies responsible for gathering and interpreting this kind of evidence contributed to the research that went into this report. Without their co-operation and help, it obviously would not have been possible.

The specific cases cited herein have been presented, as they occurred, to the International Control Commission in Saigon by the government of the Republic of Viet-Nam. Most recently, that government made an elaborate presentation to the I.C.C. on October 24, 1961, of the data available at that time of Communist-directed subversion in South Viet-Nam. The presentation was accompanied by a request that the I.C.C. investigate. The government in Saigon generously made available this same information for the compilation of this report.

What emerges from this study is a detailed, but by no means exhaustive, picture of Viet-Cong operations and of the program of the Communist government in Hanoi to win power over all Viet-Nam. The government of the United States believes that picture should be presented to the world.

There can be no doubt that the government of the Republic of Viet-Nam is fighting for its life. Those who would help the people of South Viet-Nam to remain outside the Communist orbit must have a thorough appreciation of the nature of that fight and of the way it is being conducted by the authorities in Hanoi and their disciplined followers in the South.

White Paper, 1965*

South Viet-Nam is fighting for its life against a brutal campaign of terror and armed attack inspired, directed, supplied, and controlled by the Communist regime in Hanoi. This flagrant aggression has been going on for years, but recently the pace has quickened and the threat has now become acute.

The war in Viet-Nam is a new kind of war, a fact as yet poorly understood in most parts of the world. Much of the confusion that prevails in the thinking of many people, and even many governments, stems from this basic misunderstanding. For in Viet-Nam a totally new brand of aggression has been loosed against ‾ an independent people who want to make their own way in peace and freedom.

Viet-Nam is *not* another Greece, where indigenous guerrilla forces used friendly neighboring territory as a sanctuary.

Viet-Nam is *not* another Malaya, where Communist guerrillas were, for the most part, physically distinguishable from the peaceful majority they sought to control.

---

* From Department of State Publication 7839, released February, 1965.

Viet-Nam is *not* another Philippines, where Communist guerrillas were physically separated from the source of their moral and physical support.

Above all, the war in Viet-Nam is *not* a spontaneous and local rebellion against the established government.

There are elements in the Communist program of conquest directed against South Viet-Nam common to each of the previous areas of aggression and subversion. But there is one fundamental difference. In Viet-Nam a Communist government has set out deliberately to conquer a sovereign people in a neighboring state. And to achieve its end, it has used every resource of its own government to carry out its carefully planned program of concealed aggression. North Viet-Nam's commitment to seize control of the South is no less total than was the commitment of the regime in North Korea in 1950. But knowing the consequences of the latter's undisguised attack, the planners in Hanoi have tried desperately to conceal their hand. They have failed and their aggression is as real as that of an invading army.

This report is a summary of the massive evidence of North Vietnamese aggression obtained by the government of South Viet-Nam. This evidence has been jointly analyzed by South Vietnamese and American experts.

The evidence shows that the hard core of the Communist forces attacking South Viet-Nam were trained in the North and ordered into the South by Hanoi. It shows that the key leadership of the Viet-Cong (VC), the officers and much of the cadre, many of the technicians, political organizers, and propagandists have come from the North and operate under Hanoi's direction. It shows that the training of essential military personnel and their infiltration into the South is directed by the Military High Command in Hanoi.

The evidence shows that many of the weapons and much of the ammunition and other supplies used by the Viet-Cong have been sent into South Viet-Nam from Hanoi. In recent months new types of weapons have been introduced in the VC army, for which all ammunition must come from outside sources. Communist China and other Communist states have been the prime suppliers of these weapons and ammunition, and they have been channeled primarily through North Viet-Nam.

The directing force behind the effort to conquer South Viet-

Nam is the Communist Party in the North, the Lao Dong (Workers) Party. As in every Communist state, the party is an integral part of the regime itself. North Vietnamese officials have expressed their firm determination to absorb South Viet-Nam into the Communist world.

Through its Central Committee, which controls the government of the North, the Lao Dong Party directs the total political and military effort of the Viet-Cong. The Military High Command in the North trains the military men and sends them into South Viet-Nam. The Central Research Agency, North Viet-Nam's central intelligence organization, directs the elaborate espionage and subversion effort. The extensive political-military organization in the North . . . directs the Viet-Cong war effort . . .

Under Hanoi's over-all direction the Communists have established an extensive machine for carrying on the war within South Viet-Nam. The focal point is the Central Office for South Viet-Nam with its political and military subsections and other specialized agencies. A subordinate part of this Central Office is the Liberation Front for South Viet-Nam. The front was formed at Hanoi's order in 1960. Its principal function is to influence opinion abroad and to create the false impression that the aggression in South Viet-Nam is an indigenous rebellion against the established government.

For more that ten years the people and the government of South Viet-Nam, exercising the inherent right of self-defense, have fought back against these efforts to extend Communist power south across the 17th Parallel. The United States has responded to the appeals of the government of the Republic of Viet-Nam for help in this defense of the freedom and independence of its land and its people.

In 1961 the Department of State issued a report called *A Threat to the Peace*. It described North Viet-Nam's program to seize South Viet-Nam. The evidence in that report had been presented by the government of the Republic of Viet-Nam to the International Control Commission (I.C.C.). A special report by the I.C.C. in June, 1962, upheld the validity of that evidence. The Commission held that there was "sufficient evidence to show beyond reasonable doubt" that North Viet-Nam had sent arms and men into South Viet-Nam to carry out subversion with the aim of overthrowing the legal government there. The I.C.C.

found the authorities in Hanoi in specific violation of four provisions of the Geneva accords of 1954.

Since then, new and even more impressive evidence of Hanoi's aggression has accumulated. The government of the United States believes that evidence should be presented to its own citizens and to the world. It is important for free men to know what has been happening in Viet-Nam, and how, and why.

WHITE HOUSE STATEMENT

U. S. Policy on Viet-Nam*

Secretary [of Defense Robert S.] McNamara and General [Maxwell D.] Taylor reported to the President this morning and to the National Security Council this afternoon. Their report included a number of classified findings and recommendations which will be the subject of further review and action. Their basic presentation was endorsed by all members of the Security Council and the following statement of United States policy was approved by the President on the basis of recommendations received from them and from Ambassador [Henry Cabot] Lodge.

1. The security of South Viet-Nam is a major interest of the United States as other free nations. We will adhere to our policy of working with the people and government of South Viet-Nam to deny this country to communism and to suppress the externally stimulated and supported insurgency of the Viet-Cong as promptly as possible. Effective performance in this undertaking is the central objective of our policy in South Viet-Nam.

2. The military program in South Viet-Nam has made progress and is sound in principle, though improvements are being energetically sought.

3. Major U.S. assistance in support of this military effort is needed only until the insurgency has been suppressed or until

---

* Statement, October 2, 1963.

the national security forces of the government of South Viet-Nam are capable of suppressing it.

Secretary McNamara and General Taylor reported their judgment that the major part of the U.S. military task can be completed by the end of 1965, although there may be a continuing requirement for a limited number of U.S. training personnel. They reported that by the end of this year, the U.S. program for training Vietnamese should have progressed to the point where 1,000 U.S. military personnel assigned to South Viet-Nam can be withdrawn.

4. The political situation in South Viet-Nam remains deeply serious. The United States has made clear its continuing opposition to any repressive actions in South Viet-Nam. While such actions have not yet significantly affected the military effort, they could do so in the future.

5. It remains the policy of the United States, in South Viet-Nam as in other parts of the world, to support the efforts of the people of that country to defeat aggression and to build a peaceful and free society.

MARCUS G. RASKIN

A Citizen's White Paper on American Policy in Viet-Nam and Southeast Asia*

The diplomatic policy of the American government by the end of December, 1964, was almost totally militarized. Those who were interested in negotiation without expanding the war into North Viet-Nam were eclipsed by those who merely wanted to expand the war *per se* or who wanted to bomb and negotiate. The latter policy became the policy of the "doves." The previous deterrent to a substantial military involvement in Southeast Asia, war with China, seemed to become the spur or objective. "No more sanctuaries," the Chinese were warned, thus leaving the

---

* Excerpts from Congressional Record, May 5, 1965.

direct implication that the source (China) would be struck if the war continued.

The growing American involvement in Viet-Nam was little understood in the United States. Although Congress was silent on the course of the war, privately there was anger and disbelief at the policies of the Johnson Administration. Some blamed the policies on carry-overs from the Kennedy Administration. They believed that President Johnson was a neophyte in foreign affairs and had counted too heavily on the advice of the military, the C.I.A., State, the National Security Council machinery: those who had a vested interest in the militarized foreign policy. By April of 1965, newspapers, liberal and conservative, called for a definition of American aims. University professors and students held marches and "teach-ins" in favor of negotiation. The President spoke on April 7, 1965, to the American people in reply both to the critics of his policy and to the March 15 declaration of the nonaligned nations calling for negotiation. President Johnson's speech on April 7 was predicated on the official American position that North Viet-Nam controls the Viet-Cong and the course of the guerrilla war. This view, enunciated in the Department of State's White Paper (released February, 1965), is open to serious question. A special Japanese envoy to study the situation in Viet-Nam for the government of Japan, Mr. Matsumoto, pointed out that the Viet-Cong is much like the French underground during World War II, representing different groups in the country. "It can be said that the Viet-Cong is not directly connected to Communist China or the Soviet Union. Consequently, it is not certain that the Viet-Cong will give up fighting because of the bombing of North Viet-Nam. . . . In Viet-Nam I often heard it said that the Viet-Cong is a nationalist movement. This means the Viet-Cong will not give up resistance until they have achieved their objectives."

Mr. Matsumoto said that no one could really define the character of the Viet-Cong and that even our own administration in Saigon estimates that only 30 per cent of the Viet-Cong are Communists. The Japanese findings are consistent with the dynamics of revolutionary or resistance movements. Those who in fact do the fighting and live through hardship and misery will not easily hand over their power to another, be it Ho Chi Minh or Mao Tse-tung. Ironically, the interests of the North Vietnamese and the Viet-Cong further diverged once the United States began to bomb North Viet-Nam. Although the North Vietnamese were now suffering in their own country, the Viet-Cong continued to flourish. In view of this, Ho Chi Minh may find it very difficult to stop the war.

There are four ways of looking at this "reality" in terms of American policy:

(1) The official U.S. position is correct; that Ho has sufficient control over the Viet-Cong to stop the war.

(2) The U.S. has been fooled by its own ideology which insists that revolution or civil war movements are the result of an over-all Communist conspiracy.

(3) The U.S. wishes to stabilize the Southeast Asia area and in due time will offer Ho Chi Minh and his group leadership in an attempt to countercheck the power of Communist China.

(4) U.S. planners in actuality accept the interpretation of the Japanese. They know that there is little connection between the Southern rebels and North Vietnamese, but are using this line to expand the war to North Viet-Nam and possibly China.

If this is the rationale to the American diplomatic position, it appears to be predicated on the third point, viz., that the U.S. wishes to use Ho Chi Minh and the anti-Chinese felings of the North Vietnamese to counterbalance the power of Communist China. The insistence on negotiating with Ho Chi Minh to the virtual exclusion of the Viet-Cong seems to fly directly in the face of our stated policy toward an independent South Viet-Nam. It would appear that it is to the American advantage to negotiate or to agree to negotiate with the Viet-Cong and National Liberation Front since they would be likely (given the regional character of the country) to build their own political power relatively independent of North Vietnamese domination.

The Mekong River Delta project outlined by the President in April, 1965, while it could not immediately yield results, would have the positive effect of diverting war energies to more constructive ends. What is important in this case is not that the Mekong project would take a decade before it "bore fruit," but that it reflects a new possibility toward co-operation and activity in the name of man. In that sense (although both parts of the speech reflected the terrible *hubris* of the United States) the second half of the President's speech should be taken as an indication of ways in which the United States is prepared to participate —not as boss but as good neighbor. That view is quite far from the views set forth in the first part of the speech, which left the impression that our purposes in international affairs derive from our values and principles, since we do not fight for such mundane things as territory or colonies. No price, it would seem, is too great to pay for what we believe is "right."

Not surprisingly, the speech was read by the Chinese in the context of the military build-up by the United States in Viet-Nam, increased raids, and military titillation of the Chinese border. The North Vietnamese, while rejecting the offer of "unconditional discussions," seemed more disposed, according to East European sources, to take the President's offer seriously, even to the extent of accepting a neutralized North and South Viet-Nam. The Ho Chi Minh interview printed in *Pravda* in June, 1965, also alluded to this position. Most diplomats in the East and West agreed that no negotiations or unlimited discussions could be entered into until the United States limited its military efforts to South Viet-Nam, stopped bombing North Viet-Nam, was willing to negotiate with the Viet-Cong, and accepted Article 7 of the Final Declaration of the Geneva Conference which provided for elections to name a government for all of Viet-Nam at some future determinate time. If these conditions were to be met by the United States, it would mean that the United States is prepared for diplomatic negotiations and is motivated by a foreign policy in Southeast Asia that is not primarily based on its military power. Military power has failed in Southeast Asia because it was employed by the United States to achieve results that are inherently nonmilitary. This has been the great tragedy of American statecraft in this generation.

Since the Second World War, American policy-makers have developed a foreign policy that casts America in the role of world policeman. We assumed this role in Viet-Nam, a place where we did not begin to comprehend the complex crosscurrents of politics, nationalism, personality, tradition, history, and other people's interests. To support our role as policeman, our military and C.I.A. programs in Southeast Asia grew to mammoth proportions without rhyme or reason. These programs often reflected little more than the power struggles of the agencies of

American bureaucracy, rather than the reality of the Asian situation. A report on Viet-Nam and Southeast Asia prepared in 1963 by four Senators, at the request of President Kennedy, stated:

It should also be noted, in all frankness, that our own bureaucratic tendencies to act in uniform and enlarging patterns have resulted in an expansion of the U.S. commitment in some places to an extent which would appear to bear only the remotest relationship to what is essential, or even desirable, in terms of U.S. interests.

The United States, by the military and covert way it has operated in Viet-Nam in the past ten years, has nurtured strong anti-white and anti-Western feelings in Southeast Asia. Whether we called it "responsibility" or empire, the fact is that the United States succeeded to the Japanese and French hegemony in Asia without really knowing why or with what purpose. Empires are very seldom built by design. They start almost accidentally: their dynamics and actions define what they are. Each empire has its own characteristics, although historically they all seem to involve the defense of allies, the suppression of certain regimes in favor of others, and a powerful ideology. Ultimately, a common characteristic is a lack of judgment on the part of leaders, who are no longer able to distinguish between real and chimeric interests because of the empire's octopus-like tentacles. Those tentacles, especially if they include extensive military involvement, strangle the judgment of the leaders.

Our military involvement in Viet-Nam has camouflaged America's real interests and distorted our diplomatic and political vision of the means that should be employed there. The methods we have followed in Viet-Nam may not be without cost in terms of our own nation's stability and freedom of choice. Thus, when we ask the military to undertake projects which are inherently unmilitary, we are courting great danger. It is perhaps overdramatic to say that the United States will be faced with a French Organisation de l'Armée Secrète (OAS) situation if we substantially expand the war, and then attempt an accommodation—but such seeds are easily sown. For example, the official American policy in South Viet-Nam is to support a civilian government, but the rank-and-file military as well as high-ranking American military officers in Viet-Nam support the South Vietnamese military. Bad habits are learned in such wars and they may too easily be applied at home.

It is hard for American civilian leadership to learn that the military is not a machine which can be started and stopped by pressing a button. By definition of their mission, the military want to follow through to a military victory. We will find that each day that American policy-makers procrastinate on a political settlement, the war will escalate just by its own momentum. In this regard the military bureaucratic course of the war is quite instructive. The Special Forces and the Army were given responsibility for the war, under President Kennedy. After the apparent failure of these forces, the Air Force lobbied for involvement. Using the Gulf of Tonkin as the pretext, the Air Force sent planes to South Viet-Nam as a "deterrent." But "deterrents" are vulnerable and can be easily destroyed by guerrillas, as these were at Bien Hoa. Here the psychology of the paper tiger played its part. The pride of the Air Force was wounded and it decided to involve itself more fully so that it could prove itself. Once this occurred, the Marines and the Navy (but less so) lobbied for an expanded role, which was granted. Not wanting to be left out, the Army also petitioned for greater involvement. This was also granted by the White House. Finally, the S.A.C., in a non-nuclear way, also wanted to be involved. Paradoxically, the military may have wished for involvement because they feared that the war would end, that the "politicians" would negotiate a military withdrawal before they had had a chance to test themselves in battle. While our military may have feared that the war would be over, it was very hard to impress on our opponents our peaceful intentions, or to counter those groups in the American government and the public who wanted a military "win."

As a military venture, the Vietnamese operation is not one in which very many can take any particular pride. The bad habits of that war have included torture, napalming, and defoliation, as well as an inability to understand which means could yield suitable ends. Although governments are, by their nature, notoriously uncritical of themselves, democracies, by their nature, have a better chance of holding to account their governments and the actions of the individuals in those governments (even though accepting personal responsibility for actions is not a very fashionable virtue in government). Too often governments, that is, men in government, are expected to operate under inverted definitions of responsibility and morality, or to forget about them while in government. (Indeed, a former Secretary of State, Dean Acheson, gave such behavior an ideological gloss in his Amherst College address in December, 1964.) This sort of "responsibility" and "morality" can be seen in Viet-Nam. Where, as in the case of Viet-Nam, three out of four Americans were not even aware until the middle of 1964 that the United States was involved militarily, officials seem to have felt themselves free to tolerate sadistic and totalitarian methods in the name of fuzzy objectives. Such methods spread easily, and unthinkingly, in governments. It is best that they be exposed and terminated.

With the realization that neither the United States alone nor the Western powers together can dictate a result in Southeast Asia, does there remain any role which these countries can play in that area? Most certainly it is not that of policeman or "white man's burden" for Asia. That lesson was learned, or should have been learned, ten years ago. Perhaps the moderately clever even learned it at the end of the Second World War. Nor is it likely that pacts such as SEATO—which does not include the great nations that have real or geographical interests in Southeast Asia: Japan, India, and Burma—can ever be really effective in maintaining the peace in Southeast Asia. If the great powers are to exercise a role, and if there is to be a long-term settlement, it will have to be in concert with other nations: that is, through the U.N. Although the present line of the Chinese Communists and the North Vietnamese is to oppose U.N. involvement, because they fear that the Geneva and Laotian agreements would be scrapped, any new settlement would necessarily be predicated on the 1954 and 1962 agreements. The purpose of U.N. involvement would be to guarantee that the terms are kept.

While the U.N. machinery appears to the West to be unwieldy and to leave much room for improvement, the facts are that the U.N. in the Southeast Asian area has done more to stabilize that region than either the SEATO arrangement or the American military intervention. For example, the U.N. was instrumental in ending the 1961 Laotian crisis, whereas SEATO was unable even to agree on what the crisis was. The probability is that America's allies in SEATO would be more likely to act under U.N. direction than under SEATO—as an international or regional institution, SEATO has absolutely no moral or political force. Furthermore, the nations of Southeast Asia are more favorably disposed to the U.N.—because of the voting power of the Afro-Asian and Latin American nations in the General Assembly—than they are to pact alliances which are comprised principally of white Western powers. The prescription for action is not an easy one, for it will mean that we shall have to reconsider how the United States is to relate to the world, and to itself.

PART THREE

The Second Indochina War

A. AS SEEN FROM WASHINGTON

Introduction

The Second Indochina War started on July 21, 1956. On that day, the deadline passed which had been set two years earlier at Geneva for reunification elections to be held between the two zones of Viet-Nam. South Viet-Nam had repeatedly refused to hold even low-level discussions with North Viet-Nam on economic relations, such as the two Germanys maintained throughout the worst periods of the Berlin Wall crisis. Hence, it was obvious that North Viet-Nam, once it was convinced that no meaningful relationships could be built up with the Saigon regime, had little reason to coexist with it—the more so as "March to the North" slogans became an everyday part of Saigon's propaganda output.

The fact that the Diem regime had failed to build up a broad following in the country and that the United States, to all appearances, was blind to the regime's shortcomings and was willing to support it to the bitter end, merely facilitated the task of the National Liberation Front and of the various other oppositionists in the country (for, it is important to remember, Hoa-Hao Buddhist guerrilla battalions held large tracts in several southern provinces until Diem's murder; and two unsuccessful attempts at killing him had been carried out by his own American-trained troops before he was finally assassinated—not by the Viet-Cong but by his own generals). The official view of events in Viet-Nam over the past decade cannot, of course, admit as yet that Diem not only lost popularity at the end, but in fact *never* had been popular and *always* had run South Viet-Nam as an iron-fisted dictator. For this admission would mean that American officials both in Saigon and in Washington would have to recognize the truth of what John Mecklin, a former American senior diplomat in Saigon, wrote in his recently-published *Mission in Torment:* ". . . the case against us was more complex than the sin of falsehood. . . . The root of the problem was the fact that much of what the newsmen took to be lies was exactly what the [U.S.] mission genuinely believed, and was reporting to Washington. . . . Our feud with the newsmen was an angry symptom of bureaucratic sickness."

There is little evidence at the time of this writing, at least on the public record, that a re-evaluation of the origins of the Second Indochina War has been made. This is abundantly clear from a variety of official statements, as shown below. The State Department's White Papers affirm, contrary to the hard statistical facts at hand, that South Viet-Nam under Diem had experienced an "economic miracle," along West German lines, the crowning piece of which was a successful land reform. In reality, South Viet-Nam was in the unenviable position of increasing insolvency even before the large-scale outbreak of the insurgency, and in mid-1965 American officials in South Viet-Nam are laying the groundwork for yet another land reform (the fourth, since 1946), thus giving practical, if not official, recognition to Diem's—and his successors—failure to effect land reform.

In views expressed by the Assistant Secretary for Far Eastern Affairs, William P. Bundy, as well as by other Administration officials, the whole Viet-Nam problem still boils down to "external aggression" and little else. According to Senator Thomas Dodd, South Viet-Nam was on the threshold of complete victory when Diem was killed, and the Buddhist leadership (much, if not all, of it pro-Communist) along with the American "neo-isolationists" who shared their distorted views, was about ready to sell South Viet-Nam to the foe. The chairman of the Senate Foreign Relations Committee,

Senator J. W. Fulbright, served notice that we should strive for a political settlement based on the Geneva Accords of 1954. He, for one, sought limits to the military escalation.

On the military side, distorted standards of what constitutes success or failure in a counterinsurgency operation have led to unrealistic and overoptimistic claims or expectations of military victory, repeatedly expressed in recent years by high civilians and military officials of the Department of Defense. Such estimates, once they were presented to the President by Secretary Robert S. McNamara or General Maxwell D. Taylor, had of necessity to lead to policy decisions whose political premises were often doubtful and whose military parameters were totally inaccurate. Yet to simply point to the discrepancies between policy and reality often brings forth little else but more of the "angry symptoms of bureaucratic sickness" of which John Mecklin spoke—and often from the highest quarters.

What for too long was tragically forgotten by the bureaucrats and the military is that even "insurgencies" or revolutionary wars are now covered by documents that outline certain rules—which the United States as well as Viet-Nam signed, and which both are treaty-bound to observe. The 1949 Geneva Conventions for the Protection of War Victims, which is in part reproduced below, is one of those documents. Although in the United States the public has paid scant attention to the type of war that is being fought in Viet-Nam which includes napalming and torture, other nations have carefully catalogued—and criticized—the use of these tactics.

Geneva Conventions for the Protection of War Victims*

The undersigned Plenipotentiaries of the Governments represented at the Diplomatic Conference held at Geneva from April 21 to August 12, 1949, for the purpose of revising the Conven-

---

* August 12, 1949.

tion concluded at Geneva on July 27, 1929, relative to the Treatment of Prisoners of War, have agreed as follows:

PART I

GENERAL PROVISIONS

ARTICLE 1

The High Contracting Parties undertake to respect and to ensure respect for the present Convention in all circumstances.

ARTICLE 2

In addition to the provisions which shall be implemented in peace time, the present Convention shall apply to all cases of declared war or of any other armed conflict which may arise between two or more of the High Contracting Parties, even if the state of war is not recognized by one of them.

The Convention shall also apply to all cases of partial or total occupation of the territory of a High Contracting Party, even if the said occupation meets with no armed resistance.

Although one of the Powers in conflict may not be a party to the present Convention, the Powers who are parties thereto shall remain bound by it in their mutual relations. They shall furthermore be bound by the Convention in relation to the said Power, if the latter accepts and applies the provisions thereof.

ARTICLE 3

In the case of armed conflict not of an international character occurring in the territory of one of the High Contracting Parties, each party to the conflict shall be bound to apply as a minimum, the following provisions:

(1) Persons taking no active part in the hostilities, including members of armed forces who have laid down their arms and those placed *hors de combat* by sickness, wounds, detention, or any other cause, shall in all circumstances be treated humanely, without any adverse distinction founded

on race, color, religion or faith, sex, birth or wealth, or any other similar criteria.

To this end the following acts are and shall remain prohibited at any time and in any place whatsoever with respect to the above-mentioned persons:

(*a*) violence to life and person, in particular murder of all kinds, mutilation, cruel treatment and torture;

(*b*) taking of hostages;

(*c*) outrages upon personal dignity, in particular, humiliating and degrading treatment;

(*d*) the passing of sentences and the carrying out of executions without previous judgment pronounced by a regularly constituted court affording all the judicial guarantees which are recognized as indispensable by civilized peoples.

(2) The wounded and sick shall be collected and cared for. An impartial humanitarian body, such as the International Committee of the Red Cross, may offer its services to the Parties to the conflict.

The Parties to the conflict should further endeavor to bring into force, by means of special agreements, all or part of the other provisions of the present Convention.

The application of the preceding provisions shall not affect the legal status of the Parties to the conflict.

ARTICLE 4

A. Prisoners of war, in the sense of the present Convention, are persons belonging to one of the following categories, who have fallen into the power of the enemy:

(1) Members of the armed forces of a Party to the conflict, as well as members of militias or volunteer corps forming part of such armed forces.

(2) Members of other militias and members of other volunteer corps, including those of organized resistance movements, belonging to a Party to the conflict and operating in or outside their own territory, even if this territory is occupied, provided that such militias or volunteer corps, including

such organized resistance movements, fulfill the following conditions:

> (*a*) that of being commanded by a person responsible for his subordinates;
> (*b*) that of having a fixed distinctive sign recognizable at a distance;
> (*c*) that of carrying arms openly;
> (*d*) that of conducting their operations in accordance with the laws and customs of war.

(3) Members of regular armed forces who profess allegiance to a government or an authority not recognized by the Detaining Power.

(4) Persons who accompany the armed forces without actually being members thereof, such as civilian members of military aircraft crews, war correspondents, supply contractors, members of labor units or of services responsible for the welfare of the armed forces, provided that they have received authorization from the armed forces which they accompany, who shall provide them for that purpose with an identity card similar to the annexed model.

(5) Members of crews, including masters, pilots and apprentices, of the merchant marine and the crews of civil aircraft of the Parties to the conflict, who do not benefit by more favorable treatment under any other provisions of international law.

(6) Inhabitants of a nonoccupied territory, who on the approach of the enemy spontaneously take up arms to resist the invading forces, without having had time to form themselves into regular armed units, provided they carry arms openly and respect the laws and customs of war.

B. The following shall likewise be treated as prisoners of war under the present Convention:

(1) Persons belonging, or having belonged, to the armed forces of the occupied country, if the occupying Power considers it necessary by reason of such allegiance to intern them, even though it has originally liberated them while hostilities were going on outside the territory it occupies, in particular where such persons have made an unsuccessful attempt to rejoin the armed forces to which they belong and which

are engaged in combat, or where they fail to comply with a summons made to them with a view to internment.

(2) The persons belonging to one of the categories enumerated in the present Article, who have been received by neutral or nonbelligerent Powers on their territory and whom these Powers are required to intern under international law, without prejudice to any more favorable treatment which these Powers may choose to give and with the exception of Articles 8, 10, 15, 30, fifth paragraph, 58–67, 92, 126 and, where diplomatic relations exist between the Parties to the conflict and the neutral or nonbelligerent Power concerned, those Articles concerning the Protecting Power. Where such diplomatic relations exist, the Parties to a conflict on whom these persons depend shall be allowed to perform toward them the functions of a Protecting Power as provided in the present Convention, without prejudice to the functions which these Parties normally exercise in conformity with diplomatic and consular usage and treaties.

This article shall in no way affect the status of medical personnel and chaplains as provided for in Article 33 of the present Convention.

DEPARTMENT OF STATE WHITE PAPER

Aggression from the North*

Hanoi Supplies the Key Personnel for the Armed Aggression Against South Viet-Nam

The hard core of the Communist forces attacking South Viet-Nam are men trained in North Viet-Nam. They are ordered into the South and remain under the military discipline of the Military

---

* Excerpts from Department of State Publication 7839, released February, 1965.

High Command in Hanoi. Special training camps operated by the North Vietnamese army give political and military training to the infiltrators. Increasingly the forces sent into the South are native North Vietnamese who have never seen South Viet-Nam. A special infiltration unit, the 70th Transportation Group, is responsible for moving men from North Viet-Nam into the South via infiltration trails through Laos. Another special unit, the maritime infiltration group, sends weapons and supplies and agents by sea into the South.

The infiltration rate has been increasing. From 1959 to 1960, when Hanoi was establishing its infiltration pipeline, at least 1,800 men, and possibly 2,700 more, moved into South Viet-Nam from the North. The flow increased to a minimum of 3,700 in 1961 and at least 5,400 in 1962. There was a modest decrease in 1963 to 4,200 confirmed infiltrators, though later evidence is likely to raise this figure.

For 1964 the evidence is still incomplete. However, it already shows that a minimum of 4,400 infiltrators entered the South, and it is estimated more than 3,000 others were sent in.

There is usually a time lag between the entry of infiltrating troops and the discovery of clear evidence they have entered. This fact, plus collateral evidence of increased use of the infiltration routes, suggests strongly that 1964 was probably the year of greatest infiltration so far.

Thus, since 1959, nearly 20,000 VC officers, soldiers, and technicians are known to have entered South Viet-Nam under orders from Hanoi. Additional information indicates that an estimated 17,000 more infiltrators were dispatched to the South by the regime in Hanoi during the past six years. It can reasonably be assumed that still other infiltration groups have entered the South for which there is no evidence yet available.

To some the level of infiltration from the North may seem modest in comparison with the total size of the Armed Forces of the Republic of Viet-Nam. But one-for-one calculations are totally misleading in the kind of warfare going on in Viet-Nam. First, a high proportion of infiltrators from the North are well-trained officers, cadres, and specialists. Second, it has long been realized that in guerrilla combat the burdens of defense are vastly heavier than those of attack. In Malaya, the Philippines, and elsewhere a ratio of at least 10-to-1 in favor of the forces of order was required to meet successfully the threat of the guerrillas' hit-and-run tactics.

In the calculus of guerrilla warfare the scale of North Vietnamese infiltration into the South takes on a very different meaning. For the infiltration of 5,000 guerrilla fighters in a given year is the equivalent of marching perhaps 50,000 regular troops across the border, in terms of the burden placed on the defenders.

Above all, the number of proved and probable infiltrators from the North should be seen in relation to the size of the VC forces. It is now estimated that the Viet-Cong number approximately 35,000 so-called hard-core forces, and another 60,000-80,000 local forces. It is thus apparent that infiltrators from the North—allowing for casualties—make up the majority of the so-called hard-core Viet-Cong. Personnel from the North, in short, are now and have always been the backbone of the entire VC operation.

It is true that many of the lower-level elements of the VC forces are recruited within South Viet-Nam. However, the thousands of reported cases of VC kidnapings and terrorism make it abundantly clear that threats and other pressures by the Viet-Cong play a major part in such recruitment.

THE INFILTRATION PROCESS

The infiltration routes supply hard-core units with most of their officers and noncommissioned personnel. This source helps fill the gaps left by battle casualties, illness, and defection and insures continued control by Hanoi. Also, as the nature of the conflict has changed, North Viet-Nam has supplied the Viet-Cong with technical specialists via the infiltration routes. These have included men trained in armor and ordnance, antiaircraft, and communications as well as medical corpsmen and transport experts.

There is no single infiltration route from the North to South Viet-Nam. But by far the biggest percentage of infiltrators follow the same general course. The principal training center for North Vietnamese army men assigned to join the Viet-Cong has been at Xuan Mai near Hanoi. Recently captured Viet-Cong have also reported an infiltration training camp at Thanh Hoa. After completion of their training course—which involves political and propaganda work as well as military subjects—infiltrating units are moved to Vinh on the east coast. Many have made stopovers at a staging area in Dong Hoi where additional training is conducted. From there they go by truck to the Laos border.

Then, usually after several days' rest, infiltrators move southward through Laos. Generally they move along the Laos–South Viet-Nam border. Responsibility for infiltration from North Viet-Nam through Laos belongs to the 70th Transportation Group of the North Vietnamese army. After a time the infiltration groups turn eastward, entering South Viet-Nam in Quang Nam, Quang Tri, Thua Thien, Kontum, or another of the border provinces.

The Communists have established regular lanes for infiltration with way-stations established about one day's march apart. The way-stations are equipped to quarter and feed the Viet-Cong passing through. Infiltrators who suffer from malaria or other illnesses stay at the stations until they recover sufficiently to join another passing group moving south.

The map on page 147 shows the infiltration route from North Viet-Nam to the South followed by VC Sgt. Huynh Van Tay and a group of North Vietnamese army officers and men in September 1963. Tay was captured during an engagement in Chuong Thien Province in April 1964.

Local guides lead the infiltration groups along the secret trails. Generally they direct the infiltrators from halfway between two stations, through their own base station, and on halfway to the next supply base. Thus the guides are kept in ignorance of all but their own way-stations. Only group leaders are permitted to talk with the guides in order to preserve maximum security. The men are discouraged from asking where they are or where they are going.

The same system of trails and guides used along the Lao infiltration routes is used within South Viet-Nam itself. Viet-Cong infiltrators may report directly to a reassignment center in the highlands as soon as they enter South Viet-Nam. But in the past year or more some groups have moved down trails in South Viet-Nam to provinces along the Cambodian border and near Saigon before receiving their unit assignment. Within South Viet-Nam infiltration and supplies are handled by VC units such as the Nam Son Transportation Group.

CHINA

NORTH

VIET

NAM

LAOS

XUAN MAI
(September 1, 1963)

HANOI

GULF

OF

TONKIN

VINH

DONG HOI
(September 3, 1963)

Demarcation Line

IN LAOS
(September 4, 1963)

CROSSED BORDER
(September 20, 1963)

THAILAND

SOUTH

CHINA

SEA

SOUTH

VIET

NAM

CAMBODIA

CAPTURED
(April 6, 1964)

DESTINATION
(November 26, 1963)

• SAIGON

Mekong R.

GULF OF SIAM

20°

110°

15°

10°

0   MILES   200

Infiltration route from the North by which a group of
North Vietnamese troops entered South Viet-Nam in September, 1963

At the Laos border crossing point infiltrators are re-equipped. Their North Vietnamese army uniforms must be turned in. They must give up all personal papers, letters, notebooks, and photographs that might be incriminating. Document control over the infiltrators has been tightened considerably over the past two years. A number of Vietnamese infiltrators have told of being fitted out with Lao "neutralist" uniforms for their passage through Laos.

Infiltration groups are usually issued a set of black civilian pajama-like clothes, two unmarked uniforms, rubber sandals, a sweater, a hammock, mosquito netting, and waterproof sheeting. They carry a 3–5 day supply of food. A packet of medicines and bandages is usually provided.

The size of infiltration groups varies widely. Prisoners have mentioned units as small as 5 men and as large as 500. Generally the groups number 40–50. When they arrive in South Viet-Nam these groups are usually split up and assigned to various VC units as replacements, although some have remained intact. . . .

Hanoi Supplies Weapons, Ammunition, and Other War Matériel to Its Forces in the South

When Hanoi launched the VC campaign of terror, violence, and subversion in earnest in 1959, the Communist forces relied mainly on stocks of weapons and ammunition left over from the war against the French. Supplies sent in from North Viet-Nam came largely from the same source. As the military campaign progressed, the Viet-Cong depended heavily on weapons captured from the Armed Forces in South Viet-Nam. This remains an important source of weapons and ammunition for the Viet-Cong. But as the pace of the war has quickened, requirements for up-to-date arms and special types of weapons have risen to a point where the Viet-Cong cannot rely on captured stocks. Hanoi has undertaken a program to re-equip its forces in the South with Communist-produced weapons.

Large and increasing quantities of military supplies are entering South Viet-Nam from outside the country. The principal supply point is North Viet-Nam, which provides a convenient channel for matériel that originates in Communist China and other Communist countries.

An increasing number of weapons from external Communist sources have been seized in the South. These include such weapons as 57 mm. and 75 mm. recoilless rifles, dual-purpose machineguns, rocket launchers, large mortars, and antitank mines.

A new group of Chinese Communist-manufactured weapons has recently appeared in VC hands. These include the 7.62 semiautomatic carbine, 7.62 light machinegun, and the 7.62 assault rifle. These weapons and ammunition for them, manufactured in Communist China in 1962, were first captured in December, 1964, in Chuong Thien Province. Similar weapons have since been seized in each of the four Corps areas of South Viet-Nam. Also captured have been Chinese Communist antitank grenade launchers and ammunition made in China in 1963.

One captured Viet-Cong told his captors that his entire company had been supplied recently with modern Chinese weapons. The re-equipping of VC units with a type of weapons that require ammunition and parts from outside South Viet-Nam indicates the growing confidence of the authorities in Hanoi in the effectiveness of their supply lines into the South.

Incontrovertible evidence of Hanoi's elaborate program to supply its forces in the South with weapons, ammunition, and other supplies has accumulated over the years. Dramatic new proof was exposed just as this report was being completed.

On February 16, 1965, an American helicopter pilot flying along the South Vietnamese coast sighted a suspicious vessel. It was a cargo ship of an estimated 100-ton capacity, carefully camouflaged and moored just offshore along the coast of Phu Yen Province. Fighter planes that approached the vessel met machinegun fire from guns on the deck of the ship and from the shore as well. A Vietnamese Air Force strike was launched against the vessel, and Vietnamese Government troops moved into the area. They seized the ship after a bitter fight with the Viet-Cong.

The ship, which had been sunk in shallow water, had discharged a huge cargo of arms, ammunition, and other supplies. Documents found on the ship and on the bodies of several Viet-Cong aboard identified the vessel as having come from North Viet-Nam. A newspaper in the cabin was from Haiphong and was dated January 23, 1965. The supplies delivered by the ship—thousands of weapons and more than a million rounds of ammunition—were almost all of Communist origin, largely from Communist China and Czechoslovakia, as well as North Viet-Nam. At least 100 tons of military supplies were discovered near the ship.

A preliminary survey of the cache near the sunken vessel from Hanoi listed the following supplies and weapons:

—approximately 1 million rounds of small-arms ammunition;
—more than 1,000 stick grenades;
—500 pounds of TNT in prepared charges;
—2,000 rounds of 82 mm. mortar ammunition;
—500 antitank grenades;
—500 rounds of 57 mm. recoilless rifle ammunition;
—more than 1,000 rounds of 75 mm. recoilless rifle ammunition;
—one 57 mm. recoilless rifle;
—2 heavy machineguns;
—2,000, 7.95 Mauser rifles;
—more than 100, 7.62 carbines;
—1,000 submachineguns;
—15 light machineguns;
—500 rifles;
—500 pounds of medical supplies (with labels from North Viet-Nam, Communist China, Czechoslovakia, East Germany, Soviet Union, and other sources). . . .

North Viet-Nam: Base for Conquest of the South

The Third Lao Dong Party Congress in Hanoi in September, 1960, set forth two tasks for its members: "to carry out the socialist revolution in North Viet-Nam" and "to liberate South Viet-Nam."

The resolutions of the congress described the effort to destroy the legal Government in South Viet-Nam as follows: "The revolution in the South is a protracted, hard, and complex process of struggle, combining many forms of struggle of great activity and flexibility, ranging from lower to higher, and taking as its basis the building, consolidation, and development of the revolutionary power of the masses."

At the September meeting the Communist leaders in the North called for formation of "a broad national united front." Three months later Hanoi announced creation of the "Front for Liberation of the South." This is the organization that Communist propaganda now credits with guiding the forces of subversion in the South; it is pictured as an organization established and run by the people in the South themselves. At the 1960 Lao Dong Party Congress the tone was different. Then, even before the front existed, the Communist leaders were issuing orders for the group that was being organized behind the scenes in Hanoi. "This front must rally . . ."; "The aims of its struggle are . . ."; "The front must carry out . . ."—this is the way Hanoi and the Communist Party addressed the "Liberation Front" even before its founding.

The Liberation Front is Hanoi's creation; it is neither independent nor southern, and what it seeks is not liberation but subjugation of the South. . . .

Organization, Direction, Command, and Control of the Attack on South Viet-Nam Are Centered in Hanoi

The VC military and political apparatus in South Viet-Nam is an extension of an elaborate military and political structure in North Viet-Nam which directs and supplies it with the tools for conquest. The Ho Chi Minh regime has shown that it is ready to allocate every resource that can be spared—whether it be personnel, funds, or equipment—to the cause of overthrowing the legitimate Government in South Viet-Nam and of bringing all Viet-Nam under Communist rule.

POLITICAL ORGANIZATION

Political direction and control of the Viet-Cong is supplied by the Lao Dong Party, i.e., the Communist Party, led by Ho Chi Minh. Party agents are responsible for indoctrination, recruitment, political training, propaganda, anti-Government demonstrations, and other activities of a political nature. The considerable intelligence-gathering facilities of the party are also at the disposal of the Viet-Cong.

Over-all direction of the VC movement is the responsibility of the Central Committee of the Lao Dong Party. Within the Central Committee a special Reunification Department has been established. This has replaced the "Committee for Supervision of the South" mentioned in intelligence reports two years ago. It lays down broad strategy for the movement to conquer South Viet-Nam.

Until March, 1962, there were two principal administrative divisions in the VC structure in the South. One was the Interzone of South-Central Viet-Nam (sometimes called Interzone 5); the other was the Nambo Region. In a 1962 reorganization these were merged into one, called the Central Office for South Viet-Nam. The Central Committee, through its Reunification Department, issues directives to the Central Office, which translates them into specific orders for the appropriate subordinate command.

Under the Central Office are six regional units (V through IX) plus the special zone of Saigon/Cholon/Gia Dinh. A regional committee responsible to the Central Office directs VC activities in each region. Each regional committee has specialized units responsible for liaison, propaganda, training, personnel, subversive activities, espionage, military bases, and the like.

Below each regional committee are similarly structured units at the province and district levels. At the base of the Communist pyramid are the individual party cells, which may be organized on a geographic base or within social or occupational groups. The elaborateness of the party unit and the extent to which it operates openly or underground is determined mainly by the extent of VC control over the area concerned. . . .

A Brief History of Hanoi's Campaign of Aggression Against South Viet-Nam

While negotiating an end to the Indochina War at Geneva in 1954, the Communists were making plans to take over all former French territory in Southeast Asia. When Viet-Nam was partitioned, thousands of carefully selected party members were ordered to remain in place in the South and keep their secret apparatus intact to help promote Hanoi's cause. Arms and ammunition were stored away for future use. Guerrilla fighters rejoined their families to await the party's call. Others withdrew to remote jungle and mountain hideouts. The majority—an estimated 90,000—were moved to North Viet-Nam.

Hanoi's original calculation was that all of Viet-Nam would fall under its control without resort to force. For this purpose, Communist cadres were ordered to penetrate official and non-official agencies, to propagandize and sow confusion, and generally to use all means short of open violence to aggravate war-torn conditions and to weaken South Viet-Nam's Government and social fabric.

South Viet-Nam's refusal to fall in with Hanoi's scheme for peaceful takeover came as a heavy blow to the Communists. Meantime, the Government had stepped up efforts to blunt Viet-Cong subversion and to expose Communist agents. Morale in the Communist organization in the South dropped sharply. Defections were numerous.

Among South Vietnamese, hope rose that their nation could have a peaceful and independent future, free of Communist domination. The country went to work. The years after 1955 were a period of steady progress and growing prosperity.

Food production levels of the prewar years were reached and surpassed. While per capita food output was dropping 10 per cent in the North from 1956 to 1960, it rose 20 per cent in the South. By 1963, it had risen 30 per cent—despite the disruption in the countryside caused by intensified Viet-Cong military attacks and terrorism. The authorities in the North admitted openly to continuing annual failures to achieve food production goals.

Production of textiles increased in the South more than 20 per cent in one year (1958). In the same year, South Viet-Nam's sugar crop increased more than 100 percent. Despite North Viet-Nam's vastly larger industrial complex, South Viet-Nam's per capita gross national product in 1960 was estimated at $110 a person while it was only $70 in the North.

More than 900,000 refugees who had fled from Communist rule in the North were successfully settled in South Viet-Nam. An agrarian reform program was instituted. The elementary school population nearly quadrupled between 1956 and 1960. And so it went—a record of steady improvement in the lives of the people. It was intolerable for the rulers in Hanoi; under peaceful conditions, the South was outstripping the North. They were losing the battle of peaceful competition and decided to use violence and terror to gain their ends.

After 1956 Hanoi rebuilt, reorganized, and expanded its

covert political and military machinery in the South. Defectors were replaced by trained personnel from party ranks in the North. Military units and political cells were enlarged and were given new leaders, equipment, and intensified training. Recruitment was pushed. In short, Hanoi and its forces in the South prepared to take by force and violence what they had failed to achieve by other means.

By 1958 the use of terror by the Viet-Cong increased appreciably. It was used both to win prestige and to back up demands for support from the people, support that political and propaganda appeals had failed to produce. It was also designed to embarrass the Government in Saigon and raise doubts about its ability to maintain internal order and to assure the personal security of its people. From 1959 through 1961, the pace of Viet-Cong terrorism and armed attacks accelerated substantially.

The situation at the end of 1961 was so grave that the Government of the Republic of Viet-Nam asked the United States for increased military assistance. That request was met. Meantime, the program of strategic hamlets, designed to improve the peasant's livelihood and give him some protection against Viet-Cong harassment and pressure, was pushed energetically.

But the Viet-Cong did not stand still. To meet the changing situation, they tightened their organization and adopted new tactics, with increasing emphasis on terrorism, sabotage, and armed attacks by small groups. They also introduced from the North technicians in fields such as armor and antiaircraft. Heavier weapons were sent in to the regular guerrilla forces.

The military and insurgency situation was complicated by a quite separate internal political struggle in South Viet-Nam, which led in November, 1963, to the removal of the Diem government and its replacement with a new one. Effective power was placed in the hands of a Military Revolutionary Council. There have been a number of changes in the leadership and composition of the Government in Saigon in the ensuing period.

These internal developments and distractions gave the Viet-Cong an invaluable opportunity, and they took advantage of it. . . .

Conclusion

The evidence presented in this report could be multiplied many times with similar examples of the drive of the Hanoi regime to extend its rule over South Viet-Nam.

The record is conclusive. It establishes beyond question that North Viet-Nam is carrying out a carefully conceived plan of aggression against the South. It shows that North Viet-Nam has intensified its efforts in the years since it was condemned by the International Control Commission. It proves that Hanoi continues to press its systematic program of armed aggression into South Viet-Nam. This aggression violates the United Nations Charter. It is directly contrary to the Geneva Accords of 1954 and of 1962 to which North Viet-Nam is a party. It shatters the peace of Southeast Asia. It is a fundamental threat to the freedom and security of South Viet-Nam.

The people of South Viet-Nam have chosen to resist this threat. At their request, the United States has taken its place beside them in their defensive struggle.

The United States seeks no territory, no military bases, no favored position. But we have learned the meaning of aggression elsewhere in the postwar world, and we have met it.

If peace can be restored in South Viet-Nam, the United States will be ready at once to reduce its military involvement. But it will not abandon friends who want to remain free. It will do what must be done to help them. The choice now between peace and continued and increasingly destructive conflict is one for the authorities in Hanoi to make.

I. F. STONE

A Reply to the White Paper*

That North Viet-Nam supports the guerrillas in South Viet-Nam is no more a secret than that the United States supports

---

* From *I. F. Stone's Weekly*, March 8, 1965.

the South Vietnamese government against them. The striking thing about the State Department's new White Paper is how little support it can prove. "Incontrovertible evidence of Hanoi's elaborate program to supply its forces in the South with weapons, ammunition and other supplies," the White Paper says, "has accumulated over the years." A detailed presentation of this evidence is in Appendix D; unfortunately few will see the appendices since even the *New York Times* did not reprint them, though these are more revealing than the report. Appendix D provides a list of weapons, ammunition, and other supplies of Chinese Communist, Soviet, Czech, and North Vietnamese manufacture, with the dates and place of capture from the Viet-Cong guerrillas, over the eighteen-month period from June, 1962, to January 29 last year when it was presented to the International Control Commission. The Commission was set up by the Geneva agreement of 1954. This list provides a good point at which to begin an analysis of the White Paper.

The Pentagon's Figures

To put the figures in perspective, we called the Pentagon press office and obtained some figures the White Paper does not supply —the number of weapons captured from the guerrillas and the number lost to them in recent years:

	Captured From Guerrillas	Lost to Them
1962	4,800	5,200
1963	5,400	8,500
1964	4,900	13,700
3-year Total	15,100	27,400

In three years, the guerrillas captured from our side 12,300 more weapons than they lost to us.

What interests us at the moment is not this favorable balance but the number of guerrilla weapons our side captured during the past three years. The grand total was 15,100. If Hanoi has indeed engaged in an "elaborate program" to supply the Viet-Cong, one would expect a substantial number of enemy-produced weapons to turn up. Here is the sum total of enemy-

produced weapons and supplies in that eighteen-month tally to
the Control Commission—

 72 rifles (46 Soviet, 26 Czech)
 64 submachine guns (40 Czech, 24 French but "modified"
       in North Vietnam)
 15 carbines (Soviet)
  8 machine guns (6 Chinese, 2 North Vietnamese)
  5 pistols (4 Soviet, 1 Czech)
  4 mortars (Chinese)
  3 recoilless 75 mm. rifles (Chinese)
  3 recoilless 57 mm. guns (Chinese)
  2 bazookas (1 Chinese, 1 Czech)
  2 rocket launchers (Chinese)
  1 grenade launcher (Czech)
_____
179 total

This is not a very impressive total. According to the Pentagon
figures, we captured on the average 7,500 weapons each eighteen months in the past three years. If only 179 Communist-
made weapons turned up in eighteen months, that is less than
2½ per cent of the total. Judging by these White Paper figures,
our military are wrong in estimating, as they have in recent
months, that 80 per cent of the weapons used by the guerrillas
are captured from us. It looks as if the proportion is considerably
higher. The material of North Vietnamese origin included only
those 24 French submachine guns "modified" in North Viet-
Nam, 2 machine guns made in North Viet-Nam, 16 helmets, a
uniform and an undisclosed number of mess kits, belts, sweaters
and socks. Judging by this tally, the main retaliatory blow should
be at North Viet-Nam's clothing factories.

Not Enough for a Battalion

There is another way to judge this tally of captured Communist
weapons. A Communist battalion has about 450 men. It needs
500 rifles, four 80 mm. mortars, eight 60 mm. mortars and at
least four recoilless rifles. The weapons of Communist origin
captured in eighteen months would not adequately outfit one
battalion. The figures in the appendix on ammunition captured

provides another index. We captured 183 (Chinese) shells for a 60 mm. mortar. This fires about twenty shells a minute, so that was hardly enough ammunition for ten minutes of firing. There were 100,000 (Chinese) cartridges for 7.26 mm. machine guns. That looks impressive until one discovers on checking with knowledgable military sources that these machine guns fire 600 rounds a minute. A machine gun platoon normally has four machine guns. This was enough ammunition for about forty minutes of firing by one platoon. Indeed, if the ratio of Communist-made weapons captured is the same for weapons used, then only twelve and a half days of those eighteen months were fought by the guerrillas on the basis of Communist-made supplies.

If these figures were being presented in a court of law, they would run up against a further difficulty: one would have to prove the arms actually came from the Communist side. There is a world-wide market in second-hand weapons. One can buy Soviet, Czech, and Chinese Communist weapons of all kinds only two miles or so from the Pentagon at Interarmco, Ltd., 7 Prince Street, Alexandria, Virginia. Interarmco, one of the world's foremost dealers, can provide more Communist weapons than we picked up in eighteen months on Vietnamese battlefields. Interarmco's East European Communist weapons come in large part from the huge stocks of Soviet and Czech arms captured by the Israelis in the Suez campaign. It has Chinese Communist weapons captured by our side in the Korean war. It also has, of course, a wide selection of our own military surplus. This has turned up in strange places.

For example, a book on the Algerian war, *Les Algériens en guerre,* by Dominique Darbois and Philippe Vingneau, was published in Milan in 1960 by Feltrinelli. It shows pictures of FLN (National Liberation Front) Algerian rebels wearing U.S. Marine Corps uniforms from which the "USMC" and the eagle and globe insignia have not even been removed. It shows Algerians carrying U.S. 81 mm. mortars and U.S. 50-calibre machine guns. Such photos could have been used by France to accuse the U.S. of supplying the Algerian rebels.

The State Department's White Paper says "dramatic new proof was exposed just as this report was being completed" in the discovery of a suspected Viet-Cong arms cargo ship on

February 16. The *New York Times* commented astringently on this in an editorial February 28—

Apparently, the major new evidence of a need for escalating the war, with all the hazard that this entails, was provided by the sinking in a South Vietnamese cove earlier this month of a 100-ton cargo ship loaded with Communist-made small arms and ammunition. A ship of that size is not much above the Oriental junk class. The standard Liberty or Victory ship of World War II had a capacity of 7,150 to 7,650 tons.

The affair of the cargo ship is curious. Until now there has been little evidence of arms coming in by ship. A huge fleet of small vessels patrols the coast and there have been glowing stories in the past of its efficiency. "About 12,000 vessels," the AP reported from Saigon (*New York Times,* February 22), "are searched each month by the South Vietnamese coastal junk patrol force but arrests are rare and no significant amounts of incriminating goods or weapons ever have been found." This lone case of a whole shipload of arms is puzzling.

Few Northern Infiltrees Cited

The White Paper's story on the influx of men from the North also deserves a closer analysis than the newspapers have given it. Appendix C provides an elaborate table from 1959–60 to 1964 inclusive, showing the number of "confirmed" military infiltrees per year from the North. The total is given as 19,550. One way to measure this number is against that of the military we have assigned to South Viet-Nam in the same years. These now total 23,500, or 25 per cent more, and 1,000 are to be added in the near future. The number of North Vietnamese infiltrees is "based on information . . . from at least two independent sources." *Nowhere are we told how many men who infiltrated from the North have actually been captured.* There is reason to wonder whether the count of infiltrees may be as bloated as the count of Viet-Cong dead; in both cases the numbers used are estimates rather than actual bodies.

The White Paper calls the war an invasion and claims "that as many as 75 per cent of the more than 4,400 Viet-Cong who are known to have entered the South in the first eight months of

1964 were natives of North Viet-Nam." But a careful reading of the text and the appendices turns up the names of only six North Vietnamese infiltrees. In Part I of the White Paper, Section B gives "individual case histories of North Vietnamese soldiers" sent South by Hanoi but all nine of these are of South Vietnamese origin. The next Section, C, is headed "Infiltration of Native North Vietnamese." It names five infiltrees but one of these is also from the South. That leaves four North Vietnamese natives. Then, in Appendix C, we are given the case histories and photographs of nine other Viet-Cong sent south by Hanoi. The report does not explain which ones were originally from the South but it does give the names of the provinces in which they were born. When these are checked, it turns out that only two of the nine were born in North Viet-Nam. This gives us a total of six northern infiltrees. It is strange that after five years of fighting, the White Paper can cite so few.

None of this is discussed frankly in the White Paper. To do so would be to bring the war into focus as a rebellion in the South, which may owe some men and matériel to the North but is largely dependent on popular indigenous support for its manpower, as it is on captured U.S. weapons for its supply. The White Paper withholds all evidence which points to a civil war. It also fails to tell the full story of the July, 1962, Special Report by the International Control Commission. Appendix A quotes that portion in which the Commission 2-to-1 (Poland dissenting) declared that the North had in specific instances sent men and material south in violation of the Geneva Accords. But nowhere does the State Department mention that the same report also condemned South Viet-Nam and the U.S., declaring that they had entered into a military alliance in violation of the Geneva Agreements. The U.S. was criticized because it then had about 5,000 military advisers in South Viet-Nam. The Geneva Accords limited the U.S. military mission to the 684 in Viet-Nam at the time of the 1954 cease-fire. The U.S. and South Viet-Nam were also criticized by the I.C.C. for hamstringing the Commission's efforts to check on imports of arms in violation of the Geneva Accords.

The reader would never guess from the White Paper that the Geneva Accords promised that elections would be held in 1956 to reunify the country. The 1961 Blue Book at least mentioned the elections, though somehow managing to make them seem a plot. "It was the Communists' calculation," the Blue Book put it, "that nationwide elections scheduled in the accords for 1956 would turn all of South Viet-Nam over to them. . . . The authorities in South Viet-Nam refused to fall into this well-laid trap." The White Paper omits mention of the elections altogether and says, "South Viet-Nam's refusal to fall in with Hanoi's scheme for peaceful takeover came as a heavy blow to the Communists." This is not the most candid and objective presentation. From the Viet-Minh point of view, the failure to hold the elections promised them when they laid down their arms was the second broken promise of the West. The earlier one was in 1946 when they made an agreement to accept limited autonomy within the French union, and welcomed the returning French troops as comrades of the liberation. Most of the French military did not want to recognize even this limited form of independence, and chose instead the road which led after eight years of war to Dien Bien Phu.[1]

That "Economic Miracle" Again

The most disingenuous part of the White Paper is that in which it discusses the origins of the present war. It pictures the war as an attack from the North, launched in desperation because the "economic miracle" in the South under Diem had destroyed Communist hopes of a peaceful takeover from within. Even the strategic hamlets are described as "designed to improve the peasant's livelihood" and we are asked to believe that for the first time in history a guerrilla war spread not because the people were discontented but because their lot was improving!

The true story is a story of lost opportunities. The Communist countries acquiesced in the failure to hold elections. Diem had a chance to make his part of the country a democratic showcase. The year 1956 was a bad one in the North. There was a peasant uprising and widespread resentment among the intellectuals over the Communist Party's heavy-handed thought control. But Diem on the other side of the 17th Parallel was busy erecting a

---

[1] See Jean Saintény's *Histoire d'une paix manquée* (Paris, 1953) and Ellen Hammer's *The Struggle for Indochina* (Stanford, 1954).

dictatorship of his own. In 1956 he abolished elections even for village councils. In 1957 his mobs smashed the press of the one legal opposition party, the Democratic Bloc, when it dared criticize the government. That was the beginning of a campaign to wipe out every form of opposition. It was this campaign and the oppressive exactions imposed on the peasantry, the fake land reform and the concentration camps Diem set up for political opponents of all kinds, which stirred ever wider rebellion from 1958 onward in the grass roots *before* North Viet-Nam gave support.[2] It was this which drove oppositionists of all kinds into alliance with the Communists in the National Liberation Front.

Long before the North was accused of interference, its government was complaining to the Control Commission of "border and air-space violations by the south and infringements of the Geneva Agreement by the introduction of arms and U.S. servicemen."[3] For four years after Geneva, both North Viet-Nam and China followed the "peaceful coexistence" policy while the U.S. turned South Viet-Nam into a military base and a military dictatorship. It is in this story the White Paper does not tell, and the popular discontent it does not mention, that the rebellion and the aid from the North had their origins.

McGEORGE BUNDY

*The Next Steps Toward Peace**

The difficult situation in the troubled country of South Viet-Nam is one which I have even less desire to discuss, in substantive terms, than the other questions I have taken as examples. The important mission of Secretary [of Defense Robert S.] McNamara and General [Maxwell D.] Taylor is only just ending, and it would be wholly inappropriate for me to comment on the

---

[2] Philippe Devillers in the *China Quarterly,* Jan.-Mar. 1962.
[3] *Survey of International Affairs 1956–58,* by Geoffrey Barraclough, a publication of Britain's Royal Institute of International Affairs, p. 420.
*Excerpts from a statement made September 30, 1963, reprinted in Department of State *Bulletin,* October 21, 1963.

course of action which may be chosen in the light of this mission and of the continuing consideration which is going forward in Saigon under the leadership of Ambassador [Henry Cabot] Lodge, and also in Washington.

Yet it is not wrong, I think, to suggest that in this case again there are two propositions, both of them true, and two kinds of error which can result from an unwillingness to accept them both. And again both propositions have been stated clearly by the President. The first is that the object of American policy in this part of the world is to assist in a most difficult and important struggle against Communist subversion—military, paramilitary, and political. The commitment of the United States to the independence of South Viet-Nam goes back many years. This commitment was intensified and reinforced two years ago, and since then a major co-operative effort has been carried forward with increasing energy—and at least until recently with increasing success—by Americans working closely with the people and government of South Viet-Nam. It is the policy of the United States to sustain that effort.

Yet it would be folly for the United States to neglect, or to regard with indifference, political developments of recent months which raise questions about the ability of the government and people of South Viet-Nam to support each other effectively in their contest with communism. The President has made it clear that the United States is not indifferent to these events and regards them with great concern. It is and must be the policy of the United States government to make clear its interest in whatever improvements it judges to be necessary, always of course with a proper regard for responsibilities which rest in the first instance upon the people of South Viet-Nam.

It is no secret that observers of the scene in South Viet-Nam have often differed sharply in their interpretation of events. From these differences there have come divergent recommendations for policy. There is nothing discreditable in the existence of such differences. In a situation in which easy solutions do not exist and in which commitments of purpose and hope are high, it is only natural that there should be a tendency in each observer to emphasize the part of the truth to which he is nearest. If a particular antisubversive effort is going well, the man who is working on that effort is bound to see that part of reality as very large. If in the cities there is repression and alienation of public support, men living in those cities, with responsibilities more civil than military, will feel a special and intense concern. Where danger comes is not in these equally right perceptions of important phenomena but in the human tendency, here as in each of my preceding examples, to suppose that one's own reality is the only reality, so that the observation of the other man is somehow misleading.

The requirement upon statesmanship, once again, is to seek ways of meeting both the need for effective prosecution of the struggle and the need for a workable relation between the people and government of a friendly country. No one can say that this task is easy. No one can even say it is certainly possible. But what can be said, and what the President has said already, is that the United States will not shrink from this responsibility or attempt to make it easier than it is by pretending that only one part of it is important.

THOMAS J. DODD

*The New Isolationism** (Continued)

Over the past several months, a number of my most respected colleagues have taken the floor to urge that we get out of Viet-Nam or that we enter into negotiations over Viet-Nam.

The propriety of our presence in Viet-Nam and the validity of our position has been challenged. It has even been suggested that we are the real aggressors in Viet-Nam. The war has been called "McNamara's War." It has been suggested that we more or less ignore Asia and Africa and concentrate on Europe and the Americas.

I have listened with growing dismay to these presentations— and with all the more dismay because of the respect and affection I have for the Senators who made them. . . .

* From a speech in the Senate of the United States, February 23, 1965. See also page 31.

A debate has been joined which is worthy of the best traditions of the Senate.

I hope that the remarks I make today will contribute at least in some measure, to the further unfolding of this debate. Out of this debate, let us hope, will ultimately emerge the kind of assistance and guidance that every President must have in dealing with vital issues of our foreign policy.

What we say here may help to guide the President. But in the final analysis the terrible responsibility of decision is his and his alone. He must listen to the exchanges which take place in this Chamber. He must endure a hundred conflicting pressures from public sources, seeking to push him in this direction or that. He must also endure the impatience of those who demand answers to complex questions today, and who accuse him of not having made the American position clear when he has in fact made our position abundantly clear on repeated occasions.

And finally, when all the voices have been heard, when he has examined all the facts, when he has discussed all aspects of the situation with his most trusted advisers, the President must alone decide—for all Americans and for the entire free world— what to do about Viet-Nam.

No President has ever inherited a more difficult situation on coming to office. No President has ever been called upon to make a decision of greater moment. At stake may be the survival of freedom. At stake may be the peace of the world.

I believe the United States can count itself fortunate that it has found a President of the stature of Lyndon B. Johnson to meet this crisis in its history. I also believe that, whatever differences we in this Chamber may have on the question of Viet-Nam, our feelings to a man are with the President in the ordeal of decision through which he is now passing.

I have said that I have been dismayed by the rising clamor for a negotiated settlement. In the type of war which the Communists are now waging against us, I fear that, although those who urge negotiation would be among the first to oppose an outright capitulation, their attitude may not be construed in this way by the Communists.

The Vietnamese war, in the Communist lexicon, is described as a "war of national liberation." Its strategy is based on the concept of what the Communists call "the long war." This strategy is premised upon the belief that the free world lacks the patience, the stamina, the fanatical determination to persist, which inspires the adherents of communism. It is based on the conviction that if the Communists keep on attacking and attacking and attacking in any given situation, they will ultimately be able to destroy the morale and the will to resist of those who oppose them in the name of freedom.

China affords the classic example of the long war. It took twenty years for Mao Tse-tung to prevail. There were several times during this period when his entire movement seemed on the verge of collapse. But, even in his blackest days, Mao Tse-tung remained confident that, if he persevered, ultimately his enemies would crack and he would emerge as China's undisputed ruler.

There is no more cruel test of courage and staying power than "the long war" as it is waged by the Communists. Five years, ten years, twenty years, means nothing to them. And if they detect any sign that those opposed to them are flagging, that their patience is growing thin or that their will to resist has weakened, the Communists can be relied upon to redouble their efforts, in the belief that victory is within their grasp.

I disagree strongly with my colleagues who have spoken up to urge negotiations.

But if there is any way in which my voice could reach to Peiping and to Moscow, I would warn the Communist leaders that they should not construe the debate that is now taking place in this Chamber as a sign of weakness; it is, on the contrary, a testimony to our strength.

Nor should they believe that those who speak up in favor of negotiations are the forerunners of a larger host of Americans who are prepared to accept surrender. Because there is no one here who believes in surrender or believes in capitulation. I believe the senior Senator from Idaho made this abundantly clear in his own presentation, in which he underscored his complete support for the retaliatory air strikes against North Viet-Nam.

I have been amazed by a number of letters I have received asking the question, "Why are we in Viet-Nam?" or "What is our policy in Viet-Nam?" I have been even more amazed to have the same questions put to me by sophisticated members of the press.

To me the reasons for our presence in Viet-Nam are so crystal clear that I find it difficult to comprehend the confusion which now appears to exist on this subject.

We are in Viet-Nam because our own security and the security of the entire free world demands that a firm line be drawn against the further advance of Communist imperialism—in Asia, in Africa, in Latin America, and in Europe.

We are in Viet-Nam because it is our national interest to assist every nation, large and small, which is seeking to defend itself against Communist subversion, infiltration, and aggression. There is nothing new about this policy; it is a policy, in fact, to which every administration has adhered since the proclamation of the Truman Doctrine.

We are in Viet-Nam because our assistance was invited by the legitimate government of that country.

We are in Viet-Nam because, as the distinguished majority leader, the Senator from Montana [Mr. Mansfield], pointed out in his 1963 report, Chinese Communist hostility to the United States threatens "the whole structure of our own security in the Pacific."

We are in Viet-Nam not merely to help the 14 million South Vietnamese defend themselves against communism, but because what is at stake is the independence and freedom of 240 million people in Southeast Asia and the future of freedom throughout the western Pacific.

These are the reasons why we are in Viet-Nam. There is nothing new about them and nothing very complex. They have never been obscure. They have never been concealed. I cannot, for the life of me, see why people fail to understand them.

The senior Senator from Idaho [Mr. Church] and several other Senators who spoke last Wednesday, repeated the proposal that we should seek negotiations for the purpose of terminating the bloodshed in Viet-Nam and of avoiding an enlargement of the war. We are told by some people that negotiations are the way of diplomacy and that if we reject negotiations now, we are in effect rejecting diplomacy.

The proposal that we negotiate now overlooks the fact that

there does exist a negotiated agreement on Viet-Nam, approved by the participants of the Geneva Conference of 1954. The final declaration of this agreement read, and I think it is worth while reading it for the *Record* and for our own recollection:

> Each member . . . undertakes to respect the sovereignty, the independence, the unity, and the territorial integrity of the abovementioned states and to refrain from any interference in their internal affairs.

Since there is no point to negotiating if it simply means reiterating the Geneva Agreement, I cannot help wondering whether those who urge negotiations envisage rewriting the agreement so that it does not "guarantee the territorial integrity of the above-mentioned states."

The history of negotiated agreements with the Communists underscores the fact that their promises are worthless and that only those agreements have validity which are self-enforcing or which we have the power to enforce. A report issued by the Senate Subcommittee on Internal Security—on which I have the honor to serve—establishes that the Soviet Union has since its inception violated more than one thousand treaties and agreements. The Communists have repeatedly violated the terms of the Korean armistice, of the Geneva agreement on Viet-Nam, and of the Laotian armistice. . . .

The Senator from Idaho has held up the Laotian armistice as an example of a rational agreement with the Communists that has served our interests. He could not possibly have picked a worse illustration for his argument.

I can think of no more dramatic proof than the Laotian armistice that agreements with the Communists are worthless, and that every time we try to escape from today's unpleasantness by entering into a new covenant with an implacable aggressor, we are always confronted on the morrow by unpleasantness compounded ten times over.

I traveled through Southeast Asia just before the conclusion of the Laotian armistice.

I talked to many people at that time. It is true that the armistice was favored by our Ambassador in Laos, and it obviously must have had the support of important members of the State Department hierarchy. But the personnel of our embassies in

Saigon and in Bangkok did not conceal from me their grave apprehensions over the consequences of such an armistice for Viet-Nam and Southeast Asia.

All of this I reported on confidentially upon my return.

At that time, the Saigon government still controlled the situation throughout most of the countryside, although the fifteen thousand Viet-Cong guerrillas were giving it increasing difficulty. Our Embassy personnel in Saigon expressed the fear that the conclusion of the Laotian armistice would enable the Communists to infiltrate men and material on a much larger scale and would result at an early date in a marked intensification of the Viet-Cong insurgency. Needless to say, the apprehensions which they expressed to me have been completely borne out by subsequent developments.

The Laotian armistice has served Laos itself as poorly as it has served the cause of freedom in Viet-Nam. The Communists have continued to nibble away at what is left of free Laos, in one aggressive act after another, so that by now they firmly control more than half the country, while their infiltrees and guerrillas are gnawing relentlessly at government authority in the rest of the country.

In mid-1964, I asked the Library of Congress to prepare for me a study of Communist violations of the Laotian armistice agreement. The study which they submitted to me listed fourteen specific violations up until that time.

That was last year. There have been many more since then. . . .

I should also like to quote from a statement made on March 30, 1963, by General Kong Le, the neutralist military commander who, as is common knowledge, had favored the conclusion of the Laotian armistice. Kong Le's statement is significant because it illustrates how Communists will deal tomorrow with non-Communist elements that they are prepared to accept into coalition governments today.

Referring to certain Communist stooges, General Kong Le said:

Despite their continual defeats, however, these people learned their lessons from their Communist bosses. . . . When the Prime Minister went abroad, they moved rapidly to destroy the neutralist forces. They used tricks to provoke the soldiers and people to overthrow Colonel Ketsana. When these did not succeed, on February 12 they used an assassin to murder Ketsana. They also savagely killed or arrested all neutralist party members, and their bloody hands caused the death of many people.

This was the statement of General Kong Le, one of those who had pressed the hardest for the Laotian armistice, after he saw what the armistice had done to his country.

Finally, I do not believe that the Laotian armistice has served the interests of the other peoples of Southeast Asia. I have in my possession a map of northern Laos showing areas where the Chinese Communists have been building roads that would give China direct access to the borders of Burma and Thailand. The construction of these roads bodes ill for the future peace of southeast Asia. That they are intended for future military use is taken for granted by everyone in the area.

So much for the example of the Laotian armistice.

All this does not mean to say that we must not under any circumstances enter into negotiations with the Communists. I do not suggest that at all. It simply means that when we do so, we must do so with our eyes open and with a clear understanding of the ingredients required to enforce compliance with the agreement about to be entered into. That is all I have ever urged.

Moreover, there is a time to negotiate and a time not to negotiate.

The demand that we negotiate now over Viet-Nam is akin to asking Churchill to negotiate with the Germans at the time of Dunkirk, or asking Truman to negotiate with the Communists when we stood with our backs to the sea in the Pusan perimeter in Korea. In either case, the free world could have negotiated nothing but total capitulation.

The situation in Viet-Nam is probably not as desperate and certainly no more desperate, than Britain's plight at the time of Dunkirk or our own plight at the time of Pusan. If we are of good heart, if we refuse to listen to the counsels of despair, if we again resolve that "we will never give in"—as Churchill put it—there is every reason to be confident that a time will arrive when we can negotiate with honor and for a more acceptable objective than a diplomatic surrender.

There are those who say that the whole of Southeast Asia will, whether we like it or not, go Communist. These people are at least consistent in urging negotiations now. But anyone who believes that we can negotiate now and not lose Viet-Nam to communism is deluding himself in the worst possible way.

It is human to oppose the cost of staying on in Viet-Nam when American boys are dying in a faraway land about which we understand very little. I am conscious of this. I am sensitive to it. I share the troubled minds of all Senators. But I am convinced that the great majority of those who advocate that we abandon Viet-Nam to communism, either by pulling out or by "negotiating" a settlement, have not taken the time to weigh the consequences of defeat.

In my opinion, the consequences of an American defeat in Viet-Nam would be so catastrophic that we simply cannot permit ourselves to think of it. This is truly an "unthinkable thought," to use an expression coined by the Senator from Arkansas. He was not applying it to this problem, I point out, but I find the words particularly apt in reference to Viet-Nam.

For the Vietnamese people, the first consequence would be a bloodletting on a genocidal scale.

In the Soviet Union and in Red China, tens of millions of "class enemies" were eliminated by the victorious Communists. While it is true that there are some slightly more moderate Communist regimes in certain countries, Vietnamese communism is characterized by utter disregard for human life of Stalinism and Maoism. What will happen to the more than one million refugees from North Viet-Nam? What will happen to the millions of peasants who resisted or bore arms against the Viet-Cong. I shudder to think of it. The massacre of innocents in Viet-Nam will be repeated in every Southeast Asian country that falls to communism in its wake, in a gigantic bloodletting that will dwarf the agony and suffering of the war in Viet-Nam.

Those who urge our withdrawal from Viet-Nam in the name of saving human lives have the duty to consider the record of Communist terror in every country that has fallen under the sway of this merciless ideology, with its total disregard for human life. . . .

And if the administration should ever succumb to their pressure and negotiate the surrender of Viet-Nam, and if the Vietnamese Communists then embark on the orgy of bloodletting which has always accompanied the establishment of Communist power, let those who are pressuring for negotiations not be heard to say, "But we didn't intend it this way." Because there is today no excuse for ignorance about communism.

Our withdrawal from Viet-Nam would immediately confront us with an agonizing choice.

If we decide to try to defend what is left of Southeast Asia against the advance of communism, it will require far more money, far more men, and far more American blood than we are today investing in the defense of Viet-Nam. What is more, it would involve a far greater risk of the major escalation which we seek to avoid.

If, on the other hand, we decide to abandon the whole of Southeast Asia to communism, as some of the proponents of withdrawal have frankly proposed, it would result in the early disintegration of all our alliances, and in the total eclipse of America as a great nation. Because no nation can remain great when its assurances are considered worthless even by its friends.

Whether we decide to abandon Southeast Asia or to try to draw another line outside Viet-Nam, the loss of Viet-Nam will result in a dozen more Viet-Nams in different parts of the world. If we cannot cope with this type of warfare in Viet-Nam, the Chinese Communists will be encouraged in the belief that we cannot cope with it anywhere else.

In the Congo, the Chinese Communists have launched their first attempt at applying the Vietnamese strategy to Africa.

In the Philippines, the Huk guerrillas, after being decisively defeated in the early 1950's, have now staged a dramatic comeback. According to the *New York Times,* the Huks are now active again in considerable strength, control large areas of central Luzon, and are assassinating scores of village heads and local administrators on the Viet-Cong pattern.

In Thailand, Red China has already announced the formation of a patriotic front to overthrow the government and eradicate American influence. This almost certainly presages the early launching of a Thai Communist insurrection, also patterned after the Viet-Cong.

An article in the Washington *Post* on January 16, pointed out that the Venezuelan Communists now have 5,000 men under arms in the cities and in the countryside, and that the Venezuelan Communist Party is openly committed to "the strategy of a long war, as developed in China, Cuba, Algeria, and Viet-Nam."

And there are at least half a dozen other Latin American countries where the Communists are fielding guerrilla forces, which may be small today, but which would be encouraged by a Communist victory in Viet-Nam to believe that the West has no defense against the long war.

It is interesting to note in this connection that, according to Cuban reports, a Viet-Cong delegation which came to Havana in 1964 signed a "mutual-aid pact" with the Venezuelan guerrilla forces. In addition, Marguerite Higgins, the distinguished correspondent for the Washington *Star* and other papers, points out that Viet-Cong experts have teamed up with experts from Communist China and the Soviet Union in training Latin Americans for guerrilla operations in the several schools maintained by Fidel Castro.

It has been suggested that if we abandon Southeast Asia, our seapower would make it possible for us to fall back on Japan and the Philippines and the other Pacific islands, and constitute a more realistic defense line there. This is nonsense. American seapower and American nuclear power have thus far proved impotent to cope with Communist political warfare. Cuba is the best proof of this.

If we abandon Southeast Asia, the Philippines may prove impossible to hold against a greatly stepped-up Huk insurgency.

Japan, even if it remains non-Communist, would probably, by force of circumstances, be compelled to come to terms with Red China, adding the enormous strength of its economy to Communist strategic resources.

Okinawa, where our political position is already difficult, would become politically impossible to hold.

If we fail to draw the line in Viet-Nam, in short, we may find ourselves compelled to draw a defense line as far back as Seattle and Alaska, with Hawaii as a solitary outpost in mid-Pacific.

To all those who agree that we must carefully weigh the conseqences of withdrawal before we commit ourselves to withdrawal, I would refer the recent words of the well-known Filipino political commentator, Vincente Villamin. The abandon-

174 •   *The Viet-Nam Reader*

ment of Viet-Nam, wrote Mr. Villamin, "would be an indelible blemish on America's honor. It would reduce America in the estimation of mankind to a dismal third-rate power, despite her wealth, her culture and her nuclear arsenal. It would make every American ashamed of his government and would make every individual American distrusted everywhere on earth."

This is strong language. But from conversations with a number of Asians, I know that it is an attitude shared by many of our best friends in Asia.

The situation in Viet-Nam today bears many resemblances to the situation just before Munich.

Chamberlain wanted peace. Churchill wanted peace.

Churchill said that if the free world failed to draw the line against Hitler at an early stage, it would be compelled to draw the line under much more difficult circumstances at a later date.

Chamberlain held that a confrontation with Hitler might result in war, and that the interests of peace demanded some concessions to Hitler. Czechoslovakia, he said, was a faraway land about which we knew very little.

Chamberlain held that a durable agreement could be negotiated with Hitler that would guarantee "peace in our time."

How I remember those words.

Churchill held that the appeasement of a compulsive aggressor simply whetted his appetite for further expansion and made war more likely.

Chamberlain's policy won out, because nobody wanted war. When he came back from Munich, he was hailed not only by the Tories, but by the Liberals, and the Labour Party people, including leftwingers like James Maxton and Fenner Brockway.

Churchill remained a voice crying in the wilderness.

But who was right—Churchill or Chamberlain?

Who was the true man of peace?

In Viet-Nam today, we are again dealing with a faraway land, about which we know very little.

In Viet-Nam today, we are again confronted by an incorrigible aggressor, fanatically committed to the destruction of the free world, whose agreements are as worthless as Hitler's. Indeed, even while the Communist propaganda apparatus is pulling out all the stops to pressure us into a diplomatic surrender in Viet-Nam, the Chinese Communists are openly encouraging a new

Huk insurgency in the Philippines and have taken the first step in opening a Viet-Cong type insurgency in Thailand through the creation of their quisling Thai patriotic front.

In signing the Munich agreement, it was not Chamberlain's intention to surrender the whole of Czechoslovakia to Hitler. The agreement was limited to the transfer of the German-speaking Sudetenland to German sovereignty. And no one was more indignant than Chamberlain when Hitler, having deprived Czechoslovakia of her mountain defenses, proceeded to take over the entire country.

While there are some proponents of a diplomatic solution who are willing to face up to the fact that negotiations at this juncture mean surrender, there are others who apparently quite honestly believe that we can arrive at a settlement that will both end the war and preserve the freedom of the South Vietnamese people. If such negotiations should ever come to pass, I am certain that the story of Czechoslovakia would be repeated. Having deprived South Viet-Nam of the political and military capability to resist, the North Vietnamese Communists would not tarry long before they completely communized the country.

And, before very long, those who urge a diplomatic solution for the sake of preventing war, may find themselves compelled to fight the very war that they were seeking to avoid, on a bigger and bloodier scale, and from a much more difficult line of defense.

I take it for granted that no one in this Chamber and no loyal American citizen believes that we should stand by indifferently while communism takes over the rest of the world.

I take it for granted that every intelligent person realizes that America could not long survive as a free nation in a world that that was completely Communist.

I take it for granted that everyone agrees that somewhere, somehow, we must draw the line against further Communist expansion.

The question that separates us, therefore, is not whether such a line should be drawn, but where such a line should be drawn.

I believe that we have been right in drawing the line in Viet-Nam and that President Johnson is right in trying to hold the line in Viet-Nam, despite the setbacks we have suffered over the past year. Because, if this line falls, let us have no illusions

about the difficulty of drawing a realistic line of defense anywhere in the western Pacific.

We have been told in many statements and articles that the
only alternative to withdrawal from Viet-Nam, with or without
negotiations, is a dramatic escalation of the war against the
North. And we have been warned that such an escalation might
bring in both Red China and the Soviet Union and might bring
about the thermonuclear holocaust that no one wants.

These are supposed to be the choices before us.

It is my belief, however, that the tide of war in Viet-Nam can
be reversed and that this war can ultimately be won without an
invasion of the North and without a significant intensification
of our military effort. It is my belief that there are many measures
we can take, primarily in the nonmilitary field, to strengthen
our posture and the posture of South Vietnamese forces in the
fight against the Viet-Cong insurgency.

Before outlining some of the measures which I believe can and
must be taken, I wish to deal with a number of widely accepted
fallacies and misconceptions about the situation in Viet-Nam,
because one cannot intelligently approach the problem of what
to do about Viet-Nam without first establishing the essential facts
about the present situation in that country.

The belief that the Vietnamese war is a civil war is one of the
most widespread misconceptions about Viet-Nam. This is frequently associated with the charge that it is the United States,
and not North Viet-Nam or Red China, which is intervening in
South Viet-Nam.

The war in South Viet-Nam is not a civil war. It was instigated
in the first place by the North Vietnamese Communists, with the
material and moral support of both Peiping and Moscow. There
is overwhelming proof that Hanoi has provided the leadership
for the Viet-Cong insurrection, that it has supplied them massively, and that it has served as the real command headquarters
for the Viet-Cong.

The present insurrection in South Viet-Nam goes back to the
third Communist Party Congress in Hanoi in September of 1960.
At this Congress it was decided "to liberate South Viet-Nam
from the ruling yoke of the U.S. imperialists and their henchmen
in order to achieve national unity and complete independence."
The Congress also called for the creation of a broad national

front in South Viet-Nam directed against the United States—
Diem clique. Several months later the formation of the front for
the liberation of the South was announced.

I understand that there is an official report, according to
which, the U.S. Military Assistance Command in Viet-Nam is
in possession of reliable evidence indicating that probably as
many as 34,000 Viet-Cong infiltrators have entered South Viet-
Nam from the North between January, 1959, and August, 1964.

The report indicates that the majority of hard-core Viet-Cong
officers and the bulk of specialized personnel such as communications and heavy weapons specialists have been provided
through infiltration. Infiltrators, moreover, apparently make up
the major part of Viet-Cong regulars in the northern half of
South Viet-Nam.

The infiltration from the North supplies the Viet-Cong with
much of its leadership, specialist personnel, key supplies such as
heavy ordnance and communications equipment, and, in some
cases, elite troops.

This information is derived from the interrogation of many
thousands of Viet-Cong captives and defectors and from captured documents.

It is this hard core that has come down from the North that
has provided the leadership cadres in all major insurgent actions,
including the series of sensational attacks on American installations.

The scale on which Hanoi has been supplying the Viet-Cong
insurgency was dramatically illustrated this weekend when an
attack by an American helicopter on a ship off the coast of
South Viet-Nam resulted in the discovery of an enormous arms
cache—almost enough, in the words of one American officer,
to equip an entire division. The haul included a thousand Rus-
sian-made carbines, hundreds of Russian submachine guns, and
light machine guns, and Chinese burp guns, and scores of tons
of ammunition. There were also a variety of sophisticated land
mines and ammunition for a new type of rocket launcher used
against tanks. A Communist guerrilla who was captured in the
action said that the ship which delivered the weapons had made
six trips to bases along the South Viet-Nam coast, dropping off
supplies.

Finally, we would do well to consider the fact that the general offensive launched by the Communist forces in Viet-Nam two weeks ago was preceded by an open call by Hanoi radio for assaults throughout the country on Vietnamese and American positions.

The public confusion on the nature of the Vietnamese war stems in large measure from the sabotage of the Communist member of the three-man International Control Commission set up to supervise the carrying out of the Geneva agreement. By 1961, reports of 1,200 offensive incidents of Communist agents, ranging from one-man assassinations to large-scale military actions, had been presented to the Commission. The Commission, however, took no action because the Polish Communist member consistently refused to investigate reports of North Vietnamese intervention in South Viet-Nam. In this way, this entire massive body of evidence of Hanoi's intervention in South Viet-Nam was muted and rendered ineffective.

In order to understand the war in Viet-Nam, we have to get away from traditional concepts in which armies with their own insignias cross clearly marked national demarcation lines after their governments have duly declared war.

Communist guerrilla warfare is waged without any declaration of war. In the case of Viet-Nam, it is waged from external sanctuaries which claim immunity to attack because the state which harbors them has not formally declared war.

It blends military cadres who have infiltrated into the country with native dissidents and conscripts, in a manner which conceals the foreign instigation of the insurgency, and which enables the Communists to pretend that it is merely a civil war.

It is time that we nail the civil war lie for what it is. It is time that we recognize it as a form of aggression as intolerable as open aggression across marked frontiers.

Why did Ho Chi Minh decide to launch the current war for the liberation of South Viet-Nam? The answer to this question is really very simple.

After the Geneva Agreement, it had been the expectation of the Communists that South Viet-Nam would collapse in administrative and political chaos before many months had passed, and that it would fall into their hands like an overripe plum. Indeed, when Ngo Dinh Diem took office as Premier after the surrender of North Viet-Nam to the Communists, 99 per cent of the Western press viewed the situation in South Viet-Nam as hopeless and predicted an early takeover by the Communist guerrillas.

Cut off from the mineral and industrial riches of the North; swamped by an influx of one million refugees; without an adequate army or administration of its own; with three major sects, each with private armies, openly challenging its authority—confronted with this combination of burdens and handicaps, it seemed that nothing could save the new born South Vietnamese Government.

But then there took place something that has properly come to be called the Diem miracle; this term was used at different times by President Kennedy and Secretary McNamara prior to Diem's overthrow, which most people, I believe, now realize was a tragic mistake.

Diem first of all moved to destroy the power of the infamous Binh-Xuyên, a sect of river pirates who, under the French, were given a simultaneous monopoly on the metropolitan police force of Saigon and on the thousands of opium dens and houses of prostitution and gambling that flourished there.

So powerful was the Binh-Xuyên and so weak were the Diem forces at the time that even the American Ambassador urged Diem not to attack them.

Diem, however, did attack them and drove them out of Saigon.

Having defeated the military sects and integrated them into the Armed Forces of the republic, Diem within a few years was able to resettle the one million refugees and to create a stable unified state where none had previously existed.

I could not help feeling indignant over articles and publications dealing with North Viet-Nam which have underscored what the Communists have done for their people. Among other things, they have stressed the fact that the Communists have greatly expanded their school system. What these articles did not mention was that from 1955 to 1963 President Diem had doubled the number of students in elementary schools, while at the secondary school level the increase has been fivefold.

The remarkable progress in the field of education was no exception. The entire South Vietnamese society scored remarkable advances in every field of economic and social endeavor, so that in 1963 South Viet-Nam for the first time had a sizable rice surplus for export. There were significant increases in all sectors of industry and agriculture, and a 20 per cent rise in per capita income.

Meanwhile, in North Viet-Nam, things were going from bad to worse. As in every other Communist country the collectivization of the peasants resulted in a dramatic reduction of food output and in chronic food shortages throughout the country. The resentment of the peasants was compounded by the brutal and indiscriminate punishment of hundreds of thousands of peasant farmers who were hailed before so-called people's courts and charged with being bourgeois elements or exploiting landlords. During the course of 1955 peasant revolts broke out in several areas. There was even a revolt in Ho Chi Minh's own village. And there was some evidence that the troops sent to suppress these revolts sometimes sympathized with the peasants. Shortages increased year by year. The people became increasingly apathetic.

The contrast between the growing prosperity of the South and the growing misery in the North confronted the Vietnamese Communists with a challenge they could not tolerate. That is why they decided that they had to put an end to freedom in South Viet-Nam. While they have scored some sensational victories in their war of subversion against the South Vietnamese government, I think it important to point out that this war has gravely complicated the already serious internal difficulties of the North, so that in 1963, for example, the per capita output of rice in Communist North Viet-Nam was 20 per cent lower than in 1960.

And I also consider it important to understand the significance of the fact that the Viet-Cong insurgency was directed not against a government that had failed to improve the lot of its people but against a government which, over a short period of time, had scored some of the most dramatic economic and social advances recorded anywhere in Asia.

There has been a good deal of talk about the United States escalating the war in South Viet-Nam. Several Senators who spoke last week warned that if we escalate the war by means of air strikes against North Viet-Nam, the escalation may get out of hand and wind up as a war with Red China or perhaps even a world war.

But it is not we who have escalated the war; it is the Communists. Peiping and Hanoi have been busy escalating the

war in South Viet-Nam for several years now. They have sent
in tens of thousands of soldiers of the North Vietnamese Army;
they have trained additional tens of thousands of dissident South
Vietnamese; they have supplied them with massive quantities of
equipment; and they have stepped up the tempo of their attacks
against the Vietnamese people.

Now we are told that if we take any action against the territory
of North Viet-Nam, which has mounted and directed the entire
attack on South Viet-Nam, it will entail the risk of world war.

If the Communists are always to be permitted the privilege of
escalating their attempts to take over new countries, while we
shrink from retaliation for fear of further escalation, we might as
well throw in the sponge now and tell the Communists the world
is theirs for the taking.

I find it difficult to conceive of Red China sending in her
armies in response to air strikes against carefully selected military targets. After all, if they did so, they would be risking retaliation against their highly vulnerable coastal cities, where most
of Red China's industry is concentrated. They would be risking
setting back their economy ten or twenty years.

Moreover, both the Chinese Communists and the Hanoi Communists are aware that the massive introduction of Chinese
troops would create serious popular resentment because of the
traditional Vietnamese suspicion of Chinese imperialism.

That there will be no invasion of the North by Vietnamese and
American forces can, I believe, be taken as axiomatic. Nor do I
believe there will be any large-scale involvement of American
troops on the Korean model. We will have to continue to provide the Vietnamese with logistical support and air support, as
we are doing now. But on the ground, the fighting can most
effectively be done by the Vietnamese armed forces, supported,
I believe, by military contingents from the other free Asian
countries.*

It has been stated by the senior Senator from Idaho and by
other critics of our foreign policy in Viet-Nam that it is pointless to talk about fighting for freedom in Asia because the Asian
people historically do not know the meaning of freedom. It has
even been implied that, because of their ignorance of freedom

* The difference between the Senator's expectations and the depth of
American on-the-ground involvement a bare six months later, must be
noted.—Eds.

and their indifference to it, communism exercises a genuine attraction for the peoples of Asia.

I am sure that most Asians would consider this analysis condescending and offensive. I myself would be disposed to agree with them. It is an analysis which, in my opinion, is false on almost every score.

We have grown accustomed to equating freedom with the full range of freedoms that we in the United States today enjoy. But, in the world in which we live, the word "freedom" has at least three separate and perhaps equally important connotations.

First, there is national freedom, or independence from foreign control.

Second, there is freedom of speech and press and the other freedoms inherent in parliamentary democracy, such as we enjoy.

And, third, there is the type of natural freedom that is enjoyed by primitive peasants and tribesmen in many backward countries, even under political autocracies.

It is true that most Asian governments are autocratic; and it is probably true that the Vietnamese people do not understand or appreciate freedom in the sense of parliamentary democracy. But they certainly understand the meaning of "freedom" when the word is used to mean independence from foreign rule. They are, in fact, a people with a long and proud history and a strong sense of national identity. Every Vietnamese schoolboy knows that his people fought and triumphed over the hordes of Genghis Khan in defense of their freedom; and he also knows that his country was free for five centuries before the French occupation. Finally, he knows and takes pride in the fact that his people drove out the French colonialists despite their army of 400,000 men. Do not tell me that these people know nothing about freedom.

To the Westernized Saigonese intellectuals, freedom of speech and freedom of the press are certainly very real issues; and even though they may have not mastered the processes, they would unquestionably like to see some kind of parliamentary democracy in their country. It is completely understandable that they should have chafed over the political controls that existed under the Diem government, and that have existed, in one degree or another, under succeeding governments.

But in the countryside, where the great mass of the people reside, the political controls that exist in the city are meaningless. The peasant is free to own his own land, to dispose of his produce, to worship according to his beliefs, to guide the upbringing of his children, and to elect his local village officials. To him, these freedoms that touch on his everyday life are the freedoms that really count, not the abstract and remote freedoms of constitutional and federal government.

And, if on top of granting him these natural freedoms, the government assists him by building schools and dispensaries and by providing seed and fertilizer, then, from the standpoint of the southeast Asian peasant, his life is full and he is prepared to fight to defend it against the Communists.

It is, in short, completely untrue that the Vietnamese people and the other peoples of Asia do not know the meaning of freedom. And it is equally untrue that communism is acceptable to the Asian peasant because of his indifference to freedom.

Communism has never been freely accepted by any people, anywhere, no matter how primitive.

It has never been accepted for the simple reason that even primitive peoples do not enjoy being pushed around and brutalized and terrorized, and told what to do and what not to do, and having their every activity ordered and supervised by political commissars.

This is why communism must govern by means of ruthless dictatorship wherever it takes power.

This is why the primitive mountain peoples of both Laos and Viet-Nam have, in an overwhelming majority, sided against the Communists.

This is why there are almost eight million refugees from Communist rule in Asia today—people who have seen the reality of the so-called People's Democracy, and who have given up everything they possessed and frequently risked their lives to escape from it.

That is why there is barbed wire and iron curtains surrounding the Communist countries. The inhabitants of the Communist countries would all leave if they could.

There is one final comment I would like to make while dealing with this subject. Too often I have heard it said that the Vietnamese people are not fighting because there is nothing to choose between communism and the kind of government they now have.

To equate an authoritarian regime like that in South Viet-Nam, or Taiwan, or Thailand with the totalitarian rule of communism is tantamount to losing all sense of proportion. Not only have these regimes never been guilty of the massive bloodletting and total direction of personal life which has characterized Communist rule in every country, but, carefully examined, it will turn out that these regimes are a mixture of natural democracy at the bottom with political controls of varying rigidity at the top.

Even at their worst, the political autocracies that exist in certain free Asian countries are a thousand times better than communism from the standpoint of how they treat their own people. And at their best, some of these autocracies have combined control of the press and political parties with remarkably progressive social programs.

But perhaps more important from our standpoint is that these free autocracies, for lack of a better term, do not threaten the peace of their neighbors or of the world or threaten our own security, whereas world communism has now become a threat of terrifying dimensions. . . .

Over and over again in recent months I have heard it said that our position in Viet-Nam is impossible because the French, who knew Viet-Nam so much better than we do, were compelled to admit defeat after eight years of war against the Viet-Minh. A recent half-page advertisement in the *New York Times* asked: "How can we win in Viet-Nam with less than 30,000 advisers, when the French could not win with an army of nearly half a million?"

Our own position is entirely different from the French position in Indochina. The French were a colonial power, exploiting and imposing their will on the Indochinese people and stubbornly denying them their freedom. The French military effort in Indochina was doomed because it had against it not only the Communists but the overwhelming majority of the Indochinese people. It was a war fought by Frenchmen against Indochinese.

The United States, however, does not seek to impose its control on Viet-Nam or exploit Viet-Nam. We are not a colonial power. We seek only to help the people of South Viet-Nam defend their freedom against an insurgency that is inspired and directed and aided by the North Vietnamese Communists. This is understood by the Vietnamese people. And that is why hundreds of thousands of Vietnamese who fought with Ho Chi Minh against the French are today fighting for the Saigon government against the Viet-Cong.

That is why the war against the Viet-Cong can be won, while the war of French colonialism against the Indochinese independence movement was doomed from the outset.

There is no similarity in the two situations that has any meaning or validity.

I believe the war in Viet-Nam can be won without a significant increase in our military effort. There are many things that can be done to improve the performance of our side, and most of them lie essentially in the nonmilitary field.

Let me set forth some of the things that I believe can be done.

One of the most obvious and most serious weaknesses of the American position in Viet-Nam is the lack of adequate liaison with the leaders of the various sectors of the Vietnamese community.

Because of this lack of communication, we have frequently been caught unawares by developments; we have remained without serious ability to influence them; and we have not been able to effectively assist the Vietnamese in communicating with each other and in stabilizing the political situation in Saigon.

No one person is to blame for this. It is, rather, the system which rotates military officers and A.I.D. officials and other Americans in Viet-Nam on an annual or two-year basis.

As one American officer pointed out in a recent interview, "It takes about eight months before you can really get to know the country and the people. And, just about the time you are beginning to understand something, you are rotated home and that is the end of your utility."

I believe that something can be done to improve this situation.

I have met a number of Americans, former soldiers and former A.I.D. officials who have spent five years or more in Viet-Nam, have built up personal friendships with leaders of every sector of the Vietnamese community, enjoy the confidence of the Vietnamese because of their understanding and dedication, and who would jump at the opportunity to return to Viet-Nam for the purpose of helping it in this critical hour. I am told that there may be as many as ten or twelve such people in this country.

I have proposed in a letter to the President that these Americans be constituted into a liaison group and that they be dispatched to Saigon immediately for the purpose of helping the Embassy to establish the broadest and most effective possible liaison with the army leaders, with the Buddhists, with the intellectual community, and with the Vietnamese political leaders.

I know that there is always a tendency on the part of World War II officers to resent World War I officers, and on the part of those who are involved in a situation today to resist the assistance of those who preceded them. There is also sometimes a tendency for those who were there yesterday to believe that they understand things better than those who are there today.

But this is a situation in which I am confident every American, no matter what his rank, will seek to rise above his personal prejudices. It is a situation that demands the utilization of every ounce of experience and dedication available to us.

It is my earnest personal conviction that the dispatch of such a liaison group to Saigon would result in an early improvement in our ability to communicate with the Vietnamese and in our ability to assist them in achieving the political stability which is essential to the successful prosecution of the war.

From many conversations with Vietnamese and with Americans who have served in various capacities in Viet-Nam, I am convinced that another one of our major weaknesses lies in the field of political warfare.

We have, by and large, been trying to meet the Communist insurgency by traditional military methods or by traditional methods slightly tailored to meet the special requirements of guerrilla warfare. In the field of political warfare, where the Communists have scored their most spectacular triumphs, our own effort has been limited, and halting, and amateurish, and, in fact, sadly ineffective.

The prime goal of political warfare, as it must be waged by freemen, is to win men's minds. The prime goal of political warfare, as it is waged by the Communists, is to erode and paralyze the will to resist by means of total terror.

An effective political warfare program requires three major

ingredients: First, a handful of basic slogans which capsulize popular desires and which are capable of striking responsive chords in the hearts of the people; second, a propaganda apparatus capable of conveying this program both to those on the government side and those on the side of the insurgents; third, specially trained cadres to direct the effort.

But the slogans we have are inadequate. Our propaganda program is dismally weak compared with that of the Communists. And according to my information, we still have not assisted the Vietnamese to set up an intensive training program in Communist cold war methods and how to counter them.

An article in the *New York Times* on August 3, 1964, pointed out that in every area "the basic cutting tool of the Viet-Cong is a squad of about ten armed men and women whose primary function is propaganda." The article also said that "Most of the experts in psychological warfare and propaganda here believe the Viet-Cong's agitprop teams have done the Saigon government more damage than even the tough Viet-Cong regular battalions." Finally, the article made the point that according to estimates there were 320 Viet-Cong "agitprop" teams working in the country, against twenty "information teams" for the government side. This gave the Viet-Cong an edge of 16 to 1 in the field of propaganda personnel. And the edge was probably even greater in terms of finesse and effectiveness.

Even if we help the South Vietnamese government intensify its propaganda effort, there would still remain the problem of basic goals and slogans.

I have pointed out that the Vietnamese people have a proud history and a strong sense of national unity. All Vietnamese, whether they live in the North or South, would like to see a unified and peaceful Viet-Nam. But as matters now stand, only the Communists are able to hold forth the prospect of the reunification of Viet-Nam. To date we have not given the South Vietnamese government the green light to set up a "Committee for the Liberation of North Viet-Nam," as counterpart to the "Liberation Front" which the Communists have set up in the South. This places the South Vietnamese side at a grave disadvantage.

There are any number of patriotic North Vietnamese refugees who have been itching for the opportunity to set up a Liberation

Committee for the North. The establishment of such a committee could, in my opinion, have an immediate and profound impact on the conduct of the war.

But above all, the situation in Viet-Nam underscores the need for an effective training program in political warfare, for our own foreign service and military personnel so that they can help to communicate this knowledge to nationals of other countries who, like the South Vietnamese, are engaged in a life-and-death struggle for survival against the most cunning and most ruthless practitioners of political warfare history has ever known.

In this connection, I wish to bring to the attention of my colleagues the fact that there has been pending before Congress for some six years a bill calling for the establishment of a Freedom Academy. This would be an institution where Americans and citizens of other free countries could receive concentrated training in Communist techniques and operations, and in tactics and methods designed to frustrate the Communists at every operational level, from elections for the control of trade unions and student organizations, to street riots, to attempted insurrections.

The Senate Judiciary Committee in reporting this measure to the floor in May of 1960, described the bill as "one of the most important measures ever introduced in the Congress." But, unfortunately, although the bill was passed by the Senate, the House took no action.

When the bill was reintroduced for the third time in early 1963, it had the sponsorship of the following Senators: Mundt, Douglas, Case, Dodd, Smathers, Goldwater, Proxmire, Fong, Hickenlooper, Miller, Keating, Lausche, and Scott.

The distinguished senior Senator from South Dakota last Friday reintroduced the measure for the fourth time, and it is now lying on the table, so that those who wish to add their names as co-sponsors may do so. It is my earnest hope that the measure will have the sponsorship of an even larger bipartisan group of Senators than it did in 1963. It is my hope too that there will be no further delay, no foot dragging, in enacting this long-overdue measure. It is time, high time, that we recognize the imperative need to equip ourselves and our allies with the knowledge and the trained personnel required to meet the Communist onslaught.

First of all, I think there is a growing acceptance of the need for punishing the North with hit-and-run raids. It would be much more effective if these raids could be carried out in the name of a North Vietnamese Liberation Front than in the name of the South Vietnamese government.

Second, I have reason for believing that increasing consideration is being given to the need for countering the Viet-Cong insurgency in the South with a guerrilla warfare effort in the North.

In May of 1961, when I returned from Laos and Viet-Nam, I made a statement, which I should like to repeat today:

The best way for us to stop Communist guerrilla action in Laos and in South Viet-Nam is to send guerrilla forces into North Viet-Nam; to equip and supply those patriots already in the field; to make every Communist official fear the just retribution of an outraged humanity; to make every Communist arsenal, government building, communications center and transportation facility a target for sabotage; to provide a rallying point for the great masses of oppressed people who hate communism because they have known it. Only when we give the Communists more trouble than they can handle at home, will they cease their aggression against the outposts of freedom.

I believe that every word I said in 1961 is doubly valid today. It is not too late to embark upon such a program. And if we do give the South Vietnamese government the green light to embark upon it on an effective, hard-hitting scale, again I think it would add significantly to the psychological impact of the entire program if all guerrilla activities were carried out in the name of the "Committee for the Liberation of the North."

I do not pretend to be a military expert. But I have discussed the situation in Viet-Nam with a number of military men of considerable experience in the area, and I have been encouraged to believe that the several suggestions which I have to make in this field are realistic.

I submit them for the consideration of my colleagues, because I think they make sense.

My first proposition is that we cannot regard the war in Viet-Nam in isolation from the rest of Southeast Asia.

The Communist Party over which Ho Chi Minh presided for many years was the Communist Party of Indochina. Indeed, to this day, there is no such thing as a Communist Party in Viet-Nam. Ho Chi Minh's thinking and strategy are directed toward the reunification of all the former territories of French Indo-china under his personal sway. This makes it imperative for us to develop a co-ordinated strategy for the entire area if we are to cope effectively with the Communist strategy.

Proposition No. 2 is that there are certain dramatic military actions open to us that do not involve the territory of North Viet-Nam.

The hub of the Ho Chi Minh trail is the town of Tchepone, inside the Laotian frontier, just south of the 17th Parallel, the dividing line between North Viet-Nam and South Viet-Nam. Through Tchepone pour most of the reinforcements and equipment from North Viet-Nam. From Tchepone the men and equipment are infiltrated into South Viet-Nam along hundreds of different jungle trails.

I recall that when I met with President Diem in April of 1961, he urged that the Americans assist him and the Laotian Government in pre-emptive action to secure three key centers in the Laotian Panhandle—Tchepone, Saravane, and Attopeu—in order to prevent the large-scale infiltration which is today taking place. I still have a copy of the marked map which he gave me in outlining his project. Had Diem's advice been followed there would have been no Ho Chi Minh trail. But this was at the time of the Laotian armistice and we were not disposed to take any actions which might provoke the Laotian Communists. So nothing was done.

The seizure of Tchepone by Laotian and Vietnamese forces, with American air support would, I have been assured, be a feasible military operation and one that could be carried out with the means available to us on the spot. It would do more to put a crimp in the Ho Chi Minh trail than any amount of bombing we could attempt. And it would have as dramatic an impact on the situation in Laos as on the situation in Viet-Nam.

Finally, there is the matter of collective action by the SEATO nations.

As late as April of 1961, the SEATO nations in the immediate area of the Philippines, Thailand, Australia, New Zealand, and Pakistan—all favored common action against the Communist menace in Laos. But the British and French were opposed to such action, and we ourselves sat on the fence; and the result was that nothing was done.

The charter of SEATO will have to be modified so that one nation cannot veto collective action by all the other nations. Britain, I am inclined to believe, would now be disposed to support collective action by SEATO because of the situation in Malaysia. But, perhaps France should be invited to leave SEATO, on the grounds that she has no vital interests in the area, and her entire attitude toward Red China is one of appeasement. In view of the fact that something has to be done immediately, however, the sensible course is to encourage collective action by the free nations in the area, outside the framework of SEATO, until SEATO can be reorganized in a manner that makes it effective.

In this connection, I am most encouraged by the news that South Korea has decided to send a contingent of several thousand military engineers to South Viet-Nam, and the Philippines have decided to do likewise. It is infinitely better from every standpoint to have Asian troops supporting the Vietnamese forces against the Viet-Cong on the ground, than it is to have American troops actively involved.

The retaliatory strikes ordered by President Johnson against the North have had the effect of reiterating our commitment in a manner that the Communists understand; and this, in the long run, is probably more important than the damage wrought by these strikes.

But if the Communists are to be discouraged from continuing this costly war, we must seek every possible means of underscoring our determination to stand by the people of South Viet-Nam, to pay whatever cost may be necessary, and to take whatever risk may be necessary to prevent the Communists from subjugating the Vietnamese people and other peoples in the area.

It is important to reiterate our resolve at every opportunity. And it is even more important to translate this resolve into hard political and military actions.

The American Friends of Viet-Nam have suggested another dramatic measure. They have suggested a commitment to a massive Southeast Asian development program based on the harnessing of the Mekong River—a kind of Tennessee Valley

Authority for Southeast Asia. Such a plan, they point out, would offer incredible promise to Laos, Cambodia, and Thailand as well as to South Viet-Nam, and it would offer equal promise to the people of North Viet-Nam, which only the continued belligerence and noncooperation of their government could frustrate.

This, to me, sounds eminently sensible.

If we decide to withdraw from Viet-Nam we can certainly find plenty of excuses to ease our path. We can blame it on the geography; or on the topography; or on local apathy; or on political instability; or on religious strife; or even on anti-Americanism. But that will fool no one but ourselves. These conditions make our success there difficult, but only our own timidity and vacillation can make it impossible.

It has become obvious that we cannot go on fighting this undeclared war under the rules laid down by our enemies. We have reached the point where we shall have to make a great decision, a decision as to whether we are to take the hard steps necessary to turn the tide in Viet-Nam or whether we are to refrain from doing so and thus lose inevitably by default.

The ultimate outcome of the Cold War depends upon an affirmative decision to do whatever is necessary to achieve victory in South Viet-Nam. The events of recent weeks demonstrate again that the administration is not lacking in resolve and that it is rapidly approaching such a decision.

Whether that means a larger commitment of forces, or continued retaliatory strikes against the North, or carrying guerrilla warfare to the enemy homeland, or completely sealing off South Viet-Nam from Communist aid—I say to the administration, "Give us the plan that will do the job, and we will support you."

Whether our victory be near or far, can we, dare we, turn away or begin to turn away from the task before us, however frustrating or burdensome it may be?

Here surely is a time for us to heed Santayana's maxim, "Those who will not learn from the past are destined to repeat it."

And so I speak today not merely to urge that we stand fast in Viet-Nam, but also to urge that we meet head on the new isolationism in its incipient stages, before the long months and years of discontent, frustration, and weariness that lie ahead have swelled the chorus urging disengagement and withdrawal to a deafening roar.

Let us expound a foreign policy nurtured in our constantly growing strength, not one fed by fear and disillusionment; a policy which each year is prepared to expend more, not less, in the cause of preserving our country and the decencies of man.

Let us insist upon a defense budget based upon the dangers we face abroad, not upon the benefits we seek at home.

Let us embrace a doctrine that refuses to yield to force, ever; that honors its commitments because we know that our good faith is the cement binding the free world together; a doctrine that recognizes in its foreign aid program not only that the rich are morally obligated to help the poor, but also that prosperity cannot permanently endure surrounded by poverty, and justice cannot conquer until its conquest is universal.

Let us, above all, encourage and inspire a national spirit worthy of our history, worthy of our burgeoning, bursting strength, in our arms, in our agriculture, in industry, in science, in finance, a spirit of confidence, of optimism, of willingness to accept new risks and exploit new opportunities.

And let us remember that providence has showered upon our people greater blessings than on any other, and that, great though our works have been, much greater is expected of us.

In recent days, the free world has paid tribute to its greatest champion of our age, Winston Churchill.

It is a curious thing that though Churchill is acknowledged on all sides as the pre-eminent figure of our time and as the highest embodiment of Western statesmanship, he was, throughout his life, and remains today, a prophet unheeded, a statesman whom men venerate but will not emulate.

It may well be that Winston Churchill's greatest legacy will prove to be, not the legacy of his immortal deeds, but that of his example and his precepts; and that freemen of the future will pay him the homage denied by his contemporaries, the tribute of imitation and acceptance of his message.

As we ponder the passing of this heroic figure and reflect upon his career and try to draw from it lessons which we might apply to the aggressive onslaught that we face today in a hundred ways on a hundred fronts, we might take to heart this advice which he gave in the dark days of 1941 to the boys of Harrow, his old school:

Never give in. Never, never, never, never. Never yield to force and the apparently overwhelming might of the enemy. Never yield in any way, great or small, large or petty, except to convictions of honor and good sense.

Let us resolve to nail this message to the masthead of our ship of state in this year of decision.

ROBERT S. McNAMARA

*Response to Aggression**

U.S. Objectives

I turn now to a consideration of United States objectives in South Viet-Nam. The United States has no designs whatever on the resources or territory of the area. Our national interests do not require that South Viet-Nam serve as a Western base or as a member of a Western Alliance.

Our concern is three-fold.

First, and most important, is the simple fact that South Viet-Nam, a member of the free-world family, is striving to preserve its independence from Communist attack. The Vietnamese have asked our help. We have given it. We shall continue to give it.

We do so in their interest; and we do so in our own clear self-interest. For basic to the principles of freedom and self-determination which have sustained our country for almost two centuries is the right of peoples everywhere to live and develop in peace. Our own security is strengthened by the determination of others to remain free, and by our commitment to assist them. We will not let this member of our family down, regardless of its distance from our shores.

The ultimate goal of the United States in Southeast Asia, as in the rest of the world, is to help maintain free and independent nations which can develop politically, economically, and socially,

---

* From an address before the James Forrestal Memorial Awards Dinner of the National Security Industrial Association, Washington, D.C., March 26, 1964.

and which can be responsible members of the world Community. In this region and elsewhere, many peoples share our sense of the value of such freedom and independence. They have taken the risks and made the sacrifices linked to the commitment to membership in the family of the free world. They have done this in the belief that we would back up our pledges to help defend them. It is not right or even expedient—nor is it in our nature—to abandon them when the going is difficult.

Second, Southeast Asia has great strategic significance in the forward defense of the United States. Its location across east-west air and sea lanes flanks the Indian subcontinent on one side and Australia, New Zealand, and the Philippines on the other, and dominates the gateway between the Pacific and Indian Oceans. In Communist hands, this area would pose a most serious threat to the security of the U.S. and to the family of free-world nations to which we belong. To defend Southeast Asia, we must meet the challenge in South Viet-Nam.

And third, South Viet-Nam is a test case for the new Communist strategy. Let me examine for a moment the nature of this strategy.

Just as the Kennedy Administration was coming into office in January, 1961, Chairman Khrushchev made one of the most important speeches on Communist strategy of recent decades. In his report on a Party conference entitled "For New Victories of the World Communist Movement," Khrushchev stated: "In modern conditions, the following categories of wars should be distinguished: world wars, local wars, liberation wars and popular uprisings." He ruled out what he called "world wars" and "local wars" as being too dangerous for profitable indulgence in a world of nuclear weapons. But with regard to what he called "liberation wars," he referred specifically to Viet-Nam. He said, "It is a sacred war. We recognize such wars . . ."

I have pointed out on other occasions the enormous strategic nuclear power which the United States has developed to cope with the first of Mr. Khrushchev's types of wars; deterrence of deliberate, calculated nuclear attack seems as assured as it can be. With respect to our general purpose forces designed especially for local wars, within the past three years we have increased the number of our combat-ready Army divisions by about 45 per cent, tactical air squadrons by 30 per cent, air lift capabilities by 75 per cent, with a 100 per cent increase in ship construction and conversion. In conjunction with the forces of our allies, our global posture for deterrence and defense is still not all that it should be, but it is good.

President Kennedy and President Johnson have recognized, however, that our forces for the first two types of wars might not be applicable or effective against what the Communists call "wars of liberation," or what is properly called covert aggression or insurgency. We have therefore undertaken and continue to press a variety of programs to develop skilled specialists, equipment and techniques to enable us to help our allies counter the threat of insurgency.

Communist interest in insurgency techniques did not begin with Khrushchev, nor for that matter with Stalin. Lenin's works are full of tactical instructions, which were adapted very successfully by Mao Tse-tung, whose many writings on guerrilla warfare have become classic references. Indeed, Mao claims to be the true heir of Lenin's original prescriptions for the world-wide victory of Communism. The North Vietnamese have taken a leaf or two from Mao's book—as well as Moscow's—and added some of their own.

Thus today in Viet-Nam we are not dealing with factional disputes or the remnants of a colonial struggle against the French, but rather with a major test case of communism's new strategy. That strategy has so far been pursued in Cuba, may be beginning in Africa, and failed in Malaya and the Philippines only because of a long and arduous struggle by the people of these countries with assistance provided by the British and the U.S.

In Southeast Asia, the Communists have taken full advantage of geography—the proximity to the Communist base of operations and the rugged, remote, and heavily foliated character of the border regions. They have utilized the diverse ethnic, religious, and tribal groupings, and exploited factionalism and legitimate aspirations wherever possible. And, as I said earlier, they have resorted to sabotage, terrorism, and assassination on an unprecedented scale.

Who is the responsible party—the prime aggressor? First and foremost, without doubt, the prime aggressor is North Viet-Nam, whose leadership has explicitly undertaken to destroy the independence of the South. To be sure, Hanoi is encouraged on its aggressive course by Communist China. But Peiping's interest is hardly the same as that of Hanoi.

For Hanoi, the immediate objective is limited: conquest of the South and national unification, perhaps coupled with control of Laos. For Peiping, however, Hanoi's victory would be only a first step toward eventual Chinese hegemony over the two Viet-Nams and Southeast Asia, and towards exploitation of the new strategy in other parts of the world.

Communist China's interests are clear: It has publicly castigated Moscow for betraying the revolutionary cause whenever the Soviets have sounded a cautionary note. It has characterized the United States as a paper tiger and has insisted that the revolutionary struggle for "liberation and unification" of Viet-Nam could be conducted without risks by, in effect, crawling under the nuclear and the conventional defense of the free world. Peiping thus appears to feel that it has a large stake in demonstrating the new strategy, using Viet-Nam as a test case. Success in Viet-Nam would be regarded by Peiping as vindication for China's views in the world-wide ideological struggle.

Taking into account the relationship of Viet-Nam to Indochina —and of both to Southeast Asia, the Far East and the free world as a whole—five U.S. Presidents have acted to preserve free-world strategic interests in the area. President Roosevelt opposed Japanese penetration in Indochina; President Truman resisted Communist aggression in Korea; President Eisenhower backed Diem's efforts to save South Viet-Nam and undertook to defend Taiwan; President Kennedy stepped up our counterinsurgency effort in Viet-Nam; and President Johnson, in addition to reaffirming last week that the United States will furnish assistance and support to South Viet-Nam for as long as it is required to bring Communist aggression and terrorism under control, has approved the program that I shall describe in a few minutes.

The U.S. role in South Viet-Nam, then, is: *first,* to answer the call of the South Vietnamese, a member nation of our free-world family, to help them save their country for themselves; *second,* to help prevent the strategic danger which would exist if communism absorbed Southeast Asia's people and resources; and *third,* to prove in the Vietnamese test case that the free world can cope with Communist "wars of liberation" as we have coped successfully with Communist aggression at other levels.

The Current Situation

I referred earlier to the progress in South Viet-Nam during 1954-1959. In our concern over the seriousness of the Viet-Cong insurgency, we sometimes overlook the fact that a favorable comparison still exists between progress in the South—notwithstanding nearly fifteen years of bitter warfare—and the relative stagnation in North Viet-Nam.

The so-called "Democratic Republic of Viet-Nam," with a greater population than the South and only a marginally smaller area, appears to be beset by a variety of weaknesses, the most prominent of which is its agricultural failure. Mismanagement, some poor weather, and a lack of fertilizers and insecticides have led to a serious rice shortage. The 1963 per capita output of rice was about 20 per cent lower than 1960. Before the June, 1964, harvests, living standards will probably decline further in the cities, and critical food shortages may appear in some of the villages. Furthermore, prospects for the June rice crops are not bright.

The internal transportation system remains primitive, and Hanoi has not met the quotas established for heavy industry. As for the people, they appear to be generally apathetic to what the Party considers the needs of the state and the peasantry has shown considerable ingenuity in frustrating the policies of the government.

In contrast, in the Republic of South Viet-Nam, despite Communist attempts to control or inhibit every aspect of the domestic economy, output continued to rise. In 1963, South Viet-Nam was once more able to export some 300,000 tons of rice. Add to this the pre-1960 record: up to 1960, significant production increases in rice, rubber, sugar, textiles, and electric power, a 20 per cent rise in per capita income, three-fold expansion of schools, and restoration of the transportation system. One cannot but conclude that, given stability and lack of subversive disruption, South Viet-Nam would dramatically outstrip its northern neighbor and could become a peaceful and prosperous contributor to the well-being of the Far East as a whole.

But, as we have seen, the Communists—because South Viet-Nam is not theirs—are out to deny any such bright prospects.

In the years immediately following the signing of the 1954 Geneva Accords, the Communists in North Viet-Nam gave first priority to building armed forces far larger than those of any other Southeast Asian country. They did this to establish iron control over their own population and to ensure a secure base for subversion in South Viet-Nam and Laos. In South Viet-Nam, instead of withdrawing fully, the Communists maintained a holding guerrilla operation, and they left behind cadres of men and large caches of weapons for later use.

Beginning in 1959, as we have seen, the Communists realized that they were losing the game and intensified their subversive attack. In June, 1962, a special report on Viet-Nam was issued by the International Control Commission, a unit created by the Geneva Conference and composed of a Canadian, an Indian, and a Pole. Though it received little publicity at the time, this report presented evidence of Hanoi's subversive activities in South Viet-Nam, and specifically found Hanoi guilty of violating the Geneva Accords.

Since then, the illegal campaign of terror, violence, and subversion conducted by the Viet-Cong and directed and supported from the North has greatly expanded. Military men, specialists, and secret agents continue to infiltrate into South Viet-Nam both directly from the North and through Laos and Cambodia. The flow of Communist-supplied weapons, particularly those of large caliber, has increased. These include Chinese 75 mm. recoilless rifles and heavy machine guns. Tons of explosive-producing chemicals smuggled in for use by the Viet-Cong have been intercepted along with many munitions manufactured in Red China and, to a lesser extent, elsewhere in the Communist bloc. In December, 1963, a government force attacked a Viet-Cong stronghold in Dinh Tuong province and seized a large cache of equipment, some of which was of Chinese Communist manufacture. The Chinese equipment included a 90 mm. rocket launcher, 60 mm. mortars, carbines, TNT, and hundreds of thousands of rounds of various kinds of ammunition. Some of the ammunition was manufactured as recently as 1962.

When President Diem appealed to President Kennedy at the end of 1961, the South Vietnamese were quite plainly losing their fight against the Communists, and we promptly agreed to increase our assistance.

Fourteen months later, in early 1963, President Kennedy was able to report to the nation that "the spearpoint of aggression has been blunted in South Viet-Nam." It was evident that the government had seized the initiative in most areas from the insurgents. But this progress was interrupted in 1963 by the political crises arising from troubles between the government and the Buddhists, students, and other non-Communist oppositionists. President Diem lost the confidence and loyalty of his people; there were accusations of maladministration and injustice. There were two changes of government within three months. The fabric of government was torn. The political control structure extending from Saigon down into the hamlets virtually disappeared. Of the forty-one incumbent province chiefs on November 1 [1963], thirty-five were replaced. Nine provinces had three chiefs in three months; one province had four. Scores of lesser officials were replaced. Almost all major military commands changed hands twice. The confidence of the peasants was inevitably shaken by the disruptions in leadership and the loss of physical security. Army and paramilitary desertion rates increased, and the morale of the hamlet militia—the "Minutemen"—fell. In many areas, power vacuums developed causing confusion among the people and a rising rate of rural disorders.

The Viet-Cong fully exploited the resultant organizational turmoil and regained the initiative in the struggle. For example, in the second week following the November coup, Viet-Cong incidents more than tripled from 316, peaking at 1,021 per week, while government casualties rose from 367 to 928. Many over-extended hamlets have been overrun or severely damaged. The January change in government produced a similar reaction.

In short, the situation in South Viet-Nam has unquestionably worsened, at least since last fall.

The picture is admittedly not an easy one to evaluate and, given the kind of terrain and the kind of war, information is not always available or reliable. The areas under Communist control vary from daytime to nighttime, from one week to another, according to seasonal and weather factors. And, of course, in various areas the degree and importance of control differ. Although we estimate that in South Viet-Nam's 14 million population, there are only 20 to 25 thousand "hard core" Viet-Cong guer-rillas, they have been able to recruit from among the South

Vietnamese an irregular force of from 60 to 80 thousand—mainly by coercion and "band-wagon" effect, but also by promising material and political rewards. The loyalties of the hard core have been cemented by years of fighting, first against the Japanese, then against the French, and, since 1954, against the fledgling government of South Viet-Nam. The young men joining them have been attracted by the excitement of the guerrilla life and then held by bonds of loyalty to their new comrades-in-arms, in a nation where loyalty is only beginning to extend beyond the family or the clan. These loyalties are reinforced both by systematic indoctrination and by the example of what happens to informers and deserters.

Clearly, the disciplined leadership, direction, and support from North Viet-Nam is a critical factor in the strength of the Viet-Cong movement. But the large indigenous support that the Viet-Cong receives means that solutions must be as political and economic as military. Indeed, there can be no such thing as a purely "military" solution to the war in South Viet-Nam.

The people of South Viet-Nam prefer independence and freedom. But they will not exercise their choice for freedom and commit themselves to it in the face of the high personal risk of Communist retaliation—a kidnaped son, a burned home, a ravaged crop—unless they can have confidence in the ultimate outcome. Much therefore depends on the new government under General Khanh, for which we have high hopes.

Today the government of General Khanh is vigorously rebuilding the machinery of administration and reshaping plans to carry the war to the Viet-Cong. He is an able and energetic leader. He has demonstrated his grasp of the basic elements—political, economic and psychological, as well as military—required to defeat the Viet-Cong. He is planning a program of economic and social advances for the welfare of his people. He has brought into support of the government representatives of key groups previously excluded. He and his colleagues have developed plans for systematic liberation of areas now submissive to Viet-Cong duress and for mobilization of all available Vietnamese resources in the defense of the homeland.

At the same time, General Khanh has understood the need to improve South Viet-Nam's relations with its neighbors, Cambodia and Laos; he has taken steps toward conciliation, and he has been quick and forthright in expressing his government's regret over the recent Vietnamese violation of Cambodia's borders. In short, he has demonstrated the energy, comprehension, and decision required by the difficult circumstances that he faces.

A Program to Meet Our Objectives

Before describing the means by which we hope to assist the South Vietnamese to succeed in their undertaking, let me point out the options that President Johnson had before him when he received General Taylor's and my report last week.

Some critics of our present policy have suggested one option —that we simply withdraw. This the United States totally rejects for reasons I have stated.

Other critics have called for a second and similar option—a "neutralization" of Viet-Nam. This, however, is the game of "what's mine is mine and what's yours is negotiable." No one seriously believes the Communists would agree to "neutralization" of North Viet-Nam. And, so far as South Viet-Nam is concerned, we have learned from the past that the Communists rarely honor the kind of treaty that runs counter to their compulsion to expand.

Under the shadow of Communist power, "neutralization" would in reality be an interim device to permit Communist consolidation and eventual take-over. When General Taylor and I were in Hué, at the north end of South Viet-Nam, two weeks ago, several Vietnamese students carried posters which showed their recognition of the reality of "neutralization." The signs read: "Neutralize today, Communize tomorrow."

"Neutralization" of South Viet-Nam, which is today under unprovoked subversive attack, would not be in any sense an achievement of the objectives I have outlined. As we tried to convey in Laos, we have no objection in principle to neutrality in the sense of nonalignment. But even there we are learning lessons. Communist abuse of the Geneva Accords, by treating the Laos corridor as a sanctuary for infiltration, constantly threatens the precarious neutrality. "Neutralization of South Viet-Nam"—an ambiguous phrase at best—was therefore rejected.

The third option before the President was initiation of military actions outside South Viet-Nam, particularly against North Viet-Nam, in order to supplement the counterinsurgency program in South Viet-Nam.

This course of action—its implications and ways of carrying it out—has been carefully studied.

Whatever ultimate course of action may be forced upon us by the other side, it is clear that actions under this option would be only a supplement to, not a substitute for, progress within South Viet-Nam's own borders.

The fourth course of action was to concentrate on helping the South Vietnamese win the battle in their own country. This, all agree, is essential no matter what else is done.

The President therefore approved the twelve recommendations that General Taylor and I made relating to this option.

We have reaffirmed U.S. support for South Viet-Nam's government and pledged economic assistance and military training and logistical support for as long as it takes to bring the insurgency under control.

We will support the government of South Viet-Nam in carrying out its Anti-Insurgency Plan. Under that plan, Prime Minister Khanh intends to implement a National Mobilization Program to mobilize all national resources in the struggle. This means improving the quality of the strategic hamlets, building them systematically outward from secure areas, and correcting previous overextension. The security forces of Viet-Nam will be increased by at least 50,000 men. They will be consolidated, and their effectiveness and conditions of service will be improved. They will press the campaign with increased intensity. We will provide required additional matériel. This will include strengthening of the Vietnamese Air Force with better aircraft and improving the mobility of the ground forces.

A broad national program is to be carried out, giving top priority to rural needs. The program includes land reform, loans to tenant farmers, health and welfare measures, economic development, and improved status for ethnic minorities and paramilitary troops.

A Civil Administrative Corps will be established to bring better public services to the people. This will include teachers, health technicians, agricultural workers, and other technicians.

204 •   *The Viet-Nam Reader*

The initial goal during 1964 will be at least 7,500 additional persons; ultimately there will be at least 40,000 men for more than 8,000 hamlets, in 2,500 villages and 43 provinces.

Farm productivity will be increased through doubled use of fertilizers to provide immediate and direct benefits to peasants in secure areas and to increase both their earnings and the nation's export earnings.

We have learned that in Viet-Nam, political and economic progress are the *sine qua non* of military success, and that military security is equally a prerequisite of internal progress. Our future joint efforts with the Vietnamese are going to apply these lessons.

Conclusion

To conclude: Let me reiterate that our goal is peace and stability, both in Viet-Nam and Southeast Asia. But we have learned that "peace at any price" is not practical in the long run, and that the cost of defending freedom must be borne if we are to have it at all.

The road ahead in Viet-Nam is going to be long, difficult, and frustrating. It will take work, courage, imagination and—perhaps more than anything else—patience to bear the burden of what President Kennedy called a "long twilight struggle." In Viet-Nam, it has not been finished in the first hundred days of President Johnson's Administration, and it may not be finished in the first 1,000 days; but, in co-operation with General Khanh's government, we have made a beginning. When the day comes that we can safely withdraw, we expect to leave an independent and stable South Viet-Nam, rich with resources and bright with prospects for contributing to the peace and prosperity of Southeast Asia and of the world.

J. W. FULBRIGHT

The War in Viet-Nam*

I wish to say a few words about Viet-Nam.

It is clear to all reasonable Americans that a complete military victory in Viet-Nam, though theoretically attainable, can in fact be attained only at a cost far exceeding the requirements of our interest and our honor. It is equally clear that the unconditional withdrawal of American support from South Viet-Nam would have disastrous consequences, including but by no means confined to the victory of the Viet-Cong in South Viet-Nam. Our policy therefore has been—and should remain—one of determination to end the war at the earliest possible time by a negotiated settlement involving major concessions by both sides.

I am opposed to an unconditional American withdrawal from South Viet-Nam because such action would betray our obligation to people we have promised to defend, because it would weaken or destroy the credibility of American guarantees to other countries, and because such a withdrawal would encourage the view in Peiping and elsewhere that guerrilla wars supported from outside are a relatively safe and inexpensive way of expanding Communist power.

I am no less opposed to further escalation of the war, because the bombing thus far of North Viet-Nam has failed to weaken the military capacity of the Viet-Cong in any visible way; because escalation would invite the intervention—or infiltration—on a large scale of great numbers of North Vietnamese troops; because this in turn would probably draw the United States into a bloody and protracted jungle war in which the strategic advantages would be with the other side; and, finally, because the only available alternative to such a land war would then be the further expansion of the air war to such an extent as to invite either massive Chinese military intervention in many vulnerable areas in Southeast Asia or general nuclear war.

---

* Congressional Record, June 15, 1965.

With the coming of the monsoons the Viet-Cong has undertaken expanded offensive action against the American-supported South Vietnamese Army. This new phase of the war has been going badly for our side and it is likely that the Viet-Cong offensive will be sustained until the end of the monsoons in October or November. As the ground war expands and as American involvement and American casualties increase, there will be mounting pressures for expansion of the war. For the reasons indicated, I believe that expansion of the war would be most unwise.

There have already been pressures from various sources for expanding the war. President Johnson has resisted these pressures with steadfastness and statesmanship and remains committed to the goal of ending the war at the earliest possible time by negotiations without preconditions. In so doing, he is providing the leadership appropriate to a great nation.

The most striking characteristic of a great nation is not the mere possession of power but the wisdom and restraint and largeness of view with which power is exercised. A great nation is one which is capable of looking beyond its own view of the world, or recognizing that, however convinced it may be of the beneficence of its own role and aims, other nations may be equally persuaded of their benevolence and good intent. It is a mark of both greatness and maturity when a nation like the United States, without abandoning its convictions and commitments, is capable at the same time of acknowledging that there may be some merit and even good intent in the views and aims of its adversaries.

The United States has made repeated efforts over the last four and a half years to reach reasonable settlements in Southeast Asia. Continuous talks have been held at the ambassadorial level with the Chinese Communists in Warsaw without any indication that the Chinese are prepared to accept any settlement in Southeast Asia short of the complete withdrawal of the United States and the establishment of their own hegemony. In 1962 the United States adhered to the Geneva Agreement for the neutralization of Laos; thereafter the United States withdrew all of its military personnel while North Viet-Nam has continued to support the Pathet-Lao militarily against the other Laotian factions. In 1964 and again in 1965, the United States responded favorably to proposals for conferences on the neutrality and

territorial integrity of Cambodia, clearly in the hope that such
a conference would also provide an opportunity for informal discussions with the Communist powers on Viet-Nam; the Communist powers have thus far been unresponsive to this proposal.

In April, 1965, the Secretary General of the United Nations
proposed to visit Peiping and Hanoi in order to discuss Viet-
Nam; Communist China replied that "the Viet-Nam question
has nothing to do with the United Nations" and North Viet-
Nam replied that "any approach tending to secure United Nations intervention in the Viet-Nam situation is inappropriate."
On February 20 of this year the United Kingdom, with American encouragement, proposed to the Soviet Union that Britain
and Russia, as co-chairmen of the Geneva Conference, explore
the possibilities of a Viet-Nam settlement with all the Geneva
signatories; the Soviet Union declined to participate in such an
effort. The British government then proposed to send former
Foreign Secretary Patrick Gordon Walker to explore the bases
of a Viet-Nam settlement with interested countries; both Communist China and North Viet-Nam replied that Mr. Gordon
Walker would not be welcome.

The clearest and strongest, but by no means the first, American indication of support for a negotiated settlement came in
President Johnson's now famous Johns Hopkins speech of last
April 7. In this speech the President stated explicitly and
forcefully that the United States was prepared to enter unconditional discussions for the termination of the Vietnamese war;
Hanoi and Peiping, as we all know, rejected the President's
offer out of hand. On April 8, in reply to the appeal of seventeen
nonaligned nations—and I congratulate them for it—for a peaceful settlement through negotiations without preconditions, the
United States reiterated its willingness to enter unconditional
discussions; the United States further indicated that it was prepared to withdraw its forces from South Viet-Nam as soon as
conditions were created in which the South Vietnamese people
could determine their future without external interference. In
reply to an Indian proposal for the cessation of hostilities and
the policing of boundaries by an Afro-Asian force, the United
States expressed interest and undertook discussions of the proposal with the Indian government; Communist China and North
Viet-Nam have rejected and denounced the Indian proposal.

The United States suspended bombing operations against

North Viet-Nam from May 13 to May 17 in the clear hope that the other side would respond to previous offers of negotiations. My own feeling is that the period of suspension of bombing was too short, but it must also be noted that the suspension elicited no response whatever from Hanoi and Peiping, who in fact denounced the suspension of bombing in harsh language. Finally, at the end of May the Canadian representative on the International Control Commission in Viet-Nam went to Hanoi to discuss the reaction of North Viet-Nam to the pause in American bombing; on the basis of the Canadian representative's report, Canadian Foreign Minister Martin has concluded that North Viet-Nam and Communist China are not receptive to peace overtures at this time.

The United States has been patient and remains patient in its efforts to bring about a negotiated settlement of the Vietnamese war. It cannot be denied that there have been mistakes over the years in our policy in Viet-Nam, not the least of which was the encouragement given in the mid-1950's to President Ngo Dinh Diem to violate certain provisions of the Geneva Accords of 1954. Even when past mistakes are admitted, the fact remains that over the past four and a half years the United States has consistently sought to negotiate compromise settlements on Southeast Asia. I believe that President Kennedy and President Johnson have been wise in their restraint and patience, that indeed this patience has quite possibly averted a conflict that would be disastrous for both the Communist countries and for the United States and its associates. I believe that continued restraint and continued patience, even in the face of expanded Viet-Cong military activities, are essential to avert a catastrophe in Southeast Asia.

It seems clear that the Communist powers still hope to achieve a complete victory in South Viet-Nam and for this reason are at present uninterested in negotiations for a peaceful settlement. It would be a mistake to match Communist intransigence with our own. In the months ahead we must try to do two things in South Viet-Nam: First we must sustain the South Vietnamese Army so as to persuade the Communists that Saigon cannot be crushed and that the United States will not be driven from South Viet-Nam by force; second, we must continue to offer the Communists a reasonable and attractive alternative to military victory.

For the time being it seems likely that the focus of our efforts will have to be on persuading the Communists that they cannot win a complete military victory; only when this has become clear is it likely they will respond to our proposals for unconditional negotiations.

The short-term outlook is by no means bright but neither is it without hope. It may well be, if we are resolute but also restrained in the conduct of the war, that when the current Viet-Cong offensive has run its course without decisive result the Communists will be disposed to take a different view of our standing proposal for unconditional negotiations. At such time as it becomes clear to all interested parties that neither side can expect to win a complete military victory, I would think it appropriate and desirable for the United States to reiterate forcefully and explicitly its willingness to negotiate a compromise peace and thereafter to join with other countries in mounting a large-scale program for the economic and social development of Southeast Asia.

The possible terms of a settlement cannot now be foreseen or usefully speculated upon. As a general proposition, however, I think there may be much to be said for a return to the Geneva Accords of 1954, not just in their essentials but in all their specifications. Should such a settlement be reached, it is to be hoped that both sides will recall the unrewarding consequences of their past violations of the 1954 Agreements.

Looking beyond a possible settlement of the Vietnamese war, it may be that the major lesson of this tragic conflict will be a new appreciation of the power of nationalism in Southeast Asia and, indeed, in all of the world's emerging nations. Generally, American foreign policy in Asia, in Africa, and in Latin America has been successful and constructive insofar as American aims have coincided with the national aims of the peoples concerned. The tragedy of Viet-Nam is that for many reasons, including the intransigence of a colonial power and the initial failure of the United States to appreciate the consequences of that intransigence, the nationalist movement became associated with and largely subordinate to the Communist movement.

In the postwar era it has been demonstrated repeatedly that nationalism is a stronger force than communism and that the association of the two, which has created so many difficulties for the United States, is neither inevitable nor natural. In the past it has come about when, for one reason or another, the West has set itself in opposition to the national aspirations of the emerging peoples. It is to be hoped that we will not do so again; it is to be hoped that in the future the United States will leave no country in doubt as to its friendship and support for legitimate national aspirations. If we do this, I do not think that we will soon find ourselves in another conflict like the one in Viet-Nam.

B. THE OTHER SIDE

Introduction

There is another side to the Viet-Nam war. In fact, there are several "other" sides to it, in contradiction to the oversimplified view that the insurgency is directed entirely by one small group of masterminds in Hanoi or Peking. Actually, it would not be inaccurate to say that it is the Johnson Administration that enjoys the short-term tactical advantage of being undivided: there are no "doves" left among President Johnson's official advisers; therefore, no conflicting advice is being heard. For better or worse, consensus has been achieved.

This was certainly not the case within the Communist orbit from 1963 until June, 1965, when the open commitment of American combat troops also narrowed the range of choices for the Communist nations. Until then, the major divisions of opinion (or even strategy) ran about as follows:

(a) Moscow, while paying lip service to the principle of favoring "liberation wars," was unwilling to forgo its *détente* with the United States and its growing trade with the West as the price for a guerrilla victory in as marginal an area as Viet-Nam; (b) Peking, while being most vocal in support of the principle of "liberation wars," was unwilling to confront the United States directly and risk its modest economic recovery for the sake of guerrilla victories in such marginal areas as the Congo and Viet-Nam; (c) Hanoi, witnessing the gradual disintegration of South Viet-Nam, was willing to risk a modest support program for the South Vietnamese guerrilla effort on the assumption that American reaction (in view of the admitted ineffectualness of the Saigon regime) would be, as in the case of Laos, in favor of a compromise settlement; and (d) the National Liberation Front (NLF) apparently expected to be able to defeat the South Vietnamese government politically and on the ground before a large-scale American countereffort could make itself felt. In any case, the relative smallness of the North Vietnamese "input" into the South Vietnamese insurgency up to the time of the massive American escalation of 1965, and the total absence until then in Hanoi and all of North Viet-Nam of the sophisticated air-defense weapons necessary to withstand a military confrontation with the United States even on a Korean scale, suggest that no one on the Communist side was seriously prepared for a major war over Viet-Nam. As in the case of the Soviet missiles in Cuba, Communist policy-makers may well have misread the "signals" from Washington.

Yet to each of the Communist regimes involved, the American position is a test of sorts: to the U.S.S.R. it is a test as to whether Washington will henceforth risk a world war or sally forth militarily every time even a well-localized revolution upsets the status quo—no matter how distasteful or retrograde the latter is. To Peking it is a test both of the continued militancy of "American imperialism" and of the naïveté of those (i.e., the Russians) who are willing to coexist with the United States. This is expressed in part in Mao Tse-tung's statement below. To such a guerrilla leader as North Viet-Nam's General Vo Nguyen Giap, the validity of the "liberation war" theory seems to ride on the American reaction; just as, on the American side, "counterinsurgency" is being put to the test.

But to those most immediately concerned—the NLF fighters within South Viet-Nam—the war takes on yet another aspect. These men fight against a heavily-armed enemy now directly allied to the mightiest military power in the world. The Department of State's White Book of 1961 bears unwitting witness to their enthusiasm, their determination to resist, as well as to the hardships they must endure. The Liberation Front Program seems to strike a note of moderation but, as Bernard Fall points out, this may not be the Front's last word on the subject once it rises to power. And warns Fall, the very strength of the NLF would make it difficult to ignore at the conference table and perhaps even hard to "deliver" by Hanoi. Indeed, as the American commitment to South Viet-Nam hardened to include troop support (beginning with the landing of a Marine brigade in early March, 1965), the political line of the NLF also hardened, as shown by its March 22 statement (see page 232). As the footnotes to the statement show, it apparently failed to receive the whole-hearted endorsement of Hanoi, since the latter considerably toned down the original text when it was rebroadcast from North Viet-Nam. This adds further weight to the belief that, at least until the spring of 1965, the Liberation Front and North Viet-Nam were far from being of one mind in their view of how to deal with the whole crisis.

The North Vietnamese leaders indeed have their own problems. They have become the major targets of American military operations—thus far without commensurate support from either Peking or Moscow. The North Vietnamese–Soviet joint statement of April, 1965, seems to have been an attempt at that time to present the United States with an acceptable basis for discussion, in which Russia could perhaps have exercised a moderating influence. As the Second Indochina War broadened in its geographic scope and in its level of violence in the following months, one may well wonder whether a last chance for a workable solution had not been allowed to pass by.

MAO TSE-TUNG

*In an Interview with Edgar Snow**

Comments on Viet-Nam

"Some American commentators in Saigon have compared the strength of the Viet-Cong there with the 1947 period in China, when the People's Liberation Army began to engage in large-scale annihilations of Nationalist forces. Are the conditions comparable?"

The Chairman thought not. By 1947 the People's Liberation Army already had more than a million men, against several million troops on Chiang Kai-shek's side. The P.L.A. had then used divisional and group army strength, whereas the Vietnamese liberation forces were now operating at battalion or at most regimental strength. American forces in Viet-Nam were still relatively small. Of course, if they increased they could help

---

* Excerpts from the *New Republic*, February 27, 1965. Mr. Snow was permitted to publish Mao's comments without direct quotation.

speed up the arming of the people against them. But if he should tell that to United States leaders they would not listen. Had they listened to Diem? Both Ho Chi Minh and he (Mao Tse-tung) thought that Ngo Dinh Diem was not so bad. They had expected the Americans to maintain him for several more years. But impatient American generals became disgusted with Diem and got rid of him. After all, following his assassination, was everything between heaven and earth more peaceful?

"Can Viet-Cong forces now win victory by their own efforts alone?" Yes, he thought that they could. Their position was relatively better than that of the Communists during the first civil war (1927–37) in China. At that time there was no direct foreign intervention, but now already the Viet-Cong had the American intervention to help arm and educate the rank and file and the army officers. Those opposed to the United States were no longer confined to the liberation army. Diem had not wanted to take orders. Now this independence had spread to the generals. The American teachers were succeeding. Asked whether some of these generals would soon join the liberation army, Mao said yes, some would follow the example of Kuomintang generals who had turned to the Communists. . . .

In reply to a specific question, the chairman affirmed that there were no Chinese forces in northern Viet-Nam or anywhere else in Southeast Asia. China had no troops outside her own frontiers.

(In another context, it was said that unless Indian troops again crossed China's frontiers, there would be no conflict there.)

"Dean Rusk has often stated that if China would give up her aggressive policies then the United States would withdraw from Viet-Nam. What does he mean?"

Mao replied that China had no policies of aggression to abandon. China had committed no acts of aggression. China gave support to revolutionary movements but not by sending troops. Of course, whenever a liberation struggle existed China would publish statements and call demonstrations to support it. It was precisely that which vexed the imperialists. . . .

Some Americans had said that the Chinese revolution was led by Russian aggressors, but in truth the Chinese revolution was armed by Americans. In the same way the Vietnamese revolution was also being armed by Americans, not by China. The liberation forces had not only greatly improved their supplies of America weapons during recent months but also expanded their forces by recruiting American-trained troops and officers from the puppet armies of South Viet-Nam. China's liberation forces had grown in numbers and strength by recruiting to their side the troops trained and armed by the Americans for Chiang Kai-shek. The movement was called "changing of hats." When Nationalist soldiers changed hats in large numbers because they knew the peasants would kill them for wearing the wrong hat, then the end was near. "Changing hats" was becoming more popular now among the Vietnamese puppets.

Mao said that the conditions of revolutionary victory in China had been, first, that the ruling group was weak and incompetent, led by a man who was always losing battles. Second, the People's Liberation Army was strong and able and people believed in its cause. In places where such conditions did not prevail the Americans could intervene. Otherwise, they would stay away or soon leave.

"Do you mean that the circumstances of victory for the liberation front now exist in South Viet-Nam?"

Mao thought that the American forces were not yet ready to leave. Fighting would go on perhaps for one to two years. After that the United States troops would find it boring and might go home or somewhere else.

"Is it your policy now to insist upon the withdrawal of United States forces before participating in a Geneva conference to discuss the international position of a unified Viet-Nam?"

The Chairman said that several possibilities should be mentioned. First, a conference might be held and United States withdrawal would follow. Second, the conference might be deferred until after the withdrawal. Third, a conference might be held but United States troops might stay around Saigon, as in the case of South Korea. Finally, the South Vietnamese front might drive out the Americans without any conference or international agreement. The 1954 Geneva Conference had provided for the withdrawal of French troops from all Indochina and forbade any intervention by any other foreign troops. The United States had nevertheless violated the convention and that could happen again.

"Under existing circumstances," I asked, "do you really see any hope of an improvement in Sino-American relations?"

Yes, he thought there was hope. It would take time. Maybe

there would be no improvement in his generation. He was soon going to see God. According to the laws of dialectics all contradictions must finally be resolved, including the struggle of the individual.

PROGRAM OF THE NATIONAL LIBERATION FRONT OF SOUTH VIET-NAM*

[On December 20, 1960, the day of its founding, the National Liberation Front of South Viet-Nam issued a manifesto and published its ten-point program, the text of which follows:]

I. *Overthrow the camouflaged colonial regime of the American imperialists and the dictatorial power of Ngo Dinh Diem, servant of the Americans, and institute a government of national democratic union.*

The present South Vietnamese regime is a camouflaged colonial regime dominated by the Yankees, and the South Vietnamese government is a servile government, implementing faithfully all the policies of the American imperialists. Therefore, this regime must be overthrown and a government of national and democratic union put in its place composed of representatives of all social classes, of all nationalities, of the various political parties, of all religions; patriotic, eminent citizens must take over for the people the control of economic, political, social, and cultural interests and thus bring about independence, democracy, well-being, peace, neutrality, and efforts toward the peaceful unification of the country.

II. *Institute a largely liberal and democratic regime.*

1. Abolish the present constitution of the dictatorial powers of Ngo Dinh Diem, servant of the Americans. Elect a new National Assembly through universal suffrage.

2. Implement essential democratic liberties: freedom of opin-

---

* English translation from B. B. Fall, *The Two Viet-Nams*, New York, 1963, reprinted by permission of Frederic A. Praeger, Inc.

ion, of press, of assembly, of movement, of trade-unionism; freedom of religion without any discrimination; and the right of all patriotic organizations of whatever political tendency to carry on normal activities.

3. Proclaim a general amnesty for all political prisoners and the dissolution of concentration camps of all sorts; abolish fascist law 10/59 and all the other antidemocratic laws; authorize the return to the country of all persons persecuted by the American-Diem regime who are now refugees abroad.

4. Interdict all illegal arrests and detentions; prohibit torture; and punish all the Diem bullies who have not repented and who have committed crimes against the people.

III. *Establish an independent and sovereign economy, and improve the living conditions of the people.*

1. Suppress the monopolies imposed by the American imperialists and their servants; establish an independent and sovereign economy and finances in accordance with the national interests; confiscate to the profit of the nation the properties of the American imperialists and their servants.

2. Support the national bourgeoisie in the reconstruction and development of crafts and industry; provide active protection for national products through the suppression of production taxes and the limitation or prohibition of imports that the national economy is capable of producing; reduce customs fees on raw materials and machines.

3. Revitalize agriculture; modernize production, fishing, and cattle raising; help the farmers in putting to the plow unused land and in developing production; protect the crops and guarantee their disposal.

4. Encourage and reinforce economic relations between the city and country, the plain and the mountain regions; develop commercial exchanges with foreign countries, regardless of their political regime, on the basis of equality and mutual interests.

5. Institute a just and rational system of taxation; eliminate harassing penalties.

6. Implement the labor code: prohibition of discharges, of penalties, of ill-treatment of wage earners; improvement of the living conditions of workers and civil servants; imposition of wage scales and protective measures for young apprentices.

7. Organize social welfare: find work for jobless persons; assume the support and protection of orphans, old people, in-

valids; come to the help of the victims of the Americans and Diemists; organize help for areas hit by bad crops, fires, or natural calamities.

8. Come to the help of displaced persons desiring to return to their native areas and to those who wish to remain permanently in the South; improve their working and living conditions.

9. Prohibit expulsions, spoliation, and compulsory concentration of the population; guarantee job security for the urban and rural working populations.

IV. *Reduce land rent; implement agrarian reform with the aim of providing land to the tillers.*

1. Reduce land rent; guarantee to the farmers the right to till the soil; guarantee the property right of accession to fallow lands to those who have cultivated them; guarantee property rights to those farmers who have already received land.

2. Dissolve "prosperity zones," and put an end to recruitment for the camps that are called "agricultural development centers." Allow those compatriots who already have been forced into "prosperity zones" and "agricultural development centers" to return freely to their own lands.

3. Confiscate the land owned by American imperialists and their servants, and distribute it to poor peasants without any land or with insufficient land; redistribute the communal lands on a just and rational basis.

4. By negotiation and on the basis of fair prices, repurchase for distribution to landless peasants or peasants with insufficient land those surplus lands that the owners of large estates will be made to relinquish if their domain exceeds a certain limit, to be determined in accordance with regional particularities. The farmers who benefit from such land distribution will not be compelled to make any payment or to submit to any other conditions.

V. *Develop a national and democratic culture and education.*

1. Combat all forms of culture and education enslaved to Yankee fashions; develop a culture and education that is national, progressive, and at the service of the Fatherland and people.

2. Liquidate illiteracy; increase the number of schools in the fields of general education as well as in those of technical and professional education, in advanced study as well as in other fields; adopt Vietnamese as the vernacular language; reduce the expenses of education and exempt from payment students who are without means; resume the examination system.

3. Promote science and technology and the national letters and arts; encourage and support the intellectuals and artists so as to permit them to develop their talents in the service of national reconstruction.

4. Watch over public health; develop sports and physical education.

VI. *Create a national army devoted to the defense of the Fatherland and the people.*

1. Establish a national army devoted to the defense of the Fatherland and the people; abolish the system of American military advisers.

2. Abolish the draft system, improve the living conditions of the simple soldiers and guarantee their political rights; put an end to ill-treatment of the military; pay particular attention to the dependents of soldiers without means.

3. Reward officers and soldiers having participated in the struggle against the domination by the Americans and their servants; adopt a policy of clemency toward the former collaborators of the Americans and Diemists guilty of crimes against the people but who have finally repented and are ready to serve the people.

4. Abolish all foreign military bases established on the territory of Viet-Nam.

VII. *Guarantee equality between the various minorities and between the two sexes; protect the legitimate interests of foreign citizens established in Viet-Nam and of Vietnamese citizens residing abroad.*

1. Implement the right to autonomy of the national minorities:

Found autonomous zones in the areas with a minority population, those zones to be an integral part of the Vietnamese nation.

Guarantee equality between the various nationalities: each nationality has the right to use and develop its language and writing system, to maintain or to modify freely its mores and customs; abolish the policy of the Americans and Diemists of racial discrimination and forced assimilation.

Create conditions permitting the national minorities to reach the general level of progress of the population: development of their economy and culture; formation of cadres of minority nationalities.

2. Establish equality between the two sexes; women shall have equal rights with men from all viewpoints (political, economic, cultural, social, etc.).

3. Protect the legitimate interests of foreign citizens established in Viet-Nam.

4. Defend and take care of the interests of Vietnamese citizens residing abroad.

VIII. *Promote a foreign policy of peace and neutrality.*

1. Cancel all unequal treaties that infringe upon the sovereignty of the people and that were concluded with other countries by the servants of the Americans.

2. Establish diplomatic relations with all countries, regardless of their political regime, in accordance with the principles of peaceful coexistence adopted at the Bandung Conference.

3. Develop close solidarity with peace-loving nations and neutral countries; develop free relations with the nations of Southeast Asia, in particular with Cambodia and Laos.

4. Stay out of any military bloc; refuse any military alliance with another country.

5. Accept economic aid from any country willing to help us without attaching any conditions to such help.

IX. *Re-establish normal relations between the two zones, and prepare for the peaceful reunification of the country.*

The peaceful reunification of the country constitutes the dearest desire of all our compatriots throughout the country. The National Liberation Front of South Viet-Nam advocates the peaceful reunification by stages on the basis of negotiations and through the seeking of ways and means in conformity with the interests of the Vietnamese nation.

While awaiting this reunification, the governments of the two zones will, on the basis of negotiations, promise to banish all separatist and warmongering propaganda and not to use force to settle differences between the zones. Commercial and cultural exchanges between the two zones will be implemented; the inhabitants of the two zones will be free to move about throughout the country as their family and business interests indicate. The freedom of postal exchanges will be guaranteed.

X. *Struggle against all aggressive war; actively defend universal peace.*

1. Struggle against all aggressive war and against all forms

of imperialist domination; support the national emancipation movements of the various peoples.

2. Banish all warmongering propaganda; demand general disarmament and the prohibition of nuclear weapons; and advocate the utilization of atomic energy for peaceful purposes.

3. Support all movements of struggle for peace, democracy, and social progress throughout the world; contribute actively to the defense of peace in Southeast Asia and in the world.

DIARIES OF VIET-CONG SOLDIERS*

Excerpts from the Diary of Viet-Cong Capt. Nguyen Dinh Kieu

(page 82)

May 30, 1961

Under the heading *Bch toc* (probably the abbreviation for "Command Staff Organization"), Captain Kieu assembled notes and ideas on the current situation and on what had to be done, apparently in preparation for the move to the South. ("We still have enough time to get ready. . . ."):

1—Alertness is necessary ("We should not relax in political matters . . .").

2—Better combat disposition is needed ("more mobility . . .").

3—Party activities must be stepped up during operations.

("Before departure, GH [probably a political cadre] must come and discuss the situation, the difficulties we are going to face, our objectives, etc. . . .").

4—Command staff must realize our problems ("There will be long marches, no transportation, little food . . .").

(page 83)

5—Indoctrination (propaganda for the population and international affairs).

* From Department of State Publication 7308, released December, 1961.

("Our allies have great admiration for us. But precisely at this moment we must not show any vanity which could lead our allies to think that the Vietnamese do not have any modesty.")

"See to it that our troops use only our own dry food supply and do not touch the property of the population. Beware of relationships with women. . . . Political cadres must reaffirm this before departure. . . ."

6—Protect secrecy ("Never leave used packages of cigarettes at camp sites . . .").

7—"Think of the problem of unity between the army and the population, between the political
(page 84)
cadres and the army."

8—"We must organize a system for relations with families."

9—Administrative problems ("Avoid carrying too bulky items.").

May 31 (in pencil) "The sandals and shoes distributed are a little tight."

(pages 85–86)

(Notes on a Party cell meeting dated June 30.)

(page 87)

(On this date, it is apparent the unit was in Laos.)

June 21. "We rest at Thapachon, Khan Muon (Laotian province of Khammouane). . . . It has taken us two and a half days of walking to reach here. This friendly country is really beautiful and rich. Why are its people so poor? . . ."

June 22. We arrive at Muong Xuan. This place has been burned down once by the French. Now it is again burned down by Fu Mi [Phoumi, a Laotian leader]. How much devastation! How many losses! . . ."

(page 88)

June 27. "We are leaving for Nam Mi. So far, the troops' morale is good. . . . We must be careful with the rice; we may run short of it. . . ."

June 28. "We arrive at Nam Mi. We rest here for one day. This area has been liberated only recently. The people are kind but show no understanding of politics. . . . We shall go southeast through Ban Ca Den. . . ."

June 29. "We arrive at Sepon [Tchepone]."
June 30. ⎫
July 1. ⎬ "Rest. Heavy rain. Party activities."
July 2. ⎭

(The following few entries are in pencil, apparently written before the above which are in ink:)

June 15, 1961. "At 1515 we depart, direction southeast."

"At 1820 we stop for a rest at a place 4 kilometers away from Y Ly."

"At 2400 we take the ferry at Huong Khe across the river."

"At 0300 on the 16th of June we arrive at T. Lang [probably Thanh Lang]."

"D goes and contacts the border defense corps to get help with food." (end of portion in pencil)

(page 89)

(notation on forces)

C1 + 4+ command staff + 4
C2
C3

"Sepon-Tusa (Tchepone to Tusa) took us 8 days of travel, 4 days marching, one of rest, etc. . . . ."

June 16–17. "rest at Thanh Lang"

June 18. "departure for Fong Khai . . ."

July 8. "There is no rice at the places where there should be. Then how can we continue, and it is already the 8th of July . . ."

July 9. "We sleep at Thanh Cau (or Can)."

July 10. "We sleep at Cape (or Cabe). At night we depart from Cape for Tusa. . . ."

"At 4 A.M. we arrive at the foot of the mountain. Why is it that the South is located in the skies? We keep going but when shall we reach the blue clouds and when shall we reach our beloved South?"

July 11. "We have been on the road for almost a month now. The mountain slopes are cruel. . . ."

July 12. "Rest at Tusa. The road from Cape to Tusa, where we arrived only at 1630 today, has been

(page 90)

the most difficult and the longest."

July 18. "We have departed [several illegible words] for the border. We have been on the road for 5 days."

224 · *The Viet-Nam Reader*

(notes on trouble with food supply, illness, etc.)
(page 91)
July 18. "From this day on, I am in the Fatherland again. . . .
We take along only a 2-day supply of food. . . . The capacity of the population here for understanding politics seems
higher. . . ."

"We pass an area with enemy posts. There are three of them
where we cross National Highway 14. Let's watch out for
enemy patrols from Highway 14 to Dakley. Enemy planes
are flying all day long. But we are relatively safe. . . . ."

"Our relay stations are distant from one another. Some of
them can be reached only after 7 P.M. and sometimes much later
than that. These stations have more security. They are built
near the mountains and have living quarters. . . ."
(page 92)
". . . We must do all we can to take care of the health and
morale of the troops. A group of political cadre is accompanying
us. We must avoid the enemy. That is why we have to take a
longer route. We rest for one day after passing two or three
relay stations. . . ."
(page 93)
". . . We passed Cadou-Sedang. We do not reveal the area
where we are going to operate. We must ask about our route.
The signals are provided by the relay stations and each day we
check in with one station. . . ."
(page 94)
". . . We return for three days to the relay station in the
western zone of Quang Nam. I feel here as though I were in a
'free area.' Enemy planes follow us. What are they looking for?
. . . Here is a place which used to be a safe zone during the
war against the French. . . . The problems of rice and salt have
become critical. The maximum ration is 2 lon a day. . . .
July 23. "I was seriously ill. . . . Fortunately, the 24th is a day
of rest.
July 25–26. "Although very tired, I must have the necessary
courage to continue. What is more thrilling than to stand here
on my beloved Fatherland looking at the beautiful Truong Son
mountain range?"
(page 95)
Aug. 5. "Rest at BTC [?]. We have one day to prepare to go to

Quang Ngai. Here is Tra My, in the province of Quang Nam, rich and fertile."

Aug. 13. "Arrive at Co Lo.

"Effectives were 37 at departure. Now the following are missing: Hrim, Dich, Mom, Du.

"Preparations, equipment, weapons, everything is in good shape."

(page 96)

(Notes on the qualifications of members of the company.)

(Notes on meeting of Party committee covering pages 96–99.)

(pages 101–2)

(A note to his wife, Thu Huong.)

"After fighting here, on our glorious Fatherland, I am writing to you and to our child. I have already written to you on the way. Thu Huong, I have not received any letters from you for 4 months. The working conditions are difficult. . . ."

(page 103)

"Duty situation—

"Prepare a safe base from which we can start operations to harass the enemy . . ."

(page 104)

". . . Exploit then the situation in the plains (Binh Son, Son Tinh, Quang Ngai, Mo Duc)."

"Winter-Spring 1961–62 operations: Start with small operations. Gather all military power in Safe Base No. 1 (CKI), then launch simultaneous attacks

(page 105)

all over the mountain area. After this, leave the mountain area to local forces and go as far as possible toward the midlands. . . . D_5 operate on Highway No. 5. Konbrai, Mangden, Konklung: attack enemy rescue groups, paralyze their transport, reduce their manpower. . . ."

(Pages 105–16 contain notes on military matters, evaluations of personnel, new recruits, etc.)

(page 117)

(brief evaluation at Party meeting of battle of Konbrai):

"Good secrecy was observed. No man left to visit his family. No sign of low morale. We have not yet proceeded to the counting of our casualties. The spirit of the army is high with this first victory. . . ."

(page 118)

(lists new weapons received)

Diary concludes with an entry on September 15 which discusses plans for operations at Kon Mong and includes a hand-drawn map of the area north of Konbrai.

Capt. Kieu was killed on Sept. 26, 1961, at Dakakoi and the diary was picked up on that date.

The Diary of a Viet-Cong Soldier, Do Luc

Do Luc made his first entry in his homemade diary on May 4, 1961. On that date he wrote:

"Leaving temporarily the beloved North to return to my native South to liberate my compatriots from the yoke of misery imposed by My-Diem (U.S.-Diem). This has been my ideal for a long time."

An entry of the same date with the time 1:30 A.M. noted:

"Here is the Viet-Nam–Laos border. I will always remember the international love which is engraved deep in my heart."

This was apparently a reference to his earlier service in Laos, which he described later.

By the middle of June, Do Luc and his companions had passed through Laos and had entered South Viet-Nam. On June 17 he wrote:

"Having been away for several years from the territory of Interzone 5 'Quang Nam,' my heart is both happy and sad. What shall I do now to be a worthy son of Interzone 5?"

On August 6, Do Luc wrote as follows:

"A few lines to remind me of this remote place! Not enough rice; meals tasteless because there is not enough salt; clothing is not warm enough for this very high peak.

"Nevertheless, in his determined heart, the fighter for liberation of the South remains faithful to the Party, to the people of the South, and he remains faithful to his only love."

Beginning on August 14, 1961, Do Luc began a review of some of his experiences. He wrote:

"Memory!

"One afternoon which is turning into evening. I am sitting on the peak of a high mountain. This is a famous scenic place. This is the highest peak of the whole chain of mountains, and it is all covered with mist. All this scenery arouses nostalgia in my heart! I try to recall my life since I was a young boy.

"I answered the call of the Party when I was very young, and what did I do for the people of my village? I devoted myself to the people. I took part in propaganda and aroused the people to carry out the policy of the Party and the Government and helped organize village defense and fighting forces. On March 25, 1954, I began my fighting career and I contributed my part in fighting the French Expeditionary Force. With the army of Interzone 5, I saw the end of the war on July 20, 1954, and then on April 26, 1955, I left my native place and all the ties with my family and friends to go north as a victorious fighter. Since that day, my spirit has matured together with that of the regular army. We have built up a beautiful and prosperous and strong North; the construction sites and factories spring up quickly everywhere under a bright sky and under the superior socialist regime. Close to me there was a unique source of consolation in my life. My life was beautiful, my happiness immeasureable. Enough to eat; warm clothing in my daily life; earning a living was fairly easy; often I enjoyed songs and dances which deal with the healthy life of all the people in the North and with the maturity of the Army."

In the following entry Do Luc wrote:

"Then, one morning, while my life was touched with a fresh, joyous and peaceful atmosphere, in harmony with the reconstruction program in the North, while my life was a normal one and I was happy with my only love . . .

"Suddenly, on December 15, 1960, . . .

"I answered the needs of the international solidarity of the Vietnamese-Laotian proletariat. I had to leave my beloved Fatherland and my sweet life and go to help our friends with a spirit of unselfishness, of class solidarity, of love for my Fatherland, and the spirit of the international proletarian revolution, in order to annihilate the reactionary clique of Pumi Buon Um (Phoumi-Boun Oum) so that mankind and the two countries, Viet-Nam and Laos, could achieve prosperity and happiness.

"Thus, I succeeded in meeting the needs of a friendly country.

"Our friends' war has stopped and the guns are silent. On

the call of the Party, I returned to my beloved Fatherland! My life returned to normal. I enjoyed again the peaceful atmosphere and my happiness. I continued training daily for the defense of the territory of the North and for the continuation of the liberation of the South. But I was back with my only love. Hurrah! How happy and how sweet. But my life could not continue that way!

"For the third time my life turned to war again. For the liberation of our compatriots in the South, a situation of boiling oil and burning fire is necessary! A situation in which husband is separated from wife, father from son, brother from brother is necessary. I joined the ranks of the liberation army in answer to the call of the front for liberation of the South.

"Now my life is full of hardship—not enough rice to eat nor enough salt to give a taste to my tongue, not enough clothing to keep myself warm! But in my heart I keep loyal to the Party and to the people. I am proud and happy.

"I am writing down this story for my sons and my grandsons of the future to know of my life and activities during the revolution when the best medicine available was the root of the wild banana tree and the best bandage was the leaf of rau lui, when there was no salt to give a taste to our meals, when there was no such food as meat or fish like we enjoy in a time of peace and happiness such as I have known and left behind. But that day will not take long to return to my life."

On the back pages of his diary, Do Luc had listed a number of Vietnamese words with their equivalents in the language of one of the mountain tribes in the area where he was stationed.

In the back pages of his diary, Do Luc also listed "10 disciplinary rules for military security" as follows:

"1. Do not disclose army secrets. Do not be curious about your own responsibilities and duties.

"2. Do not discuss the duties you must carry out.

"3. You must respect absolutely the regulations which protect documents during your activities. Do not carry with you those things that regulations prohibit you from carrying. If you are captured by the enemy, be determined not to give in."

(Ironically, this regulation on documents was violated by the diary in which he wrote down the rule!)

"Slogans:—absolute loyalty to the revolution
　　　　　—death is preferable to slavery

"4. Keep secret our method of hiding weapons.

"5. Do not take the liberty of listening to enemy broadcasts or of reading their newspapers or documents. Do not spread false rumors.

"6. Do not have any relations with any organization with evil segments of the population which are harmful to the revolution.

"7. Do not take your family or relatives or friends to military camp sites.

"8. Keep order and security among the population as well as among yourselves.

"9. Do not cease to carry out self-criticism or being vigilant, and continue your training.

"10. Implement seriously these ten rules, mentally as well as in deeds."

Excerpts from the Diary of a Viet-Cong Medical Officer, Mai Xuan Phong

On October 3, 1961, in Darlac Province a unit of the Army of the Republic of Viet-Nam overran a Viet-Cong camp. The VC group had included a small medical detachment. The A.R.V.N. forces captured some medical supplies and a diary kept by the Viet-Cong medical officer, a man named Mai Xuan Phong. The first dated entry in the diary is for April 20, 1961; the final one, for September 21, 1961. In the back pages of his notebook Phong wrote the words of a popular Vietnamese song. Excerpts from the Mai Xuan Phong diary follow:

(page 4)

"The most precious thing for a man is his life, because one has only one life. One must, then, live in such a way that one does not have to regret the wasted years and months, that one does not have to be ashamed of a pitiful past, that one is able to say before passing away: my whole life, my whole strength have been devoted to the most elevated and the most beautiful cause—the struggle for the liberation of mankind. . . ."

(page 5)

". . . And one has to live in a hurry. A stupid accident, disease, or any tragic hazard may suddenly put an end to one's life. . . ."

(page 6)

April 20, 1961. "Departure for a new mission to which I have been assigned. There are so many happy memories which will encourage me to fulfill my duty. . . ."

April 22, 1961. "We left the beloved fatherland at exactly five minutes to 12. Here is a friendly country. We have to cross a very mountainous border region."

(page 7)

May 14, 1961. "At 15 minutes before 9:00 we arrived at Highway No. 9 which has just been liberated. On the highway lie the remnants of four enemy GMC trucks and two armored cars which our forces have destroyed. We arrived at the post of Muong Phin (Muong Phine) which has just been liberated. We slept at Muong Phine and, next day, we cross Highway No. 9.

(unintelligible code sign "6–5 * +")

"We stop here and help build a road to allow trucks to bring in rice supplies. For two days, we have been short of food and had only glutinous rice. This portion of our route is really hard. The sun is burning hot. We do not have enough drinking water. . . ."

(page 8)

"but our patriotism and our determination to liberate the native land will help us overcome all the difficulties and accomplish our duty."

(signature)

June 1, 1961. "At 15 minutes to 2:00 we arrived at the regrouping station located on the border between Laos and Viet-Nam, at the border of Quang Nam [Province]. I have been away from the beloved fatherland for one month and 20 days (Note: bad arithmetic, should be one month and 10 days!), and I have been away from my native South for 6 years."

(signature)

(page 9)

"At exactly 3:00 P.M. on the 10th of June '61 we arrived at the boundary of Contum (Kontum) province. . . ."

(signature)

"We entered Cambodia on July 10, 1961—across the border of Cambodia and Viet-Nam in the province of Gia Rai. . . ."

(page 10)

"We arrived at the operational base in Dac Lac (Darlac) province, in the southwest highlands, on August 7, 1961. . . .

"On August 9, I received orders to go on a mission and join

an armed unit. This unit has just been organized. It does not have living quarters yet and is not yet fully equipped. The unit is composed of only two squads, all mountain tribesmen except for two Vietnamese who came from the North. As for me, in my capacity as medical assistant, I find that there are no conditions or means for me to operate. There is not sufficient medicine. Life in this base is really difficult. . . ."

(page 11)

"But I shall overcome all these difficulties in order to fulfill my duty in the revolution in the South.

"After three months and nine days, after having crossed many a border—Laos, Cambodia, Viet-Nam—after having gone through all this hardship and danger, I think that I have accomplished at this point a part of my duty.

"August 9, 1961"

(signature)

(page 12)

September 20, 1961. "Today we begin our tour of armed propaganda. We shall attack the enemy and establish popular bases among the population of the land development centers in Dac Lac (Darlac) province, in the southwest highlands. . . ."

September 21, 1961. "I received instructions to report to K (note: probably the Viet-Cong operational headquarters in the Ban Me Thuot area) in order to be assigned a new mission. . . ."

(page 14)

September 21, 1961. "At 5:30, our forces launched a massive attack on the land development center of Quang Nhieu, Ba Moi Thuoc (Ban Me Thuot), and we proceeded to armed propaganda. We gathered together about 400 people and propagandized on the policy of the Front for Liberation of the South.-. . .

"We have secured good results. We have awakened these people after the dark years they lived under My-Diem. We seized many documents and much military equipment. . . ."

(signature)

The inside cover of the Mai Xuan Phong diary bears the seal of the Tong Cong Ty Bach Hoa (literally, General Company for a Hundred Things), a state-owned enterprise in North Viet-Nam.

NATIONAL LIBERATION FRONT ON U.S. ESCALATION OF WAR,* WITH NOTES ON CHANGES MADE BY HANOI

[Liberation Radio (Clandestine) in Vietnamese to South Viet-Nam 0500 GMT 23 March 1965]

On 22 March in a certain place in the liberated areas, the NFLSV Central Committee held an important press conference to proclaim the front's five-point statement about the intensification and enlargement by the U.S. imperialists of their aggressive war in South Viet-Nam. The press conference was attended by all the members of the NFLSV Central Committee; many delegates of the front delegation and other mass organization delegations which had just returned from the Indochinese people's conference; many delegates of mass organizations and political parties; correspondents of newspapers, Liberation Press Agency, and Liberation Radio, and so forth.

At the press conference, Chairman Nguyen Huu Tho proclaimed an important five-point statement condemning the systematic war-seeking and aggressive policy of the U.S. imperialists in South Viet-Nam and enunciating the heroic South Vietnamese people's unchanged standpoint which is resolutely to kick out the U.S. imperialists in order to liberate the South, build an independent, democratic, peaceful, and neutral South Viet-Nam, and achieve national unification. Here is the NFLSV statement about the intensification and enlargement by the U.S. imperialists of their aggressive war in South Viet-Nam:

During the last ten years, the U.S. imperialists continuously intervened in and aggressed against South Viet-Nam. Recently they introduced into South Viet-Nam a series of U.S. combat

---

* March 22, 1965. The changes made by Hanoi, for the purpose of toning down the original statement, are added in the form of notes at the end of the NLF statement.

units—including missile units, marines, and strategic B-57 planes
—and many units of South Korean, Formosan, Filipino, Australian, Malay, and other mercenaries. They were so crazy that they
sent their air force and that of their lackeys to repeatedly bomb
North Viet-Nam and Laos. Faced with their[1] imminent complete defeat, the U.S. imperialists dropped their neocolonialist
mask and appeared as the most cruel soldier of old colonialism,
which actually they are. At present, not only are they stubbornly
stepping up their criminal aggressive war in South Viet-Nam, but
they are also planning to extend this war to all Indochina and
Southeast Asia.

It is clear that the puppets, lackeys, and bootlickers of the
Americans in South Viet-Nam are committing more and more
monstrous and treacherous crimes. It is clear that those shameful traitors are kowtowing before the enemies and introducing
additional troops from the United States and satellite countries
into South Viet-Nam to exterminate our race, trample on and
occupy our sacred territory, and oppress and exploit (several
words indistinct) our people. The Vietnamese people, the Indochinese peoples, the Asian peoples, and the peace- and justice-
loving peoples the world over are angrily and energetically protesting against the criminal, war-seeking, aggressive actions of
the U.S. imperialists.

Faced with the present and extremely grave situation, the
NFLSV deems it necessary to solemnly proclaim once more its
unchanged stand of struggling against the Americans to save
the country. The U.S. imperialists[2] are saboteurs of the Geneva
Accords, extremely rude and cruel aggressors and warmongers,
and deadly enemies of the Vietnamese people.

It is general knowledge that the glorious resistance of the
Vietnamese people defeated the aggressive war of the French
colonialists who were aided by the U.S. imperialists. Indeed,
during the previous protracted resistance of the Vietnamese
people, the U.S. imperialists gave the French colonialists aid
consisting of 2.6 billion dollars, 180,000 tons of weapons[3] and
200 advisers in order to repress the Vietnamese people's aspirations for independence and freedom. Thanks to their indomitable
spirit, their determination to prefer death over enslavement,
their courage, and their great combativity, and thanks to the
whole-hearted support of the world peoples, the heroic Vietnamese people achieved great victories, liberated half of their

beloved country from the enemies' grip, and [arrived at?][4] international accords in Geneva in 1954, accords which solemnly
recognized the sovereignty, independence, and territorial integrity of Viet-Nam, Laos, and Cambodia, re-established peace
in these areas, and [foresaw?][5] a reunification of Viet-Nam
through peaceful means.

The Vietnamese people are well aware of the value of those
accords. The Vietnamese people have always and correctly
applied those accords and resolutely struggled so that those
accords would be implemented in accordance with the spirit
and letter of this international document which has all the
characteristics of legality. On the other hand, U.S. imperialists
and their lackeys in South Viet-Nam have gradually and in an
increasingly brazen manner trampled on the Geneva Accords
and [word indistinct] destroying those accords by openly waging
an atrocious war in South Viet-Nam[6] over the past eleven years
with a view to enslaving and oppressing the South Vietnamese
people, turning South Viet-Nam into one of their colonies and
military bases, and partitioning Vietnamese territory forever.

Immediately after the signing of the Geneva Accords, the U.S.
imperialists hurriedly wooed their lackeys into creating the
so-called SEATO bloc and deliberately placed South Viet-Nam
under the protection of this bloc, thus actually placing South
Viet-Nam under the rule of the Americans and [their satellites,
and enabling them to intervene?][7] more and more deeply and
rudely in the affairs of South Viet-Nam. From late 1954 to 1959,
the U.S. imperialists and the puppet Ngo Dinh Diem authorities
launched a series of terrorist and mopping-up operations, such
as the Truong Tan Buu, Thoai Ngoc Hau, and other operations,
during which they frantically massacred the people who love
peace and the country, and the former resistants, and extermi-
nated the faithful of various religions and all those who did not
collaborate with them.

From the first days that peace was re-established, the South
Vietnamese people's blood[8] has been spilled in Duy Xuyen,
Huong Dien [Cho Duoc, Vinh Trinh—phonetic], and other
places, even in Saigon. To step up these savage mass massacres
and operations, the U.S. imperialists and their lackeys promulgated the fascist 10/59 law outlawing the South Vietnamese
people, and all factions and individuals who opposed the im-

perialists, calling them Communists. At the same time, they moved their guillotine from place to place throughout South Viet-Nam. During that period, according to still incomplete statistics, the U.S. executioners and their lackeys jailed and killed hundred of thousands of South Vietnamese patriots who committed no crime other than to struggle for peace, for the strict implementation of the Geneva Accords, and for the peaceful unification of Viet-Nam, or who were guilty of refusing to kowtow before them.

Naturally the criminal actions of the U.S. imperialists and their lackeys aroused hatred throughout Viet-Nam and gave rise to a wave of boiling anger throughout the world. Public opinion in Viet-Nam, public opinion in Asia, and the impartial public opinion the world over severely condemned and energetically protested against the cruel actions of the U.S. imperialists and their lackeys and loudly demanded that they put an end to their war-seeking and aggressive actions against the South Vietnamese people and that they correctly implement the 1954 Geneva Accords. But all this fell on deaf ears. The U.S. imperialists[9] continued to trample on justice and to rush ahead with their piratical war in South Viet-Nam.

In accordance with the spirit and letter of the 1954 Geneva Accords,[10] the U.S. Military Advisory Group set up during the Indochinese war and composed of 200 men should have been disbanded. But not only have they maintained it, they have also developed it illegally, so that now the total number of U.S. officers and soldiers in South Viet-Nam amounts to 30,000 men, including military policemen, men serving in missile units, paratroopers, marines, and so forth.

This is not to mention the combat units—composed of thousands of men—of their satellites: South Korea, Formosa, Australia, the Philippines, and so forth. Recently, after publicly introducing 2,000 South Korean mercenaries into South Viet-Nam, the Americans openly introduced into South Viet-Nam their own entire Ninth Marine Brigade, composed of 3,900 men and belonging to the U.S. Pacific forces, and garrisoned them in Da Nang. At the same time, as revealed by Western news agencies, they planned to introduce into South Viet-Nam a division of U.S. infantrymen.

While introducing additional military personnel into South

Viet-Nam, the Washington authorities, with the view of justifying their action, engaged in a propaganda campaign, saying that these men are only instructors, *aides-de-camp*, and so forth. In the recent past, however, the U.S. imperialists openly introduced into South Viet-Nam, first, the so-called command advisers and combat advisers, and then units, including combat units. In the past the U.S. military personnel, who commanded the aggressive war machinery in South Viet-Nam, were of high rank, but gradually they came to command directly and fought at the lowest ranks [several words indistinct] on the civil guard force, the militia force, and the regular forces. At the same time, the U.S. advisers gradually and directly managed the rebel administrative machinery from the central level down to the provincial and district levels.

Applying the bandits' traditional policy of using the Vietnamese to fight Vietnamese and using the Asians to fight Asians, the U.S. imperialists ordered their lackeys to actively recruit new soldiers, whom the Americans trained, equipped, and organized into a 500,000-man armed force that they directly commanded in order to pursue their aggressive war in South Viet-Nam. Recently, along with introducing U.S. Marines into South Viet-Nam, the Americans ordered the rebel authorities to recruit 100,000 new soldiers.

To equip the U.S. troops and the mercenaries, the U.S. imperialists introduced into South Viet-Nam an enormous [quantity of weapons?] and war matériel—namely, 1,200 planes of various types, including units of strategic B-57 jets; over 100 large and small warships, including aircraft carriers; thousands of M-113 amphibious vehicles and tanks; hundreds of thousands of tons of weapons, including over 600 artillery guns; and tens of thousands of tons of chemical poisons and phosphorus bombs. Recently, the U.S. imperialists sent two Hawk missile battalions, many jet aircraft units, and tens of tons of modern weapons to Da Nang. They have at their disposal in South Viet-Nam 111 military airfields, including 9 strategic airfields for jet aircraft, 9 naval bases, 20 radar bases, 4 strategic roadways, and many military camps and bases. Moreover, the U.S. Seventh Fleet routinely conducts maneuvers off the coast of South Viet-Nam and is used as a base from which the combat units of the U.S. Air Force and Navy have conducted airstrikes against the territory of Viet-Nam and Laos.

For the past three years, the U.S. Government has spent between 1.5 and 2 million dollars daily for its aggressive war in South Viet-Nam. Over the past eleven years to carry out its aggressive colonialist policy in South Viet-Nam, the U.S. government has spent 4 billion dollars under the "aid" label, 80 per cent of which went for military expenditures.

The aggressive war in South Viet-Nam has been a special concern for the U.S. ruling circles. U.S. President Kennedy in the past and President Johnson at present, the U.S. Security Council, the U.S. Defense Department, the U.S. Department of State, and the U.S. Central Intelligence Agency have daily followed all developments in this country. Honolulu has become a permanent meeting place where the ringleaders of the White House and Pentagon and the piratical U.S. generals in the Pacific meet every month to discuss the plan of aggression against South Viet-Nam and directly control and command the aggressive war in South Viet-Nam.

Along with the Military Assistance Advisory Group, the U.S. imperialists set up the Harkins command and the so-called Vietnamese–U.S. Joint Command, which is really the supreme U.S. military organ in South Viet-Nam directly commanded by the U.S. President and Defense Department, in order to step up the aggressive war in South Viet-Nam. Most high-ranking officials, secretaries, and generals of the United States have come to South Viet-Nam to inspect the situation, to work out plans of aggression, and to command on-the-spot the war of banditry. The U.S. Government has sent to Saigon a series of well-known U.S. generals such as O'Daniel, Collins, McGarr, Williams, Harkins, and recently Chairman of the U.S. Joint Chiefs of Staff Taylor, General Westmoreland, and General Throckmorton.

In sum, the U.S. imperialists and their henchmen have made full use of all the modern weapons and war matériel except atomic bombs to terrorize and massacre the South Vietnamese people to achieve their only objective—to place the Vietnamese people under their yoke and to turn South Viet-Nam into their colony and military base. Over the past eleven years, they have conducted more than 160,000 large and small scale mopping-up operations, killed about 170,000 people, wounded and crippled through torture about 800,000 people;[11] detained more than 400,000 people in more than 20,000 prisons; raped more than 40,000 women, including old women, children, and religious people; cut open the bellies of and buried alive more than 5,000 people; destroyed innumerable villages and hamlets; herded more than 5 million people into 8,000 concentration camps disguised as agrovilles, land development centers, and strategic hamlets;[12] and sprayed chemicals over many areas to destroy tens of thousands of hectares of crops and fruit trees and poisoned thousands of people. They have, moreover, demolished thousands of pagodas, churches, and temples and killed thousands of faithful of various religions.

Under the cruel policy of the U.S. aggressors and their henchmen, this beautiful and prosperous territory of South Viet-Nam has become ragged and desolate. Their tyrannical, fascist regime in South Viet-Nam is more cruel than the Hitlerite fascist regime and has likewise committed barbarities and cruelties equal to those of the middle ages.

All these facts written in blood revealed the criminal acts of the U.S. imperialists and their henchmen and their faces as belligerents, aggressors, and country-sellers. Their criminal actions have condemned them and are strong proof that the U.S. imperialists and their henchmen have not only violated articles 14 and 19 of the armistice agreement and points 4 and 5 of the concluding statement of the 1954 conference, banning the introduction of troops,[13] military personnel, weapons, and ammunition into South Viet-Nam, the construction of new military bases and military alliances with foreign countries, but have also brazenly torn up these international accords. The Washington authorities and the Vietnamese traitors not only disregarded the Geneva Accords, but also rudely violated the spirit and letter of international law and the Bandung conference resolution. The present realities[14] in South Viet-Nam [several words indistinct] reflect an undeniable truth that the so-called[15] Johnson–Ngo Dinh Diem joint communiqué issued in late May, 1961, was actually a bilateral military treaty and that the so-called friendship [several words indistinct] and a series of accords signed between them, although concealed under the "aid" label or other deceitful labels, were only country-selling and country-taking acts. Yet, no matter how cunning they were, they could not conceal the truth.

It is also necessary to recall that the so-called White Paper which Washington published recently is fully valueless. This cheap psychological warfare trick has no real base and is aimed only at deceiving people. This rather clumsy trick of a thief who cries "stop thief" unmasks their intention to distort the truth and change white to black in order to divert the attention of world opinion, which is energetically condemning their brazen plot of intensifying and enlarging the war. The truth is that in South Viet-Nam the U.S. imperialists are engaging in a criminal, aggressive war; the U.S. imperialists are brazenly sabotaging the Geneva Accords; the U.S. imperialists are the most dangerous warmongers and aggressors; and the U.S. imperialists are the deadly enemies of the Vietnamese people, the Indochinese peoples, and world peoples.

2—[preceding part not numbered] The heroic South Vietnamese people are determined to kick out the U.S. imperialists in order to liberate South Viet-Nam; build an independent, democratic, peaceful, and neutral South Viet-Nam; and advance toward national unification.

The South Vietnamese people are fond of peace, but the South Vietnamese people cannot stand idle and let the U.S. aggressors and their lackeys freely trample on the country and dominate the nation. They prefer death to bondage. The 14 million people have risen in one bloc and struggled gallantly to defeat the U.S. invaders and the country-sellers, liberate South Viet-Nam, achieve independence, democracy, peace, and neutrality in South Viet-Nam, and contribute to maintaining [peace in Indochina?] and Southeast Asia.

This patriotic war in South Viet-Nam is fully consistent with the most fundamental points of international law on the self-determination right of nations and the right to undertake defensive war against foreign aggression. During their sacred liberation war, the South Vietnamese people have used all sorts of weapons to fight the enemy, and the greatest supplier of weapons to the armed forces in South Viet-Nam is none other than the U.S. imperialists, following their heavy and repeated defeats during the recent past. Relying on their invincible[16] strength and enjoying the positive support of the world people, the South Vietnamese people during their extremely glorious defensive war have achieved victory after victory. Recently, the more often they fought, the stronger they became and the greater were their victories. That is why they are enthusiastically supported and encouraged by the world's people. From the beginning of 1961 to the end of the 1964 the southern armed forces and people put 200,000 of the enemy out of action, including 3,566 U.S. aggressors who were killed, wounded, or taken prisoner. The southern armed forces and people captured 47,569 weapons of all sorts including many guns and mortars; downed, damaged, and destroyed 1,892 planes; sunk and damaged 969 warships and motor boats including aircraft carriers; and destroyed and damaged 2,552 military vehicles of all sorts including many M-113 vehicles.

According to still incomplete statistics, in January and February of this year the southern armed forces and people put 32,109 of the enemy out of action, including 817 U.S. aggressors who were killed, wounded, or taken prisoner; captured 5,569 weapons of all sorts; downed, damaged, and destroyed 151 planes; and so forth.

The so-called national policy on strategic hamlets of the U.S. imperialists and their lackeys basically failed. Now, the southern people have reconquered three-fourths of the territory, on which lives more than one-half of the population. Linked together and composed of rich and densely populated areas, the liberated areas are becoming the firm rear for the sacred resistance of the South Vietnamese people.

With empty hands, the South Vietnamese people have fulfilled a great task and achieved many glorious victories. The South Vietnamese people are firmly convinced that with their own strength and with the whole-hearted support of the world's people the South Vietnamese people will surely achieve complete victory. The repeated and[17] resounding victories achieved by the South Vietnamese armed forces and people during this spring are precipitating the collapse of U.S. colonalism in South Viet-Nam. The U.S. imperialists and their lackeys are in a desperate deadlock. They are being overthrown by the extremely powerful revolutionary storms set in motion by the South Vietnamese people, but they are squirming and writhing before yielding.

To escape this dangerous situation, the U.S. imperialists are engaging in extremely dangerous adventurous military actions. The fact that they introduced into South Viet-Nam combat units of their air, naval, and ground forces, additional U.S. weapons, and mercenaries from South Korea and other satellites and used planes to bomb the D.R.V. and the Laotian Kingdom and so forth does not reflect their strength at all. On the contrary, these are the crazy actions of a [hooligan?][18] who, faced with deadlock, engages in adventurous actions. They cannot threaten anyone. By its nature, the U.S. imperialist scheme of intensifying and enlarging their present aggressive war reflects one of their humiliating defeats. It proves that their eleven-year-old colonialist and aggressive policy in South Viet-Nam and their so-called special war have gone bankrupt.

Since the U.S. imperialists have bogged down and almost died during the special war, they will be completely wiped out in [the regional war?].[19] If they dare to extend the war to North Viet-Nam, to all of Indochina, and further, they will face more humiliating defeats more quickly. Previously, with empty[20] hands the southern people dealt heavy blows on the U.S. imperialists and their lackeys and fulfilled a great and glorious revolutionary task. Now, with their own strength, with the whole-hearted support of powerful North Viet-Nam and the rich and powerful Socialist countries, and with the sympathy, support, and encouragement of the Asian, African, and Latin American countries and all peace- and justice-loving peoples the world over, the South Vietnamese people will surely and gloriously triumph over the U.S. aggressors and their lackeys in any regional or special war waged by the latter. Now more than ever before, the South Vietnamese people must firmly hold rifles in hand and struggle to achieve their fundamental goal, which is to kick out the U.S. imperialists and build an independent, democratic, peaceful, and neutral South Viet-Nam.

The NFLSV asserts once more that the U.S. scheme of introducing U.S. and satellite air, naval, and ground force units into South Viet-Nam and bombing North Viet-Nam and Laos to reduce the[21] combativity of the South Vietnamese people, to stop the aid of the North Vietnamese and world peoples to the just struggle of the South Vietnamese people, and to create a strong position from which they can force the NFLSV and the South Vietnamese people to sell their fatherland to them cheaply through certain negotiations is only an empty dream of men who are crazy politically and adventurous militarily.

The South Vietnamese people inform the U.S. imperialists

and their lackeys: "You are hooligans.[22],[23] You are stupid. How can you hope to deceive people when each time after hitting the North without warning you repeat again and again that you do not intend to enlarge the war, that the attacks are retaliatory measures, that the attacks are aimed at bringing about negotiations, and so forth? You are more stupid when you say you want to negotiate from a position of strength." The South Vietnamese people point their fingers in the faces of the U.S. imperialists and their lackeys and tell them: "Your only way out is to withdraw from South Viet-Nam. If you stubbornly pursue the war, you will suffer the greatest and most humiliating defeat you have ever suffered."

On behalf of 14 million people of the heroic South, the NFLSV solemnly states: Rivers can dry up, mountains can erode, but[24],[25] the South Vietnamese people and their armed forces will never drop their weapons as long as the South Vietnamese people's fundamental objectives—independence, democracy, peace, and neutrality—have not been achieved. The South Vietnamese people are determined to deal the heaviest blows on the heads of the U.S. imperialists and their lackeys and to achieve final victory. [several words indistinct][26] 3,000 U.S. and satellite soldiers—who have been and will be introduced into South Viet-Nam—are only stupid May flies which allow themselves to be burned needlessly by the fire of the patriotic war of 14 million people of the heroic South.

At present all negotiations are useless as long as the U.S. imperialists do not withdraw all the troops, weapons, and means of war of the United States and its satellites from South Viet-Nam and destroy their military bases in South Viet-Nam; as long as the sacred rights of the South Vietnamese people— rights to independence and democracy—[are still sold?][27] by the Vietnamese traitors to the U.S. imperialists; and as long as the NFLSV—true and only representative of 14 million South Vietnamese people—does not have the decisive voice. With regard to[28] the South Korean clique and other satellites of the Americans who are planning to introduce mercenaries into South Viet-Nam, the South Vietnamese people tell them the following: Although you are involved in waging the war, you will never be given your share. You are simply shameful scapegoats for U.S. imperialism. Since nearly 30,000 U.S. generals, field grade officers, and men with nearly half a million lackey troops are being heavily beaten by the army and people in South Viet-Nam, what can a handful of you do?

The South Vietnamese people warn those following the U.S. imperialists: If you stupidly join the war of banditry of the U.S. imperialists in South Viet-Nam, your fate will be that of the May flies before the fire of the patriotic war of the South Vietnamese people, and the inevitable result will be that, jumping into the fire, you will be burned by the fire.

3—The heroic South Vietnamese people and liberation troops are determined to fulfill their sacred mission which is to chase away the U.S. imperialists, to liberate South Viet-Nam, and to defend North Viet-Nam. Viet-Nam is one, the Vietnamese people are one, North and South are one. Their affection is as high as a mountain and as deep as the sea. This truth is as sure as the sun rises in the east. Nothing can change it. In their hot[29,30] and deadly struggle against the U.S. imperialists and their lackeys, the South Vietnamese people have always received the great and extremely precious assistance of 17 million northern brothers. The northern compatriots are enthusiastically working day and night for the southern part of the country.

On behalf of the 14 million South Vietnamese people, the NFLSV wishes to extend its full confidence and unchangeable promise to the 17 million northern compatriots. The South Vietnamese[31] people are determined to fight and defeat the U.S. imperialists. The heroic South Vietnamese people and liberation troops are determined to fulfill their sacred mission: to chase away the U.S. imperialists, to liberate South Viet-Nam, to defend the north, and to advance toward the reunification of the country.

In the recent past, to remedy their desperate situation and unavoidable collapse in South Viet-Nam, the U.S. imperialists and their lackeys madly sent aircraft and warships to pound North Viet-Nam. But these U.S. pirates and their lackeys were punished appropriately by the troops and people of North Viet-Nam. More than 40[32] U.S. jet aircraft were downed. The South Vietnamese troops are extremely happy over and warmly acclaim these brilliant performances by the troops and people of the North.

In sharing the suffering of their northern compatriots and

to defend beloved North Viet-Nam, the troops and people of South Viet-Nam have repeatedly directed their anger at the heads of the U.S. aggressors and their lackeys. The more the U.S. imperialists and their lackeys step up their acts of war against North Viet-Nam, the more strongly—two or three times more strongly—the South Vietnamese troops and people will hit the enemy.

In February, 1965, when the invaders and traitors pounded North Viet-Nam, the South Vietnamese liberation troops directed lightning attacks against the important military bases and main forces of the enemy, putting 20,706 of the enemy out of action—among whom about 600 U.S. aggressors were killed, wounded, or captured alive—seizing 3,144[33] weapons of all kinds, downing, destroying, or hitting 111 aircraft of all types, and so forth.

The NFLSV and the South Vietnamese people warn the U.S. imperialists and the Vietnamese traitors: As you are unable to vanquish the 14 million South Vietnamese people, you will have no hope of vanquishing 30 million Vietnamese people as a whole. Your adventurous military actions, which involve expanding your aggressive war, will definitely fail to drag you out of the mud of failure which is up to your necks; but they will promptly lead you to suicide.

Also to get out of their deadlock in South Viet-Nam, the U.S. imperialists and their lackeys have sent planes to attack the liberated areas in Laos, to violate the frontier and territory of Cambodia, to spray poisonous chemicals, and to drop bombs to massacre the Cambodian people. But the U.S. imperialists and their cliques have been dealt appropriate retaliatory blows by the armies and people of Laos and Cambodia.

The South Vietnamese people heartily applaud the spirit of courageous and indomitable struggle of the peoples of the fraternal neighboring countries. The South Vietnamese people pledge to stand side by side with the Laotian and Cambodian people in the struggle against the common enemy—the U.S. imperialists and their lackeys. The people and liberation troops in South Viet-Nam are determined to defeat the U.S. aggressors and their henchmen in South Viet-Nam which is a base for the acts of war and banditry of the Americans and their lackeys against the Kingdoms of Laos and Cambodia.

Once again, the South Vietnamese people greet the brilliant success of the recent conference for solidarity and against the Americans of the Indochinese people. The NFLSV and the South Vietnamese people warn the U.S. imperialists and their lackeys: If you take risks by expanding your war of banditry throughout all of Vietnam and if you intend to blow the flames of war to spread them to all of Indochina, the invincible strength of the 30 million Vietnamese people and the mountain-displacing and ocean-filling strength of hundreds of millions of people in Indochina and Asia will overflow and bury you alive.

4. The Vietnamese people express their gratitude for the whole-hearted support of the world peoples eager for peace and justice and are ready to receive their assistance, including weapons and other war matériel. The just and patriotic struggle of the South Vietnamese is whole-heartedly supported and encouraged by the peace- and justice-loving peoples of the world. The world peoples support the South Vietnamese people, not only in the moral, but also the material field. Of course, the South Vietnamese people and their representatives, the NFLSV, have the full right to receive and warmly acclaim this just assistance, especially when the[34] U.S. imperialists are introducing troops to expand the war in South Viet-Nam throughout Indochina.

The NFLSV always relies primarily on its own force and ability, but is ready to continue to receive all assistance, moral and material, including assistance in weapons and war matériel from the Socialist countries and nationalist countries, all world organizations and all peace-loving peoples throughout the world. Moreover, the front reserves for itself the right to buy weapons and war matériel from any country and organization ready to sell them to the South Vietnamese people[35] to help them strengthen their defensive potential.

The world conference of solidarity with the Vietnamese people against the U.S. aggressors and for the defense of peace held last May,[36] gathering the representatives of more than 50 countries and 16 world organizations, concretely answered our just request. If the U.S. imperialists continue to send their troops and the troops of their satellites into South Viet-Nam and to expand the war to the North and Laos, the NFLSV will call on the world peoples to send troops and youths to come and side with the South Vietnamese people in the struggle to exterminate the common enemy. The NFLSV will[37] call on the South Vietnamese children, who in compliance with the cease-fire agreements were regrouped in the north and have lived far from South Viet-Nam for ten years, to return to take up weapons to exterminate the enemy to save their country. There is a Vietnamese people's saying, "Diamond cuts diamond." The South Vietnamese people and the peace-loving peoples throughout the world are determined not to forgive the U.S. aggressors and their lackeys. They will have to bear all extremely serious consequences of their warlike and aggressive acts.

Once again, on behalf of the 14 million South Vietnamese people, the NFLSV begs to express its deep gratitude to the peoples of the Socialist countries, the nationalist countries, the world organizations, and peace- and justice-loving peoples throughout the world for their whole-hearted support for the patriotic and just struggle of the South Vietnamese people. More than ever, we assert our glorious international duty: To do our utmost and to be determined to sacrifice ourselves to contribute worthily to the common and grandiose struggle for the peoples for national independence, democracy, peace, and progress in Indochina, Southeast Asia, and the world for the defeat of the international gendarmes—the U.S. warmongers and aggressors.

5. All people must be united. All people must be armed and must heroically continue to move forward with the determination to fight to win over the U.S. enemy and the Vietnamese traitors.

The armed struggle of the South Vietnamese people against the U.S. imperialist aggressors and their lackeys has won very great victories. The South Vietnamese[38] people are moving forward, determined to achieve the greatest victory. The South Vietnamese people are winning victories, and their victories are great. They are enjoying the sympathy, support, and encouragement from the peace- and justice-loving people throughout the world. Outwardly, the U.S. imperialists and their lackeys look like a stronger tiger; but inwardly, they are weakened and confused and, more than ever before, isolated. The South Vietnamese people have engraved deeply in their minds their vow that they prefer to die rather than live as slaves. We must definitely crush the ruthless, wicked enemy.

Not only do the NFLSV and the South Vietnamese have the just cause, but they have been and are developing rapidly their material strength and their organization. They have been and are being heroic victors. The more they fight, the more enthusiastic they will be. The more they fight, the more victories they will achieve and the greater their victories will be. We are worthy successors of the Dien Bien Phu tradition and the heroic tradition of the Vietnamese people with a 4,000-year history of struggle against foreign invaders. We are developing to a high degree these traditions.

Moreover, the NFLSV and the South Vietnamese people are fighting under the extremely favorable conditions of the present era, an era in which the oppressed people in Asia, Africa, Latin America, and other continents are surging ahead like storms. The Socialist countries and the peaceful democratic forces throughout the world are an important factor pushing mankind to progress and to squelch and annihilate colonialism and imperialism concealed in whatever form. If the U.S. imperialists and their lackeys run the risk of blowing the war flames to all of Indochina, the people of the Indochinese countries and in all of Southeast Asia will unanimously and resolutely rise up to sweep them into the ocean. The South Vietnamese people and their only true representative—the NFLSV—will certainly be able to achieve the final victory.

The NFLSV Central Committee calls on the 14 million valiant South Vietnamese people and the people's armed forces, who are raising their determination to fight to win on all battlefields, more than ever before to hold their rifles firmly and develop their spirit of indomitable and patient struggle. They must be resolved to fulfill the following tasks:

All people must be united in an iron- and stone-like bloc. All people must be armed and must unanimously rise up to fight and chase away the U.S. enemy and the Vietnamese traitors. The liberation troops and the people's armed forces must bravely and strongly move forward to strike repeatedly, very strongly, very accurately, and in such a way that the U.S. aggressors and their lackeys will not have time to breathe, so as to destroy as much enemy strength as possible.

The rural people must continue to revolt to destroy the remaining strategic hamlets, to smash the enemy's oppressive machinery, to enlarge the liberated areas, and to carry out the slogan, "People living in hamlets, villages, and districts must take power in their respective places." They must set up solid combat fortresses. They must fight when the enemy comes. They must insure victory in each battle. They must be determined to cling to firmly and maintain their homes, gardens, and rice fields.

The compatriots in Saigon, Hué, Da Nang, and other cities in South Viet-Nam must urgently develop their revolutionary organizations. They must continue to take to the streets to step up their struggle in all fields, on a large scale, and decisively. They must demand that the U.S. imperialists and their lackeys end the aggressive war in South Viet-Nam. They must pinpoint those traitors who have given a helping hand to the enemy and have cheaply sold the interests of the fatherland and the people.

All compatriots, cadres, and combatants must bravely follow the liberation banner and resolutely move forward to fight and chase the U.S. enemy and his lackeys away to save the country. If the fighting would last for twenty years or longer, we must be determined and ready to fight to the end until there is not a single U.S. enemy on our ancestors' territory.

We must fight to force the U.S. enemy and his lackeys to pay their blood debts to our compatriots.[39] Our people have a 4,000-year history, which is the valiant history of a valiant people. Fighting the U.S. aggressors and their lackeys for over ten years, our people and the liberation armed forces in South Viet-Nam have written another sparkling golden page in the glorious history of our people.

We have been and are victorious. The U.S. imperialists and their lackeys have been and are vanquished. This demonstrates that our strength is invincible and that the U.S. aggressors and their lackeys are weakening. If, after ten years, we succeed in defeating the U.S. enemy, we are now in a very good position to triumph over the U.S. aggressors and their lackeys. During the past ten years the U.S. aggressors and their lackeys have been vanquished; today, they will have to suffer bitter defeats. In particular, if the U.S. imperialists escalate the war to the north, it is certain that they will court more horrible defeats.

We are absolutely convinced that we will certainly be victorious. We also pledge to our beloved Viet-Nam that we are determined to strike strongly, truly strongly; to strike to the last man, to the last breath, to the last drop of blood; and to strike very accurately at the heads of the U.S. enemy and his lackeys. We are determined to liberate the south, protect the north, and reunify the fatherland.

Notes on NFLSV Central Committee Statement

[Hanoi Domestic Service in Vietnamese at 1515 GMT on 23 March and Hanoi VNA International Service in English at 1617 GMT on 23 March carry what is termed the "text" of the 22 March NFLSV Central Committee statement which was published on 24 March. A comparison of the two Hanoi versions with the published Liberation Radio version indicates the following:]

1. Radio Hanoi and VNA omit the sentence beginning "Faced with their . . ."
2. The sentence beginning "The U.S. imperialists . . ." is identified by VNA as the beginning of part 1.
3. The initial words are rendered as "hundreds of thousands of tons" by VNA.
4. The bracketed words are rendered as "leading to" by VNA.
5. The bracketed word is rendered as "laid the basis for" by VNA.
6. In this paragraph, lines 7–10 are given by VNA as "in an increasingly brazen manner trampled on the Geneva Accords and have, in fact, scrapped those accords by openly waging an atrocious war in South Viet-Nam over the . . ."
7. Beginning with "Americans and" through the end of the sentence, this portion of the sentence is rendered by VNA as "Americans. Ever since, the United States has undertaken deeper and more and more brazen intervention in South Viet-Nam."
8. Given by VNA as "blood has been spilled in Duy Xuyen, Huong Dien, Cho Duoc, Vinh Trinh . . ."
9. The sentence beginning "The U.S. imperialists . . ." is rendered by Radio Hanoi as "But in defiance of the protests of the peace- and justice-loving peoples throughout the world, the U.S. imperialists have arrogantly stepped up their piratical war in South Viet-Nam."
10. Both Radio Hanoi and VNA omit this paragraph and the following five paragraphs as well as the first sentence

of the sixth paragraph down, ending with the words "in South Viet-Nam."

11. VNA renders this portion as "about 800,000 people; detained more than 400,000 people in more than 7,800 prisons; raped tens of thousands of women, including old women, children, and religious people . . ."

12. VNA renders these lines as "hamlets; and sprayed chemicals over many areas to destroy hundreds of thousands of hectares of crops and fruit trees and affecting tens of thousands of people. They have, moreover, demolished thousands of pagodas, churches, and holy sees or temples, killing tens of thousands of faithful of various religions."

13. Radio Hanoi and VNA omit the following, beginning with: "banning the introduction of troops, military personnel, weapons, and ammunition into South Viet-Nam, the construction of new military bases and military alliances with foreign countries . . ."

14. VNA omits the passage beginning with the sentence "The present realities . . ." through "country-taking acts" in the penultimate sentence.

15. Radio Hanoi omits the passage beginning with the words "that the so-called" through the end of the paragraph and substitutes the following: "To camouflage their faces as pirates, the U.S. imperialists have to resort to deceitful labels. But they still fail to fool the world peoples."

16. Radio Hanoi and VNA omit the passage beginning with "Relying on their . . ." through the next two paragraphs, ending with "South Vietnamese people."

17. Radio Hanoi and VNA omit the sentence beginning with "The repeated and . . ."

18. VNA renders the bracketed word as "truculent enemy."

19. VNA renders this as "they will be completely tied up if they launch a local war. If they dare to extend the . . ."

20. Radio Hanoi and VNA omit the passage beginning with "Previously, with empty . . ." through the end of the paragraph.

21. Radio Hanoi and VNA omit the words that begin "to reduce the . . ." through "South Vietnamese people . . ." in the same sentence.

22. Radio Hanoi omits the passage beginning with " 'You are hooligans" and ending with "and tell them:" on line 9.

23. VNA omits the passage beginning with "'You are hooligans" and ending with "position of strength" on line 7.

24. Radio Hanoi omits the words "Rivers can dry up, mountains can erode, but".

25. VNA omits the words "Rivers can dry up, mountains can erode, but the South Vietnamese people and their armed forces will never drop their weapons . . ."

26. Radio Hanoi and VNA omit the passage beginning with the indistinct words through the end of the paragraph.

27. VNA renders the bracketed words as "are still surrendered . . ."

28. Radio Hanoi and VNA omit the passage beginning with "With regard to . . ." through the end of the next paragraph.

29. Beginning with "In their hot . . ." through the end of the paragraph, VNA renders this portion as: "In the present state of blood and fire, in a life-and-death struggle against the U.S. imperialists and their lackeys, the heart cannot but suffer when the hand is cut. That the people in North Viet-Nam are resolved to fulfill their duty toward their kith and kin in South Viet-Nam fully conforms to sentiment and reason."

30. Beginning with "In their hot . . ." through the end of the paragraph, Radio Hanoi renders this portion as: "In their hot and deadly struggle against the U.S. imperialists and their lackeys and sharing the misfortune of the southern brothers, the northern compatriots have done their utmost to fulfill their obligations with respect to their brothers in South Viet-Nam. This is a perfectly correct and rational act."

31. Radio Hanoi omits the sentence beginning "The South Vietnamese . . ."

32. Radio Hanoi states 50 U.S. planes were downed.

33. Radio Hanoi and VNA both give the number of weapons captured as 4,144.

34. Radio Hanoi and VNA omit the portion beginning with "especially when the . . ." through the end of the paragraph.

35. Radio Hanoi omits the words "and organization ready to sell them to the South Vietnamese people. . . ."

36. VNA gives the date of the conference as "late last year."

37. VNA renders the portion beginning with "The NFLSV will . . ." through the end of the paragraph as: "While the U.S. imperialists are constantly sowing sufferings and death in South

Viet-Nam, the NFLSV, if need be, cannot but call back the sons and daughters of South Viet-Nam who have regrouped to the north in observance of the cease-fire agreement and who had to live far from South Viet-Nam during ten long years to take arms to annihilate the enemy to save their country and families. A Vietnamese proverb runs: 'To peel the thick skin of a mandarin, there must be a sharp fingernail.' The invincible fingernail of the Vietnamese people and the peace-loving people all over the world decidedly will not forgive the U.S. imperialists and their lackeys. They will have to bear all extremely serious consequences of their warlike and aggressive acts."

38. Radio Hanoi and VNA omit the portion beginning with "The South Vietnamese . . ." through the sentence ending ". . . throughout the world" four lines below.

39. Radio Hanoi and VNA omit the initial sentence: "We must fight to force the U.S. enemy and his lackeys to pay their blood debts to our compatriots."

BERNARD B. FALL

Viet-Cong—The Unseen Enemy in Viet-Nam *

Much has been said and written lately about the war in Viet-Nam, the bombs and the aircraft that are being used, and the large political issues that are involved. But relatively little is being said by either side about the furtive enemy who actually holds much of South Viet-Nam's terrain and effectively administers perhaps as much as 50 per cent of the country's rural population.

To the South Viet-Nam government in Saigon, the enemy is simply the Viet-Cong, or VC, which stands for "Vietnamese Communist." To the United States and its closest allies, the VC is an Orwellian unperson. It simply does not exist, except as an

---

* From *New Society*, London, April 22, 1965. © 1965 by Bernard B. Fall.

emanation of North Viet-Nam's People's Army and its political masters in Hanoi. The State Department devoted in recent weeks a whole White Book to prove that, by contrast with such guerrilla wars as Greece, Malaya, or the Philippines, "the war in Viet-Nam is *not* a spontaneous and local rebellion against the established government . . . In Viet-Nam a Communist government has set out deliberately to conquer a sovereign people in a neighboring state."

If that view were entirely correct, then the whole Viet-Nam insurrection would be little else but an invasion from the outside, like Germany's aggression against Poland; and any measures taken against North Viet-Nam would fall within the inherent right of a nation to self-defense against attack.

The insurrectionists in South Viet-Nam must, for obvious reasons, convince the world of the opposite—namely, that they represent a genuine uprising against a series of unpopular regimes and are willing to offer the South Vietnamese people a valid alternative both to the current Saigon regimes and to domination by Hanoi. For the time being, neither the United States (and Saigon) nor the guerrillas (and their backers in Hanoi) seem to have made their case to the point where it carries full conviction. That may be mainly so because the actual truth lies somewhere in between the two views.

First of all, it must be understood that armed opposition to the Ngo Dinh Diem regime inside South Viet-Nam, in one form or another, had never ceased between Viet-Nam's partition in 1954 and the demise of the Diem regime in November, 1963. Apart from the Communists, there existed in South Viet-Nam a variety of political-religious sects, such as the Hoa-Hao and the Cao-Dai; and at least one well-organized semipiratical band, the Binh-Xuyên, which never fully surrendered to the South Viet-Nam government.

The Binh-Xuyên were soundly beaten in May, 1955, at the outskirts of Saigon and were finally cornered in the Rung-Sat swamps a few months later. But some of the Hoa-Hao units held the field for years in the western plains of Viet-Nam. Four Hoa-Hao battalions—called Lê-Loi, Bay-Dom, 104 and 117—though hard pressed at times, were never fully destroyed. Battalion 104, under the command of "General" Truong Kim Cu, was finally cornered in 1962 in a pincer operation between Viet-Cong battalion 510 and the South Viet-Nam Army's 7th division with its American advisers. Its members were slipped to internment into neighboring Cambodia. The other units joined hands with the South Viet-Nam Army after Diem's overthrow and now hold for Saigon the same terrain which they held against it for nine years.

In the absence of any kind of legal opposition, even for the staunchest anti-Communists, all opposition to the Diem regime had perforce to be conspiratorial and, sooner or later, of a true "resistance" nature. This was true long before Communist subversion became a major menace to South Viet-Nam, and before North Viet-Nam had any logical reason to "invade" South Viet-Nam. Diem's presidential ordinance No 6 of January 11, 1956, provided for the indefinite detention in concentration camps of anyone found to be a "danger to the state." This went far beyond the preventive detention acts so dear to some Commonwealth countries. The ordinance was followed by other repressive acts which hit harder at non-Communists than at Communists, whose apparatus was better geared to clandestine operations.

Between the partition of 1954 and July, 1956 (the date originally set for a reunification election between the two zones by the Geneva Conference), the Communist network in South Viet-Nam retained a prudently calm attitude. About 80,000 raw recruits and dependents had left for areas north of the 17th Parallel. What stayed behind were an elite guerrilla cadre force of perhaps less than 5,000 and the traditional left-wing elements in Saigon. In Saigon, as late as 1953, a Trotskyite was elected to the city council, and even Diem's brother Nhu ran a Catholic Labor Movement for Peace.

As President Eisenhower was to remark in his memoirs later, every responsible observer estimated that the North Viet-Nam leader Ho Chi Minh would win even an uncoerced pan-Vietnamese election by 80 per cent of the popular vote. With elections only two years away, there was no reason for the Communists to risk precious cadre personnel on short-term adventures.

This is exactly what the later leader of the "National Liberation Front of South Viet-Nam" (NLF), a Saigon barrister named Nguyen Huu Tho, meant when he explained to the Australian Communist writer Wilfred Burchett: "There were mixed feelings about the two years' delay over reunification but the general sentiment was that this was a small price to pay for the return to peace and a normal life, free of foreign rule."

Nguyen Huu Tho had first been involved in politics when he led, in March, 1950, a student demonstration in Saigon against the presence of three American warships on a courtesy call to the French. He paid for this with three years' detention in the northern mountain town of Lai-Chau. In August, 1954, he set up what in Communist parlance is called a "legal-struggle" organization in the form of a "Committee of Defense of Peace and the Geneva Agreements," whose aim was to keep up the pressure on the South Viet-Nam government of Diem, as well as on the still-present French, to make sure that the Geneva Agreements would be observed.

But Diem had already made up his mind not to observe the agreements (which South Viet-Nam had not signed), and his repression against all oppositionists also covered Nguyen Huu Tho's peace committee and the local branches it had set up in various provincial towns.

On November 11, 1954, security police closed in on the peace committees and arrested its members. These included Nguyen Huu Tho, who now found himself jailed in the Central Viet-Nam detention house at Tuy-Hoa. He escaped only in 1961, after his appointment as president of the NLF.

"We had no idea at that time," Tho told Burchett in 1964, "but . . . we had created the embryo for the National Liberation Front, set up more than six years later."

When the South Viet-Nam government, with the open encouragement of most Western powers, defied the July, 1956, deadline for elections, it was obvious that a struggle to the death would ensue with Hanoi, unless Hanoi could be made to see that it was to its advantage to coexist with a southern rival too strong for overthrow through subversion. That could have happened if the Diem regime had chosen a set of policies which would have provided it with maximum popular support and left the Communists reduced to the role of an ineffectual harasser. The regime did exactly the opposite.

By a presidential decree of June, 1956, Diem abolished elected village councils and mayors. This imposed directly on the Viet-Nam peasantry the dictatorial regime which he already wielded at the center. In March, 1957, the regime openly violated the last restraints placed upon it by the Geneva Agreements with regard to reprisals exercised against "former resistance members"—that is, ex-guerrillas of the Viet-Minh who had fought against the French, and many of whom were not Communists. Such highly respected, non-Communist French observers as *Le Monde*'s Jean Lacouture and Philippe Devillers (author of the French classic *Histoire du Viet-Nam de 1940 à 1952*) aver that, faced with physical extermination along with the sect units, some of the former Viet-Minh guerrillas simply banded together for survival. In Devillers's words, "the overriding needs of the world-wide strategy of the socialist camp meant little or nothing to guerrilla fighters being hunted down in Nam-Bô [South Viet-Nam] . . . Hanoi preferred diplomatic notes, but it was to find that its hand had been forced."

In my view, the actual situation probably lay somewhere in between: Hanoi, to be sure, was distressed about what was happening to its faithful followers in the South. But other Communist regimes had abandoned failing guerrilla movements before: in Greece, Azerbaijan, Indonesia, Malaya, and elsewhere. In the case of Viet-Nam, however, Hanoi may well have made the judgment that:

(a) The South Viet-Nam government was in the process of alienating its own people to such an extent that even a modestly encouraged and supported guerrilla movement could well succeed in overthrowing it;

(b) Saigon's American advisers were so blinded by Diem's "successes," and so oblivious to the real weaknesses of the situation, that a rebellion might succeed before the cumbersome American apparatus could shift into high gear.

As events were to show, the plan almost worked. How well it did, even without outside aid, is best shown by the progressive shift in village official killings between 1957-58 and 1959-1960. The new guerrillas began to take over control of the only thing worth holding in a revolutionary warfare situation: people, and rural people at that. With a method showing long-standing professionalism, the guerrillas first established "resistance base areas" in certain Mekong Delta provinces such as Chau-Doc and My-Tho. They then proceeded to seal off Saigon from the rice-rich and densely populated delta area.

But terrorism was not the whole program. There were sound propaganda, like the "Three Withs" program ("a good cadre lives with, eats with, works with the population"); some modest reforms; and even a measure of physical improvement.

In a remarkable book (*Mission in Torment*) John Mecklin, whose credentials are that he was America's chief information officer in Viet-Nam during the critical 1962-64 period, writes about a village called Binh Yen Dong, only twenty miles from Saigon. The village had "gone Viet-Cong" without apparent coercion and a study was made of how the process had worked. As it turned out, the NLF had forced a local landlord to allow the farmers to take a short cut through his property to the village well, which until then they had been forced to reach via a detour.

Organizationally, the movement rose apace. In March, 1960, the "Nam-Bô Resistance Veterans Organization" met in hiding and issued a proclamation in which it announced that it had taken up "arms in self-defense." At the third congress of North Viet-Nam's Communist Lao-Dong (Workers') Party, held in Hanoi on September 5, 1960, Lê Duan, the party secretary and a former leader of the Viet-Minh in the South, issued a report which for the first time took cognizance of the "southern people's revolutionary struggle" and advocated the creation there of a "broad national united front against the U.S.-Diem clique." And on December 20, 1960, on the day after the fourteenth anniversary of Ho Chi Minh's uprising against France, a provisional Central Committee of southern resistance leaders created the National Liberation Front. The guerrilla movement had matured into a full-fledged revolutionary apparatus.

The newborn NLF led a very shadowy life for almost two years, although its military arm, the "People's Self-Defense Forces," began to roam far and wide throughout South Viet-Nam. By May, 1960, the situation had deteriorated enough for the Saigon government to report to the International Control Commission (I.C.C.) set up by the Geneva Agreements that the "southern liberation forces" constituted a "grave menace for peace."

Statistics now began to pile up inexorably: 452 village chiefs were lost by South Viet-Nam in 1957-58. By January, 1960, they were being lost at the rate of fifteen a week. On May 25, 1961, President Kennedy told Congress that minor officials were being killed in Viet-Nam at the rate of 4,000 a year: eleven a day. In 1964, over 1,500 small officials were lost, and over 400 during the first four months of 1965.

The guerrillas' strength was estimated at 3,000 in 1959. By mid-1961 they were 15,000: half of them fully armed. There were 35,000 hard-core elite troops by January this year, in addition to 60,000-80,000 "local force" guerrillas. By this month the Pentagon revised the figures to 45,000 and 100,000, respectively, grouped in five or six regimental-size units and about 60 battalions and over 150 companies.

In terms of administration, the killed or fleeing officials of the Diem administration were replaced by Administrative Committees, soon capped by District and Provincial Committees of the NLF. By February, 1962, the movement was ready to present itself to the world in the course of a clandestine congress attended by over 100 delegates. Whether by coincidence or design, the congress was convened just a few days after the United States had set up its Military Advisory Command in Saigon— just as the NLF had originally proclaimed its existence one month after Diem had almost been overthrown, in November, 1960, by his own best paratroops.

According to published accounts, the NLF congress not only grouped former Communist resistance members, but also other elements from the Vietnamese Democratic Party and the Radical Socialist Party, both of which, like all non-Communist Vietnamese political organizations, represented almost nothing. There also had appeared on the scene a small but openly Communist Party, the People's Revolutionary Party (PRP), created in December, 1961; as well as an "Afro-Asian Solidarity Committee," a Saigon-Cholon Peace Committee, representatives of minority tribes and of various front organizations such as the "Liberation Writers and Artists' Association," etc. None of these could claim much of an established following. But some of the people present had excellent reasons for being there, such as Superior Bonze Son Vong, from the Mekong's Vinh Binh province.

The thoroughly respectable Denis Warner tells Son Vong's story in his book *The Last Confucian*. In July, 1961 (that is, long before anyone spoke of Buddhist persecutions in Viet-Nam), a South Viet-Nam Army unit had swept through the province, "leaving thousands of unhappy peasants behind it," and the Buddhist Bonzes of the province had vainly petitioned against the indiscriminate shelling of hamlets and pagodas and the imprisonment of many of the Buddhist priests. "Some months later," says Warner, "their leader, Superior Bonze Son Vong, appeared on the lists of the central committee of the Viet-Cong's National Liberation Front."

The NLF congress proceeded to establish a central committee of 53 members, 31 of whom were elected then, while another 22 seats were kept open for representatives of "mass organizations, political parties and groups of personalities which will join the Front in the future." Some of the names published corresponded to aliases of unknown persons, but others were known South Viet-Nam politicians.

Nguyen Huu Tho was made president of the NLF. There are also five vice presidents: Dr. Phung Van Cung, a French-trained doctor who had fled Saigon in 1960; Vo Chi Cong, a Communist survivor of France's Poulo-Condore island prison; Y Bih Aléo, a French Army-trained mountain tribesman who is also chairman of the "Tay Nguyen [*Montagnard*] Autonomy Movement"; Huynh Tan Phat, a Saigon architect who is also secretary general of the Democratic Party; and, finally, Superior Bonze Son Vong, who happens also to be a member of the important Cambodian minority living in South Viet-Nam. The Central Committee also includes a Catholic, Josef-Marie Ho Hué Ba; a Cao-Dai leader; another Bonze; and other personalities deemed to make the committee "representative."

Several changes have occurred in the make up of the NLF since its inception. Its erstwhile secretary general, a journalist styled Professor Nguyen Van Hieu, became roving ambassador for the Front in various noncommitted countries and was replaced in his post by Huynh Tan Phat. This was said to have been a concession to the more moderate elements of the Front. Phat in turn had been replaced as vice president by a tough military commander, Tran Nam Trung, who is the highest-known leader of the Communist PRP, with the rank of assistant secretary general and who also is the representative of the "People's Self-Defense Forces" in the NLF presidium. Burchett describes him in fact as the "Liberation Front's military chief."

The program of the Front is by now well known and need hardly be repeated here. Much has been made in some quarters of the fact that the program in itself is quite moderate, which is true. Its ten points make hardly any doctrinaire references to the United States and none whatever in favor of communism. Its points dealing with foreign policy restate the Geneva Agreements' position on South Viet-Nam's nonengagement in military alliances, and reunification is left to later negotiations rather than to an iron clad two year provision as provided for in 1954. It must, however, be remembered that this program represents at best a set of "electoral promises." After all, North Viet-Nam had a constitution until 1960, which embodied phrases from the American Declaration of Independence. It was changed for a strikingly doctrinaire document once North Viet-Nam had been made secure for its regime.

A significant fact in the Front's existence is—and this point may well be argued in favor of the theory of its being a total puppet of the North—that it has failed to transform itself into a "Liberation government." To be sure, it has quasi-ministries, but they are significantly known as "committees" (Committee on Military Affairs, External Affairs, Information and Education, etc.) and are not attributed to a single person. The NLF representatives abroad—in Algiers, Havana, Cairo, Jakarta, Berlin, Prague and, recently Moscow and Peking—do not claim diplomatic status though they probably could do so in certain countries. This may simply be caution born out of previous dire experience, when such "Liberation governments," too hastily constituted, collapsed or were (as with Cambodia's Khmer Resistance Government in 1954) simply negotiated away.

In the American official view, there can be no doubt but that the NLF is nothing but a suboffice of the Reunification Commission operating under the Council of Ministers of the Hanoi government. The State Department White Book shows elaborate charts which demonstrate ties with northern military and political agencies.

But to many people, that can only be part of the story. There is, for example, the high-ranking spokesman of the Front who told *Le Monde*'s Georges Chaffard that the NLF had got along without the North for "a long time" and would "prefer to settle our affairs among 'southerners'." And he added something which many a resistance fighter (as I was in France in the Second World War) will fully understand: "We have not fought all these years simply to end up by installing one set of dictators in place of the old."

It is this aspect of resistance war that seems to be too often glibly overlooked in the case of the NLF. One does not fight for eight long years, under the crushing weight of American armor, napalm, jet bombers and, finally, vomiting gases, for the sheer joy of handing over whatever one fights for to some bureaucrat in Hanoi, merely on the say-so of a faraway party apparatus. The NLF *and* South Viet-Nam have both had to pay a heavy price for NLF victories. Officially, the US Army Chief of Staff, General Harold K. Johnson, claims that 75,000 Viet-Cong had been killed between 1961 and February, 1965. By April, the "kill" figure had risen to 89,000. The French Press Agency, on the basis of earlier Saigon reports, stated that casualties between 1957 and 1961 amounted to 29,000 on the government side and 66,000 on the Viet-Cong side. This is not too far off the NLF's own claim that over 160,000 South Vietnamese (on its side, presumably) have thus far been killed in this war.

There has been increasing evidence of differences in view as well as in tone between Hanoi and the NLF, just as there have been between Hanoi and Peking or Moscow. Thus, an important policy statement issued by the Front on March 22, found itself seriously toned down by Hanoi. In recent weeks there have been reports from Paris that Peking, fearing that Hanoi might weaken under the impact of American pressure, has attempted to "leapfrog" it by dealing directly with the Front through the NLF delegation in Peking and through emissaries in Laos and Cambodia.

There are some doubts among many observers as to whether the apparent intransigence of Hanoi does not in reality hide its relative inability to "deliver" the NLF bound hand and foot at a problematical conference table. Having sold out the guerrilla movement twice before, in 1954 and 1956, it may find the task difficult, if not altogether impossible. Yet it is on this assumption —that is, that the whole southern guerrilla movement would rapidly wither away if only it were abandoned by Hanoi—that the whole present policy of bombing North Viet-Nam into negotiating the NLF out of existence is based. The next few weeks may show whether this expectation is not somewhat too simple to be entirely true.

C. THE INTERESTED BYSTANDERS

Introduction

A war which directly involves, on the one hand, one of the key nuclear powers in the world and, on the other, albeit indirectly, the world's most populous country *and* possibly another key nuclear power, cannot leave others indifferent. And the Second Indochina War does not.

What makes the present conflict so surprising is the apparent unpopularity of the American side and the equally apparent feeling on the part of even highly respected world leaders, from the Pope to the Secretary General of the United Nations and the French President, that they are totally unable—perhaps for the first time in recent history—to exercise even the slightest influence on American actions.

It would be inaccurate to say that the United States does not have any foreign support for its action in Viet-Nam. It does—in about the same measure that the Soviet Union had support for its action in Hungary: the client states and a few super-cautious neutrals. In the present case, this means that, in Asia, the United States can count on the support of South Korea, Thailand, Formosa, and the Philippines; in the Pacific, Australia and New Zealand; and in Europe, West Germany. A few more countries, such as Malaya, Great Britain, Canada, and Japan, may support the United States officially, but against much public resistance. Nor has there been much support for our position in the foreign press. More surprisingly, the protests often come from unexpected quarters, such as Saigon's own *Post,* protesting against the use of napalm and armor on peasant huts and rice fields; or the Catholic archepiscopate of Paris, issuing in its daily *La Croix* a warning against making the Viet-Nam situation into a "white man's war."

How radically different this war looks to other people not as readily influenced by the official views from Washington is best indicated by U Thant's subtle hint about "all the facts" not being known; by de Gaulle's advocating disengagement for both Viet-Nams; by Prince Sihanouk of Cambodia wishing to maintain his country outside of a war that threatens to engulf, rather than to save, it; by a former Imperial Japanese ambassador to Saigon inspecting conditions there on behalf of his conservative Japanese government—and finding much to say that does not agree with the official Japanese position; by Gunnar Myrdal, who warned in the July 18, 1965, issue of the *New York Times Magazine,* that the conviction that U.S. policy in Viet-Nam "will end in failure is commonly held in all countries outside the United States."

And, lest it be entirely forgotten, there still exists an Indian-Canadian-Polish International Control Commission (I.C.C.) in Viet-Nam. The I.C.C. periodically issues reports—in the face of bad faith on both sides, it can do very little else. Its reports have shown violations of the 1954 Geneva Accords by all sides—including the United States.

U THANT

*Press Conference on Southeast Asia and Related Matters**

QUESTION: Along what lines do you envisage a possible solution of the Viet-Nam situation? Have you any positive proposals in mind?

THE SECRETARY GENERAL: As you know, I have been consistently advocating the necessity and the advisability of resort to political and diplomatic methods of finding a solution. I have felt all along that military methods will not produce the desired result; they will not produce an enduring peace in Viet-Nam.

In my view, there was a very good possibility in 1963 of arriving at a satisfactory political solution. In 1964 the situation deteriorated still further, and the prospects for a peaceful solu-

* February 24, 1965.

tion became more remote. Today, of course, the situation is much more difficult.

Although opinions may differ on the methods of bringing about a satisfactory solution in Viet-Nam, there is, I believe, general agreement on one point: that the situation in the Republic of Viet-Nam has gone from bad to worse. I do not think that there is any difference of opinion on that.

I have always maintained the view that the prospects for a peaceful settlement of this problem will be more and more remote as time goes on and as the aggravation develops. But still I do not believe it is too late to try diplomatic and political methods of negotiation and discussion. Of course I have never advocated the immediate withdrawal of United States troops from the Republic of Viet-Nam. I am fully conscious of the fact that such a step will naturally involve questions of face and prestige, and questions of the abrogation of previous commitments, and so forth. But I feel that once the diplomatic and political methods have been tried and if there is any perceptible improvement in the situation, if an agreed formula is at hand, if some sort of stability can be restored in the country, then at that time, of course, the United States can withdraw its troops with dignity.

As I said on a previous occasion, one prerequisite for peace in any country is the existence and functioning of a stable government. As you all know, this element is completely absent in the Republic of Viet-Nam. . . .

QUESTION: You speak of the best way of attaining an enduring peace in Viet-Nam. In view of the fact that the last negotiated agreements failed to maintain a secure and enduring peace in Viet-Nam and in view of the fact that the agreements reached at that time were broken, what would your comment be in answer to this argument, which I think is the main one put up against negotiations, that it did not work in the past and therefore it will not work in the future? They were abrogated.

THE SECRETARY GENERAL: I doubt the correctness of your hypothesis. Let me elaborate a little on this theme.

When I was in Burma, prior to my departure for New York about eight years ago, I studied the situation in Southeast Asia very closely. To my knowledge, there was not a single instance— let me repeat—there was not a single instance of North

Vietnamese providing military assistance or arms to the Viet-Cong in South Viet-Nam in 1954 and 1955. So far, no evidence has been adduced to prove that the authorities in North Viet-Nam provided matériel and military assistance to the Viet-Cong in the Republic of Viet-Nam in 1954 and 1955. After the developments in the next few months and the next few years, I am sure that there must have been involvement by the North Vietnamese in the affairs of the Republic of Viet-Nam.

While on the subject, at the risk of its being deemed a digression, let me say this: As you all know, I was very much involved in the affairs of my country, Burma, for many years since independence in January, 1948, until I left Rangoon in 1957. Immediately after Burma's independence in January, 1948, the Burmese Communists went underground and started a widespread insurrection. This fact is known to everybody. The Burmese government dealt with this internal problem by its own means, without asking for any outside military assistance or outside military arms or outside military advisers—or whatever you call them. The Burmese government dealt with this internal insurrection by its own means. As you know, the Burmese Communist Party is still underground after seventeen years and still illegal. But let me tell you: there has not been a single instance of outside help to the Burmese Communists inside Burma in the last seventeen years; there has not been a single instance of one rifle or one bullet supplied to the Burmese Communists inside Burma in the last seventeen years. And Burma has maintained and still maintains the friendliest relations with all its neighbors: with Thailand, with Laos, with mainland China, with India, and with Pakistan. As you know, Burma has over 1,000 miles of land frontier with mainland China. If only the Burmese government had decided at some stage to seek outside military assistance to suppress the internal insurrections and revolts, then I am sure that Burma would have experienced one of the two alternatives: either the country would be divided into two parts or the whole country would have become Communist long ago. This proves one point: that Burma's attitude and policies both in regard to domestic affairs and foreign affairs have been very appropriate in the circumstances prevailing in Southeast Asia.

Not one American life has been lost in Burma. Not one

American dollar has been spent in Burma in the form of military assistance in the last seventeen years. We should ask the great question: Why? I just present these facts to you just to set about thinking: Why?

QUESTION: Have you any indication from the United States government that it might under certain conditions consider a negotiation of the Vietnamese dispute? Also have you any indication that the United States might withhold further reprisals against North Viet-Nam in order to see whether such negotiations could get under way?

THE SECRETARY GENERAL: I have been conducting private disussions on this question of Viet-Nam for a long time, as you all know. Of course, it will not be very helpful at this stage to reveal even some parts or some features of the negotiations I have conducted. I just want to say that I have the greatest respect for the great American leader, President Johnson, whose wisdom, moderation, and sensitivity to world public opinion are well known. I am sure the great American people, if only they know the true facts and the background to the developments in South Viet-Nam, will agree with me that further bloodshed is unnecessary. And also that the political and diplomatic method of discussions and negotiations alone can create conditions which will enable the United States to withdraw gracefully from that part of the world. As you know, in times of war and of hostilities the first casualty is truth.

QUESTION: You said that the first prerequisite is for a stable government. Perhaps you have some ideas and suggestions for the creation or the composition of an inclusive and popular regime in Saigon which might be stable.

THE SECRETARY GENERAL: Of course, I have certain ideas on this aspect of the problem. I have communicated these ideas to some of the parties primarily concerned in the last two years. As I said a moment ago, I do not think it will be helpful if I reveal some of these ideas publicly at this moment. . . .

QUESTION: Mr. Secretary-General, . . . you seem to be suggesting that it would be very desirable if the United States troops got out of South Viet-Nam, if South Viet-Nam had a stable government and if there were negotiations to possibly neutralize the whole area. There seems to be something concrete missing in this series. How are you going to achieve that? Can you pin this thing down for us a little more?

THE SECRETARY GENERAL: As I have been saying, I have presented certain ideas on my own to some of the principal parties directly involved in the question of Viet-Nam. I have even presented concrete ideas and proposals. But up to this moment the results of these consultations and discussions have not been conclusive. And I do not think it would be in the public interest for me to reveal these ideas publicly at this moment.

QUESTION: Have they been presented to the United States among the other interested parties?

THE SECRETARY GENERAL: Yes.

QUESTION: . . . If no progress is made toward negotiations, might you feel compelled unilaterally to step into the breach and bring the matter to the Security Council?

THE SECRETARY GENERAL: I do not think that is a practical proposition, for reasons that are obvious and well known to you. The government of North Viet-Nam has all along maintained that the United Nations is not competent to deal with the question of Viet-Nam since, in its view, there is already in existence an international machinery established in 1954 in Geneva. They have all along maintained that position and, as you all know, it is a position that is also maintained by the People's Republic of China. As far as the United Nations is concerned, I think the greatest impediment to the discussion of the question of Viet-Nam in one of the principal organs of the United Nations is the fact that more than two parties directly concerned in the question are not members of this organization. I therefore do not see any immediate prospect of a useful discussion in the Security Council. . . .

QUESTION: Do you still hold to your previous view that the 1954 Geneva Conference on Indochina should be reconvened in terms of the Viet-Nam question, and do you think that such a conference should try to find means to carry out the provision in the Armistice Agreement regarding Viet-Nam whereby elections would be held in both North Viet-Nam and South Viet-Nam for the establishment of a united Viet-Nam?

THE SECRETARY GENERAL: As I have been saying, it may be rather belated to expect the same results as one could have expected, say, two years ago. But I think that it is worth trying.

On the twelfth of this month I advocated publicly that, if there are still difficulties on the part of some of the large powers as regards the immediate convening of a Geneva-type conference, it could be worth while exploring the possibilities of informal, private and confidential dialogues between some of the parties directly involved, as a preliminary step towards the convening of a more formal conference. That was my appeal. Of course, I have no way of knowing what will happen if these dialogues take place or if a formal conference takes place. I do not know what will be the result of such discussions; I do not think that anyone knows. But it is worth trying. And let me repeat what I said a moment ago: the longer we delay, the more difficult will be the achievement of an enduring peace in Viet-Nam.

QUESTION: Could I come back to the question of the elections in North Viet-Nam and South Viet-Nam, leading to the unification of the two Viet-Nams? Do you advocate that?

THE SECRETARY GENERAL: I do not want to go into the substance of the agreements arrived at in Geneva in 1954. I do not know the practical difficulties in the way of conducting free elections, both in North Viet-Nam and in South Viet-Nam. I do believe, however, that elections were possible at some stage.

QUESTION: Have you had any positive or favorable responses from any of the parties, and particularly from Peking and Hanoi, to the proposal you just mentioned—that is, the proposal for preliminary contacts?

THE SECRETARY GENERAL: I do not think that it would be in the public interest to reveal any information at this stage on that aspect of my discussions.

CHARLES DE GAULLE

*Statement on Southeast Asia**

QUESTION: General, taking into account the United States policy toward South Viet-Nam, do you hold to the suggestions which you have formulated since last year for Southeast Asia?

ANSWER: The Geneva Agreements concluded in 1954 put an end to the fighting in Indochina. At the time, everyone seemed

* News conference, July 23, 1964.

to desire it sincerely. These agreements included provisions which varied according to the countries in question, but which had in common the absolute exclusion of all outside intervention. Cambodia pledged not to enter into any alliance and not to allow any base on its territory. Laos was to prohibit the presence of any foreign troops, with the exception of a French military mission and an airfield used by France in Seno. The two Viet-Nams could not ally themselves with anyone, or introduce on their soil any outside force, or receive armaments which would increase their military potential. Moreover, general elections were scheduled to take place in Viet-Nam in 1956, so as to lead to the institution of a democratic government and to reunification. The 1954 agreements were not applied for long. That is the least that can be said about them. Cambodia alone—thanks to its national unity and to the very skillful and determined way in which it is led by its Head of State—has known how and been able to remain intact, neutral, and relatively peaceful until now. But in Viet-Nam everything conspired to bring that country back to the troubled situation from which it had just emerged, while Laos in its turn was caught up in domestic conflicts, aided from the outside.

Concerning Viet-Nam, it is clear that the existence of a Communist state installed in Tonkin—from which our troops withdrew in accordance with the agreements—and the shock caused in the South by the withdrawal of our administration and our forces, exposed the country to new perils. It was a question of discovering whether the country could find, in itself, a national cohesion and a solid government. It was then that the Americans arrived, bringing their aid, their policy, and their authority.

The United States, in fact, considered itself as being invested throughout the world with the burden of defense against communism. Since South Viet-Nam was running the risk of communism, as the regime in the North aimed at imposing itself in the South, Washington wanted to put the South in a position to protect itself. It can be added, without any intention of being derogatory, that the conviction of the United States of fulfilling a sort of vocation, the aversion which they had to any colonial work which had not been theirs, and finally the natural desire in such a powerful people to ensure themselves of new positions, determined the Americans to take our place in Indochina.

We know that, back in 1954, they sponsored the Diem government, that Diem immediately and unfortunately assumed an unpleasant attitude toward us, that once Emperor Bao Dai had left the country Diem replaced him, that he did not carry out the scheduled elections, and lastly that in all fields, particularly those of defense, economy, and administration, he placed himself in the orbit of Washington. But, as this policy was more and more unpopular, the day came when Diem tried to disentangle himself from it, while the Americans began to have doubts about him. Then a military *putsch* removed the President and established a successor. After that, a new *putsch* invested another successor, the latter closely linked with the war action which the United States is supporting, staffing, financing, and arming.

War action, indeed—for although the subversive elements of the Viet-Cong had disappeared from South Viet-Nam after the 1954 agreements, they reappeared under pretext that the agreements were not being applied. Guerrilla fighting and some action carried out by constituted units are increasingly spreading over the territory. At the same time, the people, whatever their opinion of communism, are less and less inclined to support a cause and an authority which in their view are intermingled with those of a foreign state. Thus it seems that, locally, a military solution cannot be expected. Some people imagine, it is true, that the Americans could achieve a military victory by carrying the war to the North as far as it would be necessary. But, although they certainly have at their disposal all the desired means, it is difficult to believe that they wish to take the tremendous risk of a generalized conflict.

Failing a military decision, peace must be made. Now, this implies returning to what was agreed upon ten years ago and, this time, complying with it; in other words, this implies that in North and South Viet-Nam, in Cambodia, and in Laos, no foreign power may any longer intervene in any way in the affairs of these unfortunate countries. A meeting of the same order and including, in principle, the same participants as the former Geneva Conference would certainly be qualified to make a decision and to organize a means for impartial control. That is what France is proposing to all the states concerned, in the certainty that this will have to be done—and the sooner, the better—unless Asia first, and without doubt at a later date the entire world, are to be plunged into very serious trials. This meeting, to which each participant must come without conditions or recriminations, would successively deal with the international aspects of the Laotian, Cambodian, and Vietnamese situation and as an essential first step, with their neutrality. No other road can be visualized which can lead to peace in Southeast Asia, provided that once the theoretical agreement is concluded, two practical conditions be realized. The first is that the powers which directly or indirectly bear a responsibility in what was or is the fate of Indochina—that is, France, China, the Soviet Union, and America—be effectively resolved to be involved there no longer. The second is that massive economic and technical aid be furnished to all of Indochina by the states which have the means for it, in order that development replace cruel division. France, for her part, is ready to observe these two conditions.

SOUTH VIET-NAM

*Reply to the Seventeen
Nonaligned Nations**

Following an appeal made by seventeen nonaligned countries for a negotiated peace in Viet-Nam without prior conditions, the Government of the Republic of Viet-Nam deems it opportune to reaffirm its position which was made public at a news conference on March 1:

1—Deeply attached to peace and to basic principles of the U.N. Charter, the Republic of Viet-Nam repudiates the use of force in the settlement of international conflicts and respects the self-determination right of peoples as far as the option was not put under constraint and threats.

2—In this context, the Republic of Viet-Nam shares the wish and the legitimate anxiety of the powers [which are] signatories of the above-mentioned appeal to see peace restored in Viet-Nam as soon as possible.

3—The Government of the Republic of Viet-Nam believes,

* April 4, 1965.

however, she must stress the fact that she has been compelled
to use arms and make an appeal for aid to friendly nations and
allies; it is for the safeguard of her liberty, independence, and
territorial integrity. Acting in compliance with the spirit and
letter of the U.N. Charter, which recognizes the legitimate [word
indistinct], the Republic of Viet-Nam has the right to rely on the
sympathy and the support of all nations enamored of justice and
peace to drive off the aggressor and make respected the international community's ruling principles which the Communists
have openly violated.

4—The Republic of Viet-Nam cannot therefore rally itself to
every solution which would have the effect of dedicating and
awarding the armed aggression, more especially as a cease-fire
without prior withdrawal of troops and Communist cadres would
amount to a pure and simple capitulation of our side—this because of the absence of frontlines and the Viet-Cong infiltrations
into South Viet-Nam would permit them to reorganize and re-
group their forces in view of an eventual resumption of their subversive activities.

The present conflict must be considered, but [not?] in terms of
a conventional war and every lasting peace must be matched with
necessary guarantees. All negotiations in view of a cease-fire
which ignore these imperative conditions would bring in themselves the germs of a resumption of hostilities or a return to
status-quo-ante.

5—The Republic of Viet-Nam deems, in consequence, that
negotiations in view of restoring peace could only have a chance
of success if the Communists show their sincere desire of putting
an end to the war, of which they are the authors, by withdrawing
beforehand their armed units and their political cadres from
South Viet-Nam territory.

6—The Republic of Viet-Nam considers that every international solution which would not pay attention to the legitimate
aspirations of the Vietnamese government and people, would
affect the principles of self-determination brought up in the
appeal of the seventeen nonaligned countries and compromise
the restoration of peace in Southeast Asia.

INTERNATIONAL COMMISSION FOR SUPERVISION AND CONTROL IN VIET-NAM

Special Report to the Co-Chairmen of the Geneva Conference on Indochina

June 25, 1962

. . . (2) Having examined the complaints and the supporting material sent by the South Vietnamese Mission, the Committee has come to the conclusion that in specific instances there is evidence to show that armed and unarmed personnel, arms, munitions and other supplies have been sent from the zone in the North to the zone in the South with the object of supporting, organizing, and carrying out hostile activities, including armed attacks, directed against the Armed Forces and Administration of the zone in the South. These acts are in violation of Articles 10, 19, 24, and 27 of the Agreement on the Cessation of Hostilities in Viet-Nam.

(3) In examining the complaints and the supporting material, in particular documentary material, sent by the South Vietnamese Mission, the Committee has come to the further conclusion that there is evidence to show that the P.A.V.N. [People's Army of Viet-Nam] has allowed the zone in the North to be used for inciting, encouraging, and supporting hostile activities in the zone in the South, aimed at the overthrow of the Administration in the South. The use of the zone in the North for such activities is in violation of Articles 19, 24, and 27 of the Agreement on the Cessation of Hostilities in Viet-Nam. . . .

(20) Taking all the facts into consideration, and basing itself on its own observations and authorized statements made in the United States of America and the Republic of Viet-Nam, the Commission concludes that the Republic of Viet-Nam has violated Articles 16 and 17 of the Geneva Agreement in receiving the increased military aid from the United States of America in

the absence of any established credit in its favor. The Commission is also of the view that, though there may not be any formal military alliance between the governments of the United States of America and the Republic of Viet-Nam, the establishment of a U.S. Military Assistance Command in South Viet-Nam, as well as the introduction of a large number of U.S. military personnel beyond the stated strength of the M.A.A.G. [Military Assistance Advisory Group], amounts to a factual military alliance, which is prohibited under Article 19 of the Geneva Agreement.

(21) The Commission would also like to bring to the notice of the co-chairmen a recent and deliberate tendency on the part of both the Parties to deny or refuse controls to the Commission's Teams, thereby completely immobilizing their activities and hindering the Commission in the proper discharge of its obligations to supervise the implementation of Articles 16 and 17 of the Geneva Agreement. During the last few months, there has been a near-complete breakdown so far as this important function of the Commission is concerned. The Commission considered the situation and addressed detailed communications to the two Parties recommending the resumption of normal controls immediately. (Copies of the letters sent to the two Parties are attached as Annexure I to this Report.) The Commission, however, regrets to inform the co-chairmen that there has been no improvement in this regard. . . .

(*Signed*)

G. Parthasarathi   F. G. Hooton
India   *Canada*

February 13, 1965

The International Commission for Supervision and Control in Viet-Nam presents its compliments to the co-chairmen of the Geneva Conference and wishes to draw their immediate and earnest attention to the following situation.

(While in full agreement that a report should be made to the co-chairmen, the Canadian Delegation dissents from the terms of this majority Report and has expressed its views in the attached Statement.)

On February 7, 1965, a joint communiqué was issued by the Acting Premier of the Republic of Viet-Nam (R.V.N.), acting under the authority of the National Security Council, and the Ambassador of the United States, acting under the authority of his government. This communiqué announced that military action had been taken against military installations in the Democratic Republic of Viet-Nam (D.R.V.N.).

On the same day, the Liaison Mission of the People's Army of Viet-Nam (P.A.V.N.) transmitted the text of a communiqué which was issued by the Ministry of Defense of the government of the Democratic Republic of Viet-Nam referring to the bombing and strafing of the D.R.V.N.; subsequently the government of the Democratic Republic of Viet-Nam issued on February 8, 1965, a communiqué on these events, which was communicated by the P.A.V.N. Liaison Mission in their letter to the International Commission. The Liaison Mission of the P.A.V.N. brought to the notice of the International Commission that again on February 8, 1965, bombing and strafing of a number of places had taken place and requested the International Commission "to consider and condemn without delay these violations of utmost gravity and report them to the co-chairmen of the Geneva Conference on Indochina."

On February 8, 1965, it was officially announced that further military action on the territory of the D.R.V.N. had been undertaken by R.V.N. and U.S. aircraft.

These documents point to the seriousness of the situation and indicate violations of the Geneva Agreement.

The International Commission is examining and investigating these and connected complaints still being received by it concerning similar serious events and grave developments, and will transmit a report to the co-chairmen as soon as possible.

In the meanwhile, this Special Report is submitted for the earnest and serious attention of the co-chairmen in view of the gravity of the situation. The International Commission requests the co-chairmen to consider the desirability of issuing an immediate appeal to all concerned with a view to reducing tension and preserving peace in Viet-Nam and taking whatever measures are necessary in order to stem the deteriorating situation.

The International Commission for Supervision and Control in Viet-Nam takes this opportunity to renew to the co-chairmen of the Geneva Conference on Indochina the assurances of its highest consideration.

Signed

(M. A. RAHMAN)
Representative of India on the International Commission for Supervision and Control in Viet-Nam

(R. B. STAWICKI)
Acting Representative of the Polish People's Republic on the International Commission for Supervision and Control in Viet-Nam

LA CROIX

*The War Which Is Becoming the Best Ally of Communism**

In Viet-Nam, the escalation continues, implacably. Hate grows on both sides as the immense means at the disposal of the United States come into play. Already in use are phosphorus bombs, napalm bombs and "improved" tear gas, and weapons which, it is said, utilize californium and pulverize everything within a radius of forty meters, while in Saigon and elsewhere, cases of terrorism multiply. The distinct impression which emerges from this alarming situation is that the United States is enraged to find itself facing a small adversary which it is unable to overcome. The United States would like to see that adversary brought to its knees. Unfortunately, the adversary does not consider itself beaten, and is resisting.

Where are we going in such a context? It is a good question to ask, inasmuch as the world seems generally indifferent to this conflict, including the Christian world.

Certainly, the Pope has spoken out, and the Ecumenical Council of Churches has not been friendly. During the recent colloquium in New York, there were protests from religious figures, and very recently the Australian Episcopate raised its voice. But generally, it seems, the destruction of South Viet-Nam goes forward without protest.

---

* From a correspondent in Viet-Nam, published in *La Croix*, the daily of the Catholic Archepiscopate in Paris, April 7, 1965.

This has serious implications for the future of Christianity among the huge number of pagan masses of Asia and Africa. How, in reality, will the missionary of tomorrow be able to preach love of Christ in the face of such actions by Christian countries? Because these masses, subjected as they are to well-orchestrated propaganda from the other side, already identify Christianity with the white races which claim to be the defenders of Christianity, they will thereafter have the greatest contempt for a religion authorizing such massacres.

One might say that South Viet-Nam itself participates in its own destruction through its own armed forces. It is understandable, but not justifiable. In fact, are we not dealing with the military? Militarism, it will be remembered, was designated by Pope Paul VI, in his Christmas message, as being responsible for many excesses.

An effort has been made to create the impression that this war has the approval of the people of South Viet-Nam—that they are in favor of "battering" the North. We object to such a gratuitous affirmation, because what the people want—especially the rural people, who are often victims of misdirected shooting, and are caught between two targets, but also the city youths, who try by all possible means to escape conscription—is peace, a cease-fire, and a cease-fire immediately. There is, evidently, a bourgeois group, city residents who profit from the war in business dealings, but they are only a minority, though not the most "interesting" one. There are also, and foremost, Catholic refugees for whom this war has become a sort of crusade, and who, consequently, approve all and every means. Have they considered, blinded as they are by their hatred of Communists, that they are in conflict with the Gospel and the spirit of the Second Vatican Council by not making the essential distinction between the sin and the sinners? Have they reflected that such a war, which accumulates dead and wounded, material and moral destruction, will finally become the best ally of communism?

In our view, this short-sighted policy and its consequences are to be deplored because, whatever the issue of the present conflict, South Viet-Nam will not rid itself of communism and of Communists, who have multiplied throughout the years.

A recent article in *La Croix*[1] warned against the danger of a

[1] March 23, 1965.

too open intervention by the United States in the war being fought by South Viet-Nam against the Viet-Cong aggressor.

Even if one justifies this intrusion by citing South Viet-Nam's appeal for aid to the powerful U. S., the fact remains that this is a war in which the whites are implicated (as in the Congo, with mercenaries coming for the most part from racist South Africa) and in which, consequently, it is easy for adverse propaganda to distort this aid on racial grounds. We know the slogan: Asia for the Asians, and its corollary: Africa for the Africans. Who would dare to say that such slogans do not impress the masses!

It must be admitted, moreover, that the U. S., with its own internal problems concerning integration, is ill equipped to declare itself the champion of human liberty and equality.

Then it is high time, it seems to us, that the United States renounce its "false pride"—to take up the words used by the Ecumenical Council of Churches—and that it enter a spirit of dialogue. There is nothing to keep the United States from so doing, as it is incontestably in a position of power; indeed, it constitutes the greatest military power in the world.

By holding a dialogue, Americans will not lose their prestige, but will show to the world that they belong to the "men of good will" to whom peace was promised two thousand years ago. Is this not an attitude that conforms to the Gospel, to which both Catholics or Protestants lay claim? Then why continue this bludgeoning, this "battering," which could lead to the worst, if Russia and China, who are beginning to give unequivocal signs of unrest, were to intervene in the near future!

SAIGON POS

To Rally the Peasants[*]

The main obstacle barring the government from reaching the peasants' hearts stems from the peasants' innate mistrust of officials. This mistrust, accumulated through decades of colonist

---

[*] January 10, 1964.

rule, has been compounded even more by the misrule and mishandling of Diem's lieutenants.

Peasant grievances against local officials of the Ngo Dinh Diem government have become almost endemic. Most of these grievances were justified. Cases of extortion, bribery, intimidation, arbitrary arrest, summary execution and mass torture were commonplace.

In many instances, peasant grievances are the result of tactical errors committed by well-meaning commanders. Cases have been reported of wanton bombing or shelling of entire villages where, it was later learned, only a handful of VC had been detected. Sometimes these grievances are explained away as the consequences of war. The merciless destruction of unharvested rice-fields under a column of armored personnel carriers, or the scorched earth of napalm bombing are examples of this type of grievance.

Yet all these indirect causes are forgivable. What cannot be forgiven is the sad but commonplace case of abuse by district chiefs—more often, by their deputy chiefs for security. Name a single delta province where the deputy's name is not whispered with fear among the peasant population, and with a furtive, over-the-shoulder glance.

In the days of the late Ngo Dinh Diem, the deputy chief for security's name was synonymous with affluence, quick money, and several wives. And no one dared complain. Under Diem, an accusation against a district chief, province chief, or their deputy was tantamount to subversive propaganda.

Since the Revolution, a massive overhaul of personnel has been effected, down to the district level. Yet, is there any assurance that the same mistakes as those which drove millions of peasants into the arms of the Viet-Cong will not be repeated? What are a peasant's chances against an abusive official, under the new government?

On the answers to these questions depend whether the peasant will look to the government for protection of his person, his rights, and his property, or to the Viet-Cong. And we must not forget that as long as there is one aggrieved peasant, there are ten potential Viet-Cong sympathizers, and as many potential recruits. And every new case of abuse will widen the gap between this essential war factor and the government.

D. PUBLIC ASSESSMENT

Introduction

In the summer of 1964 President Johnson, while campaigning for election to the Presidency on an antiwar platform, received the reluctant support of Congress to undertake a wide variety of military actions in Viet-Nam in response to aggression. In the early spring of 1965 he secured the support of an even more reluctant Congress for a $700 million authorization for further military expenditures. (The expenditures were recognized by the Congress and the Department of Defense as unnecessary.) Under pressure to maintain the façade of bipartisan foreign policy, the Congress did not air its frustrations publicly. There were of course exceptions. For example, Senator Morse criticized the policy, root and branch. Although a majority of the Senate Foreign Relations Committee may privately have doubted the Administration course in Viet-Nam, only Morse—as early as 1961—announced his fundamental disagreement.

The Kennedy and Johnson Administration seemed to have no satisfactory explanation to offer for American military engagement in Viet-Nam. Consequently, many representatives of the press and members of Congress felt that the news of the war as well as the reasons for it was being kept from the public. In part they were right, since only the "positive" side of news reporting was encouraged. David Halberstam of the *New York Times* makes this poignantly clear in his book, *The Making of a Quagmire*. Editorially, the press was divided, much of it critical. But in Congress there was virtually no debate on our actions in Viet-Nam. The seeming abdication of Congressional responsibility in foreign policy gave rise to a new institutional form— the teach-in—so that criticism by the informed could be heard. Two of the major antagonists at the national teach-in in Washington were George Kahin and Robert Scalapino, excerpts from whose remarks are included below.

A greater numbers of articles began to appear that cried out for public discussion and reappraisal of our Viet-Nam policy and its consequences: both political and moral (see for example

Hans J. Morgenthau, page 37, and the account by I. F. Stone, below, of our disregard for international law). The seeming breakdown in understanding of what was going on in Asia led Joseph Kraft and Bernard Fall to call for a reassessment of our position. The public mood continues to be one of confusion.

WAYNE MORSE

*American Policy in Viet-Nam**

The daily American air raids on North Viet-Nam which began on February 7 and the landing of American troops, now numbering 45,000, on the mainland of Asia, are markers in the tragic failure of the Viet-Nam policy begun by this country in 1954. At that time, the many American voices who wanted the United States to join France in re-establishing French dominion over its old colony of Indochina were deterred by President Eisenhower's precondition that we would do so only if joined by Britain. British Prime Minister Churchill declined to embark on the venture, and after the French defeat at Dien Bien Phu, a peace conference was held at Geneva which produced the Geneva Accord of 1954.

Right up to the minute of that defeat, official French sources remained optimistic about the final outcome. French airpower was unchallenged; French armor and equipment were the best that American aid could furnish, and we furnished more material for her forces than France spent herself on the war.

Nonetheless, after eight years of fighting and after 240,000 casualties, the French people had had enough of war. Mendès-France became premier on the promise to end it.

As the peace conference progressed among representatives of France, Britain, the United States, Russia, China, the Viet-Minh, Laos, Cambodia, and Viet-Nam, many Americans expressed a deep bitterness at what they viewed as a triumph for the Chinese

* Remarks at St. Mary's University, San Antonio, Texas, May 14, 1965.

Communists. The head of the U.S. military mission, General John W. O'Daniel, said on July 8, 1954, in a classic statement of the blindness to reality in Viet-Nam that has characterized an entire generation of French and later American military officers: "The war in Indochina can still be won without bringing in one single American soldier to fight. The Vietnamese have ample manpower and even today outnumber the enemy by 100,000 with superior firepower at least in a ratio of two to one and probably more. And we are ready to assist them in training an adequate national army for the security of their homeland."

The Senate Majority Leader at the time was Senator William Knowland of California. He called the Geneva Conference a step toward bringing China into the U.N., and declared he would resign his position as party leader in the Senate if Red China were admitted. For a time, it appeared that the United States representatives at Geneva would withdraw from the conference due to what was called "great Congressional pressure."

In the end, our Secretary of State did return home before the conference ended, leaving only an undersecretary to represent this country. And we did not sign the final product. We issued a statement saying only that we would regard the Accord as binding on all parties and "would view any renewal of the aggression in violation of the aforesaid agreements with grave concern." But in a separate statement in Washington, the President said: "The United States has not itself been party to or bound by the decisions taken by the Conference," attributing this position to the questionable contention that we were not a co-belligerent.

Almost simultaneously, a new government of Viet-Nam was established in Saigon under Ngo Dinh Diem. Diem had for years been an exile, living in the United States. In later years, his admirers would point to the complete absence of any organized political or economic support for him when he took over, something they regard as a compliment to his relative longevity in the job but which also testified to the extent to which he was imposed upon the country.

The 1954 agreement provided for the withdrawal from Indochina of France, and the division of the country into three parts —Laos, Cambodia, and Viet-Nam. Each was to be free of military alignment and military aid from outside. Viet-Nam was

divided into two zones for purposes of military occupation—
North and South. In July of 1956, general elections to reunite
the country under one government were to be held under the
supervision of an International Control Commission.

Historical evidence of who began violating the agreement first
is hard to come by. But it is certain that the most significant
violation was the refusal of South Viet-Nam, now headed by
Diem, to proceed with the elections. He pointed out that like the
U.S., his "government" had not signed the agreement and was
not bound by it. Although Diem said he would favor elections
supervised by the United Nations, this was not the arrangement
of the Accord, and he refused to enter into the discussions called
for in the agreement to fix the details of the I.C.C-supervised
election. This gross violation was viewed not with "grave concern" by us but with great approval.

Undoubtedly, the Viet-Minh under Ho Chi Minh would have
won such a free election. President Eisenhower declares in his
Mandate for Change that all the experts he talked to in that
period believed Ho would get at least 80 per cent of the vote. Ho
was the nationalist patriot of Viet-Nam who had our favor and
our help in World War II when he organized local resistance to
the Japanese occupation. Thereafter, he led the resistance to the
effort of France to resume its prewar colonial dominion in Indochina. A Moscow-trained and avowed Communist, Ho had
reflected the ancient Vietnamese hostility to the Chinese and was
considered closer to Moscow than to Peking.

By 1957, the International Control Commission, charged with
investigating complaints of violations, found both North Viet-
Nam and South Viet-Nam and the United States to have violated
the terms of the agreement, we through our massive aid program.
A retired police official who was part of a U.S. foreign-aid team
sent to train local police officials there in 1959, wrote me recently
that one morning he found one of his subordinates, who was a
C.I.A. agent, handing out unmarked submachine guns to the
local gendarmerie. From his knowledge of weapons, he felt sure
they had been made by an American manufacturer. Their distribution was illegal.

In light of the insistence of our government that we are there
only to enforce the agreement, it must be pointed out that the
State Department White Paper places the date of the renewal of

guerrilla warfare on the part of the Viet-Cong "after 1956." It is our government's contention that guerrilla warfare was resumed by the North after a disparity began to appear between living conditions in the North and South, to the disadvantage of the North. But it is also true that the purpose of the 1954 Accord was to end the fighting and remove the competition to the political arena, whereas we and our agent, Diem, frustrated that purpose by refusing to allow the election to proceed.

Moreover, the veneer of economic improvement in the South was certainly due in very large part to the massive American aid. It even took the form of sending millions of dollars worth of rice to what was supposed to be a rice-surplus area. Subsequently, we have continued to send millions of dollars worth every year of such foods as wheat products and dried milk, besides the cotton and tobacco we furnish for resale by the South Viet-Nam government. Much of the economic aid took the form of subsidizing key military and governmental people, until it was commonly said in foreign-aid debates that there were more Mercedes-Benz autos on the streets of Saigon than any other city of the world.

Our aid to South Viet-Nam ran about $200 million a year after 1954, in a country of only 14 million people. Even so, by 1963, Diem had become so remote from the general population and had allowed so much arbitrary power to be exercised by his family that more and more elements of the population went into opposition against him. The raids of the security police upon the Buddhists' pagodas, the suicide by fire of the monks, and the reaction against the terror of the police finally led to an overthrow of the Ngos that had at least the tacit support of the United States.

We made it quite clear that our interest was in the prosecution of the war against the rebels. What hindered that effort was bad and what helped it was good. When Diem no longer suited the American purpose, he was deposed.

Since then, the internal situation in Viet-Nam has steadily deteriorated. Putting together a government in Saigon became a major challenge to the U.S. embassy. The Viet-Cong have come to control more and more of the people and territory of the South.

With a regularity that was laughable in Western capitals that had abandoned colonialism years earlier, our top government officials went back and forth from Washington to Saigon, repeating the time-worn phrases that things never looked better, and that these additional "advisers" and these helicopters, and this new civic-action program in the hamlets, and then air raids on the North, would finally do the job of defeating the Viet-Cong.

Not once has any of these predictions proved accurate. The total of all the increments in aid has brought the cost of aid to South Viet-Nam alone to over $700 million a year, exclusive of the $700 million the President asked to pay the cost of the U.S. military operations. The original 600-man military mission of 1954 has grown to 45,000 in May, 1965.

Having stated repeatedly that the war was a civil war that had to be fought and won in the South, we found that the war there was about to be lost. So we have tried to rewrite the history of the last five years to show that it was North Viet-Nam that was doing the fighting all along. That was the purpose of the State Department White Paper that was published to justify the raids into the North. But the White Paper proved only that the Viet-Cong guerrillas had received between 10 and 20 per cent of their equipment and personnel from the North, a fact that had been known throughout the period when our government insisted it was basically a civil war and while President Johnson was rejecting the Goldwater proposals to take the war into the North.

After three months of air raids, presumably designed to drive North Viet-Nam to the bargaining table, the President tells us that North Viet-Nam shows no signs at all of wanting to talk peace. So far, North Viet-Nam has not responded to the raids on her territory with any action of her own. But we have put 45,000 men into the field in the South, and we have yet to encounter the highly regarded North Vietnamese army whose strength is put at around 350,000.

Over this whole dreary picture hangs China. At what point she may consider her territory to be threatened is anyone's guess. We found out in Korea that there are limits to where Western powers can conduct military operations on her near borders without drawing in Chinese manpower.

Altogether too many American officials brush aside all this recital of what went before. They insist that even if it was a mistake to take up where the French left off, that is all water over the dam and now we can do nothing but keep on fighting, else we will lose "face" and no one anywhere will believe we mean what we say.

But it is unthinkable to me that the United States should be talking about backing up a policy with full-scale war, if that is what it takes, when that policy admittedly was a mistake when it was started! How can any nation consider making war for reasons so many of its leaders agree were unsound?

How can a policy that was unsound to begin with ever be made to work? Are Americans so confident of the miracles to be wrought with nuclear bombs and billion-dollar aid programs that we think they will make a success of anything, no matter how badly conceived? I fear this is our assumption.

Considered on the facts of what it has cost so far and what it has achieved, the Eisenhower-Kennedy-Johnson policy in Viet-Nam has been a total failure. It has not saved the area from communism, nor from war. Its fruits today are: (1) the unifying of the large non-Communist nations of Asia—India, Japan, Pakistan, Indonesia—*against* the United States; (2) the exposure of the United States as the only foreign power engaging in the war in Viet-Nam, and a white Western power, at that; (3) the revelation that the overwhelming force of the United States is ineffective when it operates through a "front" government against indigenous revolutionary forces.

For ten years, the United States has been implementing its Viet-Nam policy with more money and more military power. The air attacks on the North were justified only by reversing the entire presentation of the war as a civil war; they were supposed to drive North Viet-Nam to the bargaining table. But in requesting $700 million to finance the American forces, President Johnson said that nothing of the kind is likely to happen, and that our intelligence indicates the North has no interest in negotiations. If negotiations were their purpose, then the air raids, too, have failed.

In the midst of this situation, our government has reacted as so many foreign governments have reacted throughout history— by trying to stifle all debate and criticism of its policy. That is one of the surest signs of failure. It is undertaken on the ground that if Americans do not appear united, the enemy will be encouraged. But that is always the excuse given to silence opposition to a disastrous foreign policy. The "pro-Communist" label is dragged out and applied to critics everywhere. I do not know of as much damage we have done to relations with any free country as Undersecretary of State Ball did to our relations with Japan when he attributed Japanese press criticism of U. S. air raids to Communist infiltration of newspaper editorial boards. The Japanese have been virtually unanimous in denying the charge; and they have been outraged that the United States should fall back upon such a scurrilous device by way of answer to the criticism.

In my opinion, our effort to "save face" has lost us not only face in Asia but much more. It is making enemies and frightened neutrals out of people who once respected us. It is making the Communists look like people whose main purpose is to rid Asia of unwanted white domination, a purpose behind which the vast bulk of Asians are united.

The Administration's effort to shut off debate in the United States begs all the great questions of how communism in Asia can be most effectively combated. Where it seizes upon national-ist aspirations to oust a Western ruler, it cannot be restrained by military force exercised by the West. France, Britain, and the Netherlands have already learned that lesson, and the United States is well on the way to learning it, too.

The one effective restraint on Communist expansion—which at this stage is still primarily Chinese Communist expansion— is strong neighbors around her. Historically, the natural counter-poise to China has been the subcontinent below the Himalayas. The era of British imperialism weakened the influence of India throughout the subcontinent and it has not yet been rebuilt. In more recent years, Japan has been the major Asian counter-weight to China.

Today, neither Japan nor the countries of the subcontinent are accepting American force as the answer to China's rise to power. The continued acceleration of American force will do more to drive these countries into neutralism or into support of China than anything the Communists might do.

Unfortunately, many high officials in the State and Defense departments and around the President have staked their careers and reputations upon our present policy. They are determined to continue it at any cost to the United States. This cost now con-templates the landing of more U.S. Army divisions in Viet-Nam, an increase in draft calls from 7,000 a month last year to 17,000 for June of 1965, a take-over from South Viet-Nam of responsibility for running the war, and the expansion of air raids in the North to industrial targets.

These people are no longer able to change the policy. Only the American people themselves can do it.

A U. S. military stronghold in Viet-Nam can only be maintained by perpetual war. This war will be fought by Americans, with the South Vietnamese increasingly becoming mere bystanders.

I do not believe there is anything worth such a war to be gained, or even preserved, by the United States. In fact, it is more to our interest to stop it than to continue it. It can be stopped through any one of many procedures. Direct negotiations is one procedure, though they must include the Viet-Cong who control at least half of South Viet-Nam.

Another is to seek a peace force from members of the Southeast Asia Treaty Organization. Of the eight SEATO members, only the U.S. and Australia have any combat troops in Viet-Nam, and those from Australia are not yet on the scene. The Philippines may or may not send some. But SEATO forces should be sought as a peacekeeping mission to pacify South Viet-Nam and separate the combatants pending a political settlement.

Another means of handling the war is through the United Nations. Our war policy is in violation of many provisions of the U.N. Charter which require members to seek peaceful settlement of disputes and to lay before the U.N. those they cannot settle peacefully alone. Either the Security Council or the General Assembly affords the means of handling the issue.

Above all, it has been demonstrated that the United States cannot enforce alone those provisions of the Geneva Agreement that we want to see enforced, while we violate the others. Other parties must be brought in, and whether we go back to the 1954 agreement or fashion a new one, the United States must honor all of it.

We must get over the idea that whoever we do not control in Asia is against us. A modern epigram has been coined which says: "He who would save face in Asia should keep his body in his own country." Some form of neutralism for Viet-Nam would probably emerge from third-party intervention. But a neutralism guaranteed by many nations, especially those of Asia itself, would do more to further our long-term objective of containing communism in Asia than a war which comes down to one of white man versus Asian. In that kind of war only communism will prosper.

GEORGE McT. KAHIN and ROBERT A. SCALAPINO

Excerpts from National Teach-In on Viet-Nam Policy*

George McT. Kahin

. . . Since the end of the last war, American officials have made such grave errors in policy towards Southeast Asia that we have every right to be skeptical about their ability to respond intelligently to the present situation in Viet-Nam. Their most consistent failure has been an inability both to appreciate the importance of Asian nationalism and to work with rather than against this powerful force. This is a major reason why Burma, Cambodia, Indonesia have become so distrustful of the United States, and why they have either broken or come close to breaking their relations with us.

Moreover the obsession of American policy-makers with what they still see as monolithic communism has blinded them to the fact that communism in Asia has adapted itself to nationalism. And they have confused the broad but nationally differentiated force and potential of communism with the threat of specifically Chinese power.

Despite the immense information-gathering facilities of the government, serious policy mistakes have been made because decisions have been taken on the basis of inappropriate criteria,

*May 15, 1965.

wrong analyses, and a disregard for the relevant facts. At the same time, essential information has been withheld from the American public and crucial policy decisions concerning Southeast Asia have been made before the public has even been aware that a problem exists. And once taken, these decisions have set in motion events which severely circumscribed any moderating influence which an informed public opinion might bring to bear.

Moreover in recent months the tendency has increased to dismiss even thoughtful criticism of government policy as irresponsible meddling.

In Viet-Nam, American policy has been wrong from the outset. In the decade following World War II, because of our illusory hope that we could induce France to become the keystone in an American-designed European military organization, we temporized with our commitment to national self-determination and backed France in her efforts to reestablish control over Viet-Nam.

By supporting her attempt to establish a Vietnamese regime which lacked nationalist support, we helped insure that Vietnamese patriots would have no real alternative but to rally to the banner of Ho Chi Minh. France's humiliating defeat at Dien Bien Phu in 1954 was a military defeat but it was made inevitable by the political failure that preceded it.

Then came the Geneva Agreements clearly specifying that Viet-Nam was one country. They stipulated that the 17th Parallel was a temporary demarcation line, not in any way to be interpreted—and here I'm using the text of the agreement—not in any way to be interpreted as constituting a political or territorial boundary.

The United States in its own unilateral declaration at Geneva spoke only of one Viet-Nam, not of a South, and not of a North, and with respect to the conference's provision for national elections, the United States also stated—again in its own unilateral declaration—that it would continue to seek to achieve unity through free elections supervised by the United Nations.

Nevertheless the United States soon thereafter set out to build up a separate state in the South. And again we made the mistake of thinking we could establish a viable government on an inadequate nationalist base. The United States supported Ngo Dinh Diem, giving him, as you know, massive amounts of—economic initially and later—military assistance.

But American aid was no substitute for nationalist support, something Diem's regime never really acquired, despite what our officials told Congress and the American people.

Diem himself had said in 1953—repeatedly, I might add—that Ho Chi Minh—and I'm quoting him—"gained in popularity as a leader of the resistance, not as a Communist," and that the vast majority of his followers were nationalist and in no way pro-Communist.

What the United States failed to recognize was that in these conditions Ho Chi Minh, who for at least nine years had been the acknowledged head of the Vietnamese nationalist movement, could not be replaced as the leader of the Vietnamese people by a man supported from the outside, a man little known and who had spent the critical years—nearly all of them—of the independence struggle abroad.

America's failure, of course, to build up an effective government under Diem is now well known, but this was not immediately apparent, for after Geneva his regime enjoyed several years of grace during which Ho Chi Minh's followers left it pretty much alone.

Essentially this was due to the fact that the Geneva Agreements had promised nationwide elections for 1956 and it was primarily because of this provision and because the agreements also stipulated that France would be responsible for carrying out the accords—carrying out the accords south of the 17th Parallel—and that France would remain there until the elections were held—it was primarily because of those reasons that the Viet-Minh withdrew its armies from the South and for a considerable period suspended revolutionary activity there.

But with American encouragement Diem refused to permit the elections in 1956 and France washed her hands of the responsibilities which she had assumed at Geneva.

Regardless of what sophistry has been employed to demonstrate otherwise, by encouraging Diem to defy this central provision of the Geneva agreements, the United States reneged on the position it had taken there in its own unilateral declaration.

Civil war in Viet-Nam became inevitable, for when a military struggle for power ends on the agreed condition that the competition will be transferred to the political level, can the side which violates the agreed conditions legitimately expect that the military struggle will not be resumed?

Despite the initial period of insulation from Viet-Minh militancy and despite unstinted American economic and political backing, Diem failed to develop a real base of popular support. Programs urged by the United States for social and economic reform, and for winning the allegiance of the non-Vietnamese hill-dwelling people, were never effectively carried out.

The Saigon regime remained all too isolated from the Vietnamese peasantry. As a result, it was unable to compete with the Viet-Cong guerrillas when, from 1958 on, these guerrillas adopted increasingly militant policies.

And in the nineteen months since the assassination of Diem, the situation has continued to deteriorate and the shifting combinations of army officers and bureaucrats controlling the government have remained just as isolated from the villagers of Viet-Nam.

Faced with this decline in political cohesion, and the evident inability of the South Vietnamese military to stave off the Viet-Cong, the present Administration has enlarged the war in Viet-Nam by bombing the North and increasing American military activity in the South.

It has endeavored to compensate for the continuing erosion of Saigon's political and military base by introducing more American troops, more American air power.

It has justified this in terms of our pledge to support Viet-Nam, a commitment which, as you know, the Administration regards as a test case.

And here I think it might be appropriate to recall the caveat of Secretary Acheson in 1950 when he stated that America could not by itself create politically stable states in Asia.

President Kennedy also recognized these limitations when, in September of 1963, he said of the South Vietnamese, "In the final analysis it's their war—they're the ones who have to win it or lose it. We can help them, give them equipment. We can send our men out there as advisers, but they have to win it."

In the context of these cautions, does an unconditional American military pledge to a weak and factious regime which lacks popular backing—does that make common sense? Is our pledge of support completely unqualified? Does it not demand a minimum degree of performance and co-operation from Saigon—political as well as military? Is our pledge automatically to any military or civilian group which happens to control Saigon? What happens if our current policy of brinkmanship induces Hanoi to send its 300,000-man army into South Viet-Nam?

Because this it may very well do if the damage inflicted by the United States becomes so great that the North has little to lose by undertaking a retaliatory attack and little to save through compromise and negotiation.

The well-known military analyst, Hanson Baldwin, has estimated that to cope effectively with such a force the United States might have to use as many as a million men.

The United States, of course, does not have these forces immediately available and even to send in a small proportion would use up our entire strategic reserve.

This same trend toward a rapprochement with Russia started by President Eisenhower, continued by President Kennedy, that trend has already been seriously affected by our policy in Viet-Nam and it will be further undermined if we continue on our present course.

Among Communist parties throughout Asia as well as among the nonaligned states generally, China's scornful derision of Russia's policy of peaceful coexistence has been gaining ever wider approval.

The possibility of co-operation between the United States and Russia to contain China's power—China's power and influence in Southeast Asia—is becoming ever more remote. Our major aim in Asia is to contain China and thus to provide the opportunity for the states of South and Southeast Asia to develop free from Peking's dominating influence.

And it is this consideration which should govern American policy toward Viet-Nam. No matter how much military power we pour into Viet-Nam, the present American policy of trying to sustain a separate state in the South may very well fail because the local political factors necessary to insure success are simply not there.

If we are going to salvage anything in Vietnam, we will achieve more through a ceasefire and a negotiated political settlement than through the futile infusion of more and more American military power.

The United States must recognize that the historic Viet-Nam fear of—fear of and antagonism toward—China continues despite the common adherence to Communist ideology. And inasmuch as the character of Vietnamese communism is inseparable from Vietnamese nationalism, Vietnamese power will not necessarily be exerted in concert with Chinese power.

This is likely to depend upon whether such actions conform with Vietnamese national interest as the Vietnamese people define that interest.

Those who still are impressed by the simplistic domino theory must realize that non-Communist governments of Southeast Asia will not automatically collapse if the Communists should come to control all of Viet-Nam. So long as Southeast Asian governments are in harmony with their nations' nationalism, so long as they are wise enough to meet the most pressing economic and social demands of their people, they are not likely to succumb to communism.

Nationalism and the demand for social and economic progress are the dominant forces in Southeast Asia today. If we can work with these forces, if we can work with them we will make a major contribution to maintaining the territorial integrity of the states of Southeast Asia and provide them with a better opportunity to develop along non-Communist lines.

The first step in that direction must be to negotiate a settlement in Viet-Nam.

What has our position been thus far? I think you know it well. The Administration tells us that it is prepared to negotiate unconditionally but in effect on condition that the Viet-Cong cease all operations immediately and on condition that the state of South Viet-Nam—and this is the most important condition, I would say—on condition that the state of South Viet-Nam continue its separate existence in permanent violation of the Geneva Agreements.

Furthermore, we have made clear that the Viet-Cong and its political arm, the National Liberation Front, cannot be party to such negotiations. Not only is that one more condition, but it flies squarely in the face of reality—political reality.

It is, I think, widely acknowledged that at least half of the South is today under the control of the Viet-Cong. Is it not utopian to assume that Hanoi is in a position to insist upon the Viet-Cong's yielding up the position it has won there?

In 1954, the Viet-Minh could induce its numerous supporters

in the South to accept Viet-Nam's partition and to abandon
their gains south of the 17th Parallel, because partition was regarded as a temporary measure to last only until elections.

But we cannot assume that once again the insurgents in the
South will give up what they have won through long and difficult
campaigns.

Over the last five years, the doctrine of uncompromising struggle and a real expectation of victory have been assiduously nurtured among the Viet-Cong. While there is undoubtedly a
considerable congruence of interest between Hanoi and the Viet-
Cong, under these circumstances we cannot assume that Hanoi
can abruptly call off the southerners' resistance.

And whatever influence Hanoi can exert over the Viet-Cong,
we cannot expect it to exert this so long as we continue bombing
the North.

The morale of the North Vietnamese is, of course, no more
likely to be broken by bombs than was that of the British or the
Russians in the last war. Indeed their will is likely to be stiffened.
President Johnson said after our Embassy in Saigon had been
bombed that outrages like this will only reinforce the determination of the American people and government. What is true for
Americans is true for the Vietnamese.

Halting our bombardment of the North would be our first
genuine indication of an interest in negotiations. Our quite
cavalier dismissal of the United Nations Secretary General's
efforts hardly constituted a serious American interest in negotiations. I submit that we should give him an unequivocal mandate to pursue negotiations and that we should make clear that
we want not just discussions but serious negotiations.

And I would suggest that concurrently we should give much
more encouragement than we have to those nonaligned Asian
and African states which wish to help promote a peaceful settlement in Viet-Nam.

And finally, for those many Americans who still regard full
public discussion of vitally important national issues as essential
to our brand of democracy, there is a particularly disquieting
domestic aspect of this situation:

Realizing as they do that an informed public discussion requires access to the relevant facts, these Americans can only be
deeply disturbed when a spokesman for the newspaper editors

of this country feels compelled to state as he did last month that the American press in Viet-Nam faces stronger restrictions than it ever has in wartime and that we are getting contradictions, double-talk and half-truths from the government concerning the situation in Viet-Nam.

And surely Americans have grounds for concern when the *New York Times* can editorialize, as it did shortly after this, less than three weeks ago, that high-ranking representatives of government in Washington and in Saigon have so obscured, confused or distorted news from Viet-Nam or have made such fatuously erroneous evaluations about the course of the war that the credibility of the United States government has been sacrificed.

When the American public faces the prospect of war it has the right to full and honest answers.

I had indeed hoped that Mr. Bundy's appearance would be an indication of a change in the Administration's attitude as to the value of informed public discussion. I can only hope that his indispensability in meeting some major crisis of policy-making is really of greater importance than the contribution he might have made this afternoon toward our better understanding of the Administration's aims and to that kind of enlightened public discussion which is so essential to the wisest conduct of foreign policy.

Robert A. Scalapino

. . . I believe that we can all agree that the Viet-Nam crisis constitutes one of the most complex and serious crises faced by the United States since World War II. There are no easy answers. Probably, very few individuals in this audience concur specifically upon every detail relating to the crisis, or upon the most logical steps to be taken in attempting to resolve it. And I am quite certain that there are no two people on this panel who agree precisely upon such matters.

We have the right, and we are now exercising the right to engage in free and uninhibited discussion on this highly important, extremely difficult problem. Along with that right, moreover, we have the responsibility to raise the level of debate as high as possible, avoiding undue emotionalism and seeking to penetrate the basic issues, complex though they may be. That responsibility, my predecessor in this debate, Professor George Kahin, fulfilled nobly, and I shall seek to maintain his standards.

Rather than begin with an historical background, as did Professor Kahin, I should prefer to blend history into an analysis of certain critical contemporary questions to which I intend to address myself.

First, is the Viet-Cong a truly indigenous force in South Viet-Nam, and has it achieved such support as it has acquired primarily through its promotion of social and economic reforms? To me, the answers to this question, however complicated, are on balance, "No." Let me begin by citing an editorial from the Peking *Daily Worker* of April 15, 1965, reproduced in the *Peking Review* on April 23. Said Peking, "The Vietnamese people's entire struggle for national salvation is a just revolutionary struggle against aggression. It is certain to win because there is the wise leadership of the Marxist–Leninist Workers' Party of Viet-Nam, because there is the unity of the thirty million Vietnamese people, and because there is sympathy and support from people the world over."

I call to your attention the first phrase in the above trilogy, "because there is the wise leadership of the Marxist–Leninist Workers' Party of Viet-Nam." There is little question that the Viet-Cong is a carbon copy of the Viet-Minh which preceded it. That is certainly not to say that the Viet-Cong has no indigenous support, or indigenous leadership. Clearly, most of the publicized leaders of the National Liberation Front of South Viet-Nam are of southern origin. I am also prepared to state that a significant segment of the NLF rank-and-file are native to the South.

But what are the truly critical factors? First, who really knows or recognizes "leaders" of the National Liberation Front like Nguyen Huu Tho? How many individuals—in or out of South Viet-Nam—accept them as true leaders?

The real leaders of the Viet-Cong are—and always have been —the small, hard-core group who are also leaders of the Vietnamese Communist movement. And the Vietnamese Communist Party has its headquarters in Hanoi, now as in the past. The South Vietnamese Revolutionary Party (the Communist Party of South Viet-Nam) numbers no more than 500 or so. It could not be expected to dominate the 500,000–man Party of the North.

Not only is the leadership of the National Liberation Front

shadowy indeed. Take a close look at its basic principles. I urge you to read them carefully, because I suggest that although there may have been differences in tactics between the Southern National Liberation Front and the Northern Workers' Party, there have been no discernible differences, up to date, on questions of basic policies or fundamental programs.

The Viet-Cong is not a unique movement. The Viet-Minh also had numerous non-Communist elements in it at one point. Until it came to power, indeed, the Viet-Minh claimed to be a multi-class, united front organization dedicated solely to the national liberation of Viet-Nam. As you well know, however, it ended completely under the domination of the Communist Party, with all opponents liquidated, silenced, or "reformed."

It is vital to understand that we face in Viet-Nam a five-stage revolutionary program which borrows heavily from the tactics pioneered by the Chinese Communists in the past. The first stage is always to construct a tightly disciplined, fully controlled Communist Party, not susceptible to penetration from the outside. The second stage is to develop a united front movement, using available nationalist and socio-economic issues to solicit support from the peasantry, the intelligentsia, and the national bourgeoisie. The third stage is to move from this "united front" phase into guerrilla warfare. If guerrilla warfare proves basically successful and the cities can be surrounded, the fourth stage is reached, with the movement into positional warfare. Then victory follows and the fifth stage: the establishment of a "People's Democracy," in which the Party takes full command, liquidating its significant opponents. In North Viet-Nam, I know of no force that has been able to survive this five-stage progression to remain in true opposition to the *Lao Dong* Party.

It is important to appreciate these facts, because they are not unique to Viet-Nam, nor for that matter, to China or North Korea where they also applied in certain degree. We are dealing with a phenomenon moreover, that involves a combination of civil war and international assistance. Unless both ingredients are given their proper weight and role, one misunderstands both the complexity of the problem and the difficulty of its solution.

Let me raise another question. Does the Viet-Cong really command the respect and allegiance of a majority of the people of South Viet-Nam? Again, although the answer is complicated, in my opinion, on balance, it must be "No." What is truly remarkable is that although the Diem government made many mistakes—and I am not here to defend that government—very few if any significant anti-Diem leaders in the South have joined the Viet-Cong. One of the most revealing facts is that the leaders of the great, populous functional groups in South Viet-Nam are not a part of the Viet-Cong today, nor have they ever been.

I refer first to the Buddhist leaders. Buddhist solutions to the Viet-Nam crisis do not involve the movement of the Viet-Cong into power. The latest Buddhist proposal which I have seen urges that all Viet-Cong elements go North, Americans go out, and some type of international force come in. It is a truly neutralist proposal.

Secondly, what about the Cao-Dai and the Hoa-Hao? These are groups that command the allegiance of millions of Vietnamese. The Cao-Dai alone reportedly has some two million members. Have the leaders of these organizations joined the Viet-Cong? Have they supported this so-called National Liberation Movement? There are a few exceptions, of course. The Communists are always able to pick up for "united front" purposes "five Catholics, three Hoa-Hao, and ten Buddhists," but in meaningful terms, the leaders who represent the central stream of the truly important functional groups of South Viet-Nam are not and have never been a part of the Communist-dominated National Liberation Front. This is not to say that they necessarily support the present government, although my own opinion is that Quat is an able man. But what is more important is that through the changes, travails, and uncertainties of months and years of warfare, they have not joined the Communist movement.

It is also essential to underline the fact that the successes of the Viet-Cong with the masses cannot be attributed to their nationalist or socio-economic appeals alone. I would not depreciate those appeals, nor their results in some quarters. I would, however, emphasize and reemphasize the fact that Communist strength in South Viet-Nam, as in many other areas, stems heavily from organizational skills. If one utilizes the full range of organizational techniques available today, creating a political movement based upon mass mobilization and effective organization, one has fashioned a powerful political force, especially when one works in a truly heterogeneous, nonorganized society. This does not necessarily mean, however, that because one has effective organizational control, one also has "public support." Anyone familiar with American big-city politics must understand this fact.

Organization is critical to success in Asia as elsewhere. Moreover, coercion is frequently involved quite as much as persuasion. How many village officials—good, bad and indifferent—have been killed by the Viet-Cong in recent years? Some estimates are six thousand. I have no doubt that some of these men were "bad," many of them "indifferent," and some of them "good." But the only question which the Viet-Cong asked was, "Do they support the Government or not?" If they did, they were finished.

To root out the local bases of power has been critical to the success of the Viet-Cong movement. Quite frankly, this application of terrorism has little to do with appeals based upon social or economic issues. I make these points because in my opinion, if the true allegiance of the people of South Viet-Nam could be thoroughly tested, it is very doubtful whether they would vote for the Viet-Cong.

Let us turn to the question of elections. On this point, the Geneva Agreement of 1954 troubles me greatly. I do not know of a single instance where a state controlled by the Communists was prepared to allow free elections. Quite frankly, moreover, I have seen nothing in recent announcements coming out of Hanoi to indicate that the North Vietnamese leaders are interested in such elections in the North. I have seen nothing to indicate that they would really share the mass media with opponents for the purpose of establishing a true dialogue, or that they would allow the creation of "class enemy" parties. I have seen nothing to indicate that the formula of "free elections," meaningful in the democratic context, can be meaningful in the Communist context.

If this is correct, was not the Geneva Agreement always fraudulent in this respect? Was it not fraudulent from the beginning to assume that free elections could be held in a society dominated by men who regard class enemies as susceptible to control by whatever means possible? Have there been any discussions of free elections throughout Korea, or Germany? In sum, I do not believe that we can afford to be unrealistic concerning the matter of elections in Viet-Nam. I do not think that we can return to a theory that somehow actions that contravene the most basic, sincere Marxist–Leninist principles are going to be the basis for a solution in Viet-Nam.

Next, let me make it clear that the Viet-Nam struggle has involved external commitments for a long time. One could cite, for example, Le Duan's statement of 1960 in which he exhorted the North Vietnamese to be "vital participants" in the movement in the South, not to be reluctant to take part in this "great revolutionary movement." That statement and many others antedate Peking's most recent pronouncements by five years. From numerous quotations, one can prove a strong commitment both from North Viet-Nam and from Peking to this war. It is more than a civil war, and it has always been more than a civil war.

Briefly, now, let me outline what has happened recently in North Viet-Nam, because this too is critical to an understanding of the Viet-Nam crisis. Beginning in late 1962 and extending into early 1963, the Lao Dong Party of North Viet-Nam underwent serious internal tensions. By the spring of 1963, the young, militant, pro-Chinese elements within the Party who generally acknowledge men like Truong Chinh as their leader had acquired predominant influence in the Central Committee and also in the Politburo.

These men had argued the case for greater militancy and increased involvement in the southern war; this was one critical issue in the internal debate. Beginning in the spring of 1963, the North Vietnamese Communist Party abandoned its stance of strict neutrality between Russia and China, moving toward a position of support for Peking on every "litmus paper" issue. On such questions as Cuba, Albania, Yugoslavia, and the critical issue of "modern revisionism," Hanoi now stood with Peking. In sum, the internal balance of power shifted in North Viet-Nam about two years ago, and in my opinion, this shift has greatly influenced the fact of increased Northern involvement in the South Vietnamese war.

There is some reason to believe that these issues have been reopened, perhaps partly because of the American bombings of the North. These bombings produced a new military—and political—situation. The Soviet Union alone could provide such sophisticated weaponry as ground-to-air missiles to meet American planes. Also, these bombings contravened the fervent militant thesis that the United States could not be provoked into large-scale action in Southeast Asia and that, therefore, further Northern involvement could take place without danger.

Such factors are, in my opinion, critical both to an analysis of developments in Hanoi and developments within the international Communist world. Once we had proven that the United States was not a paper tiger and that certain types of Communist actions could produce American reactions, we may very well have opened a whole new dialogue inside the Communist world, or at least, reoriented some of the forces involved.

When it comes to the basic issues that confront us today, Professor Schlesinger outlined these very well this morning. In theory, we are confronted with three broad alternatives: withdrawal, negotiations, or escalation. It seems to me clear that the arguments against American withdrawal are so powerful that they have not been answered, at least as yet. It is not merely that withdrawal would reduce American credibility with her allies and the neutrals around the world. It is also that a green light would be given to the new Communist-dominated National Liberation Movements even now getting underway.

I do not need to remind you that Peking has repeatedly broadcast its intent to support the Thai National Liberation Movement, and has already launched its first propaganda in this connection. Does this mean that the Thai people are seriously dissatisfied with their government? Is this really going to be an appeal to socio-economic issues? Can we assume that nationalist questions are really burning in the minds of either the Thai intellectuals or the Thai peasantry, and that this movement truly springs out of the indigenous source-springs of Thailand?

I see no evidence to that effect. I see problems in Thailand, as in all other parts of the emerging world. There are problems in the Northwest—with poverty and with the North Vietnamese minority. There are also ethnic problems in the Malayan border regions. However, I do not believe that anyone who is a specialist on this region would argue that Thailand is a logical spot for a National Liberation Movement from the standpoint of its indigenous problems. Indeed, the Thai peasant probably lives better than any other peasantry in Southeast Asia. In passing, one should also comment that until recently at least, the South Vietnamese peasant, despite all of his problems, undoubtedly lived better than his North Vietnamese counterpart. If socio-economic issues, therefore, were the truly critical question, some curious new analyses would be in order.

We cannot ignore the crucial element of power, and central to this, in my opinion, is the fact that for more than five years, Peking and Moscow have been arguing vigorously—with no holds barred—about the way in which to handle American imperialism. That argument, which has continued down to the present month, can be summarized as follows: American imperialism, asserts Peking, is a paper tiger. Maintain pressure and attack, and it will retreat. One must not submit to "nuclear blackmail." The problem with the Russians, argues Peking, is that they have been too sensitive to American power, too willing to compromise, and too reluctant to push the revolutionary movement forward.

American withdrawal from Viet-Nam would prove the Peking thesis correct, and make it virtually impossible for moderation to prevail within the Communist world. If the strategy of pushing America and forcing it into unilateral retreat works in Viet-Nam, it will work elsewhere and be tried everywhere.

I do not subscribe precisely to the "domino theory." It would be more appropriate to advance a "checkers theory." Peking will jump over states—and possibly even continents—if they can be "neutralized." She will move to those areas where she can combine the ingredients necessary for her revolutionary formula. But as long as she had the advantages of privileged sanctuaries both within her own territory and within those of her allies wherein to mobilize manpower and assemble equipment for their training and support, she had a strategy well-nigh foolproof. The assault upon Thailand is an instructive illustration of seizing upon an illogical base from which to start a revolution—except in terms of its geography and Peking's national interests.

Let me then move to the question of negotiations. I suspect that the overwhelming majority of individuals in this room, and listening to us, favor negotiations. The critical issue is who is willing to negotiate and upon what terms? Up to date—and we can certainly hope that this will change—the Chinese have indicated very little willingness to negotiate. They have refused U Thant's proposed visit to Peking, a visit which had our support. They have also declined all overtures of the British and

French—public and private. Their comments upon the recent proposal of the Indians for an Afro-Asian international force to operate in Viet-Nam was made in one word: "ridiculous." Their sabotage of the Cambodian Conference is well known. On the other hand, whatever may have been the qualms of the United States about coming to the conference table, we have explored and we have allowed our allies to explore all possibilities that seemed promising. We are still doing this, and we are still hoping that at least Hanoi will come forward, break its two-year old tie with Peking, and move into a new orbit of independence.

This last question bears upon the concept of Ho Chi Minh as a potential Vietnamese Tito. It seems to me that a powerful case can be developed against this thesis, granting certain strong points in its favor. As was noted this morning, Titoism developed in a given historical and geopolitical setting. Tito emerged quite literally between East and West. He also emerged as a result of certain deliberate, ruthless policies taken in the final days of the Stalinist era by the Russians.

There is no indication, incidentally, that Peking will make the same mistakes in this respect as did the Soviet Union. I would cite North Korea to you as an example of a state which has recently been extremely close to Peking and which the Chinese have treated very differently from the Russian method. The Peking approach is more subtle, with much less overt pressure applied against indigenous regimes than was the case with Moscow in the late 1940's.

Quite apart from this, however, the evolution of Ho Chi Minh and that of Tito have been very different. Ho and his Party have always had strong regional ambitions, and commitments to the Communist movements in Laos and Cambodia—indeed, to the movement throughout Southeast Asia. For a considerable period, Ho was Comintern agent for this entire area. There is no element of containment in the Vietnamese Communist movement as yet, even among the so-called "moderates."

Moreover, Ho Chi Minh himself is now 75 years of age, and his lifespan cannot be predicted—nor the man or men who will replace him. As noted earlier, young militants have been emerging in this movement who may well have strong pro-Chinese sentiments. And if Vietnamese communism contains significant regional, expansionist interests, it will need support. This support is most likely to come from China. Indeed, the whole history of Viet-Nam indicates that while there has periodically been stout resistance to Chinese control on the one hand, there has also been a powerful element of cooperation with China on the other, as the extensive Sinicization of North Vietnamese culture indicates so well.

This brings us to the central problem, namely, the question of containing China. I agree heartily with Professor Kahin when he speaks of the importance of generally aligning ourselves with Asian nationalism. I did feel that I detected some discrepancy in two themes which he presented: that the nationalist and Communist movements are by nature antithetical, and that they can be united. Both views, of course, are possible. Communism and nationalism can be united for certain purposes and periods of time, but in their purest forms, they are antithetical. It is certainly important to note that Asian communism has been closely connected with the Asian nationalist surge—it has generally been successful only where it has been able to capture or use the nationalist movement.

There is another side to this picture, however. North Korean communism, for instance, was implanted as a result of Soviet power. And I suggest that the power and pressures which Communist China is applying to the small neutralist Asian states at present, unless these are counteracted by some balance of power in this region, will result in increasing *anti-nationalist* trends, and satellite-type states. Observe what Peking did to Sihanouk in connection with the abortive Cambodian Conference. Look at the situation in Burma which, in my opinion, is by no means as good as Professor Kahin suggests. The Burmese government still has white and red flag Communist guerrillas fighting in the jungle, and Peking has given indications that it is very unhappy that the Communists have not been brought into the government.

If these small states are to survive, some balance of power must be established in Asia. Such a balance of power, if it is to be effective, must be a combination of both Western and Asian power; it must represent a true fusion. Thus, it is critical today that we interact more closely with such major Asian societies as Japan and India—and I would hope some day—Indonesia. These are the nations with which we can work in forwarding the social, economic and nationalist revolutions over time. The indications of recent years, however, are that if Communist power is allowed to operate unchecked in Asia, it will ultimately impose its own version of socio-economic revolution, its own sense of national interests upon other nations and peoples. Working with Asian nationalism requires a heterogeneous policy that accepts this fact among others.

What should our basic objective be? Our first goal should be a truly neutral, nonaligned Southeast Asia, not the type of "neutralism" advanced speciously by the Communists. We should seek to develop more Finlands and fewer Bulgarias in this region —more truly independent states and fewer satellites. This requires a balance of power, and certain international guarantees for the area, and both should be developed as quickly as possible.

Second, we should, of course, negotiate on the Viet-Nam issue when we can, but we should make it clear that we are not negotiating just with "leaders"—we are negotiating with men representing various defined groups. We should negotiate with the Viet-Cong in South Viet-Nam *as Communists,* and we should negotiate with other elements in terms of the groups they truly represent. It should be remembered that the Buddhists are the largest functional group in South Viet-Nam. They dwarf the Viet-Cong in numbers and supporters.

Lastly, we should develop a "two-channels policy" not only for the neutralists but for the Communists as well. On the one hand, we should urge socio-economic development, cultural exchange, and a general policy of peaceful coexistence. We should make it clear that we earnestly desire an exchange of scholars, journalists, and a program of economic development for all people, including the Chinese. At the same time, however, we should also make it clear that we will not surrender unconditionally in the face of force, that we will not be compelled to capitulate to a philosophy that regards compromise as evil. As long as we define and defend both of these channels, keeping them open and operative in an imaginative sense, we cannot fail, in the long run, to reach a solution to our problems.

I. F. STONE

International Law and the Tonkin Bay Incidents*

The American government and the American press have kept
the full truth about the Tonkin Bay incidents from the American
public. Let us begin with the retaliatory bombing raids on North
Viet-Nam. When I went to New York to cover the U.N. Security
Council debate on the affair, U.N. correspondents at lunch recalled cynically that four months earlier Adlai Stevenson told the
Security Council the U.S. had "repeatedly expressed" its em-
phatic disapproval "of retaliatory raids, wherever they occur and
by whomever they are committed." But none mentioned this in
their dispatches.

When Britain Staged Reprisals

On that occasion, last April, the complaint was brought by
Yemen against Britain. The British, in retaliation for attacks
from Yemen into the British protectorate of Aden, decided to
strike at the "privileged sanctuary" from which the raids were
coming. The debate then might have been a preview of the
Vietnamese affair. The British argued that their reprisal raid was
justified because the Fort they attacked at Harib was "a centre
for subversive and aggressive activities across the border." The
Yemeni Republicans in turn accused the British of supporting
raids into Yemen by the Yemeni Royalists. "Obviously," Stevenson said, "it is most difficult to determine precisely what has
been happening on the remote frontiers of southern Arabia." But
he thought all U.N. members could "join in expressing our disapproval of the use of force by either side as a means of solving
disputes, a principle that is enshrined in the Charter," especially
when such "attacks across borders" could "quickly escalate into
full-scale wars." The outcome was a resolution condemning "re-

---

* From *I. F. Stone's Weekly*, August 24, 1964.

prisals as incompatible with the purposes and principles of the United Nations." That resolution and Stevenson's words are as applicable to Southeast Asia as to southern Arabia. Though the Czech delegate cited them in his speech to the Council on August 7 about the Vietnamese affair, no word of this appeared in the papers next day.

In the August 7 debate, only Nationalist China and Britain supported the U.S. reprisal raids. The French privately recalled the international uproar over the raid they had made under similar circumstances in February, 1958, into the "privileged sanctuary" afforded the Algerian rebels by Tunisia. They struck at the Sakiet-Sidi-Youssef camp just across the border. Senators Kennedy, Humphrey, Morse, and Knowland denounced the raid and Eisenhower warned the French the U.S. would not be able to defend their action in the Security Council.

Reprisals in peacetime were supposed to have been outlawed by the League of Nations Covenant, the Kellogg Pact and the United Nations Charter. All of them pledged peaceful settlement of disputes. Between nations, as between men, reprisals are lynch law. Some White House ghost writer deserves a literary booby prize for the mindless jingle he turned out to defend ours in Viet-Nam. "The world remembers, the world must never forget," were the words he supplied for Johnson's speech at Syracuse, "that aggression unchallenged is aggression unleashed." This gem of prose is a pretty babble. What the world (and particularly the White House) needs to remember is that aggression is unleashed and escalated when one party to a dispute decides for itself who is guilty and how he is to be punished. This is what is happening in Cyprus, where we have been begging Greeks and Turks to desist from the murderous escalation of reprisal and counter-reprisal. Johnson practices in Southeast Asia what he deplores in the Mediterranean.

More Reprisal Raids Coming?

Public awareness of this is essential because the tide is running strongly toward more reprisal raids in the Far East. The first was the raid by U.S. Navy planes in June on Pathet-Lao headquarters in Laos in retaliation for shooting down two reconnaissance planes. We would not hesitate to shoot down reconnaissance planes over our own territory; such overflights are a clear violation of international law. But the U.S. now seems to operate on the principle that invasion of other people's skies is our right, and efforts to interfere with it (at least by weaker powers) punishable by reprisal. This is pure "might is right" doctrine.

The very day we took the Vietnamese affair to the Security Council, Cambodia illustrated a sardonic point to be found in Schwarzenberger's *Manual of International Law*—"military reprisals are open only to the strong against the weak." The U.N. distributed to Security Council members the latest in a series of complaints from Cambodia that U.S. and South Vietnamese forces had been violating its borders. It alleged that at dawn on July 31 "elements of the armed forces of the Republic of Viet-Nam, among them Americans in uniform," opened fire "with automatic weapons and mortars," seriously wounding a peasant and killing a bull. If Cambodia could only afford a fleet large enough, we suppose it would be justified by Johnsonian standards in lobbing a few shells into the U.S.A.

The Law We Applied at Nuremberg

Even in wartime, reprisals are supposed to be kept within narrow limits. Hackworth's *Digest,* the State Department's huge Talmud of international law, quotes an old War Department manual, *Rules of Land Warfare,* as authoritative on the subject. This says reprisals are never to be taken "merely for revenge" but "only as an unavoidable last resort" to "enforce the recognized rules of civilized warfare." Even then reprisals "should not be excessive or exceed the degree of violence committed by the enemy." These were the principles we applied at the Nuremberg trials. Our reprisal raids on North Viet-Nam hardly conformed to these standards. By our own account, in self-defense, we had already sunk three or four attacking torpedo boats in two incidents. In neither were our ships damaged nor any of our men hurt; indeed, one bullet imbedded in one destroyer hull is the only proof we have been able to muster that the second of the attacks even took place. To fly sixty-four bombing sorties in reprisal over four North Vietnamese bases and an oil depot, destroying or damaging twenty-five North Vietnamese PT boats, a

major part of that tiny navy, was hardly punishment to fit
the crime. What was our hurry? Why did we have to shoot from
the hip and then go to the Security Council? Who was Johnson
trying to impress? Ho Chi Minh? Or Barry Goldwater?

This is how it looks on the basis of our own public accounts.
It looks worse if one probes behind them. Here we come to the
questions raised by Morse of Oregon on the Senate floor August
5 and 6 during debate on the resolution giving Johnson a pre-
dated declaration of war in Southeast Asia. Morse was speaking
on the basis of information given in executive session by Secretaries Rusk and McNamara to a joint session of the Senate
Committee on Foreign Relations and Armed Services. Morse
said he was not justifying the attacks on U.S. ships in the Bay of
Tonkin but "as in domestic criminal law," he added, "crimes are
sometimes committed under provocation" and this "is taken into
account by a wise judge in imposing sentence."

Morse revealed that U.S. warships were on patrol in Tonkin
Bay nearby during the shelling of two islands off the North
Vietnamese coast on Friday, July 31, by South Vietnamese ves-
sels. Morse said our warships were within three to eleven miles of
North Vietnamese territory, at the time, although North Viet-
Nam claims a twelve-mile limit. Morse declared that the U.S.
"knew that the bombing was going to take place." He noted that
General Khanh had been demanding escalation of the war to the
North and said that with this shelling of the islands it was escalated. Morse declared the attack was made "by South Vietnamese naval vessels—not by junks but by armed vessels of
the PT boat type" given to South Viet-Nam as part of U.S.
military aid. Morse said it was not just another attempt to
infiltrate agents but "a well-thought-out military operation."
Morse charged that the presence of our warships in the proximity "where they could have given protection, if it became
necessary" was "bound to be looked upon by our enemies as an
act of provocation." The press, which dropped an Iron Curtain
weeks ago on the antiwar speeches of Morse and Gruening,
ignored this one, too.

Yet a reading of the debate will show that Fulbright and
Russell, the chairmen of the two committees Rusk and Mc-
Namara had briefed in secret session, did not deny Morse's facts
in their defense of the Administration and did not meet the

issue he raised. Fulbright's replies to questions were hardly a model of frankness. When Ellender of Louisiana asked him at whose request we were patrolling in the Bay of Tonkin, Fulbright replied:

These are international waters. Our assistance to South Viet-Nam is at the request of the South Vietnamese government. The particular measures we may take in connection with that request is our own responsibility.

Senator Nelson of Wisconsin wanted to know how close to the shore our ships had been patrolling:

MR. FULBRIGHT: It was testified that they went in at least eleven miles in order to show that we do not recognize a twelve-mile limit, which I believe North Viet-Nam has asserted.

MR. NELSON: The patrolling was for the purpose of demonstrating to the North Vietnamese that we did not recognize a twelve-mile limit?

MR. FULBRIGHT: That was one reason given. . . .

MR. NELSON: It would be mighty risky if Cuban PT boats were firing on Florida, for Russian armed ships or destroyers to be patrolling between us and Cuba, eleven miles out.

When Ellender asked whether our warships were there to protect the South Vietnamese vessels shelling the islands, Fulbright replied:

The ships were not assigned to protect anyone. They were conducting patrol duty. The question was asked specifically of the highest authority, the Secretary of Defense and the Secretary of State. They stated without equivocation that these ships, the *Maddox* and the *C. Turner Joy,* were not on convoy duty. They had no connection whatever with any Vietnamese ships that might have been operating in the same general area.

Fulbright did not deny that both destroyers were in the area at the time of the July 31 shelling and inside the territorial limits claimed by North Viet-Nam. He did not deny Morse's charge that the U.S. knew about the shelling of the islands before it took place. He merely denied that the warships were there to cover the operation in any way. Our warships, according to the official account, just happened to be hanging around. Morse's point—which neither Fulbright nor Russell challenged—was that they had no business to be in an area where an attack was about to take place, that this was bound to appear provocative. Indeed the only rational explanation for their presence at the time was that the Navy was looking for trouble, daring the North Vietnamese to do something about it.

Why Our Ships Moved Out to Sea

Morse made another disclosure. "I think I violate no privilege or secrecy," he declared, "if I say that subsequent to the bombing, and apparently because there was some concern about the intelligence that we were getting, our ships took out to sea." Was this intelligence that the ships were about to be attacked within the territorial waters claimed by North Viet-Nam? Morse said our warships went out to sea and "finally, on Sunday, the PT boats were close enough for the first engagement to take place." This dovetails with a curious answer given by Senator Russell at another point in the debate to Senator Scott of Pennsylvania when the latter asked whether Communist China had not published a series of warnings (as required by international law) against violations of the twelve-mile limit. Russell confirmed this but said, "I might add that our vessels had turned away from the North Vietnamese shore and were making for the middle of the gulf, *where there could be no question,* at the time they were attacked."

The italics are ours and call attention to an evident uneasiness about our legal position. The uneasiness is justified. A great many questions of international law are raised by the presence of our warships within an area claimed by another country as its territorial waters while its shores were being shelled by ships we supplied to a satellite power. There is, first of all, some doubt as to whether warships have a right of "innocent passage" through territorial waters even under peaceful circumstances. There is, secondly, the whole question of territorial limits. The three-mile limit was set some centuries ago by the range of a cannon shot. It has long been obsolete but is favored by nations with large navies. We make the three-mile limit the norm when it suits our purposes but widen it when we need to. We claim another nine miles as "contiguous waters" in which we can enforce our laws on foreign ships. While our planes on reconnaissance operate three miles off other people's shores, we enforce an Air Defense Identification Zone on our own coasts, requiring all planes to identify themselves when two hours out. In any case, defense actions may be taken beyond territorial limits. The law as cited in the U.S. Naval Academy's handbook, *International Law for Sea-Going Officers* is that "the right of a nation to protect itself from injury" is "not restrained to territorial limits . . . It may watch its coast and seize ships that are approaching it with an intention to violate its laws. It is not obliged to wait until the offense is consummated before it can act."

If the Cubans Shelled Key West

More important in this case is the doctrine of "hot pursuit." The North Vietnamese radio claims that in the first attack it chased the U.S. warships away from its shores. "The right of hot pursuit," says Schwarzenberger's *Manual of International Law,* "is the right to continue the pursuit of a ship from the territorial sea into the high sea." The logic of this, our Naval Academy handbook explains, is that "the offender should not go free simply because of the proximity of the high seas." It is easy to imagine how fully these questions would be aired if we spotted Russian ships hanging around in our waters while Cuban PT boats shelled Key West. Our actions hardly fit Johnson's description of himself to the American Bar Association as a champion of world law.

There are reasons to believe that the raids at the end of July marked a new step-up in the scale of South Vietnamese operations against the North. These have been going on for some time. In fact, a detailed account in *Le Monde* (August 7) says they began three years before the rebellion broke out in South Viet-Nam. Ever since January of this year the U.S. press has been full of reports that we were planning to move from infiltration and commando operations to overt attacks against the North. *Newsweek* (March 9) discussed a "Rostow Plan No. 6" for a naval blockade of Haiphong, North Viet-Nam's main port, to be followed by PT boat raids on North Vietnamese coastal installations and then by strategic bombing raids. In the middle of July the North Vietnamese radio reported that the U.S. had given South Viet-Nam five hundred "river landing ships" and four small warships from our mine-sweeping fleet. A dispatch from Hong Kong in the *New York Times* (August 14) quoted an "informed source" as saying that the North Vietnamese had concealed the fact "that the shelling of the islands" on July 31 "had been directed at a sensitive radar installation." The shelling of radar installations would look from the other side like a prelude to a landing attempt.

How the Public Is Brain-Washed

These circumstances cast a very different light on the *Maddox* affair, but very few Americans are aware of them. The process of brain-washing the public starts with off-the-record briefings for newspapermen in which all sorts of far-fetched theories are suggested to explain why the tiny North Vietnamese navy would be mad enough to venture an attack on the Seventh fleet, one of the world's most powerful. Everything is discussed except the possibility that the attack might have been provoked. In this case the "information agencies," i.e., the propaganda apparatus of the government, handed out two versions, one for domestic, the other for foreign consumption. The image created at home was that the U.S. had manfully hit back at an unprovoked attack—no paper tiger we. On the other hand, friendly foreign diplomats were told that the South Vietnamese had pulled a raid on the coast and we had been forced to back them up. As some of the truth began to trickle out, the information agencies fell back on the theory that maybe the North Vietnamese had "miscalculated." That our warships may have been providing cover for an escalation in raiding activities never got through to public consciousness at all.

The two attacks themselves are still shrouded in mystery. The *Maddox* claims to have fired three warning shots across the bow of her pursuers; three warning shots are used to make a merchantman heave-to for inspection. A warship would take this as the opening of fire, not as a warning signal. The North Vietnamese radio admitted the first encounter but claimed its patrol boats chased the *Maddox* out of territorial waters. The second alleged attack North Viet-Nam calls a fabrication. It is strange that though we claim three boats sunk, we picked up no flotsam and jetsam as proof from the wreckage. Nor have any pictures been provided. Whatever the true story, the second incident seems to have triggered off a long-planned attack of our own. There are some reasons to doubt that it was merely that "measured response" against PT bases it was advertised to be. Bernard Fall, author of *The Two Viet-Nams,* who knows the area well, pointed out in the Washington *Post* August 9 that "none of the targets attacked" in the reprisal raids "was previously known as a regular port or base area. Hon-Gay, for example, was one of the largest open-pit coal mining operations in Asia, if not the world." Was this one of the strategic industrial targets in Rostow's "Plan No. 6"?

JOSEPH KRAFT

A Way Out in Viet-Nam*

In the manuscript room of a half-ruined abbey a nineteenth-century English divine discovered an account of the Battle of Hastings as set down by a Saxon general. Harold's men, according to that account, had held their own, and were about to put the Normans to rout when William sued for peace. Harold delegated a team of political and diplomatic advisers to negotiate. These, in the course of the talks, sold out to William. And thus there took place the Norman Conquest.

I was reminded of that story, a cautionary tale told by Hilaire Belloc, on a recent trip to South Viet-Nam. Something there has obviously gone wrong. The United States pours into the country about $2 million a day. It has dispatched as military advisers to the Vietnamese government armies 20,000 crack troops, most of them officers. It has staffed its diplomatic aid and information missions with the cream of the American bureaucracy. Still, the Communist Viet-Cong holds most of the countryside and puts steady pressure on the government's shaky base in the cities. Optimists say that it would take five years of close fighting to

* From *Harper's,* December, 1964. Copyright 1964 by Harper's Magazine, Inc. Reprinted by permission of the author.

clear the country, but acknowledge that the government and its armies have neither the stomach nor the popular backing for such a campaign. The pessimists throw up their hands. "I feel," one American put it, "as though I was standing on the deck of the *Titanic.*"

In that atmosphere, self-justification and the foisting of blame upon others flourish on the grand scale. The civilians charge the soldiers with having no political sense, while the military claim that the diplomats cut the political ground from under their feet. The American Army and Air Force are in a perpetual wrangle; the regular bureaucrats and the area specialists are constantly at odds; the official establishment and the press are at all times hostile and suspicious. And, taken individually, their apologies and complaints are about as useful in explaining what went wrong as the tale of the beaten Saxon general. And about as believable.

But put them together, and there emerges a larger and more impersonal outline of the American failure. Basically what has happened is that the United States has been acting out of character in South Viet-Nam. To guide its efforts, this country has adopted a doctrine fit for the circumstances but unsuitable for the American military and inconsistent with the political instincts of the American government. A process is to blame, not a villain. And once the process is understood, it can be seen that the failure could have been much worse and that there still exists a way out.

The ruling doctrine, of course, is the famous doctrine of counterinsurgency. It was developed chiefly by the French in their long-drawn-out wars in Indochina and Algeria. Elements were added by the British in their pacification of Malaya. And the Americans had some prior experience as advisers to the Philippine government in its successful campaign against the Communist-dominated "Huks."

The point of departure for the doctrine lies in the theory that the Communists have developed a new kind of war—revolutionary war. Their object in these combats is to use semimilitary means for the accomplishment of a revolutionary end—the overthrow of an existing system and its social base. The aim is less to take territory and inflict casualties on enemy forces than to win over the population. The insurgents, as one well-worn phrase goes, must be to the people as "a fish is to water." To that end, the insurgents arm themselves with some popular cause—independence or social justice or land reform. They conduct ambushes and acts of terror and sabotage to undermine local authority. Generally, they move by night and in small units, away from the main population centers which are left to the authorities. Preferably, they hit and then run to a privileged sanctuary in jungle or mountain fastnesses or across a national border. Usually, the conflict is protracted, and the insurgents win less by overwhelming than by wearing down their enemies.

The sovereign prescription against revolutionary war is counterinsurgency warfare. As a first step, the defending forces, themselves moving in small, mobile units, apply military pressure to force the insurgents to disperse and hide. With the insurgents on the run, the next move is to cut contacts between the population and the guerrillas. The population is moved from exposed areas to easily defensible garrisons. All inhabitants are registered, given identity cards, and screened politically. Those found to be agents for the insurgents are imprisoned or sent off for "rehabilitation." The others are formed into paramilitary units for self-defense. A major effort is then made to remove the causes of popular unrest by elections and reform programs of civil action. The regular army becomes the "sons of the people." By these means, the tables are turned on the insurgents. The pacification campaign becomes what is called a "pro-people fight."

In the spring of 1961, after two years of unsuccessful conventional military resistance, counterinsurgency was accepted as the official American policy for winning in South Viet-Nam. The decision was made known in two widely publicized talks on guerrilla warfare—by the State Department's Counselor of Policy Planning, Walt Rostow, and by Roger Hilsman, who was then the Department's Director of Intelligence. That newest U.S. defense industry—the community of civilian strategists—jumped to the challenge. From their workshops flowed an extraordinary stream of books on revolutionary war, guerrilla tactics and strategy, counterinsurgency, the teachings of Mao Tse-tung and of the Cuban leader "Che" Guevara: fourteen of them were published by one house (Frederick A. Praeger) alone. Even before publication, the manuscripts were in use as texts for courses given at the military staff schools and the Foreign Service Institute. Almost overnight, talk of pacification campaigns, clear-

and-hold tactics, population control, paramilitary forces entered into the American military lexicon. Now even the greenest lieutenant in South Viet-Nam can recite on the need for the army to be to the people as a fish to water.

But if the doctrine flourished, the practice languished. For the theory ran against the fact of the whole American military and political tradition. And in countless encounters, habit and custom, as they always do, overcame the abstract ideal. Take, for example, the ideal of meeting the insurgents on their own ground in small, mobile units. It is easy to talk about. But the use of machines instead of manpower is something that runs close to the American bone. In line with that basic approach, the United States Army has been, for half a century at least, an army of big battalions, equipped with heavy weapons of enormous firepower requiring elaborate supply and service organizations to the rear. In keeping with that tradition, American military advisers back in 1954 organized the Vietnamese forces into a system of massive army corps which stretch down into divisions and regiments and companies.

Doctrine or no doctrine, that organization has never changed. The Vietnamese and their American advisers hardly ever move into battle in less than battalion strength. Wherever possible, planes and artillery are brought to bear in the fighting. Supporting these operations to the rear is a top-heavy staff. At one point, the American forces had a score of generals in Saigon—that is, one for every thousand officers and men. While the exact figure is not available, probably half the American military contingent is employed on staff work in the capital. The symbol of the whole operation is the main Saigon PX. It is a metropolitan department store with cigarettes, whiskey, clothing, books, tape recorders, cameras, records, furniture, tennis rackets, broilers, refrigerators, and all the other appurtenances of gracious living in the affluent society.

Thus organized and equipped, the government forces and their American advisers are inevitably set far apart from the population. Hardly any of the American advisers even speak the language; those with the closest contacts are usually moved after a year, in accord with an army rotation program for men serving away from their families. As to the Vietnamese army, far from being a collection of the "sons of the people," it has become something like a privileged caste. Its soldiers drive pell-mell through villages, taking food and roughing up the population. Its draft call, in some places anyway, is a mass kidnaping. Many of the leading generals have acquired private fortunes, and sent their children off to France for schooling and safety. A prominent Vietnamese Air Force general has been known to enter a bar with his retinue, run up a bill for more than $100 in food and drink, and then leave without paying the check. Sensing themselves to be a mercenary army, the Vietnamese forces, by the admission of their own commanders, are not keen to fight. And whenever there is fighting, the bombing of villages and the inevitable harm done to innocent civilians only widen the gap between the people and the military.

Because the gap is so great, political screening by the Army is a joke. Back in 1961 and 1962, true to the counterinsurgency doctrine, the Army regrouped much of the population in strategic hamlets, equipped with their own paramilitary defense units and supposedly under close military control. But in the weeks following the coup that unseated President Ngo Dinh Diem, perhaps a half to two-thirds of the hamlets fell apart. Under the very eyes of the Army and its advisers, they had been infiltrated by Viet-Cong agents. A similar incident took place several weeks ago among a group of tribesmen directly organized and equipped by American Special Forces to guard against Viet-Cong forays from across the Cambodian border. Even though the Americans were with them night and day in fixed camps, the tribesmen put together a highly organized revolt against the government, in which pro-Communist literature was distributed and at least a score of Vietnamese were murdered— before the rebellion was finally under control.

Typical of how little the American military have penetrated into the life around them is what happened at the time of the abortive *coup d'état* of last September 13. The coup was attempted by units of the Vietnamese Fourth Corps and Seventh Division stationed south of Saigon. As these units moved on the capital, their American advisers went with them. It was only when the troops reached the outskirts of the city that the Americans came to realize they were not embarked on a normal military operation.

In these circumstances, it is hard to say that the counterinsurgency campaign has failed. In sober truth it has not even been begun. Nor could it be. For the basic requirements of counterinsurgency—the operations conducted in remote corners by small units in close touch with the local population—go against the very nature of the American military establishment. There may be exceptions for small, specially trained elite units, but by and large American forces are no more fit for counterinsurgency than an elephant is suited to act like a mouse. Moreover, if the adjustment had been made, if the countryside had been pacified and control asserted over the population, matters would almost certainly have been worse. For the American government has proved no more capable of meeting the political requirements of counterinsurgency than the American soldiers have been able to perform its security tasks.

The essential political requirement is a popular regime. But for that purpose it is not enough to have good slogans, millions of dollars in aid, and hearts pure of colonial intent. In any area where revolutionary war has really taken hold, there is required a basic change in regime, a turn of the wheel that ousts the old governors and puts new masters in their place.

But the United States government has no mechanism, no rationale even, for making such choices. It has no system for distinguishing the party or class or clique it wants to back in power. Unlike the Russians, who normally favor the local Communists, or the British and French, who tend to support their trading partners, Americans are neutral and color-blind when it comes to picking and choosing among competing foreign claimants for support. Except in the case of Communist regimes, or when authority is usurped by one agency or another, the American way is to accept the status quo, scrubbing it up a little with land reforms. The prevailing neutrality of the American approach is one reason that military and intelligence agencies have so much weight in U.S. Missions abroad. Even if these agencies have no special political bias, they work with, and tend to favor, their opposite numbers in foreign governments. Within the context of the normal American mission, they are, thus, one-eyed men in the kingdom of the blind.

In South Viet-Nam, the bent toward the status quo meant that the U.S. backed the continued supremacy of the Catholic minority, which had initially been made top dog by the French colonial system and which was confirmed in that role under the regime of President Diem. It is true that, in the fall of 1962, Washington flashed signs that encouraged the top Vietnamese generals to overthrow Diem. But the signs came only after the corruption, weakness, and ineffectiveness of the regime had been made scandalously clear. Even to reach that decision inside the American government took almost superhuman efforts on the part of a tiny, well-placed group of officials that happened to have the ear of the President.

And once the change at the top was accomplished, the American effort was exhausted. Instead of pressing for a new regime, with a voice for the Buddhist majority and a place for the students and the younger officers, the Americans accepted the old regime plus the first strong man to come along, General Minh. When he proved not strong enough, they then accepted the old regime plus the second strong man to come along, General Khanh. And ever since, they have been throwing their weight into the scales to preserve a semblance of legitimacy.

Given the political failure, the military failure is almost a blessing. For if the military phase of the counterinsurgency program had succeeded, the American Army would have had the sensation of having defeated the enemy. It would have taken on the missionary zeal of the doers of good works. It would have knitted up infinite commitments and loyalties to local leaders and communities. It would thus have become attached beyond untangling to what at bottom remained an unworkable government.

As it is, there is no such attachment, and a way out presents itself. The escape hatch lies in encouraging a combination of Buddhist leaders and younger officers to take over the government. Almost certainly they would move to negotiate a local peace with the Viet-Cong. Probably, such an arrangement would in time bring the Communists into the Saigon government. It would also mean the withdrawal of the American military mission, though not necessarily the end of the American presence. But the American purpose has never been to keep Communists out of the Saigon government, still less to keep its own forces on the ground. The purpose has been to provide a barrier against the extension of Chinese power, and the collapse of other regimes in Southeast Asia that would follow a Chinese take-over.

Within the context of a localized peace negotiation, that purpose can still be served. It is not clear that the Viet-Cong will necessarily dominate a coalition government; it is at least possible that with peace on their side, the Buddhists and Army can draw support away from the Communists and contain them within a government. Even if the Viet-Cong does come to dominate the Saigon government, moreover, it need not necessarily be an extension of Ho Chi Minh's Communist regime in North Viet-Nam; there is sufficient bad blood between North and South to make possible a long-term divorce. Finally, even if Hanoi does come to dominate Saigon, it is not written in the stars that Peking has to dominate Hanoi. On the contrary, there is a possibility for a revisionist regime, Communist-dominated, but with lines to Moscow rather than Peking.

None of these settlements, of course, would be perfect, or even without serious risks. But neither would the United States be powerless to influence events. It could apply military pressure to Hanoi and Peking. It could bring to bear its weight in the United Nations and in its standing with the Soviet Union. For once the purpose is to make a safe peace rather than to win an impossible war, the United States can begin to play a useful role. It can at last stop acting like an elephant trying to be a mouse.

GARY PORTER

Globalism—The Ideology of Total World Involvement

Americans are well aware of the fact that their nation has shifted from a foreign policy of isolationism to one of deep involvement since the last world war. They are aware that the United States is, in military capacity and economic potential, the greatest power in the world. But it is too little understood that the alliances, the aid programs, and the military presence of the United

States are all justified by what can only be termed a revolutionary ideology in foreign policy.

Walter Lippmann referred to this ideology as "globalism," but the word does not convey the full meaning of the idea. It is not the global extent of U.S. foreign policy which is revolutionary, but the depth of involvement and the radical objective on which that involvement is based. Undersecretary of State George Ball, in a Department of State publication released in November, 1964, perhaps more accurately labeled the concept "total world involvement" and summarized our role as one of "world responsibility divorced from territorial or narrow national interest." The new conception of national interest, according to Ball, cannot be expressed "in terms of defense of bits and pieces of real estate with which we enjoy a special relation." W. W. Rostow declares that we must go beyond "conventional national interest" to build an "orderly world community."

This orderly world community, as envisioned in the new concept of globalism, was described by Secretary of State Dean Rusk (in an address on March 4, 1965) as

a world of independent national states, each with its own institutions, co-operating with other nations to further their mutual welfare, a peaceful world, a world increasingly responsible to the rule of law, a world in which all human beings enjoy their natural rights, regardless of nationality or creed or color, and a world in which all can share in the abundance which modern science and technology make possible.

The salient feature of the globalist ideology is the abandonment of the traditional idea of definable and limited national interest, and its replacement by the idea of world order is not presented as something for the distant future, but as something to which American power and prestige are to be committed here and now. Deputy Assistant Secretary of State Leonard Unger expressed the opinion that the old and honored conception of spheres of influence is "out of keeping with the kind of peaceful world that must come into being in the next generation." And Dr. Rostow, in a panel discussion at the national teach-in, spoke of the U.S. hope for world order "perhaps in the next generation."

President Johnson himself emphasized the immediacy of the

purpose at Johns Hopkins University, when he talked about the dream of our generation: "It is a very old dream but we have the power and now the opportunity to make that dream come true. For centuries nations have struggled among each other. But we dream of a world where disputes are settled by law and reason. And we will try to make it so."

Never has a more expansive and idealistic goal been declared for the foreign policy of any nation—not even by the Communist globalists. If the President's rhetoric means anything at all, it means that the United States, leading a coalition of free nations, considers itself powerful enough to bring an end to the violence of international life once and for all.

Secretary of State Rusk recently identified U.S. objectives with the "purposes and principles of the United Nations Charter" and said that these purposes and principles must "at least animate enough states with enough will and enough resources to see to it that others do not violate these rules with impunity." The unavoidable implication is that it is the will and the resources of the United States which must be central to the task.

And the attainment of this orderly world community will follow upon the abolition of the ancient legal and political problem of aggression. Rusk has warned that the elimination of aggression is absolutely necessary "if freedom is to survive on this small planet" and even "if mankind is to survive."

According to the new theory of globalism, the objective of ending aggression once and for all has been prosecuted successfully on the levels of nuclear attack and conventional attack. Having made it clear that neither nuclear nor conventional attack can succeed, we now need only solve the problem of what Secretary Rusk calls "illegal support for so-called wars of liberation" to complete the grand purpose of making the world pacific. "Once we remove this kind of aggression," Secretary Rusk recently wrote, "as we are trying to do in Viet-Nam, the human race can perhaps look forward to peace, to the solutions of lesser problems, and to the benefits deriving from the conquests of science."

The identification of U.S. globalism with the purposes of the United Nations suggests a transcendence of mere national interest. But the reverse is equally true: the interests of the United States have now become universal and can be satisfied in theory only by the absence of any threat to world order. The Chief of Staff of the Army, General Harold K. Johnson, declared earlier this year, "the moment that freedom is eroded, I thing that we have a chink in our own security." And Secretary Rusk puts it very simply: "We have a deep national interest in peace, the prevention of aggression, the faithful performance of agreements. the growth of international law."

In an interview this year, Ambassador Henry Cabot Lodge said the U.S. might be justified in staying in Viet-Nam even if a Saigon government asked us to leave. Asked if this meant that "we have a right to be there in the interest of world peace," he answered that our withdrawal would have "world consequence and would certainly shake our position in Berlin."

Thus our self-delegated global responsibility has not only erased the distinction once maintained between those interests which were vital to us and those which were peripheral; it has also broken down the old limits of U.S. interventionary power.

This dedication to global responsibility presumes that there exists an elementary commonality of interest among all decent nations—a kind of "general will" which the United States, as the global power, unequivocally and unfailingly recognizes, and identifies by the term "free-world interests."

Mr. Ball points out that the consequences of the irresponsible actions of smaller nations are limited. "But," he adds, "for America to act in the same fashion would produce consequences on a giant scale that could seriously endanger free-world interests." Thus the views of those nations in the free world that differ from ours on specific issues may be dismissed *a priori* as irresponsible, because these nations have not in fact accepted the responsibility for maintaining the interests of the free world.

The nations of Western Europe lack "a sense of world involvement," according to Mr. Ball, because they have a psychological problem. The answer is to be found in the size and resources of these countries as compared with the United States. He concludes that the epic developments of the postwar world have "created a new concept of scale in world affairs" which make it "necessary for nations to command vast resources if they are to play a major world role." World responsibility, Mr. Ball concludes, "may, in today's world, be possible . . . only for nations such as the United States which command resources on a scale adequate to the requirements for leadership in the twentieth century."

The globalist ideology, in short, replaces specific and limited national interest with generalized and universal national interest; it promises an orderly world community once the immediate problem of aggression has been eliminated; it tends to presume that the global role of the U.S. uniquely qualifies its government to discern the true interests of the free world. And finally, it explains the failure of other free-world allies to play such a global role as a function of their lack of the requisite size and scale.

Secretary of State Rusk told an audience of former Peace Corps volunteers, in complete sincerity, that we must "revisit Lord Acton." He is convinced, he said, that the United States has not been corrupted by the great power which she has amassed, since it has been used only in pursuit of the "simple and decent" objectives of the American people.

To imagine that "power corrupts" by making men suddenly wicked and malicious is to miss the point. It corrupts in much subtler ways: by creating pressures for the use of the power which is available, by increasingly expanding a nation's legitimate security needs, and by becoming the object of pride and prestige. It clearly lays the ideological foundation for American intervention in the affairs of others nations whenever America unilaterally decides to commit U.S. military power in order to forestall communism.

Globalism is most deeply at issue in Viet-Nam. There the "responsibility" of the United States is explained in terms of the U.S. confrontation with Chinese-sponsored revolutionary militance, which is seen as the real source of international disorder in the future.

The falling-domino theory in Southeast Asia has been replaced by what has been called the "test-case theory," which solemnly accepts as truth all the Chinese propaganda about Viet-Nam and the future of wars of national liberation: that the success or failure of the Viet-Cong campaign in Viet-Nam will determine the success or failure of Communist insurgency in Venezuela.

The defense of Viet-Nam—or more precisely, the denial of Viet-Nam—thus becomes a vital interest, not because of its intrinsic relationship to U.S. security, but because it is thought to be a symbolic meeting place of the tides of history. Any retreat from a commitment, though given conditionally and outside any formal treaty, will be taken, according to this argument, as a sign that the tide in the world has fundamentally turned.

To understand why U.S. officials have so readily accepted the Chinese Communist thesis that this is a test case, it is necessary to remember the other side of the coin, which is that with firmness the U.S. can deal a crippling blow to the Communist aggression in Viet-Nam and, by extension, discourage Communist uprisings around the world.

The belief that world order awaits only an American success in this one test case rests on the simplistic belief that disruptions of the peace are merely the result of a monolithic evil design which can be ended once the would-be aggressors learn that "aggression does not pay." But it is the height of folly to assume that the mere presence of the Marines will deter unrest and revolutionary movements.

There is an air of unreality to the notion of putting an end to aggression. There will continue to be a variety of aggressions with varying shades of Communist participation. If the millennium marked by the absence of aggressive behavior by states is ever to come, it will come about through the slow evolution of all states to the point where they have an interest in the status quo. It is beyond the capacity of any state—even the United States—to make this happen. There are obviously some things which can be done to encourage it, but they are all in the constructive areas of aid, trade, and diplomacy. The struggle in Viet-Nam may be a test of many things, but it will certainly not determine whether international aggression is to continue or cease.

BERNARD B. FALL

Viet-Nam—The Agonizing Reappraisal*

The military "kill" becomes the primary target—simply because the essential political target is too elusive for us, or worse, because we do not understand its importance. . . . The Communist challenge in Southeast Asia has yet to be faced on its real terrain: that of ideas, policies and down-to-earth effective administration. . . . North Viet-Nam is likely to be a tough and determined "adversary-by-proxy" in what can in all honesty be called "The Second Indochina War."

The above lines are taken from this writer's *Current History* article of November, 1962, written and researched in the late summer of that year; fifteen months before the overthrow of the Ngo Dinh Diem regime (and the murder of the latter) on November 2, 1963.

More than one year later, nothing has happened that would in any way tend to modify that estimate. The disintegration of South Vietnamese society, precipitated by the Diem regime's dictatorial policies but carefully plastered over until its demise, has now come into the open and manifests itself in student riots, government paralysis at most levels and in many areas, Buddhist demonstrations, and war-weariness among many South Vietnamese Army (A.R.V.N.) units. Pro-government successes may still be best measured in "kills"—23,500 for the year 1963[1] —rather than in provinces or districts made safe for unfettered local elections or for effective economic improvement.[2]

---

* From *Current History,* February, 1965. © 1965 by Current History, Inc.
[1] Military Advisory Command, Viet-Nam (M.A.C.V.), *The Observer* [weekly], March 21, 1964. The same source credits 7,500 of those kills to fixed-wing aircraft.
[2] While this is totally forgotten today, local elections took place in war-torn non-Communist Viet-Nam in January and June, 1953. The 3,650 elected town councilors were (predictably) anti-French in their majority, a few even were open "neutralists," and one successful candidate—in Saigon—was a Trotskyite Marxist. But it was felt in Saigon that the gain in representativeness was worth the gamble. The by then hopeless military situation prevented further exploitation of that initial gain.

The "Strategic Hamlet" program, launched with great fanfare in March, 1962, and designed (in slavish imitation of a Malayan pattern totally inapplicable to Vietnamese conditions) to protect the villagers and their chiefs from Communist control, was a shambles by the time Diem died, although that truth had been hidden from the outside world, and in part probably from Diem as well. Probably one of the few side benefits of Diem's demise was that it set in motion a reassessment of Viet-Nam's internal situation and occasioned a series of brutally frank studies (most of which are still unavailable to the public), which showed clearly how badly the situation had deteriorated. Of the 8,500-odd strategic hamlets—now rebaptized "New Life Hamlets"—officially declared to be in existence, less than 1,500 were viable. . . . The result was that a joint American-Vietnamese report of January, 1964, openly stated that "the war cannot be won unless immediate reforms are made at the village level."[3] At year's end, no reforms had been undertaken. . . .

It should be obvious by now that in the present state of affairs in South Viet-Nam, *everything* is Communist-infiltrated. In 1951, Bishop of Saigon Chassaigne had to dissolve the *Sao-Mai* Boy Scout units of the Saigon area, because they were Communist-infiltrated. In the kind of fratricidal war being fought in Viet-Nam, even family bonds prove little: Buddhist leaders Tam Chau or Tri Quang may have brothers in North Viet-Nam; but so have Generals Duong Van Minh and Nguyen Khanh. And it was Madame Ngo Dinh Nhu who proudly admitted, three months after her husband had been murdered along with Diem, that he had indeed contacted Viet-Cong leaders and was undertaking negotiations, allegedly for their surrender.[4]

As for the Buddhists of Viet-Nam, it would be totally futile to argue in detail with those who hold the view that the Buddhists are the sole channel of Communist infiltration in South Viet-Nam.[5] In the case of Viet-Nam's "Buddhists,"[6] persecution

---

[3] *The Saigon Post,* January 20, 1964.
[4] *Le Nouveau Candide,* Paris, February 13, 1964.
[5] See Marguerite Higgins, "Ugly Americans of Vietnam," in *America* [a Jesuit weekly], October 3, 1964; or *Time,* December 11, 1964.
[6] "Buddhists" in Viet-Nam include all the Confucianists, ancestor-worshippers, Cao-Dai and Hoa-Hao sect members who do not explicitly reject Buddha, as do the Catholic, Protestant, and Muslim minorities in Viet-Nam.

was *real,* but it was not new, nor, for that matter, one-sided. The myth of Vietnamese religious tolerance, sedulously built up by the Diem regime and some of its foreign admirers, does not stand serious examination. One of the most compelling reasons for French intervention in Viet-Nam in 1845–47 was precisely that the Vietnamese emperors, Thieu-Tri and Tu-Duc, were engaging in wholesale massacres of Vietnamese Catholics. An American Catholic source averred that "in the persecutions of the last century, tiny Viet-Nam had 100,000 martyrs, far above any single nation's quota [sic] since the early Roman persecutions."[7] Independent Vietnamese and French sources confirm this. Under the French, the pendulum swung the other way and kept on swinging that way under Diem.

As early as 1952, Vietnamese sources began to complain that French-armed Catholic militia forces, rather than fighting the Communists, preferred to use their weapons to "plunder pagodas, demolish temples, and convert by force the population."[8] And exactly nine years later, in July, 1961, a Western observer, though sympathetic to the Diem regime, was to report that an A.R.V.N. military operation failed to capture Communist insurgents but, in the process, destroyed rural villages in Tra Vinh province of the Mekong Delta:

> The following month, after the army had retired leaving thousands of unhappy peasants behind it, Buddhist bonzes petitioned the province chief in Tra Vinh against the shelling of hamlets and pagodas and to demand the release of their imprisoned fellows. Some months later their leader, Superior Bonze Son Vong, appeared on the lists of the central committee of the Viet-Cong's National Liberation Front.[9]

That case, from personal observation, was not unique; and discrimination in favor of Catholics throughout the Diem administration was sufficiently widespread for *Informations Catholiques Internationales* to devote almost a whole issue to it (and to its long-range danger for the Vietnamese Catholic community) *before* the outbreak of the Buddhist demonstrations

---

7 *Catholic Digest,* February, 1962, p. 17.
8 Van Thanh, "L'auto-défense des villages: Base de la pacification du Nord-Viet-Nam," *Orient-Occident,* Paris, November, 1952, p. 19.
9 Denis Warner, *The Last Confucian.* London: Penguin Books, 1964, p. 153.

in Viet-Nam.[10] All that did not prevent the departing American ambassador, Frederick E. Nolting, from declaring, as he left Saigon in the summer of 1963, that he had never seen "any evidence" of anti-Buddhist persecution while in Viet-Nam.

In sum, the religious tensions which rack South Viet-Nam in 1964–65 are not new, nor directly ascribable to some particularly evil phenomenon. Rather than being the *cause* of South Viet-Nam's internal malaise, Buddhist obstreperousness is a clear *symptom* of disintegration of the South Vietnamese social fabric. . . .

Another part of the Diem legacy that might well have contributed to the demise of non-Communist South Viet-Nam was the problem of the mountain tribal minorities, or *montagnards*. Here also, unwillingness to see that the Diem regime practiced discrimination on a large scale led at least one unabashed but vocal admirer of the past regime to aver that Ngo Dinh Diem was "the man who has both a greater knowledge of and a deeper concern for the [tribal] minorities than any other person in Viet-Nam."

The actual facts showed otherwise. American scholars in the field, notably Professors Gerald C. Hickey and Frederic Wickert, pointed out as early as 1957 that the *montagnards* were bitterly dissatisfied with the Vietnamese government's policies of forced assimilation of the minorities in the guise of "equality" and with the colonization of the hill areas by lowlanders.[11] . . .

Again, warnings were disregarded. The program of the "Liberation Front" (NLFSV) of December, 1960, contained specific promises of autonomy. A *montagnard,* Y Bih Aléo, was made a member of the NLFSV's central committee. A captured Viet-Cong document[12] gave detailed instructions in early 1963 on NLFSV operations designed to attract a greater following among the mountain tribesmen. And on August 1, 1964, the latter formed a *Front Unifié de Lutte pour la Race Opprimée* (FULRO) [United Front for Struggle of the Oppressed Race];

[10] No. 188, Paris, March 15, 1963.
[11] Bernard Fall, "Who's Who in Viet-Nam," *New Republic,* October 17, 1964.
[12] *VCD-22,* unclassified translation of captured document, USIS Saigon, 15 pp., n.d. See also the lead article in *Liberation Press,* No. 12, October 25, 1962 [an English-language bulletin published by the NLFSV], by Y Bih Aléo.

which, significantly, stated that tribesmen are "dying every day under the thrusts of the Viet-Cong" while [General] "Nguyen-Khanh and his servants are incapable of guaranteeing our life and our freedom and also make use of any pretext to suppress and mistreat us."

It was FULRO which, on September 20, 1964, led to the rebellion of Rhadé (also called Edé) tribesmen against both their United States Special Forces advisers and their A.RV.N. superiors and to their temporary occupation of parts of the hill area capital of Ban Mé Thuot and its radio transmitter. In their proclamation, the tribesmen again accused both Vietnamese regimes as bent on their destruction, although their appeal also spoke of the "warmaking SEATO bloc" and other favorite Communist shibboleths. When the rebellion was contained a week later through a combination of South Vietnamese force and U.S. Special Forces patience and understanding, it was still unclear (as in the case of the Buddhists) how much of this rebellion had been manufactured by the NLFSV and how much was genuine resentment of lowland Vietnamese interference with the tribes.[13] The tribesmen also addressed an appeal to the De-colonization Committee of the United Nations. In view of the importance of the area they occupy in Viet-Nam, victory—or even a successful stalemate—in South Viet-Nam would be as impossible without the co-operation of the *montagnards* as it would be without that of the peasants of the Mekong Delta.

Clearly, a heavy legacy was left by the Diem regime to its successors. Its worst shortcomings are precisely *not* in the largely irrelevant conventional military field, but in what it did (or what it allowed to happen) to relations between parts of the Vietnamese population by its constant playing-off of one group against another: refugees vs. indigenous South Vietnamese; *montagnards* vs. low-landers; Buddhists vs. Catholics; pro-French vs. pro-Americans; the army vs. the civilians; the peasantry vs. the city dwellers. These wounds, deeply embedded in the society, prove harder to heal than military losses.

This may at times be difficult to understand for people to whom "stability" seems to be the only yardstick of government

---

[13] Howard Sochurek, "American Special Forces in Action in Vietnam," *The National Geographic,* January, 1965.

effectiveness[14]—they apparently forget that the world recently has seen several "stable" governments disappear overnight, from Batista's in Cuba to Khrushchev's in Moscow. These same observers would do well to remember that it was the Vietnamese *army* (not the Buddhists or the students) who tried to murder Diem twice before, in November, 1960, and February, 1962, before it finally succeeded in overthrowing his regime in November, 1963. There is perhaps no grimmer evidence of the loss of control which had already overtaken the Diem regime in March to May, 1963 (i.e., *before* the Buddhist clashes), than the map below, based on official documentation,[15] indicating the extent of Communist tax collections throughout South Viet-Nam. In all but three provinces, the Viet-Cong was collecting taxes of some kind or another; and in twenty-seven provinces Communist taxation proceeded on a formalized basis, with bond issues, tax tables and proper receipts.

While it is always risky to state a case on the basis of might-have-beens, the realities of the situation on the ground inside South Viet-Nam, even six months before Diem's overthrow, indicate that an even more brutal collapse of South Viet-Nam might well have occurred had the regime survived the November, 1963, coup. The A.R.V.N. might have split for good into loyal and disloyal elements, and Ngo Dinh Nhu (as his wife asserted in the above-mentioned article) might have negotiated both his brother and South Viet-Nam into neutralism; or, failing this, might well have joined the rebels with his own Republican Youth movement transformed into *maquis* forces. Those who might reject such a possibility would do well to ponder the example of the American-trained and American-advised Kong-Lê forces in Laos: overnight they smashed the United States-backed right-wing regime and later joined the Pathet-Lao pro-Communist forces in an alliance that lasted just long enough to destroy all erstwhile American hopes for a right-wing Laotian regime.[16] In

[14] Joseph Alsop, "Kings Log and Stork," Washington *Post*, December 16, 1964.
[15] U.S. Operations Mission, Saigon, *Resources Control Survey*—Viet-Nam, June 14, 1963, declassified January 1, 1964. The same survey also indicated that control measures were noneffective or nonexistent in sixteen provinces; and only six were rated as "acceptably effective."
[16] See Arthur Dommen's recent book, *Conflict in Laos*. New York, 1964.

NORTH VIET NAM

Demarcation Line

LAOS

THAILAND

Da Nang

15°

CAMBODIA

SOUTH CHINA SEA

Saigon

10°

GULF OF SIAM

REPUBLIC OF VIET-NAM

Areas taxed by Viet-Cong   March-May 1963

MILES
0   100

105°

South Viet-Nam there are ample amounts of civilian and military candidates for a "Kong-Lê gambit."

Throughout 1964, the situation inside South Viet-Nam worsened considerably by every yardstick of insurgency measurement, from actual battle casualties to tonnage of rice not falling into Viet-Cong hands; from the size of the enemy units to the desertion rate of the A.R.V.N. forces; from the reduction of United States advisory forces promised in October, 1963, to the steady increase of American reinforcements until the 25,000-men mark was probably reached by early 1965. The losses of village officials through assassination, which had reached a peak rate of 4,000 a year in 1960–61, had reached the figure of 429 killed and 482 abducted between January 1 and November 15, 1964; i.e., ran at a rate of about 1,000 a year. The cumulative loss of such officials since the beginning of the insurgency in 1957 in all likelihood is now in excess of 15,000—or almost one per village.[17]

That makes the chances of a liquidation of the insurgency through simple military repression, as in the case of the Mau-Mau in Kenya, somewhat dubious. The recognition of this fact is by now almost unanimous. Yet it has brought about two exactly opposite viewpoints on how to terminate the Second Indochina War. One side, mostly on the liberal end of the spectrum, urges a rapid disengagement of the United States from the conflict;[18] while the other extreme argues for a heavier involvement, culminating—if need be—in a full-scale Korean-type ground war in North Viet-Nam.[19] An even more extreme view holds that the Viet-Nam affair could be transformed into a "golden opportunity" to "solve" the Red Chinese problem as well, possibly by a pan-Asian "crusade" involving Chinese Nationalist, Korean, and Japanese troops, backed up by United States power as needed.

Other "options" or suboptions have cropped up in recent months and have no doubt been entertained at various govern-

---

[17] Jack Foisie, in Los Angeles *Times,* November 16, 1964. The same newspaper, over the signature of Ed Meagher, reported on July 26 that "the Viet-Cong guerrillas have lost the initiative. . . ."
[18] SANE, "Southeast Asia and Vietnam," press release of October 16, 1964 [2 p., mimeog.].
[19] William Beecher, "U.S. Readies Data Could Serve To Justify 'Escalating' War on Reds," *Wall Street Journal,* November 18, 1964.

ment levels with varying degrees of success, or have been discussed in the press. In most cases, however, the arguments
failed to take into account some of the obvious difficulties
inherent in the military aspects of such an escalation; almost
none hinted at the price that would be exacted in blood, treasure
or worldwide political complications for the implementation of
any one of the options offered.

To "play through" the full set of options would be tantamount to attempting to define the total number of color, trim,
powerplant and body variations in which a major car model is
available. . . . Hence the series presented below is merely for
reference, and does not pretend to be exhaustive.

1. *"Walking away."* The option of simply and purely abandoning South Viet-Nam to its fate is hardly ever openly considered, although several nations have availed themselves of that
exit in recent years: Britain walked out of Greece and Palestine;
the United States out of mainland China; and the French out of
Guinea. In Greece, another power (the United States) stepped
into the vacuum; in Palestine, the Israelis survived; in Guinea,
the lesson proved to have no major consequences and perhaps
did keep the other French-African states in line for a time; and
in China it proved disastrous. What would happen in South
Viet-Nam is obvious.

2. *Negotiating "Out."* The liberal view points to several such
instances which did not produce major disasters or simply consolidate an already-compromised solution: Lebanon or Laos,
for example. The opposite view argues that to negotiate from the
basis of an immediate cease-fire in the field would leave the
Viet-Cong in control of about 70 per cent of the Vietnamese
countryside and, hence, in ultimate control of all Viet-Nam. It
further argues that such a negotiation would have a snowballing
"domino effect" on other countries in the path of Communist
subversion. The counterargument is that in Europe, the fall of
Czechoslovakia, Budapest and the building of the Berlin Wall
increased the West's determination to withstand Communist
pressure.

3. *Negotiating while fighting on.* This is rarely envisaged, although such a situation was faced for more than two years by
the United States in Korea, for more than four years by the
French in Algeria, and for three years by the British in Cyprus.

One respected observer reported the following Vietnamese view from Saigon, expressed in December, 1963:

> When General Minh [the then junta leader] tells us that we must fight on until final victory, nobody follows him because everybody knows that [victory] is impossible. But if you tell the Vietnamese that they must fight to restore the situation before making peace, you will see that they will go along with it.[20]

Whether this held true eighteen months later would be hard to assess. But the Korean precedent tends to show that "negotiation" as a concept did not diminish the combativeness of the Korean troops.

4. *"Diplomatic judo."* Judo is the art of defeating one's enemy by making use of leverage gained from his own body weight. In the case of South Viet-Nam's adversary-by-proxy, that weight is its justified fear of a conjugation of United States and Red Chinese pressure. That is, any sizeable American action against North Viet-Nam would no doubt bring about a Red Chinese reaction *à la* Korea; e.g., a pre-emptive occupation by Chinese forces of North Viet-Nam.

It is hardly likely that such a possibility is viewed with favor by the older North Vietnamese leadership. It did not fight against the French for thirty years and against the United States for ten years merely to become a Chinese satrapy and a battleground for a Sino-American military contest.[21]

5. *Fight on under the "ground rules."* That covers the present policy, with a variety of "escalatory" variations, involving sealing off South Viet-Nam's boundaries; the introduction of high-performance weapons; and, ultimately, of United States and other allied ground troops as combatants. The purpose of the exercise would be to gain time until the essential civilian counter-insurgency measures begin to take hold. Such tactics worked successfully in such cases as Malaya and the Philippines. They failed in Algeria (in spite of the real military successes of the French), in Cyprus and in Palestine, among many others. In either case, they bring on extremely long-lasting wars, with a

---

[20] Max Clos, "Le Viet-Nam après Diem," *Le Figaro,* December 24, 1963.
[21] For a detailed discussion of that point, see Bernard Fall, "Our Choices in Vietnam," *Reporter,* March 12, 1964.

resulting heavy burden on the civilian population: Malaya, 13 years; Algeria, 8 years; Philippines, 6 years; Cyprus, 5 years.

6. *Escalation-by-proxy.* The proxy is double, as it may involve pressure by non-American proxies and on territory not belonging to either of the direct contenders, North and South Viet-Nam. As shown earlier, the bombing of Communist supply trails or staging areas and airfields in Laos by Laotian aircraft, with Lao or mercenary pilots, is probably the mildest type of feasible escalation. If directed (as it already has been over the past year) against Communist supply bases held in violation of the 1962 Geneva Agreements on Laos, its legality is almost unquestionable. So, up to a point, would be the technological escalation to higher-performance aircraft. A similar ground escalation is possible: Laotian troops, South Vietnamese troops; and the latter with American advisers.

7. *Harassing the "sanctuary."* Here also, geographical and technological variations are almost infinite. Both American airstrikes and naval engagements against North Vietnamese fixed installations and warships have already taken place . . .

In actual military effectiveness, the worth of such operations is nil. The North Vietnamese defeated the French while operating jungle supply lines in the face of two hundred French combat aircraft. The relative invulnerability of such human-supported supply operations is best evidenced by the fact that "Operation Strangle," a United States Air Force undertaking of huge proportions designed to destroy North Korean and Communist Chinese supply lines in Korea through massive bombing of the road and rail net, proved to be an utter failure: hundreds of thousands of "A-frame" carriers made up for the destroyed transportation system.

A similar American interdiction operation against the Communist supply lines around the dying fortress of Dien Bien Phu was requested by the French in February–May, 1954. Dubbed "Operation Vulture," its effectiveness against human porters in the jungle was greatly doubted by American experts and the operation was canceled. There is no doubt that the same conditions which led to the failure of operations "Strangle" and "Vulture" still exist in Viet-Nam. Primitiveness carries its own kind of invulnerability when matched against sophisticated weapons.

8. *Repayment in kind.* When the situation in South Viet-Nam proves particularly irritating, there often arises a "spasm-reaction" of wishing to repay in kind the damage inflicted: blow up "their" military depots; kill "their" village chiefs; compel "them" to protect their cities; subvert "their" mountain tribes, and so on.

Here again, the variation goes from the small saboteur group parachuted or infiltrated for a few isolated missions, to the large-scale American "D-Day" force landing from an armada of amphibious craft and paratroop planes in the heart of the Red River Delta. The first type of operation has been carried out constantly at least since 1956. The casualty rate is very high and successes, if any, are few and far between.

In view of the countrywide police and intelligence network prevailing in North Viet-Nam, in typically Communist fashion, even a more massive effort in that direction is likely to encounter difficulties.

And invasion of North Viet-Nam would almost surely run into most of the problems the French encountered in the same undertaking. In addition, it would have two likely consequences: (a) with the gloves off in South Viet-Nam, the North Vietnamese regime would immediately retaliate as best it knows how, and that would be with its fearsome jungle-going ground combat divisions. There are at least fourteen such divisions available in North Viet-Nam, and a defensive operation against a conventional United States landing in the North could be conducted with about one-half of them, in addition to the local militia forces constantly available and armed.

That would leave perhaps six to eight divisions to invade sorely pressed South Viet-Nam. And, lest this be forgotten (it is, of course), the Japanese took all of mainland Southeast Asia from Singapore to Mandalay with *six* divisions.

What a Red Chinese intervention would do to such an operation is anyone's guess, but Korea permits a few good estimates.

Conclusion

That leaves the West in general, and the United States in particular, in the throes of a dilemma aptly described by Walter Lippmann as the choice between "unattainable victory and unacceptable defeat." As the year 1964 ended, the consensus seemed to converge toward a more or less temporary stabilization along the lower reaches of points 5 to 7 of the above scale. The advantage of such an approach is that it stays within the realm, for good or ill, of what has already been experienced; and there exist some remote chances that alternate approaches by third parties on both sides may bring about a "thaw" in the presently-frozen positions.

Some sources aver that Hanoi and Peking, and these two and the Liberation Front, may not be as unified as it appears on the surface. The usually reliable *Le Monde* expert Georges Chaffard reported in November, 1964, that Peking might be in the process of "leapfrogging" Hanoi with the NLFSV to take over directly the backing of the latter's operations. Chaffard (echoing other French views) feels that Hanoi, now truly worried about an extended American "spasm-reaction" or a deliberate shift toward policy ranges 7–8 of the above scale, might be willing to settle for a compromise that neither Peking nor the NLFSV find acceptable.[22]

Approaches made by Dr. Pham Ngoc Thach (a South Vietnamese guerrilla leader during the First Indochina War and now Minister of Health in the North Vietnamese government) to Vietnamese exiles in France during a recent visit seem to have echoed a similar tendency.

If such a fissure indeed exists within the Asian Communist complex involved in Viet-Nam, then perhaps application of a solution within the 3–4 range of the above scale could become conceivable without endangering the ever fragile and volatile South Vietnamese political-military gossamer. As often before, American policies—indeed, the West's whole position—in Southeast Asia are at a crossroads. But that crossroads is dangerously close to the point of no return.

---

[22] Georges Chaffard, "Par-dessus Ho Chi Minh," *L'Express*, November 15, 1964.

PART FOUR

The Negotiating Positions

INTRODUCTION

The stated diplomatic position of the contending nations and groups in Viet-Nam, except for the South Vietnamese military, suggest that there are common elements to negotiate about. Pham Van Dong's statement, the Ho Chi Minh interview in *Pravda* during the spring of 1965 and President Johnson's speech at Johns Hopkins in April, 1965, outline a diplomatic settlement from which negotiation and successful advancement of the American national interest could be achieved.

One of the obstacles to negotiations, however, has been American reluctance to negotiate with the National Liberation Front. The official rationale for this position has been that the U.S. negotiates only with governments. American diplomatic history is full of examples in which the U.S. successfully negotiated with revolutionary groups, military establishments and armies, rather than governments—the most recent case being the various contending factions in the Dominican Republic. Ironically, the posture taken by the Department of State *vis à vis* negotiations with the NLF has been contradictory to American diplomacy precedent. Since President Johnson's press conference of July 30, 1965, the possibility of contacts with the NLF as "part" of a North Vietnamese delegation at a conference no longer seems excluded by the U.S.

Still, as the following items show, a great deal needs to be done by both sides to bring the Viet-Nam problem to the level of a fruitful diplomatic confrontation.

PREMIER PHAM VAN DONG OF NORTH VIET-NAM

Policy Declaration*

Following is the text of an English-language report by Hsinhua, the Chinese Communist press agency, on the essentials of a policy declaration by Premier Pham Van Dong of North Viet-Nam, as monitored in the United States:

Pham Van Dong, Premier of the Democratic Republic of Viet-Nam, elucidated the unswerving stand of the government of the D.R.V. [Democratic Republic of Viet-Nam] on the Viet-Nam question in his report on government work at the second session of the United National Assembly. The [North] Vietnamese News Agency issued the full text of the report today.

Premier Pham Van Dong said that it is the unswerving policy of the government of the D.R.V. to strictly respect the 1954 Geneva Agreements on Viet-Nam and to correctly implement their basic provisions as embodied in the following points:

1. Recognition of the basic national rights of the Vietnamese people—peace, independence, sovereignty, unity and territorial integrity. According to the Geneva Agreements, the United States government must withdraw from South Viet-Nam United States troops, military personnel, and weapons of all kinds, dismantle all United States military bases there, cancel its "military alliance" with South Viet-Nam. It must end its policy of intervention and aggression in South Viet-Nam. According to the Geneva Agreements, the United States government must stop its acts of war against North Viet-Nam, completely cease all encroachments on the territory and sovereignty of the D.R.V.

2. Pending the peaceful reunification of Viet-Nam, while Viet-Nam is still temporarily divided into two zones, the military provisions of the 1954 Geneva Agreements on Viet-Nam must be strictly respected. The two zones must refrain from joining any military alliance with foreign countries. There must be no

---

* Reprinted in the *New York Times*, April 14, 1965.

foreign military bases, troops, or military personnel in their respective territory.

3. The internal affairs of South Viet-Nam must be settled by the South Vietnamese people themselves, in accordance with the program of the NFLSV [the South Vietnam National Liberation Front, or political arm of the Viet-Cong] without any foreign interference.

4. The peaceful reunification of Viet-Nam is to be settled by the Vietnamese people in both zones, without any foreign interference.

Pham Van Dong said that the aforementioned stand of the D.R.V. government unquestionably enjoys the approval and support of all peace and justice-loving governments and peoples in the world. The government of the D.R.V. is of the view that the stand expounded above is the basis for the soundest political settlement of the Viet-Nam problem.

If this basis is recognized, favorable conditions will be created for the peaceful settlement of the Viet-Nam problem, and it will be possible to consider the reconvening of an international conference along the pattern of the 1954 Geneva Conference on Viet-Nam.

The government of the D.R.V. declares that any approach contrary to the above-mentioned stand is inappropriate. Any approach tending to secure a United Nations intervention in the Viet-Nam situation is also inappropriate because such approaches are basically at variance with the 1954 Geneva Agreements on Viet-Nam.

LYNDON B. JOHNSON

American Policy in Viet-Nam*

Last week seventeen nations sent their views to some two dozen countries having an interest in Southeast Asia. We are joining

---

* Remarks at Johns Hopkins University, Baltimore, Maryland, April 7, 1965.

those seventeen countries and stating our American policy to-night which we believe will contribute toward peace in this area of the world.

I have come here to review once again with my own people the views of the American government.

Tonight Americans and Asians are dying for a world where each people may choose its own path to change.

This is the principle for which our ancestors fought in the valleys of Pennsylvania. It is a principle for which our sons fight tonight in the jungles of Viet-Nam.

Viet-Nam is far away from this quiet campus. We have no territory there, nor do we seek any. The war is dirty and brutal and difficult. And some four hundred young men, born into an America that is bursting with opportunity and promise, have ended their lives on Viet-Nam's steaming soil.

Why must we take this painful road?

Why must this nation hazard its ease, its interest, and its power for the sake of a people so far away?

We fight because we must fight if we are to live in a world where every country can shape its own destiny, and only in such a world will our own freedom be finally secure.

This kind of world will never be built by bombs or bullets. Yet the infirmities of man are such that force must often precede reason and the waste of war, the works of peace.

We wish that this were not so. But we must deal with the world as it is, if it is ever to be as we wish.

The world as it is in Asia is not a serene or peaceful place.

The first reality is that North Viet-Nam has attacked the independent nation of South Viet-Nam. Its object is total conquest.

Of course, some of the people of South Viet-Nam are participating in attack on their own government. But trained men and supplies, orders and arms, flow in a constant stream from North to South.

This support is the heartbeat of the war.

And it is a war of unparalleled brutality. Simple farmers are the targets of assassination and kidnaping. Women and children are strangled in the night because their men are loyal to their government. And helpless villages are ravaged by sneak attacks. Large-scale raids are conducted on towns, and terror strikes in the heart of cities.

The confused nature of this conflict cannot mask the fact that it is the new face of an old enemy.

Over this war—and all Asia—is another reality: the deepening shadow of Communist China. The rulers in Hanoi are urged on by Peking. This is a regime which has destroyed freedom in Tibet, which has attacked India and has been condemned by the United Nations for aggression in Korea. It is a nation which is helping the forces of violence in almost every continent. The contest in Viet-Nam is part of a wider pattern of aggressive purposes.

Why are these realities our concern? Why are we in South Viet-Nam?

We are there because we have a promise to keep. Since 1954 every American President has offered support to the people of South Viet-Nam. We have helped to build, and we have helped to defend. Thus, over many years, we have made a national pledge to help South Viet-Nam defend its independence.

And I intend to keep that promise.

To dishonor that pledge, to abandon this small and brave nation to its enemies, and to the terror that must follow, would be an unforgivable wrong.

We are also there to strengthen world order. Around the globe from Berlin to Thailand are people whose well being rests in part on the belief that they can count on us if they are attacked. To leave Viet-Nam to its fate would shake the confidence of all these people in the value of an American commitment and in the value of America's word. The result would be increased unrest and instability, and even wider war.

We are also there because there are great stakes in the balance. Let no one think for a moment that retreat from Viet-Nam would bring an end to conflict. The battle would be renewed in one country and then another. The central lesson of our time is that the appetite of aggression is never satisfied. To withdraw from one battlefield means only to prepare for the next. We must say in Southeast Asia—as we did in Europe—in the words of the Bible: "Hitherto shalt thou come, but no further."

There are those who say that all our effort there will be futile—that China's power is such that it is bound to dominate all Southeast Asia. But there is no end to that argument until all of the nations of Asia are swallowed up.

There are those who wonder why we have a responsibility there. Well, we have it there for the same reason that we have a responsibility for the defense of Europe. World War II was fought in both Europe and Asia and when it ended we found ourselves with continued responsibility for the defense of freedom.

Our objective is the independence of South Viet-Nam and its freedom from attack. We want nothing for ourselves—only that the people of South Viet-Nam be allowed to guide their own country in their own way.

We will do everything necessary to reach that objective and we will do only what is absolutely necessary.

In recent months attacks on South Viet-Nam were stepped up. Thus, it became necessary for us to increase our response and to make attacks by air. This is not a change of purpose. It is a change in what we believe that purpose requires.

We do this in order to slow down aggression.

We do this to increase the confidence of the brave people of South Viet-Nam who have bravely borne this brutal battle for so many years with so many casualties.

And we do this to convince the leaders of North Viet-Nam— and all who seek to share their conquest—of a simple fact:

We will not be defeated.

We will not grow tired.

We will not withdraw, either openly or under the cloak of a meaningless agreement.

We know that air attacks alone will not accomplish all of these purposes. But it is our best and prayerful judgment that they are a necessary part of the surest road to peace.

We hope that peace will come swiftly. But that is in the hands of others besides ourselves. And we must be prepared for a long continued conflict. It will require patience as well as bravery— the will to endure as well as the will to resist.

I wish it were possible to convince others with words of what we now find it necessary to say with guns and planes: armed hostility is futile—our resources are equal to any challenge— because we fight for values and we fight for principle, rather than territory or colonies, our patience and our determination are unending.

Once this is clear, then it should also be clear that the only path for reasonable men is the path of peaceful settlement.

Such peace demands an independent South Viet-Nam—securely guaranteed and able to shape its own relationships to all others—free from outside interference—tied to no alliance—a military base for no other country.

These are the essentials of any final settlement.

We will never be second in the search for such a peaceful settlement in Viet-Nam.

There may be many ways to this kind of peace: in discussion or negotiation with the governments concerned; in large groups or in small ones; in the reaffirmation of old agreements or their strengthening with new ones.

We have stated this position over and over again fifty times and more to friend and foe alike. And we remain ready with this purpose for unconditional discussions.

And until that bright and necessary day of peace we will try to keep conflict from spreading. We have no desire to see thousands die in battle—Asians or Americans. We have no desire to devastate that which the people of North Viet-Nam have built with toil and sacrifice. We will use our power with restraint and with all the wisdom that we can command.

But we will use it.

This war, like most wars, is filled with terrible irony. For what do the people of North Viet-Nam want? They want what their neighbors also desire—food for their hunger—health for their bodies—a chance to learn—progress for their country, and an end to the bondage of material misery. And they would find all these things far more readily in peaceful association with others than in the endless course of battle.

These countries of Southeast Asia are homes for millions of impoverished people. Each day these people rise at dawn and struggle through until the night to wrestle existence from the soil. They are often wracked by diseases, plagued by hunger, and death comes at the early age of forty.

Stability and peace do not come easily in such a land. Neither independence nor human dignity will ever be won though by arms alone. It also requires the works of peace. The American people have helped generously in times past in these works, and now there must be a much more massive effort to improve the life of man in that conflict-torn corner of our world.

The first step is for the countries of Southeast Asia to associate themselves in a greatly expanded co-operative effort for development. We would hope that North Viet-Nam would take its place in the common effort just as soon as peaceful co-operation is possible.

The United Nations is already actively engaged in development in this area, and as far back as 1961 I conferred with our authorities in Viet-Nam in connection with their work there. And I would hope tonight that the Secretary General of the United Nations could use the prestige of his great office and his deep knowledge of Asia to initiate, as soon as possible, with the countries of that area, a plan for co-operation in increased development.

For our part I will ask the Congress to join in a billion dollar American investment in this effort as soon as it is underway.

And I would hope that all other industrialized countries, including the Soviet Union, will join in this effort to replace despair with hope and terror with progress.

The task is nothing less than to enrich the hopes and existence of more than a hundred million people. And there is much to be done.

The vast Mekong River can provide food and water and power on a scale to dwarf even our own T.V.A.

The wonders of modern medicine can be spread through villages where thousands die every year from lack of care.

Schools can be established to train people in the skills needed to manage the process of development.

And these objectives, and more, are within the reach of a cooperative and determined effort.

I also intend to expand and speed up a program to make available our farm surpluses to assist in feeding and clothing the needy in Asia. We should not allow people to go hungry and wear rags while our own warehouses overflow with an abundance of wheat and corn and rice and cotton.

So I will very shortly name a special team of outstanding, patriotic, and distinguished Americans to inaugurate our participation in these programs. This team will be headed by Mr. Eugene Black, the very able former president of the World Bank.

This will be a disorderly planet for a long time. In Asia, and elsewhere, the forces of the modern world are shaking old ways and uprooting ancient civilizations. There will be turbulence

and struggle and even violence. Great social change—as we see
in our own country—does not always come without conflict.

We must also expect that nations will on occasion be in dispute with us. It may be because we are rich, or powerful, or because we have made some mistakes, or because they honestly
fear our intentions. However, no nation need ever fear that we
desire their land, or to impose our will, or to dictate their
institutions.

But we will always oppose the effort of one nation to conquer
another nation.

We will do this because our own security is at stake.

But there is more to it than that. For our generation has a
dream. It is a very old dream. But we have the power, and now
we have the opportunity to make that dream come true.

For centuries nations have struggled among each other. But
we dream of a world where disputes are settled by law and
reason. And we will try to make it so.

For most of history men have hated and killed one another in
battle. But we dream of an end to war. And we will try to make
it so.

For all existence most men have lived in poverty, threatened
by hunger. But we dream of a world where all are fed and
charged with hope. And we will help to make it so.

The ordinary men and women of North Viet-Nam and South
Viet-Nam—of China and India—of Russia and America—are
brave people. They are filled with the same proportions of hate
and fear, of love and hope. Most of them want the same things
for themselves and their families. Most of them do not want their
sons to ever die in battle, or to see their homes, or the homes of
others, destroyed.

Well, this can be their world yet. Man now has the knowledge
—always before denied—to make this planet serve the real needs
of the people who live on it.

I know this will not be easy. I know how difficult it is for
reason to guide passion, and love to master hate. The complexi-
ties of this world do not bow easily to pure and consistent
answers.

But the simple truths are there just the same. We must all try
to follow them as best we can.

We often say how impressive power is. But I do not find it

impressive at all. The guns and the bombs, the rockets and the warships, are all symbols of human failure. They are necessary symbols. They protect what we cherish. But they are witness to human folly.

A dam built across a great river is impressive.

In the countryside where I was born, and where I live, I have seen the night illuminated, and the kitchen warmed, and the home heated, where once the cheerless night and the ceaseless cold held sway. And all this happened because electricity came to our area along the humming wires of the REA. Electrification of the countryside—yes, that, too, is impressive.

A rich harvest in a hungry land is impressive.

The sight of healthy children in a classroom is impressive.

These—not mighty arms—are the achievements which the American nation believes to be impressive.

And—if we are steadfast—the time may come when all other nations will also find it so.

Every night before I turn out the lights to sleep I ask myself this question: Have I done everything that I can do to unite this country? Have I done everything I can to help unite the world, to try to bring peace and hope to all the peoples of the world? Have I done enough?

Ask yourselves that question in your homes—and in this hall tonight. Have we, each of us, all done all we can do? Have we done enough?

We may well be living in the time foretold many years ago when it was said: "I call heaven and earth to record this day against you, that I have set before you life and death, blessing and cursing: therefore choose life, that both thou and thy seed may live."

This generation of the world must choose: destroy or build, kill or aid, hate or understand.

We can do all these things on a scale that has never been dreamed of before.

Well, we will choose life. And so doing, we will prevail over the enemies within man, and over the natural enemies of all mankind.

GILBERT F. WHITE

Viet-Nam—The Fourth Course*

A peaceful and honorable resolution of the conflict in South Viet-Nam and Laos may be found in a bold plan for land and water development which already unites factions in four nations of Southeast Asia. For seven years, Cambodia, Laos, Thailand, and South Viet-Nam have been working with little publicity and without disagreement on a huge development program. These four countries, which do not cooperate in anything else, have reached accord on development of the Lower Mekong Basin. . . .

The Lower Mekong River may be the key to a fourth course of action [for Viet-Nam], a more constructive and humane one than any of the others. For the imaginative scheme to manage the winding streams and alluvial soils of that great basin now provides a framework within which all nations could join their technical, financial, and police assistance under the United Nations flag in working toward a concrete goal. The attractions of taking positive international action based on indigenous plans for the Lower Mekong are obvious. The difficulties of getting agreement are great and have not been fully assessed. But they should be explored with all of the energy and skill now going into war plans. Even if the specific framework suggested by Mekong experience were to prove impracticable, other viable and constructive solutions may lie in this direction.

Planning for the Lower Mekong was begun by a committee of the four countries under auspices of the United Nations Economic Commission for Asia and the Far East in 1957. The basin below the Burmese and Chinese borders includes virtually all the area of Cambodia and Laos, the Korat Plateaus in northeast Thailand, and the delta and southwest interior of Viet-Nam. It embraces half the population of the four countries. It is a huge area drained by an untouched river of the dimensions of the Columbia.

---

* From the *Bulletin of the Atomic Scientists,* December, 1964. Copyright 1964 by the Educational Foundation for Nuclear Science, Inc.

The committee set out to gauge streams, explore damsites, chart soils, study farming, and do all the other things needed to design a program of managing water and land for the welfare of its twenty million people, mostly rice farmers. The survey effort was unique in dealing with the entire lower basin as a unit before construction began, in doing this under United Nations guidance, and in calling upon technical help from other nations. Always before, nations have joined in river development, as in the Indus or Rio Grande, under pressure of contending claims. In the Mekong, they started with a clean slate and a generous supply of both water and land. As yet there are no serious conflicts. They lacked essential data, and decided to defer construction until more facts were in hand.

More than $14 million has been spent to date on basic studies. These now involve twenty other nations and eleven international agencies. The U.S. Bureau of Reclamation helped with a reconnaissance study. Lieutenant General Raymond Wheeler, former chief of the Corps of Engineers, headed a United Nations mission which recommended a series of detailed investigations. France was the first to offer direct assistance; Canada flew the aerial photographs; the United States studied the hydrology; Australia investigated damsite geology; Japan sent reconnaissance engineering teams; the Philippines did detailed mapping; France surveyed soils and fish life. The studies and organization became more complex. India sent a team to design a large dam; Israel contributed agricultural engineers. The names of the Netherlands, Pakistan, the Scandinavian countries, New Zealand, the United Kingdom, the International Labor Organization, the World Health Organization, and the Ford Foundation began to appear in progress reports.

The Food and Agriculture Organization designed pilot farms and the World Meteorological Organization advised on flood forecasts and hydrology. These and many other basic surveys are being put together by an international staff and Advisory Board under the Committee's guidance.

With all of these nations in the picture it might seem impossible to get anything done. There was no model to follow. Skeptics in Bangkok and Saigon and Washington called the idea visionary. In fact, there have been delays and administrative snarls, but the work has moved surprisingly well. An Indian survey team uses American hydrology, Philippine maps, and Australian geology to design a dam in Cambodia which also would benefit Vietnamese farmers downstream.

The total U.S. contribution to Lower Mekong planning has cost less than four days of military aid in South Viet-Nam, now reported to exceed $1.5 million per day.

Burma has such a small and inaccessible part of the upper basin that it has not taken part. The People's Republic of China has at least 74,000 square miles in the upper basin. This lies in a long narrow segment, most of which is steep gorge cutting through high dissected plateaus. While China has not participated in the planning for the lower basin, integrated development of the entire basin ultimately should include the upper reaches. Hydroelectric storage there probably would benefit the regimen of the lower stream, but even if China were to divert its entire share into other basins—a most unlikely prospect—there still would be enough water in the Lower Mekong basin to care for major works now planned. North Viet-Nam does not have a part in the basin. However, if large-scale hydroelectric installations were to be made along the mainstream above tidewater, its cities would be a possible market for the power.

Much of the planning centers upon improvement of agriculture by supplying water for irrigation of a second crop in the dry season and by preventing drought losses. Stream regulation would cut down the heavy dislocations caused by annual floods. There are massive opportunities to increase output of rice and to diversify crops in the delta, around the Grand Lake in Cambodia, and in the winding alluvial valleys upstream. Channel, terminal, and shipping improvements would be essential to rebuilding the commercial life of the delta. Hydroelectric power plants on the tributaries would provide cheap power for urban and commercial growth, but the marketing of large blocks of power would depend upon development of industrial complexes. These have been actively discussed by Japanese interests. . . .

With the major outlines of a program in hand, work already has begun on construction of several tributary projects. West Germany is loaning funds for a multiple purpose power and irrigation project in the Nam Pong tributary basin in Thailand. France is helping with two small power and water supply projects in Laos. Part of the United States A.I.D. program supports water control and village development schemes that fit into the general plan in Laos and Thailand. In Cambodia, one multiple purpose undertaking has begun under Australian engineering supervision and a second will be ready to start if funds can be found.

More extensive water and land improvement projects are in early prospect. High priority is given to measures to rehabilitate the deteriorated inland water transport system so essential to the economy of the Delta by rebuilding waterways, barges, terminals, and ship repair yards. A combination power and irrigation dam in the Nam Ngum basin near Vientiane in Laos would bring large-scale rural improvement and cheap electricity to the doors of the capital. To meet the needs of growing population and to raise the level of living above the present per capita income of $60–$100 annually, much heavier investments will be in order. These allocations should be related to national growth requirements in other sectors. The very large main-stem projects take time to design (projects the size of Hoover Dam are on the drafting boards) and no doubt will be deferred for some years, but expenditures of the scale of $200 million per year may not be unreasonable over the next two decades. Much of this can be on village improvement schemes that benefit the farmers directly and promptly.

To approach this level of investment, innovations in financing and security are needed. Rather than relying upon separate loans or grants from contributing nations, the Mekong countries should have a central financial agency to receive and supervise expenditure of funds. All four countries probably would gain from unified administration of help from the outside. It is possible that the International Bank for Reconstruction and Development might be enlisted to play this role. Commitment to finance a long-term program would in itself be an earnest of intention by donor nations to support sound social growth along the river.

But heavy financial support will not come unless the security of the area can be assured more confidently. The United Nations might be expected to provide a blue-helmeted watch and ward service for those sectors of the project area where security is threatened. It could do this on the invitation of the country concerned. Cambodia and Thailand would have no immediate need beyond protection of their borders. Laos and South Viet-Nam would find it essential in the areas where civil unrest has been intense. United Nations measures would have to be launched with the authority of the General Assembly and with guarantee of costs and personnel contingents from interested member nations. In a more basic sense the United Nations presence would be effective only if it were grounded on agreement among the nations concerned that present national military operations should be suppressed. Reduction of violence will take time in the most favorable circumstances, for the guerrillas and army groups will be slow to disband and will have trouble finding and settling into work in their home villages.

This type of agreement would be fundamentally different from the cease fire that is envisioned under a neutralization treaty. The four countries, the United States, North Viet-Nam, and other interested nations would commit themselves primarily to advance a great development program for the welfare of the people of the lower basin on which the four governments have agreed. This would mean withdrawal of national military units. It would require support for a United Nations force to maintain security of the program—from delta canal to Laotian rice paddy. It would substitute a development goal for an indistinct battle line, and it would permit the United States to withdraw gracefully in favor of an international force committed to that goal. Financial obligations of the United States would in the future be linked with contributions of money and people from other nations.

Would this be acceptable to North Viet-Nam and the Pathet-Lao? No one can say for certain what ultimate position they would take. Developments to date are encouraging. None of the important field work has yet been halted by guerrilla activity. It is known that the head of the Pathet-Lao is highly sympathetic to multipurpose water programs in his country. The goal of harnessing a river's resources to serve the common man is widely hailed in both Communist and non-Communist countries, and the People's Republic of China and the U.S.S.R. have been distinguished practitioners of the idea. Neither has raised formal objections to its embodiment in the Lower Mekong. And while Cambodia for political reasons has cut off United States bilateral assistance, it is willing to accept help through the Lower Mekong channel.

A proposal for expanded international co-operation in the Lower Mekong would give a new choice to elements which have pushed guerrilla action in South Viet-Nam and Laos. By outright opposition they probably could block an enlarged venture toward goals they respect. On the other hand, by withholding opposition they could get the integrity of national governments in the two countries guaranteed by a United Nations presence devoted to advancing those aims. Thereafter, a weak United Nations administration with flabby assistance from the outside no doubt would favor growth of dissident groups, as in Laos in recent years. But a vigorous international effort aimed at bettering the lot of villagers and city workers might stabilize the governments and in time enable the people of Laos and South Viet-Nam to choose by nonviolent means the government they want.

Is it possible that the vision of a majestic river harnessed for the advance of twenty million people by an unprecedented piece of international co-operation would so command the imagination of the nations that the present grueling conflict could give way to a struggle for more abundant life? Could this mean to a world increasingly aware of its network of mutual responsibilities what the Tennessee Valley Authority meant to proponents of national development thirty years ago? The Mekong Committee's files are beginning to bulge with the necessary technical plans and surveys. Such investigations must continue. What is needed immediately, however, is incisive analysis by the United Nations as well as by the interested nations of practical steps to negotiate on a new basis of a common human cause. Just as the river's planning has called forth a unique degree of collaboration among scientists and nations, new forms of political and economic organization will be required to translate plans into village and city action.

If the Lower Mekong program in its present form does not prove a complete way out of the Southeast Asian dilemma, it at least suggests a route that is challenging. This is a way calling for international collaboration in advancing the economic welfare of peasants who long months ago had enough of terror in the night. It builds on plans shaped by the four nations and commands their support. It draws technical assistance, financial help, and necessary police protection from a score of other nations under the United Nations flag. In such a venture the United States could with honor and deep conviction invest its men, experience, and capital as a member of an international team. The route is broadly plotted, its technical foundations are laid, but its political surface is yet untried. That testing warrants all of the ingenuity, careful logistic planning, and determination on both sides that marks the current undeclared war of attrition in the Mekong swamps and hills. Nothing less than the same searching appraisal now should be made of a constructive solution. . . .

PRINCE NORODOM SIHANOUK

*In an Interview with Robert Scheer**

What Can Be Done in Southeast Asia

One of the reasons advanced by the Cambodian Royal Government for the rejection of United States aid is that the American foreign-aid program was designed to develop a capitalist economy. In what ways is a capitalist economy incompatible with Cambodia's plans for the future?

Our decision to reject United States aid in all its forms must be placed in a general context: repeated aggressions by the South Vietnamese; permanent and insufferable hostility of the South Vietnamese and Thai people, United States allies, who give wide support to our own rebels, the so-called "Free Khmers" of Son Ngoc Thanh and Sam Sary; the fanatic campaign against Cambodia and her regime, of almost all of the American press that speaks of us as "ingrates, pocketing the United States' money while serving Red China," etc. In passing, I would call it to your attention that if Cambodia is not able to offer herself the luxury of a capitalistic economy (which would put her under the fist of several rich businessmen and foreign powers), she has not on the other hand adopted the Communist system. Private interests still control a large sector, notably in the realm of agri-

---

* *Ramparts*, July, 1965.

culture and small and medium industry. If they are able to prove their capacities in these areas, the state will not wish to assume any new control. In taking over control of the banks, of the import-export trade and insurance, the government has assured itself of a revenue that the foreigner had in the past counted for his own profit.

What are the overall, long-term domestic objectives of the Royal Cambodian Government, and in what sense are these socialistic?

Khmer socialism stems neither from Marxism nor from any other foreign doctrine. Inspired by the sentiments of solidarity, love, and compassion for the Buddha, it is linked to our national heritage. Our kings of Angkor have always practiced it. Also, we *never* deem it contradictory to call the movement of the young people of the kingdom, the "Young Royal Socialists of Khmer."

Our objectives are those of every nation that has the desire to rise from an underdeveloped state: to complete the modernization of our country's economic structure, to continue increasing our agricultural production (especially rice, corn, rubber), through a *politique de l'eau* (dams, canals, reservoirs, etc.) and to create new industries and products in order to satisfy, without recourse to unfavorable import arrangements, our essential national needs.

What is the Cambodian view of the United States role in South Viet-Nam and what solutions does Cambodia offer towards ending this war? Would Your Royal Highness please also comment on the American fear of "losing face" if it permitted a negotiated peace in South Viet-Nam?

The answer to this very important question may be found in my speech at the opening of the Conference of the Indochinese People. There, I proposed the neutrality of South Viet-Nam, Cambodia, and Laos, by means of complete and simultaneous disengagement of the East and the West in this region, with strict guarantees and feasible international control.

I believe the "negotiated solution" to be always valuable. But the progressive escalation of the war (the American raids of terror on North Viet-Nam and the countermeasures that the Socialist world will inevitably take) might ruin attempts at compromise. An all-out conflict, that the United States will finally lose without even being able to save face, is what we are risking.

What is the reaction of Your Royal Highness to the United States argument which holds that the nations of Southeast Asia would fall like dominos to Communist rule, in the event of United States withdrawal from South Viet-Nam?

It is certain that if the United States provokes a major confrontation in this region—which will inevitably end in their humiliating retreat—all the other Asian nations, one after another (beginning with the allies of the United States), will come to know, if not domination, at least a very strong Communist influence.

That is exactly what I have tried to avoid by interceding over the years for a true neutrality for Laos and South Viet-Nam, by suggesting that they form with Cambodia, which is already neutral, a "buffer zone" separating the East and West in this troubled region of Southern Asia.

But, the United States, in Laos, has "played ball" with the extreme right and liquidated the neutralists. In perpetuating the war in South Viet-Nam, in supporting in Saigon leaders who are universally unpopular, known as her "creatures," the United States has forced the majority of the common people and the majority of the elite of South Viet-Nam into the arms of the Communists. This is not the way to combat communism in this region, or in many others. This "anti-Communist" war, by reason of the imperialist character that it forcibly assumes in the eyes of the masses, on the contrary, *favors communism.*

Could Your Royal Highness comment on the level of understanding of the United States government concerning developments in the People's Republic of China?

It concerns a total incomprehension. The People's Republic of China replaces, in the imagination of the United States, the ogres, the wolves-in-sheep's-clothing and other frightening phantoms. Your compatriots understand nothing of Asia. They are afraid of it! They mistrust it! They mistreat it! And they are astonished that they are not loved!

To what extent would United States military withdrawal from South Viet-Nam—and the effect this action would have on the South Vietnamese and Cambodian frontier issue—contribute to a friendly co-operation between the people of Cambodia and the United States?

It is very certain that when the United States will have put an end, in one way or another, to the war they are waging in South Viet-Nam and in Laos, we will no longer have any reason to be hostile to her. For our hostility stems from the fact that the United States unconditionally supports the Vietnamese and Thais, not only against the Communists, but also against us, the Cambodians, who are neutralists and nationalists. The Vietnamese and Thais are our two traditional adversaries who have, over the course of centuries, torn apart the Khmer Realm and who would like nothing better than to wipe it off the map, joining their frontiers at the Mekong.

The day when the planes supplied by the United States (and piloted by Americans) no longer bomb our territory, when the American tanks, accompanied by South Vietnamese troops, directed by American advisers, no longer penetrate our frontier villages carrying death—the day when America will have recalled her troops from our Indochina, then our relations will inevitably relax.

How would Your Royal Highness see future relations between the United States and a peaceful and disengaged Asia, once the American military presence has disappeared?

A South Asia peaceful and nonaligned, thanks to the joint understanding of East and West, can not fail to maintain good relations among the Eastern and Western camps—also with the United States. America would no longer be, in our eyes, an imperialistic nation that seeks to impose *her* policy and *her* government upon us, but a great nation from whom we would no longer have anything to fear.

Unfortunately, we are not there yet.

Prince Sihanouk on the President of the NLF (Viet-Cong)

Following the Conference of Indochinese People Prince Sihanouk invited those journalists still present in Phnom Penh to his mountain retreat for a very candid press conference. There he revealed the substance of a conversation he had held the preceding evening with Mr. Huynh Tan Phat, Vice President of the National Liberation Front and President of their delegation to the conference. His remarks offer a rare insight into the current attitudes of the NLF leadership within South Viet-Nam. I was the only American present. The following is a verbatim report of Prince Sihanouk recounting the conversation he held with Huynh Tan Phat.—Robert Scheer.

"What the Viet-Cong wants is not a confused situation which would obtain if they negotiated now—like Laos in 1962—while everything is confused—nothing good will result—the conference in 1962 has done Laos more harm than good—has not been successful for Laos. What the NLF wants, Mr. Phat says, is to clarify the situation in South Viet-Nam and to kill off all that still believes in the United States—all that still sticks to the United States and when the United States supporters, believers, followers will be wiped out, the situation will be clear and the Viet-Cong will of necessity win. Mr. Phat would like to have a clearer situation, a regroupment—the coming to the resistance of all the nationalists—national union to implement peace and independence in the country.

"I think it would be interesting for you to know that Mr. Phat has added this following judgment about Cambodia. He said that before coming to our country he already had a good idea of our way of life and our situation here. But when he arrived here with his other countrymen from South Viet-Nam it seems that our conditions of life are much better than they could have imagined. So to use his own words he said Cambodia is a very contagious example for South Viet-Nam and what South Viet-Nam wants is to have the same way of life, the same situation as Cambodia. And he revealed that he had held conversations with his countrymen from North Viet-Nam during the conference and they were in agreement with each other so far as the delay they would have before reaching the reunification of Viet-Nam. He spoke about ten or even twenty years before reaching the stage of reunification. So he said that during that time and after winning the war in South Viet-Nam we should like to be neutral like you Cambodians. To be neutral and to have the same way of life, because our conditions of life are more similar to yours than to the conditions of life in the North of our homeland. And he added—so far as foreign aid is concerned—the future independent state of South Viet-Nam would like to have the same treatment as Cambodia. That is to say—she would like to receive unconditional aid from every side—from the Socialist camp as well as from the Western camp—from France for instance. So you know, I am giving to you the words of Mr. Phat— I cannot guarantee that the future will be like that but you have to take note of this."

NORTH VIETNAMESE–SOVIET STATEMENT*

The Central Committee of the CPSU (Communist Party of the Soviet Union), the Soviet government and the Central Committee of the Vietnamese Workers Party, the government of the Democratic Republic of Viet-Nam resolutely denounce the piratical actions of American imperialism in the region of Indochina, the armed intervention spearheaded against the freedom-loving people of South Viet-Nam, the open acts of aggression and piratical attacks on the Democratic Republic of Viet-Nam.

The imperialist expansionist policy carried through by the United States of America is a flagrant violation of the Geneva Agreements of 1954 on Viet-Nam. It is aimed at the frustration of the peaceful reunification of the country and the conversion of South Viet-Nam into a factual colony and military *place d'armes* of the United States.

In violation of the Geneva Agreements, the United States set up its military bases on the territory of South Viet-Nam, and illegally sent there its armed forces and weapons. It unleashed a

---

* Joint Statement, April 17, 1965, as reported by Tass.

bloody war of extermination against the Vietnamese people, resorting to barbarous means against the peaceful population, including napalm bombs and poison gas.

It is with anger and indignation that the peoples of the world are protesting against the atrocities perpetrated by the aggressors on Vietnamese soil. They will never forgive and forget these crimes of imperialism.

The aggressive actions of the United States in Viet-Nam create a threat to the peace not only in Southeast Asia, but also aggravate tension throughout the world, increase the danger of a military conflict with grievous consequences for all the peoples of the world.

The Central Committee of the CPSU, the Soviet government, the entire Soviet people are expressing fraternal solidarity with the people of Viet-Nam who are waging a heroic, just struggle against the American aggressors.

The party and government delegation of the Democratic Republic of Viet-Nam pointed out that the international solidarity and many-sided assistance rendered by the Soviet Union make an important contribution to the strengthening of the defense of the Democratic Republic of Viet-Nam, its ability to give a rebuff to the military provocations of imperialists. The fraternal support of the U.S.S.R. and other Socialist countries strengthens the Vietnamese people's faith in the ultimate victory of their just cause.

The party and government delegation of the Democratic Republic of Viet-Nam express the profound gratitude of the Vietnamese people, the Vietnamese Workers Party and the government of the Democratic Republic of Viet-Nam to the fraternal Soviet people, the CPSU and the government of the U.S.S.R. for the great fraternal international support and assistance. This support and assistance to a great extent strengthen the forces of the Vietnamese people in their struggle in defense of the security of the Democratic Republic of Viet-Nam and in the struggle against the barbarous aggression by American imperialism in South Viet-Nam. The party and government delegation of the Democratic Republic of Viet-Nam expresses gratitude for the fraternal, hearty welcome accorded it by the CPSU Central Committee and the Soviet government during the stay in the Soviet Union.

The Vietnamese people also highly appreciate the constant support of the Soviet people, which finds its expression in numerous meetings and rallies of protest against the aggression by American imperialism, in letters of the Soviet working people expressing a desire to volunteer in order to fight shoulder to shoulder with the Vietnamese brothers against the aggressors.

If the United States aggression against the Democratic Republic of Viet-Nam is intensified, the Soviet government, in case of necessity, given an appeal by the government of the Democratic Republic of Viet-Nam, will consent to the departure for Viet-Nam of Soviet citizens who, guided by the sentiment of proletarian internationalism, express a desire to fight for the just cause of the Vietnamese people, for the maintenance of the Socialist achievements of the Democratic Republic of Viet-Nam.

Having discussed the situation in South Viet-Nam, the CPSU Central Committee, the Soviet government and the central committee of the Vietnamese Workers Party and the government of the Democratic Republic of Viet-Nam consider that the National Front of Liberation is the genuine exponent of the will and aspirations of the people of South Viet-Nam, its only legitimate representative. The program of the Front enjoys the broad support of the mass of the people because it proclaims independence, democracy, peace, an end to imperialist intervention and the formation in South Viet-Nam of a national, democratic coalition government carrying through a policy of independence and neutrality in full conformity with the Geneva Agreements of 1954.

It was noted during the talks that the statement of the central committee of the South Vietnamese National Liberation Front of March 22 this year met with a positive response in the Soviet Union and enlisted support.

The Soviet Union and the Democratic Republic of Viet-Nam express their firm confidence that the just struggle by the people of South Viet-Nam waged under the leadership of the National Liberation Front will be crowned with a complete victory. No matter what means the imperialists resort to, they will not succeed in enslaving the people upholding their independence and freedom.

During the talks the party and government delegations of the U.S.S.R. and the Democratic Republic of Viet-Nam expressed their evaluation of the recent statement made by the United States President in connection with the situation in Viet-Nam. This statement shows that the United States is still keeping a course for the extension of the acts of aggression against the Democratic Republic of Viet-Nam, for the further spreading of the war against the people of South Viet-Nam and does not seek to explore avenues leading to a peaceful solution of the Vietnamese problem.

It is significant that the statement by the United States President on a so-called peaceful settlement has been made at a time when further bombings of the territory of the Democratic Republic of Viet-Nam are taking place, when there are further movements of American military units and weapons to South Viet-Nam to step up the bloody aggression against the people of South Viet-Nam—and these aggressive actions continue.

The Soviet Union and the Democratic Republic of Viet-Nam agree that a solution of the Vietnamese problem calls for an immediate end to the aggressive actions by the United States against the Democratic Republic of Viet-Nam; in conformity with the Geneva Agreements the government of the United States must evacuate its forces, servicemen and arms from South Viet-Nam, put an end to the aggression against South Viet-Nam and the infringement of the territorial integrity and sovereignty of the Democratic Republic of Viet-Nam.

In the period before the peaceful reunification of Viet-Nam it is necessary, according to the Geneva Agreements, that the two parts of Viet-Nam have no military alliances with other countries, have no foreign military bases and servicemen on their territory.

The affairs of South Viet-Nam must be settled by itself on the basis of the program of the National Liberation Front.

The peaceful reunification of Viet-Nam must be effected by the Vietnamese people themselves without outside intervention.

There also was an exchange of opinion on questions pertaining to the situation in Laos and Cambodia in connection with the ceaseless United States intervention in the affairs of those countries. A realistic way to a solution of these problems is scrupulous compliance with the Geneva Agreements of 1954 and 1962. For these purposes it would be useful to convene the relevant international conferences.

Examining the questions of measures to strengthen the defense potential of the Democratic Republic of Viet-Nam, the party and government delegations of the Democratic Republic of Viet-Nam and the U.S.S.R. noted with satisfaction that the earlier understanding on these questions is being implemented to the envisaged extent and procedure.

The CPSU Central Committee, the Soviet government and the central committee of the Vietnamese Workers Party, the government of the Democratic Republic of Viet-Nam reached an understanding on further steps designed to safeguard the security and defend the sovereignty of the Democratic Republic of Viet-Nam, which is an objective of aggressive actions by American imperialism, and agreed on appropriate measures for these purposes. The Soviet Union reaffirmed its readiness to continue rendering the necessary assistance to the Democratic Republic of Viet-Nam for the repulsion of United States aggression.

The party and government delegations of the U.S.S.R. and the Democratic Republic of Viet-Nam emphasized that in conditions of activization of the imperialist forces, their attempts to suppress the liberation movement of the peoples, unity of action and strengthening of the solidarity of the Socialist countries, of all who are coming out against imperialism and colonialism, for freedom and independence of the peoples, is more necessary than ever before.

Guided by the interests of safeguarding peace, freedom and independence of the peoples, the Soviet Union and the Democratic Republic of Viet-Nam appeal to the governments and peoples of all countries to take the necessary steps in order to put an end to the imperialist aggression by the United States in the region of Indochina.

The continuation and extension of the American aggression in Viet-Nam is a provocation not only against one Socialist country—the Democratic Republic of Viet-Nam—but also against all Socialist countries.

At the same time this American aggression is a provocation against the national liberation movement of the peoples of Asia, Africa and Latin America, against all peace-loving peoples, against all who cherish the cause of peace and national independence. The interests of peace and international security call for curbing the forces of imperialism and aggression that encroach on the freedom and rights of the Vietnamese people.

PART FIVE

Escalation

A. AS SEEN FROM WASHINGTON

Introduction

The American phase of the Second Indochina War began on February 8, 1965, when American aircraft began 'round-the-clock bombing operations in North Viet-Nam, allegedly in retaliation for specifically "North Vietnamese" attacks against American bases—but in fact because the rapidly-deteriorating South Vietnamese internal situation required tangible proof of all-out American support for Saigon.

This occurred at a critical diplomatic juncture: in Hanoi, Soviet Prime Minister Alexey Kosygin—as became rapidly known—attempted to steer North Viet-Nam toward a less militant course; in neutral Cambodia's capital, Phnom-Penh, Prince Sihanouk had convened an "Indochina People's Conference" to establish a basis for an organization of a non-aligned state system to cover the whole Indochinese Peninsula, including North Viet-Nam. In the United States, the overwhelming mandate given President Johnson in November 1964 by the voters, provided the incoming Administration with the kind of flexibility and support which President Dwight D. Eisenhower enjoyed when in 1953 he settled the stalemated Korean War on a com-

368 · *The Viet-Nam Reader*

promise "no-win" basis. The opening of the bombing offensive smack in the middle of the Kosygin visit and the Phnom-Penh Conference understandably foreclosed the possibility of any fruitful contacts that might have been undertaken at the time.

The 1965 bombing offensive was a triple failure: it did not stem to any significant extent the flow of North Vietnamese supplies and manpower replacements (if anything, the North Vietnamese increased their commitments to match those of the U.S.); it failed to make a lasting contribution to South Vietnamese military morale or political stability (a new coup took place on June 12, 1965, which brought Air Vice-Marshal Nguyen Cao Ky to power); and, above all, it failed to achieve its aim of bringing Hanoi to its knees in short order and nullified whatever positive diplomatic effects were to be derived from President Johnson's April 1965 speech at Baltimore (cf. pp. 343, ff. above).

The resignation of General Maxwell D. Taylor as Ambassador to Viet-Nam in July 1965 in effect heralded the end of the "Flexible Response" doctrine as far as U.S. military commitments in Viet-Nam were concerned. For the first time since 1950, and against the repeated admonitions of three Presidents[*] and many senior military commanders, American ground troops were sent into combat on the Asian mainland. In two years 500,000 American troops found themselves in the presence of a restive South Vietnamese people, a dispirited local army led by ever-feuding generals primarily concerned with political power, and a determined enemy seemingly impervious to the vast deployment of American manpower and military technology.

With the radically-changed character of the American involvement, an entirely new set of political and diplomatic rationales had to be devised to insure continuity of support at home and passivity among potentially critical allies and neutrals. Within the United States, the change was marked by the need to present an objective justification for the increased military commitment. Thus early in 1966 NATO was suddenly confronted by the Secretary of Defense with the startling assertion that the Viet-Nam war contributed to preserving Western Europe from a

---

[*] Truman, Eisenhower and Kennedy.

Red Chinese threat. This resurrection of the "Yellow Peril" theory was also echoed by the Senate Majority Whip, Russell Long of Louisiana.

For both internal and external consumption, however, the Viet-Nam War itself had to be provided with at least the semblance of a negotiable solution; the more so as earlier charges that North Vietnamese diplomatic feelers had been flatly turned down, were substantiated. Matching the negotiating positions of Hanoi (cf. p. 342) and of the NLF (pp. 232, ff.), the State Department issued in January 1966 a 14-Point Program restructuring the offers contained in Johnson's Johns Hopkins' speech (pp. 343, ff.). As will be seen, Hanoi and Washington agree on making the 1954 Geneva Agreements "an adequate basis for peace in Southeast Asia." They obviously disagree, however, on how to bring about a situation in which the Geneva Accords can be implemented.

As a result of the combined pressures of public opinion at home and among our allies and the neutral powers in the United Nations (and, presumably, certain shortages of bombs and spare parts in Viet-Nam itself), there was a thirty-seven-day pause in the bombing of North Viet-Nam in January–February 1966. On the day bombing was resumed, Ambassador Arthur Goldberg explained to the United Nations the nature of America's worldwide peace efforts. However, a United Nations debate on the Viet-Nam problem failed to materialize.

The Senate Foreign Relations Committee hearings which began in January 1966 threatened to bore deeply into a wall of policy that hitherto had largely remained unbreached from within. To regain the initiative in the field of Viet-Nam policy innovation and to enhance the nonmilitary aspects of American involvement in Viet-Nam, the President and his closest advisers decided that they would meet with the senior Saigon leaders in Honolulu in February of 1966.

The Honolulu Declaration which resulted from that Conference outlined an attempt at applying Great Society solutions to the incredibly complicated situation in South Viet-Nam. The Declaration, all protests to the contrary notwithstanding, clearly reflects the irreconcilable differences in philosophy between the Americans and the Vietnamese junta leadership in Saigon. It also provided Air Vice-Marshal Ky with a direct American

Presidential endorsement, which apparently was used by Ky in his own internal feuds with other (and perhaps more representative) South Vietnamese political factions.

The decision by President Johnson on June 29, 1966, to bomb oil-storage areas within the city limits of Hanoi and Haiphong created a new level of escalation. All American allies in Europe (including Great Britain) dissociated themselves from this new move, and North Viet-Nam's Communist allies in turn began to back beleaguered Hanoi with specialists as well as weapons. On October 17, 1966, they promised an additional one billion dollars' worth of matériel to the country.

This sudden isolation of the United States from her traditional allies gave renewed impetus to the search for alternate power groupings as an outlet for the energies of the swollen National Security bureaucracy. The weak Asian and the white nations of the Pacific were that outlet.

As a result, President Johnson met in Manila with the leaders of these nations on October 25–26, 1966. That meeting resulted in a Joint Communiqué that was, in fact, to become the charter of the new "Asia-First" orientation of American policy.

In itself the Joint Communiqué of the Manila summit talks sets forth an ambiguous diplomatic position in which "The people of South Viet-Nam will ask their allies to remove their forces and evacuate their installations as the military and subversive forces of North Viet-Nam are withdrawn, infiltration ceases, and the level of violence does subside . . . not later than six months after the above conditions have been fulfilled." This was considered a fraud not only by the Chinese, the North Vietnamese, the National Liberation Front, the Soviet Union and virtually all European nations, but also by former Vice-President Nixon in his appraisal of the Manila Conference. In a later clarifying statement answering Nixon, President Johnson made clear that the United States would not leave South Viet-Nam until *all* violence ceased. In effect, he was announcing an American protectorate there for the foreseeable future.

DEPARTMENT OF STATE
14 POINTS*

United States Official Position on Viet-Nam

The following statements are on the public record about elements which the United States believes can go into peace in Southeast Asia:

1. The Geneva Agreements of 1954 and 1962 are an adequate basis for peace in Southeast Asia;
2. We would welcome a conference on Southeast Asia or on any part thereof;
3. We would welcome "negotiations without preconditions" as the 17 nations put it;
4. We would welcome unconditional discussions as President Johnson put it;
5. A cessation of hostilities could be the first order of business at a conference or could be the subject of preliminary discussions;
6. Hanoi's four points could be discussed along with other points which others might wish to propose;
7. We want no U.S. bases in Southeast Asia;
8. We do not desire to retain U.S. troops in South Viet-Nam after peace is assured;
9. We support free elections in South Viet-Nam to give the South Vietnamese a government of their own choice;
10. The question of reunification of Viet-Nam should be determined by the Vietnamese through their own free decision;
11. The countries of Southeast Asia can be non-aligned or neutral if that be their option;
12. We would much prefer to use our resources for the economic reconstruction of Southeast Asia than in War. If there is peace, North Viet-Nam could participate in a regional effort to which we would be prepared to contribute at least one billion dollars;

---

* Press release, January 7, 1966.

13. The President has said "The Viet Cong would not have difficulty being represented and having their views represented if for a moment Hanoi decided she wanted to cease aggression. I don't think that would be an insurmountable problem."

14. We have said publicly and privately that we could stop the bombing of North Viet-Nam as a step toward peace although there has not been the slightest hint or suggestion from the other side as to what they would do if the bombing stopped.

THE WHITE HOUSE DECLARATION OF HONOLULU*

Part I

The Republic of Viet-Nam and the United States of America jointly declare:

   their determination in defense against aggression,

   their dedication to the hopes of all the people of South Viet-Nam,

   and their commitment to the search for just and stable peace.

In pursuit of these objectives the leaders of their governments have agreed upon this declaration, which sets forth:

   the purposes of the Government of Viet-Nam,

   the purposes of the Government of the United States,

   and the common commitment of both Governments.

---

* Released February 8, 1966.

Part II

The Purposes of the Government of Viet-Nam

Here in the mid-Pacific, halfway between Asia and North America, we take the opportunity to state again the aims of our government.

We are a government—indeed a generation—of revolutionary transformation. Our people are caught up in a mortal struggle.

This struggle has four sides.

1. We must defeat the Viet-Cong and those illegally fighting with them on our soil. We are the victims of an aggression directed and supported from Hanoi. That aggression—that so-called "War of National Liberation"—is part of the communist plan for the conquest of all of Southeast Asia. The defeat of that agggression is vital for the future of our people of South Viet-Nam.

2. We are dedicated to the eradication of social injustice among our people. We must bring about a true social revolution and construct a modern society in which every man can know that he has a future; that he has respect and dignity; that he has the opportunity for himself and for his children to live in an environment where all is not disappointment, despair and dejection; that the opportunities exist for the full expression of his talents and his hopes.

3. We must establish and maintain a stable, viable economy and build a better material life for our people. In spite of the war, which creates many unusual and unpredictable economic situations, we are determined to continue with a policy of austerity; to make the best possible use of the assistance granted us from abroad; and to help our people achieve regular economic growth and improved material welfare.

4. We must build true democracy for our land and for our people. In this effort we shall continue to imbue the people with a sense of national unity, a stronger commitment to civic responsibility. We shall encourage a widened and more active participation in and contribution to the building of a free, independent, strong and peaceful Viet-Nam. In particular, we pledge again:

—to formulate a democratic constitution in the months ahead, including an electoral law;

—to take that constitution to our people for discussion and modification;

—to seek its ratification by secret ballot;

—to create, on the basis of elections rooted in that constitution, an elected government.

These things shall be accomplished mainly with the blood, intelligence, and dedication of the Vietnamese people themselves. But in this interdependent world we shall need the help of others:—to win the war of independence; to build while we fight; to reconstruct and develop our nation when terror ceases.

To those future citizens of a free, democratic South Viet-Nam now fighting with the Viet-Cong, we take this occasion to say come and join in this national revolutionary adventure:

—come safely to join us through the Open Arms Program.

—stop killing your brothers, sisters, their elders and their children.

—come and work through constitutional democracy to build together that life of dignity, freedom and peace those in the North would deny the people of Viet-Nam.

Thus, we are fighting this war. It is a military war, a war for the hearts of our people. We cannot win one without winning the other. But the war for the hearts of the people is more than a military tactic. It is a moral principle. For this we shall strive as we fight to bring about a true social revolution.

Part III

The Purposes of the Government of the United States

(1) The United States of America is joined with the people and Government of Viet-Nam to prevent aggression. This is the purpose of the determined effort of the American armed forces now engaged in Viet-Nam. The United States seeks no bases. It seeks no colonial presence. It seeks to impose no alliance or alignment. It seeks only to prevent aggression, and its pledge to that purpose is firm. It aims simply to help a people and government who are determined to help themselves.

(2) The United States is pledged to the principles of the self-

determination of peoples, and of government by the consent of the governed. It therefore gives its full support to the purpose of free elections proclaimed by the Government of South Viet-Nam and to the principle of open arms and amnesty for all who turn from terror toward peace and rural construction. The United States will give its full support to measures of social revolution including land reform based upon the principle of building upward from the hopes and purposes of all the people of Viet-Nam.

(3) Just as the United States is pledged to play its full part in the world-wide attack upon hunger, ignorance, and disease, so in Viet-Nam it will give special support to the work of the people of that country to build even while they fight. We have helped and we will help them—to stabilize the economy—to increase the production of food—to spread the light of education —to stamp out disease.

(4) The purpose of the United States remains a purpose of peace. The United States Government and the Government of Viet-Nam will continue in the future, as they have in the past, to press the quest for a peaceful settlement in every forum. The world knows the harsh and negative response these efforts have thus far received. But the world should know, too, that the United States Government and the Government of Viet-Nam remain determined that no path to peace shall be unexplored. Within the framework of their international commitments, the United States and Viet-Nam aim to create with others a stable peace in Southeast Asia which will permit the governments and peoples of the region to devote themselves to lifting the condition of man. With the understanding and support of the Government of Viet-Nam the peace offensive of the United States Government and the Government of South Viet-Nam will continue until peace is secured.

Part IV

The Common Commitment

The President of the United States and the Chief of State and Prime Minister of the Republic of Viet-Nam are thus pledged again:

to defense against aggression,
to the work of social revolution,
to the goal of free self-government,
to the attack on hunger, ignorance, and disease,
and to the unending quest for peace.

DEPARTMENT OF STATE:

Three Statements of the Manila Summit Conference*

Goals of Freedom

We, the seven nations gathered in Manila, declare our unity, our resolve, and our purpose in seeking together the goals of freedom in Viet-Nam and in the Asian and Pacific areas. They are:

1. To be free from aggression.
2. To conquer hunger, illiteracy, and disease.
3. To build a region of security, order, and progress.
4. To seek reconciliation and peace throughout Asia and the Pacific.

Communiqué

Introduction

1. In response to an invitation from the President of the Republic of the Philippines, after consultations with the President of the Republic of Korea and the Prime Ministers of Thailand and the Republic of Viet-Nam, the leaders of seven nations in the Asian and Pacific region held a summit conference in Manila

---

* Department of State Press Release 252, October 25, 1966.

on October 24 and 25, 1966, to consider the conflict in South Viet-Nam and to review their wider purposes in Asia and the Pacific. The participants were Prime Minister Harold Holt of Australia, President Park Chung Hee of the Republic of Korea, Prime Minister Keith Holyoake of New Zeland, President Ferdinand E. M. Marcos of the Philippines, Prime Minister Thanon Kittikachorn of Thailand, President Lyndon B. Johnson of the United States of America, and Chairman Nguyen Van Thieu and Prime Minister Nguyen Cao Ky of the Republic of Viet-Nam.

Basic Policy

2. The nations represented at this conference are united in their determination that the freedom of South Viet-Nam be secured, in their resolve for peace, and in their deep concern for the future of Asia and the Pacific. Some of us are now close to the actual danger, while others have learned to know its significance through bitter past experience. This conference symbolizes our common purposes and high hopes.

3. We are united in our determination that the South Vietnamese people shall not be conquered by aggressive force and shall enjoy the inherent right to choose their own way of life and their own form of government. We shall continue our military and all other efforts, as firmly and as long as may be necessary, in close consultation among ourselves until the aggression is ended.

4. At the same time our united purpose is peace—peace in South Viet-Nam and in the rest of Asia and the Pacific. Our common commitment is to the defense of the South Vietnamese people. Our sole demand on the leaders of North Viet-Nam is that they abandon their aggression. We are prepared to pursue any avenue which could lead to a secure and just peace, whether through discussion and negotiation or through reciprocal actions by both sides to reduce the violence.

5. We are united in looking to a peaceful and prosperous future for all of Asia and the Pacific. We have therefore set forth in a separate declaration a statement of the principles that guide our common actions in this wider sphere.

6. Actions taken in pursuance of the policies herein stated

shall be in accordance with our respective constitutional processes.

Progress and Programs in South Viet-Nam
The Military Effort

7. The Government of Viet-Nam described the significant military progress being made against aggression. It noted with particular gratitude the substantial contribution being made by free world forces.

8. Nonetheless, the leaders noted that the movement of forces from North Viet-Nam continues at a high rate and that firm military action and free-world support continue to be required to meet the threat. The necessity for such military action and support must depend for its size and duration on the intensity and duration of the Communist aggression itself.

9. In their discussion, the leaders reviewed the problem of prisoners of war. The participants observed that Hanoi has consistently refused to cooperate with the international committee of the Red Cross in the application of the Geneva conventions, and called on Hanoi to do so. They reaffirmed their determination to comply fully with the Geneva conventions of 1949 for the protection of war victims, and welcomed the resolution adopted by the executive committee of the League of Red Cross Societies on October 8, 1966, calling for compliance with the Geneva conventions in the Viet-Nam conflict, full support for the International Committee of the Red Cross, and immediate action to repatriate seriously sick and wounded prisoners of war. They agreed to work toward the fulfillment of this resolution, in cooperation with the International Committee of the Red Cross, and indicated their willingness to meet under the auspices of the ICRC or in any appropriate forum to discuss the immediate exchange of prisoners.

Pacification and Revolutionary Development

10. The participating governments concentrated particular attention on the accelerating efforts of the Government of Viet-Nam to forge a social revolution of hope and progress. Even as the conflict continues, the effort goes forward to overcome the tyranny of poverty, disease, illiteracy and social injustice.

11. The Vietnamese leaders stated their intent to train and assign a substantial share of the armed forces to clear-and-hold actions in order to provide a shield behind which a new society can be built.

12. In the field of revolutionary development, measures along the lines developed in the past year and a half will be expanded and intensified. The training of revolutionary development cadres will be improved. More electricity and good water will be provided. More and better schools will be built and staffed. Refugees will be taught new skills. Health and medical facilities will be expanded.

13. The Vietnamese Government declared that it is working out a series of measures to modernize agriculture and to assure the cultivator the fruits of his labor. Land reform and tenure provisions will be granted top priority. Agricultural credit will be expanded. Crops will be improved and diversified.

14. The Vietnamese leaders emphasized that underlying these measures to build confidence and cooperation among the people there must be popular conviction that honesty, efficiency and social justice form solid cornerstones of the Vietnamese Government's programs.

15. This is a program each of the conferring governments has reason to applaud recognizing that it opens a brighter hope for the people of Viet-Nam. Each pledged its continuing assistance according to its means, whether in funds or skilled technicians or equipment. They noted also the help in non-military fields being given by other countries and expressed the hope that this help will be substantially increased.

Economic Stability and Progress

16. The Conference was told of the success of the Government of Viet-Nam in controlling the inflation which, if unchecked, could undercut all efforts to bring a more fulfilling life to the Vietnamese people. However, the Vietnamese leaders reaffirmed that only by constant effort could inflation be kept under control. They described their intention to enforce a vigorous stabilization program, to control spending, increase revenues, and seek to promote savings in order to hold the 1967 inflationary gap to the minimum practicable level. They also plan to take further measures to insure maximum utilization of

the port of Saigon, so that imports urgently needed to fuel the military effort and buttress the civil economy can flow rapidly into Viet-Nam.

17. Looking to the long-term future of their richly endowed country, the Vietnamese representatives described their views and plans for the building of an expanded post-war economy.

18. Military installations where appropriate will be converted to this purpose, and plans for this will be included.

19. The conferring nations reaffirmed their continuing support for Vietnamese efforts to achieve economic stability and progress. Thailand specifically noted its readiness to extend substantial new credit assistance for the purchase of rice and the other nations present reported a number of plans for the supply of food or other actions related to the economic situations. At the same time, the participants agreed to appeal to other nations and to international organizations committed to the full and free development of every nation, for further assistance to the Republic of Viet-Nam.

Political Evolution

20. The representative of Viet-Nam noted that, even as the conference met, steps were being taken to establish a new constitutional system for the Republic of Viet-Nam through the work of the Constituent Assembly, chosen by so large a proportion of the electorate last month.

21. The Vietnamese representatives stated their expectation that work on the constitution would go forward rapidly and could be completed before the deadline of March 1967. The constitution will then be promulgated and elections will be held within six months to select a representative government.

22. The Vietnamese Government believes that the democratic process must be strengthened at the local as well as the national level. The Government of Viet-Nam announced that to this end it will begin holding village and hamlet elections at the beginning of 1967.

23. The Government of Viet-Nam announced that it is preparing a program of national reconciliation. It declared its determination to open all doors to those Vietnamese who have been misled or coerced into casting their lot with the Viet-Cong.

The Government seeks to bring them back to participate as free men in national life under amnesty and other measures. Former enemies are asked only to lay down their weapons and bring their skills to the service of the South Vietnamese people.

24. The other participating nations welcomed the stated expectation of the Vietnamese representatives that work on the constitution will proceed on schedule, and concurred in the conviction of the Government of the Republic of Viet-Nam that building representative, constitutional government and opening the way for national reconciliation are indispensable to the future of a free Viet-Nam.

The Search for Peace

25. The participants devoted a major share of their deliberations to peace objectives and the search for a peaceful settlement in South Viet-Nam. They reviewed in detail the many efforts for peace that have been undertaken, by themselves and other nations, and the actions of the United Nations and of His Holiness the Pope. It was clearly understood that the settlement of the war in Viet-Nam depends on the readiness and willingness of the parties concerned to explore and work out together a just and reasonable solution. They noted that Hanoi still showed no sign of taking any step toward peace, either by action or by entering into discussions or negotiations. The search for peace must continue.

26. The Government of the Republic of Viet-Nam declared that the Vietnamese people, having suffered the ravages of war for more than two decades, were second to none in their desire for peace. It welcomes any initiative that will lead to an end to hostilities, preserves the independence of South Viet-Nam and protects the right to choose their own way of life.

27. So that their aspirations and positions would be clear to their allies at Manila and friends everywhere, the Government of the Republic of Viet-Nam solemnly stated its views as to the essential elements of peace in Viet-Nam.

(1) *Cessation of Aggression.* At issue in Viet-Nam is a struggle for the preservation of values which people everywhere have cherished since the dawn of history: the independence of peoples and the freedom of individuals. The

people of South Viet-Nam ask only that the aggression that threatens their independence and the externally supported terror that threatens their freedom be halted. No self-respecting people can ask for less. No peace loving nation should ask for more.

(2) *Preservation of the Territorial Integrity of South Viet-Nam.* The people of South Viet-Nam are defending their own territory against those seeking to obtain by force and terror what they have been unable to accomplish by peaceful means. While sympathizing with the plight of their brothers in the North and while disdaining the regime in the North, the South Vietnamese people have no desire to threaten or harm the people of the North or invade their country.

(3) *Reunification of Viet-Nam.* The Government and people of South Viet-Nam deplore the partition of Viet-Nam into North and South. But this partition brought about by the Geneva Agreements of 1954, however unfortunate and regrettable, will be respected until, by the free choice of all Vietnamese, reunification is achieved.

(4) *Resolution of Internal Problems.* The people of South Viet-Nam seek to resolve their own internal differences and to this end are prepared to engage in a program of national reconciliation. When the aggression has stopped, the people of South Viet-Nam will move more rapidly toward reconciliation of all elements in the society and will move forward, through the democratic process, toward human dignity, prosperity and lasting peace.

(5) *Removal of Allied Military Forces.* The people of South Viet-Nam will ask their allies to remove their forces and evacuate their installations as the military and subversive forces of North Viet-Nam are withdrawn, infiltration ceases, and the level of violence thus subsides.

(6) *Effective Guarantees.* The people of South Viet-Nam, mindful of their experience since 1954, insist that any negotiations leading to the end of hostilities incorporate effective international guarantees. They are openminded as to how such guarantees can be applied and made effective.

28. The other participating governments reviewed and endorsed these as essential elements of peace and agreed they would act on this basis in close consultation among themselves in regard to settlement of the conflict.

29. In particular, they declared that allied forces are in the Republic of Viet-Nam because that country is the object of aggression and its Government requested support in the resistance of its people to aggression. They shall be withdrawn, after close consultation, as the other side withdraws its forces to the north, ceases infiltration, and the level of violence thus subsides. Those forces will be withdrawn as soon as possible and not later than six months after the above conditions have been fulfilled.

Continuing Consultation Among the Participating Nations

30. All the participants agreed that the value of a meeting among the seven nations had been abundantly demonstrated by the candid and thorough discussions held. It was further agreed that, in addition to the close consultation already maintained through diplomatic channels, there should be regular meetings among their Ambassadors in Saigon in association with the Government of the Republic of Viet-Nam. Meetings of their Foreign Ministers and Heads of Government will also be held as required.

31. At the close of the meeting, all the visiting participants expressed their deep gratitude to President Marcos and to the Government of the Republic of the Philippines for offering Manila as the conference site, and expressed their appreciation for the highly efficient arrangements.

Declaration on Peace and Progress in Asia and the Pacific

We the leaders of the seven nations gathered in Manila: desiring peace and progress in the Asian-Pacific region; having faith in the purposes and principles of the United Nations which call for the suppression of acts of aggression and respect for the principle of equal rights and self-determination of peoples; determined that aggression should not be rewarded; respecting the right of all peoples to choose and maintain their own forms of government; seeking a peaceful settlement of the war in Viet-Nam; and being greatly encouraged by the growing regional understanding and regional cooperation among the free nations of Asia and the Pacific hereby proclaim this declaration of principles on which we base our hopes for future peace and progress in the Asian and Pacific region:

I. Aggression must not succeed.

The peace and security of Asia and the Pacific and, indeed, of the entire world, are indivisible. The nations of the Asian and Pacific region shall enjoy their independence and sovereignty free from aggression, outside interference, or the domination of any nation. Accepting the hard-won lessons of history that successful aggression anywhere endangers the peace, we are determined to fulfill our several commitments under the United Nations Charter and various mutual security treaties so that aggression in the region of Asia and the Pacific shall not succeed.

II. We must break the bonds of poverty, illiteracy and disease.

In the region of Asia and the Pacific, where there is a rich heritage of the intrinsic worth and dignity of every man, we recognize the responsibility of every nation to join in an expanding offensive against poverty, illiteracy and disease. For these bind men to lives of hopelessness and despair; these are the roots of violence and war. It is when men know that progress is possible and is being achieved, when they are convinced that their children will lead better, fuller, richer lives, that men lift up their heads in hope and pride. Only thus can there be lasting national stability and international order.

III. We must strengthen economic, social and cultural cooperation within the Asian and Pacific region.

Together with our other partners of Asia and the Pacific, we will develop the institutions and practice of regional cooperation. Through sustained effort we aim to build in this vast area, where almost two-thirds of humanity live, a region of security and order and progress, realizing its common destiny in the light of its own traditions and aspirations. The peoples of this region have the right as well as the primary responsibility to deal with their own problems and to shape their own future in terms of their own wisdom and experience. Economic and cultural cooperation for regional development should be open to all countries in the region, irrespective of creed or ideology, which genuinely follow a policy of peace and harmony among all nations. Nations outside the region will be welcomed as partners working for the common benefit and their cooperation will be sought in forms consonant with the independence and dignity of the Asian and Pacific nations.

A peaceful and progressive Asia, in which nations are able to work together for the common good, will be a major factor in establishing peace and prosperity throughout the world and improving the prospects of international cooperation and a better life for all mankind.

IV. We must seek reconciliation and peace throughout Asia.

We do not threaten the sovereignty or territorial integrity of our neighbors, whatever their ideological alignment. We ask only that this be reciprocated. The quarrels and ambitions of ideology and the painful frictions arising from national fears and grievances should belong to the past. Aggression rooted in them must not succeed. We shall play our full part in creating an environment in which reconciliation becomes possible, for in the modern world men and nations have no choice but to learn to live together as brothers.

RUSSELL LONG

On China*

Mr. President, with my responsibilities of being chairman of a committee as well as the assistant majority leader, I was not able to be present at the hearings of the Foreign Relations Committee, but I want to say that these advocates of retreat, defeat, surrender, and national dishonor have not been doing the country any good when they went before a television network suggesting that this Nation was not committed to fighting aggression in this area. The Senate voted for the resolution last year, and Senators voted that this country would help that country resist aggression, and specifically authorized the President to take whatever steps he felt necessary to resist further aggression. We are committed. We have more than 200,000 men there. We have at stake our national honor. We are committed to resisting Communist aggression. That is what this is all about. It has been going on for some time.

* Congressional Record, February 16, 1966.

The Senator from Alaska voted against the resolution, and he was privileged to do it, but once the Congress adopted that resolution, it had taken a firm position. Once Congress authorized the President to do that which he felt necessary, the President was authorized to do it. It was authorized in the resolution and discussed specifically during the debate on the floor of the Senate. He was authorized to send troops wherever necessary to resist aggression in the area.

It is not helping our country when Senators go before the Nation and express their fears on this issue that the Red Chinese might come in, and the fact that we are losing some American boys. We are inflicting at least 10 to 1 damage on the North Viet-Nam invaders compared to the losses suffered by our forces.

If this great nation is to be humiliated, is to be defeated and run out and be downgraded to a second-class power by that little nation, then I wish Red China would come in. It would be a great humiliation for this Nation to be defeated by a small nation of 16 million people. If we must be defeated, it would be better to lose to a large nation of 700 million people.

This Nation was founded because we had courageous men. We became a great nation because the people had courage. They did not give up because they had to fight Indians. If the men who came on the *Mayflower* were frightened to helplessness the first time they had to fight Indians, they would have gone back to England on the *Mayflower*. But they fought the Indians and won, meanwhile losing some fine Americans, until this Nation became great. We are upholding our commitments in the proud tradition of our fathers, grandfathers, great-grandfathers, and many other courageous Americans who fell on the field of battle.

I only wish that back during the Civil War there had been a humorous element in the Congress that would have appeared daily before a nationwide television network and have said, "We fought and lost a Yankee today. We lost a boy today, let us quit." If they had spread that propaganda, it might have spread fear. Maybe the war would have gone the other way. Then we would have won the principles of States' rights. We would prove that we were the strong people. Having achieved victory we could have offered to rejoin the Union with considerable pride that our theory of States' rights had been sustained.

B. THE OTHER SIDE

Introduction

As seen from Hanoi and the National Liberation Front in the field, the escalation of the war by the United States has caused them to intensify their military efforts and to multiply their diplomatic efforts in order to receive military and material support from the Sino-Soviet bloc. In late 1965 the United States admitted that the North Vietnamese had made various attempts since 1964 to ascertain a common ground for negotiations. However, the United States had not taken seriously such North Vietnamese feelers, believing that even the rumor of such negotiations would lead to the collapse of the South Vietnamese client government. As such feelers failed, as every American profession of peaceful intent was matched by a further military escalation and troop commitment, Hanoi discounted altogether the argument that the United States wanted a negotiated end to the conflict.

The primary interest of the National Liberation Front remains "the prospect of a South Viet-Nam completely liberated, really independent and democratic" which, in the view of its leader, Nguyen Huu Tho, "is no longer a dream and a matter of conviction but has become a living truth." While there is no doubt that both the Liberation Front and Hanoi desire ultimate reunification—as does Hanoi-born Premier Nguyen Kao Ky of South Viet-Nam—the documentation shows a difference of priorities between Hanoi and the National Liberation Front. While the North Vietnamese appear satisfied with a return to the Geneva Agreement, and are willing to accept, for a limited time, the presence of American troops, there is no evidence that the Liberation Front is willing to adopt a similarly conciliatory attitude. As long as there is a difference in view and interest between the NLF and the North Vietnamese, there is a real policy requirement for the United States to deal directly with the National Liberation Front regardless of how much or how little it is considered controlled by Hanoi. During World War II when Italy was the junior Axis partner and Germany indeed directed the war on the other side, the allies found it in the most selfish national interest to deal directly with the Italians instead of insisting upon obtaining Berlin's surrender first.

As becomes clear from a reading of the recent statements of the NLF and of the senior leaders in Hanoi, their conviction has, if anything, hardened in their estimation of the character of this war. They firmly believe that popular support can still outweigh the effect of American military technology and, as Ho Chi Minh expressed it recently, they also feel that they would be capable of surviving the eventual destruction of the cities and industries of North Viet-Nam. If that assumption is correct then the United States may well have to face up to an enemy which is prepared to fight for a generation.

NGUYEN HUU THO

*Reply to the Japanese Newspaper "Akahata"**

Hereunder are the replies to the first three questions put to Me Nguyen Huu Tho, President of the Presidium of the South Viet-Nam NLF Central Committee:

QUESTION: Would you please describe the main features of the South Vietnamese people's heroic struggle against the U.S. imperialists and their henchmen over the last five years under the skilful and correct leadership of the NLF?

ANSWER: After defeating, together with the entire Vietnamese people, the U.S.-backed French colonialists, and winning glorious victory in the first War of Resistance (1945–1954) the South Vietnamese people have, over the last eleven years, had to cope with the utterly atrocious intervention and aggression of the U.S. imperialists, the extremely ferocious and dangerous ringleader of imperialism. Making untold sacrifices and overcoming indescribable hardships, the South Vietnamese people's patriotic movement has constantly developed and led to the

* From *Vietnam Courier*, Hanoi, February 24, 1966.

founding of the South Viet-Nam National Front for Liberation
five years ago, on December 20, 1960. With the coming into
being of the NLF the South Vietnamese people's valiant struggle
switched on to a new stage, that of big and repeated victories
in all fields. The main features of this new stage are:

1. By upholding the banner of patriotism and justice with
the aim of driving out the U.S. aggressors, overthrowing the
puppet administration, achieving independence, democracy,
peace and neutrality in South Viet-Nam and the reunification
of the country, the NLF, reflecting the most legitimate aspirations of the South Vietnamese people and meeting the most
urgent demands of patriots from all strata in South Viet-Nam,
has therefore succeeded in forming the broadest and strongest
ever solidarity bloc of the entire people to oppose the U.S.
aggressors and save the country. This first great achievement of
the NLF is precisely the most basic step which has paved the
way for later successes of the South Vietnamese people's patriotic struggle. It is also the root cause which has led to the
defeat of all colonialist maneuvers and aggressive military plans
of the U.S. imperialists at their inception.

2. Though at the beginning the odds against the South Vietnamese people were overwhelming in the balance of forces
between them on one side, and the aggressors and traitors on
the other, the NLF has resolutely led the people's self-defense
struggle and developed it into a real people's war which has
become more and more effective day after day against the U.S.
aggressive war. This was possible thanks to the Front's deep
confidence in the tremendous strength of the masses which have
risen up against oppression, its spirit of thorough-going revolution without the least illusion about the enemy's extremely stubborn and wicked nature.

From the jungle to the countryside and even in the towns
temporarily controlled by the enemy, the people's war has developed vigorously and widely, thus making a closely combined
action possible between various areas, drawing millions of people
to the frontline to wage a political and armed struggle, attack
and harass the enemy everywhere and repeatedly foil their aggressive plans.

In only five years, led and inspired by the NLF the South
Vietnamese people, starting from scratch have succeeded in

founding a powerful political army and powerful armed forces. The political army composed of millions of people of different ages, with the great contingent of women as its core is better and better organized and has constantly taken the initiative in attacking the enemy, and has shaken and disintegrated to its foundations the enemy administration in the rural and urban areas, destroyed by big chunks the "strategic hamlets" system— backbone of the enemy's aggressive plans.

The armed forces have also developed quickly in all fields— politics, tactics, technique, organization and command.

Organized into three armed forces—guerilla, regional forces and regular army—along the line of people's war defined by the NLF, the Liberation Armed Forces, together with the rest of the people, have during five years' fighting recorded brilliant achievements: wiped out or disintegrated a force of over 550,-000 American and puppet troops, captured nearly 70,000 guns of different kinds, shot down or destroyed nearly 2,500 aircraft, destroyed nearly 6,000 of the 8,000 "strategic hamlets" set up by the enemy. The tremendously quick tempo of growth in both effectives and quality of the Liberation Armed Forces have gone beyond all calculations of the U.S. aggressive ringleaders and upset all their war plans.

3. As a result of the repeated victories recorded by the South Viet-Nam armed forces and people, the South Viet-Nam NLF now controls over four-fifths of the South Viet-Nam territory inhabited by more than 10 million people.

A vast liberated area has been formed, stretching from the Ben Hai river bank [south of the 17th parallel—] through the immense High Plateaux to the fertile plains of Nam Bo [South Viet-Nam proper]. This tremendous achievement recorded by the South Vietnamese people during five years' fighting and sacrifices under the glorious banner of the South Viet-Nam NLF is of tremendous significance: It has created a material basis for the NLF to gradually translate its program into reality, and at the same time conditions for the South Vietnamese people to increase their potential in all fields and actively prepare for a long fight against the U.S. imperialists till complete victory.

For the South Vietnamese people, the prospect of a South Viet-Nam completely liberated, really independent and democratic is no longer a dream and a matter of conviction, but has become a living truth: a new and really democratic society of the people is taking shape in the liberated area. Revolutionary administrative organs have been set up down to liberated hamlet and village levels in the form of people's self-governing committees. These not only care for, mobilize and organize the people to carry out the resistance war and see to the security of the liberated areas but also do their best to improve the people's life in all fields. Two million hectares of ricefields have been allotted by the Front to the peasants, thus increasing many times the fighting power of the main army of the revolution. Developing production has been able to meet in a more and more adequate fashion the needs of the people and the resistance war. Cultural and educational work has also been developed widely and incessantly along a national, scientific and popular line. Though faced with many difficulties created by the enemy, the protection of the people's health continues to record great achievements thanks to the closely combined use of popular traditional medicine and modern medicine.

As a result of the ever greater successes of the South Viet-Nam army and people, the liberated areas have consolidated and developed continually, thereby creating a situation in which the areas still under the enemy's temporary control are subject to an encirclement and pressure. At the same time, thanks to its ever greater attraction, they have contributed to promoting the people's struggle in the enemy-controlled areas.

Frightened by the growth and influence of the liberated areas, the U.S. aggressors and their henchmen have stopped at no barbarous and cruel schemes to sabotage these tremendous achievements of the people and to misrepresent and slander the liberated areas. However, all these schemes and tricks have met with failure.

Inspired by the results gained at the cost of their own blood, the South Vietnamese people are resolved to fight to the end to safeguard and develop these gains and to march forward and sweep off the enemy from the whole country.

4. The U.S. imperialists are the sworn enemy of the South Vietnamese people and the cruel enemy number one of the peoples throughout the world. They are committing aggression in South Viet-Nam while using it as a testing ground of method of repression and aggression to be applied in other countries.

The South Vietnamese people are determined to foil this dark design.

The South Vietnamese people's just cause of national liberation is closely linked with the struggle of the world's peoples for independence, democracy, peace and social progress, and constitutes at the same time an active contribution to that common cause. That is precisely why an international front of solidarity with the South Vietnamese people against U.S. aggression has been formed in practice and has been growing in size and strength with every passing day.

The peoples and governments of all socialist countries and many Asian and African countries, and peoples of many other countries including the American people have been giving the South Vietnamese people an extremely great and effective assistance, not only political and moral but also material.

The international movement of solidarity with, and support for, the South Vietnamese people has also developed in the form of continual drives of stirring struggle on a world scale with the participation of thousands of millions of people, inspiring and encouraging us, energetically denouncing and condemning the U.S. imperialists and urging them to end their aggressive war in South Viet-Nam.

It may be said that never has a national liberation movement been so strongly supported by the world, and never have the U.S. imperialists been so isolated and decried by world public opinion.

5. The U.S. imperialists' neo-colonialist policy and "special war" have received deadly blows from the South Vietnamese people in their most fundamental aspects.

To carry out their aggressive war in South Viet-Nam, the U.S. imperialists have been relying on the puppet army and administration set up by them. But now the former is disintegrating at an increasing tempo on the battlefield, and the latter has also decayed to such a point that it has become only a moribund administration, hated by the South Vietnamese people and spurned by world public opinion. The fact that the U.S. imperialists had to resort to war as a means to realize their neo-colonialism spelled out a most basic step toward the collapse of U.S. policy of aggression in the present world situation. Now, they have been compelled to send combat troops for direct aggression in South Viet-Nam and engage deeper and deeper in the intensification and expansion of the war. This is another new step towards bankruptcy bearing a great significance for the world's peoples. Today, in spite of all kinds of double talk about "peace" and "negotiation," they have appeared under their true colors as the most cruel and bloodthirsty aggressive colonialist devil.

QUESTION: What is the political and military significance of the development of the valiant struggle of the South Vietnamese people?

ANSWER: The whole world is following with special interest the development of the South Viet-Nam war not only because the U.S. imperialists have more and more stubbornly fanned up the flames of war thus seriously threatening peace in Indo-China, Southeast Asia and the world, but also because the heroic struggle of the South Vietnamese people has given rise to a number of problems bearing an important political and military significance. The people and the NLF of South Viet-Nam through their own experiences have clearly realized that:

1. The colonialists and imperialists, especially U.S. imperialism, always remain the sworn enemy of the independence, democracy, peace and social progress of the peoples. Whatever deceitful maneuvers they may resort to, their piratical and bellicose nature remains unchanged. Since they use counter-revolutionary violence to repress the people at home and enslave others in foreign countries, the oppressed people must necessarily resort to revolutionary violence to resist them and wipe them out. The popular masses can be truly liberated and peace really safeguarded only by the line of thorough revolution.

2. In their life-and-death struggle against the oppressor and aggressor, the revolutionary people may have started with virtually nothing in their hands. But if they grow more deeply conscious of the justice of their cause, realize their own strength, and struggle with burning hatred against the enemy, they are thereby equipped with arms which no steel of the enemy, however hard, nor weapon, however destructive, can match.

3. People struggling against oppression and aggression always have to endure sacrifices and overcome hardships, and will certainly win complete victory in the end provided that there is correct leadership, that the people are united, that the struggle

enjoys widespread and strong support from the world's peoples, and that constant efforts are made to tap all revolutionary potentialities and constantly reinforce one's own strength, while paying attention to detecting and thoroughly aggravating the enemy's weaknesses, guiding the masses to march forward from minor victories to major ones, pushing back the enemy step by step and wiping them out unit by unit as a first step toward throwing off their yoke.

4. The heyday of the colonialists and imperialists has gone forever. One should not be afraid of the enemy. He can be completely defeated even if he is as brutal and bloodthirsty as the U.S. imperialists. When the oppressed people dare to stand up and know how to hit back at the enemy, improve their method of counter-attacks, develop their fight into a full-scale people's war, all aggressive wars of the enemy, in whatever form, can be defeated together with their oppression in whatever form.

QUESTION: In your opinion, what are the prospects for the South Vietnamese people's struggle?

ANSWER: The prospects for the patriotic struggle of the South Vietnamese people are: "The South Vietnamese people will certainly win! The U.S. imperialists will certainly be defeated!"

This assumption has long been not only a rocklike conviction of the fourteen million South Vietnamese people but has become that of thousands of millions of people who cherish independence, freedom, justice and world peace.

To make plain the practical basis of the above assumption, I deem it necessary to review the process of the eleven-year struggle of the South Vietnamese people through its main stages. During the first six years, opposing their bare hands to the guns and bullets, guillotines and even poison of the enemy, the indomitable South Vietnamese people never ceased to develop their patriotic movement and thereby inflicted initial failures on the U.S. imperialists' policy of intervention and neo-colonialism. In 1961 when the U.S. imperialists threw off their interventionist mask and started their "special war" in South Viet-Nam, the South Vietnamese people already enjoying the NLF leadership powerfully marched forward to frustrate all their military plans. The failure of the Staley-Taylor plan shattered the fantastic dream to pacify South Viet-Nam within eighteen months nurtured by the U.S. aggressive ringleaders. And then the Taylor-

McNamara plan, which was only designed to pacify a number of key provinces in South Viet-Nam also went bankrupt, thus driving the enemy farther into a confused and defensive position. Since early 1965, flummoxed and floundering in both strategy and tactics, the U.S. imperialists have recklessly and massively dispatched additional troops to invade South Viet-Nam, and at the same time expanded the war to North Viet-Nam, hoping to "turn the tide" and "regain the initiative." But in fact, the Johnson-McNamara clique have committed one mistake after another. Not only have they failed to "change" their tragic situation and regain any measure of "initiative," but they have also been sinking ever more deeply into the swamp of failure and impasse. The forces of the South Vietnamese army and people have rapidly grown up in all fields, and throughout the year, in the dry season as well in the rainy season and then in the dry season again they have dealt the enemy repeated telling blows. About 20,000 U.S. aggressors of the most seasoned units armed with the most modern and up-to-date equipment were put out of action. More than forty battalions of puppet main forces with hundreds of thousands of troops were wiped out.

Though suffering heavy setbacks the U.S. imperialists, still obdurately nurturing their aggressive dream, have resorted to deceitful "peace" claptrap, staged the "unconditional discussions" farce in an attempt to soothe public opinion and cover up their ever more frantic aggressive activities. But the South Vietnamese people and the progressive people in the world are ready and highly vigilant. However obdurate and bellicose they may be, whatever perfidious tricks they may resort to and however long they may prolong the war, the U.S. imperialists will finally and certainly be defeated.

The South Vietnamese people who, starting from scratch, have promoted their cause to the present stage and created for themselves all factors of victory, will shrink before no sacrifices and hardships to fulfill their glorious task of liberating South Viet-Nam and reunifying the country.

GENERAL VO NGUYEN GIAP

The Present Military Situation in Viet-Nam

DATA AND PROSPECTS

A New Stage In U.S. Aggressive War

By the end of July 1965 after General Taylor had had to resign and as McNamara, back in Washington from Saigon, had been busy pressing more troops for South Viet-Nam, the American press wrote: The reason for the new U.S. involvement is obvious . . . because the Saigon army and government have lost the war. So the 500,000 puppet troops commanded by the Americans have not been able to cope with our people's patriotic war; our people's patriotic war has prevailed over the U.S. "special war." The immediate dispatching of a U.S. expeditionary corps to the South Viet-Nam battlefield is an untoward emergency move, a strategically passive move in an attempt to retrieve the worsening predicament of the puppet clique. . . .

In the South of our country as in many parts of the world, faced with the growth of the socialist camp and the national liberation movement, to hide their aggressive nature the American imperialists have applied neo-colonialism with the customary policies and maneuvers, hoping to enslave our nation through their agents and by means of military and economic aid. In the period between 1954 and 1959 since the day when they brought Ngo Dinh Diem to Saigon and staged the "Republic of Viet-Nam" farce, the U.S. imperialists sought every means to carry out those neo-colonialist tricks. . . .

Continuing their scheme of aggression against the South, the American imperialists had to resort to new war methods to reach their goal.

To use war to achieve neo-colonialism constituted a heavy setback for the U.S. imperialists. In their passivity they still tried to hide their cruel nature under the disguise of an undeclared war, of the so-called "special war." This is a kind of war that the many American military theoreticians do not regard as a real war as far as the aggressor is concerned. As a matter of

* From *Vietnam Courier*, Hanoi, January 27, 1966.

fact, this is a kind of war waged by the native stooge reactionary force, the puppet army and administration, equipped with arms, materials and other war means supplied by the U.S., following the American imperialists' plan and commanded by the U.S. with a view to crushing the revolutionary struggle and destroying the patriotic forces in the South of our country.

The first plan mapped out by the American imperialists for this war was the Staley-Taylor plan. They reckoned that with their enormous material force they could "pacify" the whole South of our country within eighteen months. But they met with the extremely heroic resistance of the Southern people, led by the South Viet-Nam National Front for Liberation. The Staley-Taylor plan came to grief and was buried together with the Ngo Dinh Diem regime which piteously collapsed on November 1, 1963.

In 1964 the U.S. imperialists put forward a new strategic plan, the Johnson-McNamara plan aimed at "pacifying" South Viet-Nam within two years. Again they increased the flows of war means, military and economic aid and advisers. They even stated that by the end of 1965—after their victory—the withdrawal of their advisers would begin, in an endeavor to force upon the American people and world public opinion the belief that it was not an American war. However, the resistance for national salvation of the Liberation armed forces and people in the South had gained strength and great successes which culminated in the glorious Binh Gia victory. Soon the Johnson-McNamara plan shared the fate of the Staley-Taylor plan.

In face of this failure and predicament the U.S. imperialists took a step farther in their adventurist aggression by raising their "special war" to its highest degree in the hope to retrieve this strategy when the initiative is lost. Their scheme is:

1. To step up their aggressive war in the South of our country by reinforcing U.S. and satellite combat units while consolidating the puppet administration, strengthening the puppet army and bolstering the puppet reactionary forces as the mainstay and a tool of the aggressive war.

2. To expand the war mostly by intensifying their air strikes against the North of our country, regarding it as part of their neo-colonialist aggressive war to threaten the North and save the situation in the South.

3. Together with this intensification and expansion of the aggressive war they carry out a so-called diplomatic and psychological campaign with double talk about "peaceful settlement" and "unconditional discussions" in an attempt to dupe public opinion and cover up their dark design.

However, the American imperialists cannot shake the determination of our people in both zones to fight them for national salvation, cannot cause any decrease in the wholehearted assistance of the Northern people to the patriotic struggle of the Southern people, let alone stabilize the very critical position of the puppet army and administration.

In brief, in the South as well as in the North, in mid-1965 the U.S. imperialists and their henchmen were meeting with heavy setbacks:

—In the face of the repeated offensives of the South Viet-Nam Liberation armed forces, the puppet army had been driven further into a passive situation, an increasing number of puppet battalions had been wiped out and the morale of the puppet troops had been alarmingly declining.

—The Saigon puppet administration had been ever more rotten and after thirteen coups it had become utterly inefficient in the hands of the unruly "Young Turks."

—The system of "strategic hamlets" continued disintegrating while the people's movement in towns was rising. The powerful upsurge of the army and people in Central and South Trung Bo had compelled the enemy to abandon part of his scheme to concentrate on pacifying the Mekong river delta. The rural areas controlled by the U.S. imperialists and their agents had been markedly reduced while the liberated areas expanded and built into the firm rear of the liberation war.

—In their "escalation" against the North, the U.S. imperialists unable to shake our people's determination to fight them for national salvation, had been suffering heavy losses. The Northern people's hatred for the U.S. imperialists had been all the more embittered and their emulation drive of production and fighting for national salvation had become the more resolute to defeat the U.S. imperialist aggressors, to defend the North and liberate the South.

The situation described above shows that the U.S. strategy of "special war" developed to its highest degree had been foiled in the main. The fact that Johnson recalled Taylor in July while hurriedly dispatching troops to South Viet-Nam at an accelerated tempo evidences the American imperialists' panic and passiveness in face of their discomfiture. And it is due precisely to this failure and passiveness that they frenziedly stepped up their war efforts according to a new strategy aimed at reversing the situation and wresting back strategic initiative in the South. This once again proves that the U.S. imperialists' scheme to occupy the South has not changed at all. Thereupon the impudent nature of the American aggressors has been fully laid bare. The U.S. imperialists have thrown off their last mask and appeared in their true colors as colonialist aggressors.

It is not the case of an ordinary transfer from one stage to another but a shift to a new strategic stage of their aggressive war. The main characteristic of this stage is that the American imperialists not only make use of the puppet reactionary armed forces—i.e., the puppet army—as the main tool of the war, but also bring in a U.S. expeditionary corps for a direct invasion of the South while continuing to expand the war of destruction mostly by air strikes to the North of our country. . . .

The U.S. troops are the core, serving as the military mainstay of the puppet army and administration and the main mobile force, and as the occupying force in important strategic bases and the strategic and tactical reserve, taking a direct part in the combat in an attempt to wipe out our people's revolutionary force on the Southern battlefield.

The puppet army which relies on the American troops to exist, consolidate and develop, constitutes both the mobile force on the battlefield and the main force to control and pacify the people, while serving as the political mainstay of the U.S. troops.

Clearly enough, in military strategy, the American imperialists have gone beyond the limits and scope of the "special war." Of course, while they step up their aggressive war according to their new strategy, the U.S. imperialists' purpose is to continue achieving neo-colonialism in South Viet-Nam. . . .

U.S. Outward Strength and Most Fundamental Weakness

The U.S. imperialists are the international gendarme, the topmost imperialists, with the most powerful economic and military potential of all the imperialists. By taking a direct part in the aggressive war they hope to rely on their material strength to overcome all difficulties in man power and politics thereby to retrieve their predicament in the South. With a sizable expeditionary corps which is to be eventually increased they hope to give themselves new vantage-grounds on the battlefield: *First,* to strengthen their military force in general, especially their strategic mobile force, thereby to tilt the balance of forces in their favor; *second,* to control important strategic areas and set up firm bases as springboards, to launch raids or attacks against the liberated areas; *third,* to build up their air force, develop their superiority in this arm to decimate our forces and to strike deep into the liberated areas.

Their scheme is to prevent the collapse of the puppet army and administration; to launch offensives aimed at wiping out the Southern revolutionary forces, to strive to consolidate the areas still under their control and gradually to carry out a pacification with key areas, to attack the liberated areas and to wrest back some of the lost areas; to seek every means to encircle and isolate the Southern battlefield; meanwhile to intensify the war of destruction against the North and carry on their deceptive peace negotiations campaign.

Banking upon a force of over 700,000 men to be eventually increased, the American imperialists hope to realize their scheme by means of more radical and efficacious measures. They reckon that they can gradually win military and political successes, secure a position of strength to end the war with a solution favorable to them, or to prolong or expand the aggressive war when necessary.

The U.S. imperialists' design is very ambitious, their scheme most perfidious, and their military and political maneuvers extremely cruel and cunning. However, beside their definite strong points in material strength the American imperialists have most fundamental weak points in political and military fields, in both strategy and tactics. . . .

The dispatch of an expeditionary corps for a direct invasion of our country is itself afflicted with most fundamental weak points they cannot overcome.

First, the sending of their troops directly to invade our country, exposes all the clearer the U.S. imperialists' true colors as agressors and their lackeys' as traitors, whereby the contradiction between the American imperialists and our nation becomes all the sharper and fiercer. Stirred by their hatred for the aggressors our entire people broadly and firmly unite within the National United Front against the U.S. imperialists and their stooges. All patriotic forces are determined to fight for national salvation. Moreover, many Vietnamese in the enemy-temporarily controlled area, even in the puppet army and administration, in the parties and organizations under the sway of the U.S. puppets, so far unaware of the nature and scheme of the American imperialists and their minions, now begin to see the latter's true nature as aggressors and traitors.

Second, due to U.S. imperialists' dispatching of their troops to invade our country in the conditions when the strategy of their "special war" has fundamentally gone bankrupt while our people's patriotic war has developed with a very powerful mettle, the Liberation armed forces have grown up, and the liberated areas have included the major part of the Southern population and territory, though they may bring in hundreds of thousands of troops, they cannot avoid being driven into passivity in strategy, compelled to scatter their forces in the defensive as well as in the offensive, and cannot easily wrest back the initiative as they wish but instead face increasing failures and predicament.

Third, due to their above-mentioned loss of political and military initiative no matter how modern its equipment, the American expeditionary corps cannot bring into full play its combativeness, and cannot escape the inevitable defeat which is likely to befall any aggressive army facing a whole nation resolute to resist them. . . .

Fourth, the purpose of the U.S. imperialists' introduction of troops into the South being to prevent the collapse of the puppet army and administration, and create new conditions to consolidate and strengthen the puppet forces, the U.S. imperialists directly invade the South of our country at a moment when the puppet army and administration are seriously weakening. In this situation, the more direct the Americans' aggression, the more isolated and differentiated the puppet army and administration are, the greater the contradiction between the U.S. imperialists and their placement, the more conscious those who have any national feeling among the puppet army and administration become and the more numerous those who cross over to the people's side. Consequently, American military build-up not only cannot retrieve the predicament of the puppet army and administration but instead speeds up the latter's collapse in face of our people's resistance. When the American imperialists' crack troops are defeated by our people, the disintegration and collapse of the puppet army and administration will be all the more inevitable.

Fifth, the U.S. imperialists having started the war in the South, are more and more sternly condemned by the peace-loving people in the world. Now that they openly send their troops for a direct aggression against the South and use their air force to strike at the North, an independent and sovereign socialist state, they are meeting with increasing energetic opposition from the peoples of the socialist countries and the world's progressive people including the American people.

The strong points of the U.S. imperialists are limited whereas their weak points are basic ones. In the process of development of the aggressive war the latter will become more and more visible and aggravated and will surely lead the American imperialists to ignominious failure.

Decisive Factors of Our Victory

1. The first factor is the Party's correct revolutionary line. This line is the condensed expression of the clever and creative combination of Marxist-Leninist general principles with the concrete practice of our revolution. This is the line of the people's national democratic revolution progressing to socialism, in a former semi-feudal colony. . . . A correct revolutionary line is the surest guarantee for our people's ultimate victory in their just struggle against the American imperialists for national salvation.

2. The second factor is the unity of the entire people against the U.S. imperialists for national salvation: North and South are of one mind in their determination to defeat the American aggressors and their lackeys, ready to make every sacrifice rather than lose their independence and be enslaved. This iron will reflects our entire people's tradition of indomitable resistance

against foreign aggression. It has united our people, millions like one, resolute to fight to defend our country and secure independence, democracy, unity and peace.

Our compatriots in the South have closed their ranks in the fire of the revolutionary struggle, fought throughout twenty long years, overcome countless difficulties, braved a cruel enemy with a firm resolve to march forward, to fight and to win. Today our people in the South have the National Front for Liberation, a broad-based organization possessed of a correct line and program and enjoying high prestige at home and abroad. . . .

Meanwhile the people in the North of our country are steadily progressing to socialism with an ardent love for the fatherland and for socialism and with an unprecedented political and spiritual identity of mind. The North is not only a source of inspiration but also *a firm rear for the struggle against the U.S. imperialists for national salvation of our entire people,* endowed with an excellent political system and strong economic and national defense potential. This is a favorable condition which did not exist in our former resistance against the French imperialists.

Since the American imperialists extended their war of destruction to the North, our army and people there have stood up, fought resolutely and inflicted initial defeats upon the enemy's war of destruction. In response to the call of the Party Central Committee, the Government and President Ho Chi Minh, our people in the North have launched a Movement Against the U.S. Imperialists for National Salvation to carry out production while fighting, fight heroically in defense of the North, give wholehearted and all-out support to the liberation revolution in the South and make a substantial contribution to the common victory of the whole nation.

The Vietnamese nation has always had a tradition of unity and unbending resistance against foreign aggression, but if we look back to its several thousand-year old history as well as to the revolutionary struggle of the past years, we shall realize that never have the entire people united so firmly and broadly as today, never has the will to fight off aggression and defend the country been promoted to such a degree as today.

3. The third factor is the invincible people's war and the experience to lead this struggle. If one can say that at present

in military affairs apart from the great invention of atomic weapon there is a greater invention, people's war, one can safely say that the Vietnamese people have contributed to the devising and the efficient wielding of such an invincible weapon. People's war in our country has developed in the historical, political and social conditions of Viet-Nam and achieved a very high standard with an extremely varied content. . . .

4. The fourth factor is the warm sympathy and wholehearted support given us by the people of the brother socialist countries, and the progressive people the world over, including the American people. Our people's struggle against the U.S. imperialists for national salvation aims not only at liberating a half of our country still enslaved but also at defending the socialist North. This great struggle is the frontline of progressive mankind against American imperialism, it is making a great contribution to the world peoples' revolutionary struggle for peace, national independence, democracy and socialism. That is precisely why the brother socialist countries have given their unreserved support to the stand and line of struggle against the American imperialists for national salvation of our government and of the South Viet-Nam National Front for Liberation and lent an all-out assistance to our people to defeat the U.S. imperialist aggressors. . . .

What Facts Prove

The question is: Which will win in the end? Our people or the American imperialists? Throughout the past eleven years, every time the U.S. imperialists launch a new aggressive scheme that same question is raised. The liberation struggle of the heroic Southern people has supplied an eloquent answer: whatever trick the American imperialists may resort to they will inevitably fail in the end. And the fundamental law of the great patriotic struggle of our compatriots in the South throughout the various stages is: the farther the U.S. imperialists and their flunkies engage in their scheme to enslave the South of our country the deeper they sink in their morass and the greater their defeats, whereas the more determined the Vietnamese people's struggle the greater their victories.

Today the question as to which will win in the South is more pressing than ever for at the present juncture there has emerged a new factor: the introduction by the American imperialists of hundreds of thousands of troops. *Can these massive reinforcements reverse the situation? Can the Vietnamese people who have recorded many great successes in their just struggle, win new victories in face of direct aggression by such modern an army as the U.S. imperialists? Can they defeat the American expeditionary corps?*

. . . If in the past when they brought Ngo Dinh Diem to power and began to realize the Collins plan or when they put forth the Staley-Taylor plan or the Johnson-McNamara plan the American imperialists had been extremely optimistic and reckoned that their dark design would be certainly achieved, today when they begin to send a huge expeditionary corps to the South they firmly believed that they could turn the tide. They were confident that within a short time, the pattern of the aggressive war would change; that with their crack divisions and brigades, their strategic and tactical air force they were fully able to change the correlation of forces, set up solid defense positions, launch bold offensives, push ahead their pacification with key points, thereby not only preventing the collapse of the puppet army and administration but also consolidating and strengthening their stooges, the reactionary forces. The Pentagonians hastily declared that: At the very moment when big U.S. combat units were introduced into the South and the war was intensified there were wide prospects of a quick victory. When their first military operations do not yet meet with any retaliation to speak of they hastened to declare out of optimism that they had shifted to the offensive and compelled the Southern Liberation troops to disperse their forces and undertake only small formations. They also made dramatic preparations for attacks on all fronts in the coming dry season in order to wrest back the initiative and hold it more and more firmly, and drive the Southern people into an ever more serious passive position.

However, reality has fallen short of the U.S. imperialists' expectations and purposes. From the point of view of general strategy on the Southern battlefield *is the enemy applying a strategy of the offensive or that of the defensive? Is he following the strategy of lightning attack and lightning victory or that of protracted war? As regards operations on various battlefields is he making his major efforts on the coastal battlefield where he can bring into full play the power of his technical weapons, or on the hinterland battlefield where he dreads most to face defeat? Is he concentrating on the Nam Bo battlefield where lie great political and economic centres or on the Western High Plateaux regarded as an important strategic position? As regards co-ordination with the puppet troops is he concentrating on independent operations, or on joint operations?* Those are many strategic questions to which the enemy himself cannot give clear-cut answers, for the American expeditionary corps is embarking in a blind tunnel. The most outstanding feature of the military situation over the past months is that not only the Southern Liberation armed forces have kept on stepping up guerilla warfare but they have also developed large-unit actions. . . .

At present it is evident that the American imperialists are at sea as far as military strategy is concerned. But what about tactics? Though the U.S. expeditionary corps has been fighting the Liberation armed forces for only a short length of time, the latter have proved able to best their enemy's tactics. . . .

We do not feel at all complacent at these initial successes. We definitely guard against subjectivism for the U.S. imperialists are a cruel and cunning enemy with a great military potential, who is extremely obdurate and at the same time knows how to draw lessons from experience to contrive ever fiercer and ever more ruthless fighting methods. However, the living reality of the struggle against the American imperialists for national salvation over the past eleven years has brought home to our people and the people's armed forces in both zones that *we shall certainly defeat the U.S. aggressors under any circumstances.*

The heavy defeats of the American expeditionary corps right in its first actions on the Viet-Nam battlefield are causing to the U.S. imperialists and their valets many more difficulties, not only military but also political and economic. Far from improving, the situation of the puppet army and administration instead is deteriorating as it has lost faith in its master's modern army. The antiwar movement in the U.S.A. is developing with every passing day while the internal contradictions among the Washington ruling circles are increasing.

In view of this situation the American imperialists are scheming to send more reinforcements to the South, beef up the U.S.

expeditionary corps one and a half, two or more times. They are plotting to intensify their aerial war of destruction against the North, while threatening to expand the war to neutralist Laos and Cambodia. U.S. President Johnson talks about taking *"hard steps"* in Viet-Nam. U.S. Secretary of State Dean Rusk also stresses, *"We will not withdraw from Viet-Nam"* for the U.S.A. must *"keep its commitments."* The American imperialists' familiar trick has been to couple the stepping up of their aggressive war with a ballyhoo about their *"goodwill for peace"*: this time, together with its preparations for new adventurist military moves, the U.S. administration opens a large-scale *"peace campaign."* The Johnson administration's *"peace efforts"* are only aimed at placating public opinion at home and abroad which has been energetically protesting against their aggressive policy.

However, whatever honeyed words the American aggressors may use, they cannot deceive the Vietnamese people and the peace-loving people throughout the world. There has not been the slightest change to the original design of the U.S. aggressors. They want to cling to South Viet-Nam and to keep Viet-Nam permanently partitioned. They refuse to withdraw their troops from the South and to recognize the South Viet-Nam National Front for Liberation as the sole genuine representative of the South Vietnamese people; they cynically arrogate to themselves the right to bomb and strafe the territory of the Democratic Republic of Viet-Nam, an independent and sovereign socialist state, and go to the length of demanding from the Vietnamese people a compensation for the halt in the bombing of North Viet-Nam. The essence of the "unconditional discussions" hoax is to compel our people to accept the American aggressors' terms.

We must further heighten our vigilance over the enemy's perfidious scheme. We must step up our entire people's patriotic war, resolutely fight until victory, no matter how many hundreds of thousands of troops the U.S. imperialists may dispatch to Viet-Nam and how far they may escalate their war of destruction against the North. Our people are determined not to shrink from any sacrifice to bring the great struggle against the American imperialists for national salvation to final victory. . . .

STAUGHTON LYND
TOM HAYDEN

Statement on Return from North Viet-Nam*

HAYDEN: Our fact-finding effort took us first to Prague, Moscow and Peking, where we interviewed representatives of the National Liberation Front, the Democratic Republic of Viet-Nam, and the Soviet and Chinese Peace Committees. Thus when we arrived in Hanoi on December 28 we felt we had a tentative understanding of the NLF and D.R.V. positions.

During our ten days in North Viet-Nam we talked with many persons in many walks of life. These included Premier Pham Van Dong; Mr. Hoang Quoc Viet, who is head of the country's trade unions and also holds a position in the government corresponding to that of Attorney General in the United States; Colonel Ha Van Lau, liaison officer of the D.R.V. to the International Control Commission, officials of the Fatherland Front, the Workers Party, the Democratic Party, and the Socialist Party; leaders of the Buddhist and Catholic faiths and of women's organizations; student and youth leaders; and members of our host group, the North Viet-Nam Peace Committee. We talked with soldiers from the NLF army who were visiting the North. We met also with many ordinary people in Hanoi, in the countryside, and in Nam Dinh, a city which has been bombed and strafed by American planes.

We asked permission to speak with an American prisoner so as to inquire into the treatment they receive and to ask if they had grievances which we could report to both Vietnamese and American authorities. On the evening of January 3 we were allowed to speak for one hour with a captured American pilot, with his agreement. At his wish, in response to our suggestion, we will write to his family to tell them of our talk with him.

We intend not to identify this man lest in any way he suffer reprisals because of publicity. Our talk with him ranged from

* Reprinted by permission from January, 1966 *Viet-Report*. © *Viet-Report*, Inc., 133 West 72nd Street, N.Y., N.Y.

the World Series to the history of Viet-Nam, but centered on the question of his treatment as a prisoner. He said that his life was no bed of roses but that his treatment was adequate and better than he had expected. . . .

Vietnamese officers were present throughout the conversation which naturally imposed restraint on all four Americans. We came away deeply moved by the poise and courage our fellow-citizen displayed in this difficult situation. His treatment so far as we could determine was adequate and humane.

On December 30 we submitted to the D.R.V. government, through the Peace Committee, a list of those questions about the positions of the NLF and the D.R.V. which seemed to us most often asked in the United States. On January 5 we received written answers to these questions from Premier Pham Van Dong, and spoke with the Premier for 90 minutes.

Mr. Staughton Lynd and I prepared a report of our findings for you, which he will read on behalf of both of us . . .

LYND: Mr. Hayden and I wish first to explain why we will limit our comments this evening to the written statement I am about to read, rather than answering questions. Having in mind the experience of the Italian professors whose words as quoted in the press were repudiated by Hanoi, we fear the possibility of unintentional distortion which could lessen the usefulness of the report we have brought back from Viet-Nam.

For example, it would be a distortion to say or imply that we return with a dramatic concession or an explicit peace feeler. We feel we do bring back with us significant clarifications of the NLF and D.R.V. attitudes toward some of the more controversial among President Johnson's 14 points. We ask the cooperation of the press, in the interest of the concern for accuracy and responsibility which you share with us, to report our statements in this regard as what they are, namely, clarifications rather than concessions.

The first half of the remainder of our statement will deal with the pause in bombing and the reaction of D.R.V. to that pause. Then we will return to some of the specific points at issue between the United States on the one hand, and the NLF and D.R.V. on the other. . . .

For those to whom we talked in Viet-Nam, the record of events in recent weeks proves clearly the continuing inconsistency of American policy. American ambassadors have gone all over the world to "knock on any door" seeking peace. But Premier Pham Van Dong, in response to our questions, stated unequivocally that the United States government had not made contact with the government of the D.R.V., either at Hanoi or through D.R.V. ambassadors in other capitals, since President Johnson spoke of knocking on any door Dec. 20. We assume that the United States, in keeping with previous policy, has not sought to make contact with NLF representatives either. To those with whom we spoke in Viet-Nam, it appears that the United States knocks on all doors except the doors of those whom it is fighting. They wonder if the United States is searching for peace or mainly attempting to soften its image before negative public opinion abroad and at home.

To be sure, there is now a pause in the bombing of North Viet-Nam. But the Vietnamese remind us that the last pause was followed immediately by expansion of the war. During the current pause, while the United States has waited for a so-called signal from Hanoi, Vietnamese sources have emphasized that President Johnson's words are accompanied by escalation in the South. According to these sources, the day after President Johnson spoke of knocking on any door the Department of Defense admitted the widespread use of toxic chemicals and authorized "hot pursuit" by American troops into Cambodia. A week later, when President Johnson announced his 14 points, 4000 new American troops of the 25th division arrived at Pleiku. Hanoi sources also point to the arrival in Saigon between Dec. 21 and Jan. 1 of the Chief of Staff of the United States Army, the chairman of the Joint Chiefs of Staff, the Secretary of the Army, and the Secretary of the Air Force. Experience suggests to them that such conferences immediately precede new escalation.

The North Vietnamese do not trust an offer to negotiate unconditionally which, as they see it, represents only one side of America's two-sided policy. They want to know if the United States has clearly decided that Viet-Nam should be united, rather than partitioned. They want to be sure that the United States has finally abandoned any plan to make South Viet-Nam a military base for the United States in Southeast Asia. Thus "Observer" stated in Nanh Dan for Jan. 3 that the so-called unconditional negotiations offered by the United States in fact contain four conditions: 1. United States troops will stay in South Viet-Nam as long as the United States thinks it necessary; 2. South Viet-Nam must be an independent sovereign state; 3. The United States refuses to recognize the NLF; 4. "The North Vietnamese people are not allowed to support the patriotic struggle of their compatriots in the South."

In our view, the United States does make such policy demands regularly, and they do conflict directly with its other stated aim of unconditional discussions and its denial of any ambition to occupy part of Asia.

President Johnson's 14-point program appears to come close to the diplomatic statements of the NLF and D.R.V., especially in accepting the Geneva Agreements as a basis of settlement, in denying any desire to keep troops indefinitely in South Viet-Nam, and in approving reunification.

However, the North Vietnamese see two crucial inadequacies in the new United States peace position. First, they wonder how the United States can accept the Geneva Agreements as the basis for settlement but treat the D.R.V. four points merely as a matter which could be discussed. Hanoi considers its four points to be the essence of the Geneva Settlement, especially the provisions requiring withdrawal of all foreign troops from Viet-Nam and leaving all political solutions to the self-determination of the Vietnamese people.

Secondly, the United States realizes that the NLF must be in some sense a party to any final negotiation, but the United States defines the NLF simply as an arm of Hanoi. Premier Pham Van Dong told us that his government "can by no means be dissociated" from the third point in its four-point program, which calls for settling the affairs of South Viet-Nam in accordance with the program of the NLF. The Premier said that what this point involved was the principle of self-determination at the heart of the Geneva Agreements. Like many others with whom we spoke, the Premier insisted on the independence of the NLF from the D.R.V. government in Hanoi. At one point in our talk he indicated his own surprise at the apparent strength of the NLF and its success in dealing with the United States forces.

Thus the negative response of the D.R.V. to the bombing pause appears to stem, first, from observation of warlike acts in South Viet-Nam which have accompanied the pause, and second, from uncertainty as to whether the United States has really given up its plans for an indefinite occupation of South Viet-Nam and decided to return to the Geneva Agreements.

So long as American policy remains obviously two-sided, we can understand the realistic suspicion of Premier Pham Van Dong, who told us: "What is the reason for the peace offensive? To win public opinion, particularly American public opinion. Only by so doing can President Johnson escalate the war."

We feel it would be tragic, and quite frankly, irresponsible on the part of the United States government, to regard Hanoi's response to a temporary bombing pause as a conclusive demonstration that an honorable negotiated solution cannot be found with the NLF and the D.R.V. Our conversations in Viet-Nam convinced us that many ingredients of an honorable solution exist.

As you know, we have cabled Senator Fulbright asking to report our findings, at any time and under any conditions, to the Senate Committee on Foreign Relations. We sent this cable because we consider it our responsibility as American citizens to make available to the appropriate agency of the government the information we have obtained.

We hope to present to the Senate Committee on Foreign Relations the full text of our questions to Premier Pham Van Dong and his written answers, together with a summary of our interviews with the Premier and with other NLF and D.R.V. spokesmen. Both these texts will be made public no later than Sunday, January 16, when we expect to make a public report at the Manhattan Center in New York City.

However, because of the urgency of the problems involved, we also consider it our responsibility to state now what we regard as some of the key points in Premier Pham Dong's answers to our questions.

1. In his written answers, the Premier repeated the statement in the Foreign Ministry release of Jan. 4, namely, that a "political settlement of the Viet-Nam problem" could be envisaged "only when the United States has accepted the four-point stand of the Government of the D.R.V., has proved this by actual deeds, at the same time has stopped unconditionally and for good its air raids and all other acts of war against the D.R.V.

In our interview, we asked the Premier what actual deeds the government of the D.R.V. had in mind. He replied that that was something for the United States government to decide.

In the context of our other conversations, this response appears to clarify significantly the D.R.V. attitude toward American military withdrawal. On the one hand, as we were told over and over again, the NLF and D.R.V. require, as a precondition to negotiations, an unambiguous *decision* by the United States to withdraw all its troops from Viet-Nam. On the other hand, they would seem to be prepared to leave the United States considerable freedom in choosing how to demonstrate by concrete steps that this decision has been made. Every indication is that there is no explicit requirement of the physical withdrawal of all United States troops prior to negotiations.

2. The Premier categorically denied the presence of "forces of the Democratic Republic of Viet-Nam in South Viet-Nam," terming it a "sheer fabrication."

We think that this denial has not previously been made in such absolute terms by the highest governmental authorities in the D.R.V. In response to a similar question from reporter Felix Green only a few weeks earlier, President Ho Chi Minh only said that the United States is "fabricating false information" to "cover up" its aggression.

Premier Pham Van Dong's answer seems even more interesting since we prefaced our questions by saying that we would not report having asked any question that the Premier chose not to answer. We see little reason for Premier Pham Van Dong to make such a statement if it can be proven false by American authorities.

3. It has been widely assumed in the United States that the D.R.V. is no longer open to the possibility of reunification of North and South Viet-Nam by means of a free general election. In response to a question about this, Premier Pham Van Dong referred to a passage in the program of the Vietnamese Fatherland Front, which says in part: "we must conduct negotiations to arrange the holding of free general elections in order to achieve national unity without either side trying to exert pressure on, or trying to annex the other."

4. In response to a question about the possible reconvening of the Geneva Conference, Premier Pham Van Dong quoted his

words of last April to the effect that once the D.R.V. four points had been accepted "it will be possible to consider the reconvening of an international conference of the type of the 1954 Geneva Conference on Viet-Nam." We might add that one of the D.R.V. ambassadors to whom we spoke en route to Hanoi commented that determination of the "role and composition" of an international supervisory commission would be an appropriate task for such a conference.

Throughout our interview Premier Pham Van Dong, like so many others to whom we spoke, insisted that while the people of Viet-Nam were prepared to fight as long as need be to win their independence, none wanted peace more than they. If there was one message which person after person charged us to bring back to the people of the United States, it was this: Tell the American people we make a distinction between them and the American government. Explain to them that we have been fighting for twenty-five years and that many of us, having regrouped to the North under the Geneva Agreements, have not seen or heard from our families in ten years. Who could want peace more than we? But there can be no real peace unless there is independence. An end to this war, they never failed to add, would be in the interest both of our people and of yours.

At one point in our interview with Premier Pham Van Dong, he said to us: If you have the opportunity to see President Johnson, please ask him for me, why is he fighting us? We wonder if the American people are sure of the answer to this question. Before we launch a new and more terrible round of escalation, should we not stop to consider whether the possibilities of peace have really been exhausted? The present American peace initiative is not yet seen as such by the Vietnamese. They see it through suspicious eyes, for it is accompanied by American military build-up in the South and by continued United States references to the permanent partitioning of Viet-Nam. Until these policy inconsistencies have been resolved, we believe it is tragically unfair to brand our antagonists as intransigent or to conclude that an honorable negotiated settlement is impossible.

C. REAPPRAISALS

Introduction

The year 1966 saw the gradual failure of American political processes to influence the President and the Defense Establishment. At the beginning of 1966 Senator Fulbright, Chairman of the Senate Foreign Relations Committee, held hearings on the policy and course of the war in Viet-Nam in the hopes of rallying respected alternate views to the existing policies. It had no effect except to introduce the rhetoric of the witnesses into subsequent statements of the Administration. One minor side effect of the hearings was the emergence of a coalition government theory which would include the NLF, advocated by Senator Robert Kennedy.

Another unforeseen consequence of ever-widening American commitment on the Asian mainland was the emergence of a body of high level military opinion represented by Generals Gavin and Ridgeway working against "any unlimited political objective that might entail unlimited military effort."

While for the time being the military effort had not yet become unlimited, it already had become unrestrained in method as is pointed out in the large body of reliable evidence put forward by Eric Norden.

The United Nations, even at this late stage, has been unable to really face up to the dangers of the Viet-Nam issue. An attempt at debating it after the end of the thirty-seven-day bombing pause at the beginning of 1966 was abruptly closed by mutual agreement of all powers, including the absent Red China, leaving the Secretary General to deplore what was going on without being able to affect the course of events.

U THANT

Statement*

(Through spokesman on March 9, 1966, in response to inquiries)

The Secretary General is deeply concerned over the escalation in fighting in Viet-Nam and the mounting casualties, and the destruction there.

He feels that any move to bring the parties closer to negotiation must include the following:

1. The cessation of bombing of North Viet-Nam.
2. Substantial reduction by all parties of all military activities.
3. The participation of the National Liberation Front in any discussion for a peaceful settlement.

ERIC NORDEN

American Atrocities in Viet-Nam†

In the bitter controversy over our Vietnamese policies which has raged across the nation since the President's decision last February to bomb North Viet-Nam, there is only one point which supporters of U.S. policy will concede to the opposition: the sheer, mindnumbing horror of the war. Despite the barrage of official propaganda, reports in the American and European press reveal that the United States is fighting the dirtiest war of its history in Viet-Nam. The weapons in the American arsenal include torture, systematic bombing of civilian targets, the first use of poison gas since World War One, the shooting of prisoners and the general devastation of the Vietnamese countryside by napalm and white phosphorous. Not since the days of the Amer-

---

* U. N. Press Office March 9, 1966.
† From *Liberation*, February, 1966, by permission.

ican Indian wars has the United States waged such unrelenting warfare against an entire people.

Torture of prisoners and "suspects" by Vietnamese troops and their U.S. advisers is a matter of public record. "Anyone who has spent much time with Government units in the field," writes William Tuohy, *Newsweek's* Saigon correspondent, "has seen the heads of prisoners held under water and bayonet blades pressed against their throats. . . . In more extreme cases, victims have had bamboo slivers run under their fingernails or wires from a field telephone connected to arms, nipples or testicles." (*New York Times* Magazine, November 28, 1965.)

Donald Wise, Chief foreign correspondent for the London *Sunday Mirror,* reports that such torture is condoned and even supervised by U.S. officers. "No American is in a position to tell his 'pupils' to stop torturing," Wise writes from Saigon. "They are in no mood to either. . . ." Some of the standard tortures described by Wise include "dunking men head first into water tanks or slicing them up with knives. . . . Silk stockings full of sand are swung against temples and men are hooked up to the electric generators of military HQ's." (London *Sunday Mirror,* April 4, 1965.)

The "Viet-Cong" use terror also, of course, but theirs is of a more selective nature, if only to avoid estranging the peasants and villagers on whom they depend for food and shelter. They will kill and mutilate the body of a Government official, but they generally pick an unpopular and corrupt victim whose death is welcomed by the peasants. U.S. and Government troops in the countryside, on the other hand, feel themselves lost in an enemy sea and tend to strike out indiscriminately at real or imagined guerrillas. Thus, no Vietnamese is exempt from mistreatment and torture. As Wise reports, "Inevitably, innocent peasants are kneed in the groin, drowned in vats of water or die of loss of blood after interrogation. But you cannot identify VC from peasants. . . ." In fact, it is assumed that every peasant is a real or potential Viet-Cong rebel. "In a VC-controlled area the yardstick is rough: every young man of military age is assumed to be a VC soldier who has thrown away his weapon just before capture. Most areas of Viet-Nam are now VC-controlled. Therefore, most men in the countryside should be presumed to be VC soldiers or sympathizers." (*Ibid.*)

Many U.S. reporters have witnessed torture first-hand. Beverly Deepe, the New York *Herald Tribune's* correspondent in Saigon, writes:

One of the most infamous methods of torture used by the government forces is partial electrocution—or "frying," as one U.S. adviser called it. This correspondent was present on one occasion when the torture was employed. Two wires were attached to the thumbs of a Viet-Cong prisoner. At the other end of the strings was a field generator, cranked by a Vietnamese private. The mechanism produced an electrical current that burned and shocked the prisoner. (New York *Herald Tribune*, April 25, 1965.)

Electrical torture is employed all over Viet-Nam, even on the battlefront. A small U.S. field generator used to power pack radios is often "modified" for torture purposes and is prized for its high mobility. The device generates sufficient voltage to provide strong and sometimes deadly shocks. According to Malcolm Browne, the A. P. correspondent who won a Pulitzer Prize for his reporting of the war, "The 'ding-a-ling' method of interrogation involves connection of electrodes from this generator to the temples of the subject, or other parts of the body. In the case of women prisoners, the electrodes often are attached to the nipples. The results are terrifying and painful. . . ." (*The New Face of War* by Malcolm Browne, Bobbs-Merrill Co., 1965.)

Less sophisticated methods than electrical torture are also used. According to Beverly Deepe:

Other techniques, usually designed to force onlooking prisoners to talk, involve cutting off the fingers, ears, fingernails or sexual organs of another prisoner. Sometimes a string of ears decorates the wall of a government military installation. One American installation has a Viet-Cong ear preserved in alcohol. (*Op. cit.*)

There is apparently no attempt to disguise such atrocities, even for public relations reasons. Writes Malcolm Browne:

Many a news correspondent has seen the hands whacked off prisoners with machetes. Prisoners are sometimes castrated or blinded. In more than one case a Viet-Cong suspect has been towed after interrogation behind an armored personnel carrier across the rice fields. This always results in death in one of its most painful forms. Vietnamese troops also take their share of enemy heads. . . . (*Op. cit.*)

U.S. Army Special Forces men pride themselves on their advanced methods of "interrogation," often patterned after Chinese models. In his first-hand account of the Special Forces in action, *The Green Berets,* Robin Moore gives a graphic description of a torture session presided over by a Special Forces officer of Finnish origin who had served with the Nazi Army on the Russian Front in World War Two. (Because of Moore's embarrassing disclosures, his publishers, who had originally presented the book as "truthful . . . a factual account," were forced under pressure from Assistant Secretary of Defense Arthur Sylvester to label the material "fictionalized.")

Although torture of Viet-Cong suspects antedated the arrival in strength of U.S. forces, American technology has given it some interesting twists. The helicopter, introduced by the United States as a vital element in the air war, is now playing a role in the "interrogation" of prisoners. *Houston Chronicle* reporter Jonathan Kapstein reported the innovation, termed "the long step," on his return from an assignment in Viet-Nam.

A helicopter pilot looked up from his Jack Daniels-and-Coke to relate what had happened to a captive he had been flying back from a battle area. A Vietnamese army officer yelled in the ear of the suspected guerrilla who was tied hand and foot. The man did not respond, so the officer and a Vietnamese soldier heaved him, struggling against his ropes, out of the UH-1B helicopter from 2,900 feet. Then over the roar of the engine, the officer began to interrogate another prisoner who had watched wide-eyed. The answers must have been satisfactory, the flier said, because, though kicked and roughly handled, the guerrilla was alive to be marched off when the helicopter landed. . . . (*Nation,* Dec. 21, 1964.)

A prisoner who "cooperates" after watching the exit of his comrade is not always rewarded. *Herald Tribune* Saigon correspondent Beverly Deepe reports an instance when "Two Viet-Cong prisoners were interrogated on an airplane flying toward Saigon. The first refused to answer questions and was thrown out of the airplane at 3,000 feet. The second immediately answered all the questions. But he, too, was thrown out." (New York *Herald Tribune,* April 25, 1965.) Sometimes there is not even the pretense of "questioning." Jack Langguth, Saigon correspondent for the *New York Times,* reports a case where "One American helicopter crewman returned to his base in the central highlands last week without a fierce young prisoner entrusted to him. He told friends that he had become infuriated by the youth and had pushed him out of the helicopter at about 1,000 feet." (*New York Times*, July 7, 1965.)

Even if a prisoner is lucky enough to make the full trip, half the fun isn't getting there. Jimmy Breslin, in a dispatch to the New York *Herald Tribune* from South Vietnam, wrote:

At 12:00 o'clock, a helicopter came in and the shirtless Marine in the tent said it was going to Da Nang. . . . A young redheaded machine-gunner sat in the doorway, chewing on a chocolate cracker from a C-ration tin. He kicked a small spool of wire out of the doorway and made room.

"We just rode Nuongs, you can tell that by the wire here," he said.

"Why?" he was asked. Nuongs are Chinese mercenaries from Formosa. . . .

"They always want the wire for the prisoners," the kid said.

"Don't you know that? They get a VC and make him hold his hands against his cheeks. Then they take this wire and run it right through the one hand and right through his cheek and into his mouth. Then they pull the wire out through the other cheek and stick it through the other hand. They knot both ends around sticks. You never seen them with prisoners like that? Oh, you ought to see how quiet them gooks sit in a helicopter when we got them wrapped up like that. (New York *Herald Tribune*, Sept. 29, 1965.)

As the tempo of the fighting has increased, many Viet-Cong prisoners are spared the ordeal of torture—they are shot on the spot by their U.S. or Vietnamese captors. Writes *Newsweek's* Saigon correspondent, William Tuohy:

Some Viet-Cong suspects do not survive long enough for the third degree. Earlier this year, in an operation along the central coast, a Government detachment failed to flush VC troops suspected of lurking in the area. However, several villagers were rounded up and one man was brought before the company commander. The Vietnamese officer briefly questioned the suspect, then turned to his adviser . . . and said, "I think I shoot this man. Okay?"

"Go ahead," said the adviser.

The officer fired a carbine round point-blank, striking the villager below the chest. The man slumped and died. The patrol moved on. Later, a correspondent asked the adviser, who had seemed a decent enough fellow, why he had given his approval.

. . . "These people could have moved to a Government area.

In this war they are either on our side or they are not. There is
no in-between." (*New York Times* Magazine, Nov. 28, 1965.)

Houston Chronicle correspondent Jonathan Kapstein reported
on his return from Viet-Nam:

In the pleasantly dim officers' club at Vinh Long, South Viet-
Nam, a 25-year-old U.S. Army lieutenant described what he had
seen one time when soldiers of the Vietnamese 7th Infantry Division
captured prisoners. "They had four, all suspected of being Viet-
Cong—the first prisoners they had taken in a long time. They lined
'em up and shot the first man. Then they questioned the second.
His answers were unsatisfactory, I guess, because they shot him
too. . . ." (*Nation*, December 24, 1964.)

As U.S. casualties have mounted even the pretense of preliminary interrogation has been dropped. Captured and wounded
Viet-Cong are now executed summarily. Captain James Morris,
a U.S. Army Special Forces man, reports the aftermath of an
ambush he sprang on a small enemy contingent:

I moved from one dark shape to the other, making sure they
were dead. When I moved up on the last one, he raised up, his
arms extended, eyes wide. He had no weapon. Cowboy stitched
him up the middle with his AR-15. He didn't even twitch. . . . (*Es-
quire*, August, 1965.)

Pulitzer Prize winning correspondent David Halberstam re-
counts the treatment accorded a group of Viet-Cong prisoners
by Government forces after a "particularly bitter" battle near
Bac Lieu:

The enemy were very cocky and started shouting anti-American
slogans and Vietnamese curses at their captors. The Marines . . .
simply lined up the seventeen guerrillas and shot them down in cold
blood. . . . (*The Making of a Quagmire* by David Halberstam.
Random House, 1965.)

The treatment of Viet-Cong POW's seems to vary with the
severity of American losses in the action preceding their capture.
After a platoon of the U.S. 1st Air Cavalry Division was almost
wiped out in a battle in the Chu Prong foothills of the Ia Drang
valley, Reuters reported:

In one place nearby the Americans found three North Vietnamese
wounded. One lay huddled under a tree, a smile on his face. "You
won't smile any more" said one of the American soldiers, pumping

bullets into his body. The other two met the same fate. (November 18, 1965.)

Chicago Daily News correspondent Raymond R. Coffey, reporting on the same battle, accompanied U.S. relief forces to a clearing littered with dead from the previous day's fighting. He writes:

> It was almost impossible to walk twenty paces without stumbling upon a body. . . . Suddenly a few yards away a wounded enemy soldier lifted one arm weakly and an American sergeant poured a long burst of M-16 rifle bullets into him. "Was he trying to give up, Sarge?" a man asked. "I'd like to find more of those bastards trying to give up," the sergeant said bitterly. No one disagreed with him. . . . (Chicago *Daily News*, November 19, 1965.)

Apart from the moral question, U.S. and South Vietnamese torture and execution of prisoners of war is, of course, in clear violation of international law. Both South Viet-Nam and the United States are signatories to the 1949 Geneva Conventions governing the treatment of prisoners. Article 17 states: "No physical or mental torture, nor any other form of coercion, may be inflicted on prisoners of war to secure from them information of any kind whatever." In a specific provision pertaining to undeclared or civil war, the Conventions prohibit, with respect to prisoners of war, "violence to life and person, in particular murder of all kinds, mutilation, cruel treatment and torture."

The International Red Cross in Geneva, to which the Conventions assigned the right to visit POW's and insure their proper treatment, has publicly protested U.S. treatment of prisoners in Viet-Nam. The *New York Times* declared on December 1, 1965 that "the International Committee of the Red Cross in Geneva . . . complained again that the United States was violating an international accord on the treatment of prisoners. . . ." An earlier dispatch reported that "The International Red Cross Committee is dissatisfied with the way the United States and South Vietnamese Governments observe their pledge to respect the Geneva Conventions protecting war victims. . . . The Committee's representative in Saigon has been unable to visit prisoners taken by American and South Vietnamese troops despite the affirmative reply of the two governments to its appeal for the observance of the conventions. The Saigon authorities were said to have given repeated assurances that they intended to allow the International Red Cross to visit the prisoners but to date have done nothing more about it." (*New York Times,* November 26, 1965.)

If the United States is not willing to observe the Geneva Conventions itself, it is quick to point an accusing finger at others. When the North Vietnamese Government threatened to try captured U.S. airmen as war criminals, the United States denounced any such move as a violation of the Geneva Conventions and appealed to the International Red Cross. Hans Henle, a former executive of the information Service of the International Committee of the Red Cross in Geneva, commented:

The Viet-Cong fighters are as protected by the Geneva Conventions as the American G.I.s are. Dramatic protests against violations of the Geneva Conventions should have been made when the first Viet-Cong prisoners were shot, when they were tortured, when the American Army started to destroy Viet-Cong hospitals and to cut off medical supply. . . . It is utterly hypocritical to condone wholesale violations of the Red Cross principles on one side and protest reprisals against them. . . . (*New York Times,* International Edition only, October 14, 1965.)

Not content with the present level of inhumanity, some agencies of the United States Government are attempting to turn torture from a political liability to an asset. The Associated Press reported on October 16, 1965, that Senator Stephen Young, who had just returned from a fact-finding mission in Viet-Nam, "says he was told by a member of the Central Intelligence Agency in Viet-Nam that the C.I.A. committed atrocities there to discredit the Viet-Cong. Young said he was told that the C.I.A. disguised some people as Viet-Cong and they committed atrocities. . . ." (Philadelphia *Inquirer,* October 20, 1965.) Young's revelations landed like a bombshell on official Washington. "The C.I.A. and the State Department went into an uproar," the *Herald Tribune* reported. "There was deep distress among State Department officials who feared his reported remarks would have disastrous repercussions abroad." (New York *Herald Tribune,* October 21, 1965.) But Young refused to back down. "The C.I.A. has employed some South Vietnamese," he reiterated, "and they have been instructed to claim they are Viet-Cong and to work accordingly . . . several of these executed two village leaders and raped some women. I know such men have been employed, and I question the wisdom of that."

So, as the war escalates, does the human agony in its wake. The prospect is for more, not less, torture and shooting of POW's. "There comes a time in every war," James Reston writes from Saigon, "when men tend to become indifferent to human suffering, even to unnecessary brutality, and we may be reaching that point in Viet-Nam." (*New York Times,* September 5, 1965.) Frustrated and bitter, U.S. forces in Viet-Nam have dehumanized their enemy, and anaesthetized their own consciences. Graham Greene, struck by the ubiquitous photographs of torture in the U.S. press, wrote recently:

> The strange new feature about the photographs of torture now appearing is that they have been taken with the approval of the torturers and published over captions that contain no hint of condemnation. They might have come out of a book on insect life. "The white ant takes certain measures against the red ant after a successful foray." But these, after all, are not ants, but men. . . . These photographs are of torturers belonging to an army which could not exist without American aid and counsel. . . . The long, slow slide into barbarism of the Western World seems to have quickened. (The London *Daily Telegraph,* November 6, 1965.)

The New York *Herald Tribune* reported on May 23, 1965, that "Near the big coastal city of Hue, U.S. Marines set crops on fire and burned or dynamited huts. . . ." In July, 1965, U.S. Marines fought a Viet-Cong force which had landed in sampans on the island of An Hoa and attacked a Vietnamese navy post there. The two major towns on the island, Longthanh and Xuanmy, had been occupied by the guerrillas. Together the towns had about 1,500 inhabitants. After the Viet-Cong retreated, "the Marines were ordered to burn Longthanh and Xuanmy to prevent the Viet-Cong from reoccupying them. . . ." (*New York Times,* July 11, 1965.) Few Viet-Cong had been killed or captured, but two prosperous villages were razed and, according to U.S. sources, about 100 civilians died from U.S. fire. An A.P. dispatch from the island on July 11, 1965, reported that Americans had called An Hoa "Little Hawaii" because "of its rolling surf and happy people. In one day An Hoa became a little hell."

The two nearby villages of Chan Son and Camne in the Me-

kong Delta felt the brunt of U.S. "pacification" in August, 1965.
Marine patrols near the villages had received light sniper fire
from Viet-Cong guerrillas. What happened next was described
by U.S. newsmen accompanying the Marines into the villages.

A Marine shouted, "Kill them! I don't want anyone moving!"
. . . The Marines burned huts they believed were the sites of sniper
fire. A sergeant said orders called for this. . . . [After the firing died
down] U.S. Marines found a woman and two children among 25
persons they killed. . . . The woman died of a wound in the side,
perhaps from one of the 1,000 artillery shells poured into the area.
A wailing child beside her had an arm injury. A grenade hurled by
a Marine blasted two children to death in an air-raid shelter. (*New
York Times*, August 3, 1965.)

How the Marines reacted to their "victory" was described by a
U.P.I. dispatch from Chan Son:

"I got me a VC, man. I got at least two of them bastards."
The exultant cry followed a 10-second burst of automatic
weapons fire yesterday, and the dull crump of a grenade exploding
underground.
The Marines ordered a Vietnamese corporal to go down into the
grenade-blasted hole to pull out their victims.
The victims were three children between 11 and 14—two boys
and a girl. Their bodies were riddled with bullets.
Their father was still suffering from shock. A husky Marine lifted
him on his shoulder and carried him off.
"Oh, my God," a young Marine exclaimed. "They're all kids."
A moment earlier, six children nearby watched their mother die.
Her blood left a dark trail in the "air-raid shelter," where the family
fled when the Marines attacked. A wrinkled grandmother had pulled
her into a more comfortable position to let her die.
The terrified face of a 60-year-old man looked up from a hole;
his wailing mingled with the crying of the village children.
In the village, a little boy displayed his sister who was no more
than four. She had been shot through the arm.
The Marines had received a few sniper rounds from Chan Son
village. . . .

The sniper fire was enough for the Marines to open up with
everything they had: rifle fire, automatic fire and grenades. A
number of women and children were caught in the fire. Five of
them were killed and five others wounded.

Shortly before the Marines moved in, a helicopter had flown over the area warning the villagers to stay in their homes. (New York *Herald Tribune,* August 3, 1965.)

Chan Son's neighboring village of Camne fared no better. Morley Safer, a CBS television correspondent accompanying the force occupying the town, reported that U.S. Marines had burned 150 houses in the hamlet, ignoring "the pleas of old men and women to delay the burnings so that belongings could be removed." Safer's report, delivered on "Evening News with Walter Cronkite," August 4, 1965, said that:

"After surrounding the village . . . the Marines poured 3.5 in. rocket fire, M–79 grenade launchers and heavy and light machine-gun fire. The Marines then moved in, proceeding first with cigarette lighters, then with flame throwers, to burn down an estimated 150 dwellings." Safer concluded by revealing that "I subsequently learned that a Marine platoon on the right flank wounded three women and killed one child in a rocket barrage. The day's operations netted about four prisoners—old men."

It was unusual for U.S. "pacification" teams to be accompanied by U.S. reporters, and Washington was evidently embarrassed by the widespread publicity given the Chan Son and Camne incidents. Charles Mohr reported from Saigon on subsequent "attempts by public information officers to de-emphasize the importance of civilian deaths and the burning of village huts at the hands of U.S. Marines." (*New York Times,* August 9, 1965.) And Secretary of the Navy Paul Nitze publicly supported the burning of villages as a "natural and inevitable adjunct" to defense of U.S. bases in their vicinity. Nitze declared that "Where neither United States nor Vietnamese forces can maintain continuous occupancy, it is necessary to destroy those facilities." (*New York Times,* August 15, 1965.) The final word was had by a U.S. military spokesman in Saigon who told reporters that "Marines do not burn houses or villages unless those houses or villages are fortified." When a U.S. correspondent commented that the great majority of Vietnamese villages were fortified in one way or another, the spokesman said simply: "I know it."

The Vietnamese peasant is caught in a vicious vise by U.S. "pacification" tactics. If he stays in his village he may die under U.S. fire; if he flees before the advancing troops he may still be rounded up, and shot on the spot as an "escaping Viet-Cong."

Murders of such terrified peasants are a daily occurrence in Viet-Nam, and American G.I.'s are bagging their share of the game. A typical instance was reported by the A.P. from the town of Hoi Vuc, scene of a Marine "search-and-destroy" operation:

"The sweat-soaked young Leatherneck stood over the torn body of a Viet Cong guerrilla with mixed emotions flitting over his face. For Cpl. Pleas David of Tuscaloosa, Alabama, it was a day he would never forget. David had just killed his first man. 'I felt kind of sorry for him as I stood there,' said David, a lanky 17-year-old. 'And he didn't even have a weapon'. . . ." The unarmed "Viet-Cong" was walking along a paddy dike when the four Marines approached him with levelled guns. The frightened Vietnamese saw the guns and threw himself on the ground. As the Marines ran towards him he jumped up and tried to escape. "I let him get 250 yards away and then dropped him with two shots from my M-1," the A.P. quotes the young Marine, adding "The man had been hit squarely in the back. No weapons were found with him. . . ." The Marine was congratulated by his buddies. "Maybe the Viet-Cong will learn some respect for marksmanship. When we see them we hit them," one boasted. Another declared that "David is a good example. . . . Don't think we are killers. We are Marines." (New York *Post,* April 30, 1965.)

It is official U.S. military policy to shoot and ask questions later. Thus, in an operation thirty-five miles outside of Saigon, U.S. troops rushed a peasant shack believed to harbor Viet-Cong. One U.S. Lieutenant hurled a grenade through the door but the inhabitants tossed it back out. According to the A.P., "Another American soldier charged the shack, pulled the pin on a grenade and gave the fuse a few seconds count-down before pitching it in. Following the explosion the G.I. leaped into the shack with his M-14 rifle blazing. Three men and a baby died. Two women were wounded. Shrapnel took off the lower half of one woman's leg." (November 16, 1965.)

Not all G.I.'s enjoy making war on women and children. Some have written agonized letters home. Marine Cpl. Ronnie Wilson, 20, of Wichita, Kansas write the following letter to his mother:

Mom, I had to kill a woman and a baby. . . . We were searching the dead Cong when the wife of the one I was checking ran out of a cave. . . . I shot her and my rifle is automatic so before I knew

428 · *The Viet-Nam Reader*

it I had shot about six rounds. Four of them hit her and the others went into the cave and must have bounced off the rock wall and hit the baby. Mom, for the first time I felt really sick to my stomach. The baby was about two months old. I swear to God this place is worse than hell. Why must I kill women and kids? Who knows who's right? They think they are and we think we are. Both sides are losing men. I wish to God this was over.

But those American G.I.'s who react with shock and horror to their bloody mission are a distinct minority. Most American soldiers in Viet-Nam do not question the orders that lead them to raze villages and wipe out men, women and children for the "crime" of living in Viet-Cong-controlled or infiltrated areas. Extermination of the (non-white) enemy is to them a dirty but necessary job, and few grumble about it. Some have even come to enjoy it. Warren Rogers, Chief Correspondent in Viet-Nam for the Hearst syndicate, reports that:

There is a new breed of Americans that most of us don't know about and it is time we got used to it. The 18- and 19-year-olds, fashionably referred to as high-school dropouts, have steel in their backbones and maybe too much of what prize fighters call the killer instinct. These kids seem to enjoy killing Viet-Cong. . . . (New York *Journal-American*, September 16, 1965.)

To many critics of the war this "new breed of Americans" bears a disquieting resemblance to an old breed of Germans.

As the United States build-up has grown, there has been an increasing reliance on air attack. Any village in "VC territory" (which now comprises most of the country outside of the big cities) is considered a "free strike" area. U.S. planes rain death over vast areas of the countryside, killing Viet-Cong guerrillas and innocent peasants alike. No attempt is made to discriminate between military and civilian targets. American pilots, the Washington *Post* reported recently, "are given a square marked on a map and told to hit every hamlet within the area. The pilots know they sometimes are bombing women and children." (March 13, 1965.) Supersonic jets and B-52 bombers blanket vast areas of the countryside with 1,000-pound bombs, napalm and white phosphorous. According to *New York Times'* Saigon Correspondent, Charles Mohr,

This is strategic bombing in a friendly, allied country. Since the Viet-Cong doctrine is to insulate themselves among the population and the population is largely powerless to prevent their presence, no one here seriously doubts that significant numbers of innocent civilians are dying every day in South Viet-Nam. (*New York Times,* September 5, 1965.)

The victims of such raids are always reported in the official U.S. enemy casualty lists as "dead Viet-Cong." The accuracy of such reports was revealed by Jack Langguth in a dispatch from Saigon:

As the Communists withdrew from Quangngai last Monday, U.S. jet bombers pounded the hills into which they were headed. Many Vietnamese—one estimate was as high as 500—were killed by the strikes. The American contention is that they were Viet-Cong soldiers. But three out of four patients seeking treatment in a Vietnamese hospital afterward for burns from napalm or jellied gasoline, were village women. (*New York Times,* June 6, 1965.)

Quang Ngai province has been the scene of some of the heaviest fighting of the war. When U.S. and Vietnamese troops could not dislodge the Viet-Cong from their positions it was decided to destroy all villages in the province which were not garrisoned by U.S. or Vietnamese forces. The fate of Duchai, a complex of five fishing villages on the coast, is typical. Neil Sheehan told the story of Duchai in a dispatch to the *New York Times:*

In mid-August United States and Vietnamese military officials decided the Communists were using Duchai as a base for their operations in the area and that it should be destroyed. For the next two months . . . it was periodically and ferociously bombed by Vietnamese and American planes. . . . At least 184 civilians died during Duchai's two months of agony. Some reasonable estimates run as high as 600. . . . When an American visits Duchai these days, villagers . . . tell him horror stories of how many of the 15,000 former inhabitants were killed by bombs and shells. "There," said a fisherman pointing to a bomb crater beside a ruined house, "a woman and her six children were killed in a bomb shelter when it got a direct hit." Duchai's solid brick and stucco houses, the product of generations of hard-earned savings by its fishermen, were reduced to rubble or blasted into skeletons. Five-inch naval shells tore gaping holes in walls, and bombs of 750 to 1,000 pounds plunged through roofs, shattering interiors and scattering red roof-tiles over the landscape. . . . Here and there napalm blackened the ruins. (November 30, 1965.)

Sheehan reported that at least ten other villages in the province had "been destroyed as thoroughly as the five in Duchai" and another twenty-five nearly as badly damaged. Four hundred and fifty other villages have been under intermittent attack by U.S. and Vietnamese planes. "Each month," Sheehan writes, "600 to 1,000 civilians wounded by bombs, shells, bullets and napalm are brought to the provincial hospital in Quangngai town. Officials say that about thirty per cent of these cases require major surgery. A recent visitor to the hospital found several children lying on cots, their bodies horribly burned by napalm." (*Ibid.*)

An American doctor in the Quang Ngai hospital, J. David Kinzie, was moved to protest the horrors of the war in a letter to a U.S. magazine:

I have been in Quang Ngai for six months in general practice at a civilian provincial hospital, and I can remain silent no longer.

There comes a time in a doctor's life, no matter how hardened he has become, and perhaps in every man's life, no matter how cynical he may be, when he must protest as effectively as he can about the suffering of his fellow man. When one's own country is involved in the inhumanity, the responsibility becomes greater. Thus I add my belated voice.

The civilian hospital in our province in central Viet-Nam is good by Vietnamese standards. The patients, already diseased by tuberculosis, anemia, and malnutrition in many cases, are now entering more frequently from direct effects of the war. For example, a pregnant woman demonstrator with a bullet hole in her abdomen, whose fetus died later; a twelve-year-old boy brought in unconscious by relatives who described how artillery blasted their village the night before; a fifty-year-old woman, accused of being Viet-Cong who had been beaten, electrically shocked, and had her hands punctured for three days to extort information; three other civilians also accused of supporting the Viet-Cong were released to the hospital after severe beatings and their innocence determined. Many of the victims' "crimes" consisted merely in living in an area the Viet-Cong had overrun the night before. . . .

Of course, war has always been described as evil, but does this mean that America must add to it? Our military advisers teach Vietnamese modern techniques of killing each other. Our weapons aid in more thorough destruction of themselves. Rather than liberating a people, it seems that these techniques and weapons result in innocent civilians, women, and children being beaten, burned and murdered. . . .

Is America to survive on the blood of Vietnamese civilians? Does this make us great? (*Progressive*, March 1965.)

Thousands of children are dying as a result of United States air strikes. Charles Mohr writes in the *New York Times:*

In [a] delta province there is a woman—who has both arms burned off by napalm and her eyelids so badly burned that she cannot close them. When it is time for her to sleep her family puts a blanket over her head. The woman had two of her children killed in the air strike which maimed her last April and she saw five other children die. She was quite dispassionate when she told an American "more children were killed because the children do not have so much experience and do not know how to lie down behind the paddy dikes." (September 5, 1965.)

Vietnamese villagers, driven to desperation, have occasionally descended *en masse* on U.S. bases to protest the bombings of their villages. Such demonstrations have been violently repressed. In early September a group of villagers marched on the U.S. air base at Danang demanding an end to air attacks on their villages. The demonstration was dispersed and five participants, selected at random, were arrested. Their punishment was swift. The Chicago *Daily News* reported from Saigon, "At Danang, three persons were executed by a South Vietnamese firing squad. The execution, held in a soccer stadium was postponed at the last minute until midnight . . . because news photographers refused to obey an order that no pictures be taken until the final shot had been fired. The three were among five persons arrested Monday during a demonstration by about 200 persons in downtown Danang. They were protesting crop damage from artillery fire and air attacks by U.S. forces." (Chicago *Daily News,* September 23, 1965.) The fate of the other two arrested demonstrators was described in a U.P.I. dispatch from Saigon. ". . . the fourth man would be executed later, but at the moment . . . he was described as a 'singing bird.' The fifth demonstrator, a woman, was sentenced to life in prison although the demonstration had been so small that few were even aware of it." (Washington *Daily News,* October 4, 1965.)

The essence of U.S. bombing policy was expressed with unusual frankness by a U.S. officer serving with a helicopter unit in the Mekong Delta. Jack Langguth asked the officer what the answer was to Viet-Cong activity. " 'Terror.' he said pleasantly. 'The Viet-Cong have terrorized the peasants to get their coopera- tion, or at least to stop their opposition. We must terrorize the villagers even more, so they see that their real self-interest lies with us. . . . Terror is what it takes.' " (*New York Times* Maga- zine, September 19, 1965.)

But in the long run, the bombing only helps the National Liberation Front. According to Senator George McGovern: "To bomb [the Viet-Cong] is to bomb the women and children, the villages and the peasants with whom they are intermingled. Our bombing attacks turn the people against us and feed the fires of rebellion." (*Congressional Record,* June 17, 1965.) Robert Taber, an authority on guerrilla warfare, writes in his new book *The War of the Flea* [Published by Lyle Stuart, 1965.]: "The indiscriminate use of air power against presumed Viet-Cong targets does much to explain the alienation of the rural popula- tion from the Saigon Government. Country people whose only contact with the government comes in the form of napalm and rocket attacks can scarcely be expected to feel sympathetic to the government cause, whatever it may be. On the other hand, they have every reason to feel solidarity with the guerrillas, usually recruited from their own villages, who share their peril and their hardships."

More than any other single factor, our air war in Viet-Nam is turning the rest of the world against the United States.

All war, of course, is hell. There is no such thing as a "clean war," in Viet-Nam or anywhere else. But even in warfare there are certain observable norms of decency which cannot be dis- regarded. These were laid down after World War Two in the Charter of the International Military Tribunal, under which the Nuremberg Trials of top Nazi civilian and military leaders were held. Our actions in Viet-Nam fall within the prohibited clas- sifications of warfare set down at Nuremberg under Article Six, which reads:

. . . The following acts, or any of them, are crimes coming within the jurisdiction of the Tribunal for which there shall be individual responsibility:
a) Crimes against peace: namely, planning, preparation, initiation or waging of a war of aggression, or a war in violation of interna- tional treaties, agreements, or assurances, or participation in a

common plan or conspiracy for the accomplishment of any of the foregoing.

b) War crimes: namely, violations of the laws or customs of war . . . plunder of public property, wanton destruction of cities, towns or villages, or devastation not justified by military necessity.

c) Crimes against humanity: namely, murder, extermination, enslavement, deportation, and other inhumane acts committed against any civilian population, before, or during the war. . . .

Under the provisions of Aritcle 6 the United States is clearly guilty of "War Crimes," "Crimes against Peace" and "Crimes against Humanity," crimes for which the top German leaders were either imprisoned or executed. If we agree with Hermann Goering's defense at Nuremberg that "In a life and death struggle there is no legality," then no action can or should be taken against the government leaders responsible for the war in Viet-Nam. But if Americans still believe that there is a higher law than that of the jungle, we should call our leaders to account. Otherwise we shall have proved Albert Schweitzer correct when he wrote:

It is clear now to everyone that the suicide of civilization is in progress. . . . Wherever there is lost the consciousness that every man is an object of concern for us just because he is a man, civilization and morals are shaken, and the advance to fully developed inhumanity is only a question of time. . . . We have talked for decades with ever increasing lightmindedness about war and conquest, as if these were merely operations on a chessboard; how was this possible save as the result of a tone of mind which no longer pictured to itself the fate of individuals, but thought of them only as figures or objects belonging to the material world? (*The Philosophy of Civilization.*)

The issue at stake in Viet-Nam is not, as President Johnson constantly claims, what will happen if we leave. It is what will happen to us as a people, and to our judgment in history, if we stay.

GENERAL
MATTHEW B. RIDGWAY

On Viet-Nam*

One of our most deeply embedded traditions asserts the supremacy of the civilian authority over the military. It follows that the only justification for a military policy is to support and execute the policies decided by our civilian authorities. Military effort must always be so closely tied to the political objective that at no time do we risk a mushrooming, unlimited war, while the political goal remains definitely restricted.

What troubles many good citizens, people who support the President as I do, is exactly where the balance lies between our military and our political objectives in Viet-Nam, and whether, in fact, the military effort may soon be dominant if, indeed, it is not already so.

The cry of "Why are we in Viet-Nam?" echoes two of the questions I heard from soldiers and civilians in December 1950, when I took command of a defeated and dispirited army. "Why are we in Korea?" and "What are we fighting for?" were the queries then. As the new commander, intent on rebuilding confidence and the offensive spirit, I had to answer.

I told our troops that we were in Korea because we had been ordered there by properly constituted authorities. The loyalty that we gave and expected barred any questioning of those decisions. As to what we were fighting for, my answer was essentially this: "The real issues are whether Western civilization shall defy and defeat communism. This has long ceased to be a fight for freedom of our Korean allies alone. It has become a fight for our own survival in an honorable independent national existence."

Today, in Viet-Nam, I think questions like these are rarely asked. Our combat forces seem to have a better understanding

---

* From *Look,* April 5, 1966. Copyright © 1966 by General Matthew B. Ridgway. Reprinted by permission of the Harold Matson Company, Inc.

of why they are fighting than do many people at home. The soldiers draw no parallel with the Korean war, for many of them hardly recall that conflict. They know that we are using armed force to repel an armed aggression that seeks to impose Communist control over people who reject that tyranny. In Korea, our obligation was a moral one. In Viet-Nam, we have a treaty obligation: The Southeast Asia Treaty of 1954 and its protocol commit us to help with armed force when a nation in the treaty area asks for our aid, as South Viet-Nam has done.

It should be perfectly clear, then, that the President has but one basic course to pursue. He must honor our treaty commitment while concurrently making an intensive effort to find some honorable and acceptable solution. He must also enlist the greatest possible support—diplomatic, economic, and military—from the greatest possible number of nations, to bring the fighting to an end and to lessen the danger of drift into a catastrophe of unimaginable proportions.

Currently, a great deal of loose talk in the United States tends to increase the probability that our military effort will become divorced from the political objective and we will stray toward nuclear disaster. When presumably responsible citizens urge upon the Nation, "Let's get it over with now. Let's plaster Viet-Nam and China, too" or "Let's bomb North Viet-Nam back into the stone age," the danger of our losing all sight of our political objective becomes very real. These hardy folk, who, like Omar Khayyam, are ready to "take the cash and let the credit go, nor heed the rumble of a distant drum," would be talking sense only if our political objective were unlimited— the imposition of a pax Americana upon the entire world—and if we confessed no national morality whatever.

We cannot ignore this moral question. Otherwise, we retreat overnight to the jungle from which the human race took millennia to crawl. The civilian authorities themselves bear much responsibility for the widespread confusion among well-meaning people over the military situation and our political objectives. Within the past two years, pronouncements on our military efforts by highly placed authorities have ranged from rosy euphoria to grim foreboding. As for our political aims, we have been chided for not grasping "the simplicity of our basic objectives" in Viet-Nam. Yet we have been given numerous definitions of those objectives:

To contain communism; to halt aggression; to prove to Communist leaders that aggression cannot be made to pay off; to support "the right of a people to choose their own government"; to help the South Vietnamese realize their desire to "live in the way they prefer"; and to assist a helpless people "to advance toward economic prosperity and social improvement." As recently as December 7, 1965, Senator J. William Fulbright called for the negotiation of "an honorable compromise." On the same day, Secretary of State Dean Rusk was quoted: "There is no room for compromise" on Viet-Nam.

Our military objective has been frequently and beguilingly described as "victory." This word always rings gladly on American ears. What American does not want to win any fight he gets into? It is a deeply ingrained national trait to go all out for victory, using whatever force we possess. There is, we are told, and we foolishly agree, "no substitute for victory." But we are not dealing with a lawsuit, a prizefight, or a football game. We live in a world very unlike the one we were raised in. We have a potential for wholesale destruction so indescribably vast that many words, including "victory," lose their meaning. It would hardly be counted a "victory" if one football team were to defeat another through the use of knives; neither would we savor triumph in a "victory" that would reduce three-fourths of the civilized world to rubble.

With no clearcut limit upon our immediate military objective, we commit ourselves to an upward-spiraling course that may approach annihilation. If we decide to employ whatever force is needed (and no one is wise enough to estimate now how much that will be) to achieve victory in Viet-Nam, do we double, then triple, then quadruple our ground forces? And if victory even then eludes us, do we extend the war to wider and wider arenas? And if we still fail to eliminate all resistance, do we then use nuclear weapons?

We cannot thus engage to achieve victory at whatever cost unless we have already announced an unlimited political objective: i.e., the complete subjection of the outside world to American domination. And I cannot see in the current situation anything to justify the setting up of so rash a goal as that. But if, in the light of their greater knowledge of the situation, our highest civilian authorities believe that something like this should be our goal, then the public should be told immediately. If our policymakers do not believe in aiming for such a goal, and there is certainly no indication that they do, then a halt should be called soon to control our military buildup.

In my opinion, it is the immediate duty of our civilian authorities to define more precisely and pragmatically just what is our political goal—assuming it is something less than global defeat of all resisting forces. At the very least, we should have what Senator Karl Mundt called for recently in a TV debate moderated by Eric Sevareid: "A declaration of policy from the White House to the Senate, where that policy can then be debated." With that objective precisely fixed, the size of the military effort needed to attain it could be clearly determined. With our aims loosely described only as "freedom for the people to choose their way of life" or as "standing up to communism," we have drifted from a point where we were told, a scant two years ago, that our military task would be largely accomplished and our troops withdrawn by December 1965, to a point where the faint outline of a half-million troop commitment becomes a distinct possibility. And even that commitment is not offered as a final limit. The situation remains, to use Senator Mike Mansfield's apt phrase, "open-ended," and we have made, to date, I believe, an unconvincing argument to our people that our goals lie within the zone of vital national interest that cannot be compromised. The falling-domino theory—if Viet-Nam falls, then Laos, Thailand, and all south Asia will collapse— is a theory I have never accepted. Like many other premises upon which people tend to rest their position, it is deserving of more searching analysis than it generally gets.

I am fully aware that I am speaking in generalities. Whatever course I propose or whatever action I oppose, I still cannot deal in specifics. The plain truth is that no individual, outside of the top levels of Government has, or should have, access to enough inside information to do otherwise. I have no private sources of top-level intelligence and no access to top-level military plans. Yet the proper functioning of a democracy demands that the conscientious citizen speak his carefully considered views. Only then can patriotic and competent officials, civilian and military, who bear the ultimate responsibility for decisions, find the guidance they must have. The recent hearings before the Senate Foreign Relations Committee served an admirable purpose in stimulating public thought and discussion of one of the most difficult problems this country has had to face.

Many of those who have thoughtfully endorsed a widening or an intensifying of the war have spoken, I believe, from the conviction that they have been applying the lessons learned in Korea. Lessons can be learned from Korea. But there are far more dissimilarities between the two actions than there are parallels. In South Korea, we had a workable government, led by a fiercely patriotic and powerful civilian leader whose opposition to communism was widely known and who held the allegiance of the majority of his people. We acted in concert with many nations and had been deputized by the United Nations to repel the aggressor in its name.

Relatively little terrorist activity occurred in South Korea, United Nations personnel rode in open jeeps throughout our zones without ever drawing an assassin's fire. Our power easily contained guerrilla activity, even though our forces were neither as well-equipped nor as mobile as they are in Viet-Nam. A unified military command kept both United States and ROK armies under the direct control of the U.S. commander. In short, our line of battle was well-defined, the enemy clearly identifiable, and the political divisions were sharp.

None of these conditions holds for Viet-Nam today. Yet we do have a "right" to be there, for our treaty obligation is clear and specific. I think we should take care, however, not to misread history in an effort to justify unlimited military effort. Most people will agree that we face confused, complex, and unpredictable situations. Most people will agree that each contains potential perils of great and undetermined extent.

Confronted with such circumstances, would we not be wise to avoid further dispersion of our already overextended resources? Would it not be sound judgment to husband our strength and to refuse further far-flung commitments in our "open-ended situation" until we can discern more clearly the shape of things to come?

Again, we hear talk of "sanctuaries." Yet the bombing of sanctuaries never turns out to be a simple matter. During the Korean war, the Manchurian bases, the so-called sanctuary, were indeed wide open to attack from the air. We deliberately refrained from bombing them, as we refrained from taking out the vulnerable Yalu bridges. The advisability of carrying this war over the border into Manchuria in this manner was considered in the highest councils of our Nation. The decision not to bomb the sanctuary was made for reasons that seemed then, and still seem, wise to me. Had we attacked mainland China through air raids, we would have unleashed a war of unknowable dimensions. Not one of our major allies would have approved this adventure, and the coalition formed to stop Communist aggression would have dissolved. Furthermore, our "shoestring" air force (this was Gen. Hoyt Vandenberg's own description) would have dwindled, through combat losses and natural attrition, to a shadow. We would have been left without power to honor the many IOU's we had extended on a worldwide basis. The time then required to rebuild sufficient strength to honor our obligations would have been two years.

Nor should it be forgotten that the United Nations forces had their own sanctuary during the Korean conflict, just as we have one now in South Viet-Nam. Both China and the United States operated under self-imposed limitations as to the bombing of hostile bases. The Chinese air force in Manchuria and other nearby bases was strong enough to have done us major damage, not only in South Korea, but in Japan. Similarly, Red China now may possess the power to destroy Saigon and inflict heavy damage on our South Viet-Nam port facilities in one swift strike should we carry our air attack close to her own vitals.

China has the strength, too, to reopen the Korean front. Should we, in that instance, oppose her there, or should we withdraw to more defensible positions to the south and east, an unthinkable abandonment of our Korean allies? An attack upon mainland China might well bring Soviet Russia into the fray, with Western Europe open to immediate invasion. Where do we draw our line of defense then, and what weapons do we use? And where do we concentrate our strength?

These questions suggest the immensity of the problem the President and his advisers now wrestle with. Those men in public life who urge prompt and unlimited escalation of the war are neither diminishing the problem nor strengthening the President's arm. They only make it even more difficult for the President to steer the Nation on that careful course between duty and disaster.

And those who call for immediate disengagement from Viet-Nam, as if it had all been a mistake, likewise make the President's path more difficult. We cannot escape now from the obligations we took upon ourselves when we first pledged our word to the South Vietnamese. One lesson to be drawn from Korea is that we cannot pull out of a sticky situation without regard for those who have fought at our side.

During the Korean war, soon after the Chinese launched their New Year's offensive in January 1951, serious thought was given in Washington to our abandoning the peninsula and pulling our forces back to Japan. (I opposed this strongly.) It quickly became clear that such a withdrawal would require the evacuation of at least a million South Koreans, those who had been our battlefield allies or had worked with us since the invasion. To have left them to the vengeance of the Communists would have been an infamous betrayal.

We are under similar obligation in Viet-Nam not to abandon the hundreds of thousands who have been our allies there. We cannot pick up and run home without making extensive and permanent provision for all the Vietnamese who have supported our arms. A concept like the one discussed by Gen. James Gavin, for holding fast to our defensive enclaves, would enable us to fulfill our obligation to our Vietnamese allies, before committing ourselves to unlimited military effort, while we continue to seek an honorable solution.

Korea also taught that it is impossible to interdict the supply routes of an Asian army by airpower alone. We had complete air mastery over North Korea, and we clobbered Chinese supply columns unmercifully. Unquestionably, we inflicted serious damage upon the Chinese and greatly complicated their problems of reinforcement and supply. But we did not halt their offensive nor materially diminish its strength. The Chinese, like the Vietnamese, traveled light, with each man carrying his ammunition, his food, and his weapon on his back. They moved at night or on hidden footpaths and goat tracks, immune from air attack. And where we did find their concentrations and strike them, we still could not force them off the disputed ground. In Korea, I saw whole sections of railroad bombed into scrap iron by aircraft, and yet the enemy rebuilt the tracks in a single night, and the trains ran the next day. After the Chinese repulsed the ill-fated advances to the Yalu, Gen. Douglas MacArthur himself expressed disillusionment with the value of tactical airpower. It could not isolate the battlefield, he said, and its effectiveness had been greatly overrated. It is easy for the civilian mind to be seduced with talk of "easy" conquest through airpower. But the crucial battles are still won by foot soldiers.

There is yet another lesson etched by our experience in Korea: It is folly to base military strategy upon our interpretation of enemy intentions. As our forces pushed toward the Yalu in the home by Christmas offensive of November-December 1950, the high command assured all doubters that the Chinese had no intention of intervening in force because the psychological moment for this had passed, because "no commander in his right mind" would send his forces across the Yalu at this season and because of various other reasons understood only by those who had made a study of the "oriental mind." We knew, however, that the Chinese were capable of dealing us a mighty blow along the Manchurian border, where our forces would be strung out almost haphazardly, without mutual support between commands and without supplies enough to sustain more than a light engagement. We knew that close to a hundred thousand well-disciplined and well-armed Chinese troops were mobilized on the other side of the river. We knew that Chinese volunteers had already appeared in force south of the Yalu, for we had suffered severe attacks from them and had taken prisoners from units known to be in the Chinese order of battle.

Yet, despite this intelligence, we hurried forward in pursuit style, our forces thoroughly dispersed and improperly clothed for fighting in subzero temperature. We "knew" the Chinese were bluffing, and we "knew" they would never commit more than a token force of volunteers. We abandoned elemental prudence. Instead of being guided by enemy capability, we divined the enemy intentions. The mistake cost us very dearly in American lives and took us close to disaster. It might be pointed out, too, that MacArthur's earlier brilliant coup at Inchon, where he cut the enemy's lifeline in one spectacular and surprising strike, succeeded in large part because of his stated reliance on the enemy's assumption that no commander would risk the monstrous tides, the tortuous channel, and the two-mile mudflats outside Inchon Harbor. Custer likewise knew that the Indians would not attack at Little Bighorn And the French "knew" that Wolfe would never be fool enough to try to scale that precipice guarding Quebec.

We should be wary of experts who feel they can correctly interpret Chinese intentions and can predict how they will react to any move of ours. We know what the Chinese are capable of in Southeast Asia. This is the knowledge that should guide us in appraising our strategy.

The one final important lesson we can draw from what happened in Korea is that we cannot enter into agreements with the Communists unless we have ironclad sanctions, underwritten by the world's major powers, including, if possible, the Soviet Union. Viet-Nam, as Senator Joseph Clark pointed out in that TV debate I referred to previously, is only an incident. The major threat to our security and our way of life still comes from Red China and the Soviet Union. It is with our eye upon them that we must plan our global strategy. To do that calls for the best minds we can assemble in farsighted statesmanship and creative thinking.

Finally, I want to put proper emphasis on one aspect of the whole military and political problem that tends too often to be either minimized or ignored—that is the moral factor. In June 1955, when I was chief of staff of the Army, I had occasion to address a letter to the Secretary of Defense regarding the military defense of the United States. My conviction, pressed in that letter, remains unaltered:

> Just as the ultimate and most deadly threat of communism is the destruction of the religious and moral principles which have guided man to new heights of dignity and self-respect so also do we find the same threat in the increasingly significant ignoring by our planners of the consequences of omitting the moral factor in considering the use of the immense destructive capability which now exists in the world.

It is my firm belief that there is nothing in the present situation or in our code that requires us to bomb a small Asian nation "back into the stone age." While we should be prepared to pay any price in order to live up to our obligations, there must be some moral limit to the means we use to achieve victory. A victory that would require the wholesale devastation of a country by nuclear arms because it would not yield to conventional force would be the ultimate in immorality.

General Ridgway's Nine Points for Viet-Nam

1. We should emphatically reject the two extreme courses—"pullout" or "all-out war"—that have been advocated by certain groups.

2. We should give our full support to the President's determined efforts to fulfill our treaty obligations and to honor our pledges, while at the same time seeking an honorable solution of the basically political problem in Viet-Nam.

3. With due regard for diplomatic secrecy, our Government should spell out, more specifically and pragmatically, our immediate and long-range political objectives, firmly rejecting any unlimited political objective that might entail unlimited military effort.

4. We should also reject any political involvement that might gradually commit us to military efforts that would jeopardize our basic security and those vital American interests that cannot be compromised.

5. Once having announced our political objectives within the framework stated above, we should then employ whatever force is needed to attain them.

6. We should categorically reject "preventive" war, employing nuclear weapons, the use of which would be, in my opinion, a deliberate move down the road of international immorality past the point of no return.

7. We should enter into formal agreements with the Communist leaders of Southeast Asia only after establishment of enforceable sanctions to guarantee the permanent protection of the South Vietnamese people.

8. We should sign no instrument with those leaders without prior agreement in good faith among a group of nations, including, if possible, the Soviet Union, to join in fairly sharing the task of applying proper sanctions.

9. We should repose complete confidence in the capability of our military leaders in Southeast Asia to accomplish any mission they may be assigned, for these men are among the best that our Nation has produced.

J. W. FULBRIGHT

On the Arrogance of Power*

Mr. Fulbright: Mr. President, it is quite obvious, from the discussions that have taken place in the last several weeks, particularly with regard to the military authorization bill, that underlying those discussions was a deep concern about our relations with China. So this morning I want to say a few words about that subject.

Speaking of China, United Nations Secretary General U Thant recently made the point that "when a country is obsessed with fear and suspicion, all sorts of tensions are likely to develop, all sorts of unreasonable reactions are likely to come forth. Countries, like individuals," he said, "have nervous breakdowns," and it is the duty of the community to try to understand and find some remedy. The Secretary General pointed out that "China is going through a difficult stage of development and" he said, "in such a delicate stage, countries will show certain emotions, certain strong reactions, certain rigidities, and even certain arrogance." (The Washington *Post,* January 21, 1966.)

The Secretary General's words are supported by modern knowledge of human behavior.

Said the distinguished psychiatrist, Dr. Jerome D. Frank:

> Frightened, hostile individuals tend to behave in ways which aggravate their difficulties instead of resolving them, and frightened, hostile nations seem to behave similarly.[1]

A nation, like an individual, Dr. Frank suggests, is likely to respond to a feared rival by breaking off communications, by provocative behavior, or by taking measures which promise immediate relief, regardless of their ultimate consequences.

Fearful and hostile behavior is not rational but neither is it uncommon, either to individuals or to nations, including our own. In retrospect most Americans would agree that our national behavior was unduly fearful and irrational during the McCarthy

---

* Congressional Record, March 7, 1966.
[1] Letter from Dr. Frank to Senator Fulbright, Sept. 13, 1960.

period of the early fifties and the "Red scare" after World War I. And just about all of us would agree that our Nation suffered something worse than a "nervous breakdown" just over a hundred years ago.

Perhaps we southerners have a sensitivity to this sort of thing that other Americans cannot fully share. We—or our forebears —experienced both the hotheaded romanticism that led to Fort Sumter and the bitter humiliation of defeat and a vindictive Reconstruction. The indignities suffered by the South during that era have burdened not just the South but the entire Nation with a legacy of bitterness far more durable and, in retrospect, more damaging than the physical destruction wrought by the war itself. Even today, although the South has long since recovered its political rights and has begun at last to share in the Nation's economic prosperity, the very word "Yankee" still awakens in some southern minds historical memories of defeat and humiliation, of the burning of Atlanta and Sherman's march to the sea, or of an ancestral farmhouse burned by Cantrell's raiders, or a family fortune lost and never recovered, or of arrogant carpetbaggers and the helpless rage of the people they dispossessed.

These memories are irrational but not irrelevant. They are pertinent because they persist and, by persisting, continue to work a baleful influence on our national life. They may be pertinent as well in helping us to understand the bitterness and anger and unreason in the behavior of other peoples who once were great but then were struck down and finally rose again only after a long era of degradation at the hands of foreigners.

I am thinking about China. Not being an expert in such matters, I cannot claim with anything approaching certainty that the indignities suffered by China in the nineteenth century have had human consequences comparable to those of the injustices suffered by the American South in the wake of the Civil War. It may be, however, that there is a similarity. Unless we are to believe that there is a "Chinese nature" which is entirely different from the "American nature," unless we believe that there is no such thing as a common human nature, it would seem to me logical to suppose that, national differences—great as they are— notwithstanding, the people of one nation are likely to respond to success and to humiliation, to victory and to defeat, in about the same way as the people of another nation.

China has experienced very little except humiliation and defeat in its relations with the West, including Russia and, to some degree, America. One of our leading Chinese scholars, Prof. John K. Fairbank, who is the director of the East Asian Research Center of Harvard University, believes that the rapacious behavior of Europeans in China in past centuries has a great deal to do with the irrationality and hostile behavior of China's current leaders. He writes:

The sources of China's revolutionary militancy are plain enough in Chinese history. The Chinese Communist regime is only the latest phase in a process of decline and fall followed by rebirth and reassertion of national power. China's humiliation under the unequal treaties of the 19th century lasted for a hundred years. An empire that had traditionally been superior to all others in its world was not only humbled but threatened with extinction. Inevitably, China's great tradition of unity, as the world's greatest state in size and continuity, was reasserted.[2]

Words like "extraterritoriality" and "unequal treaties" are far too antiseptic, too bland, to describe China's humiliation by Western imperialism. In human terms, the coming of Western civilization to China in the nineteenth century meant the plundering of China's wealth by foreigners and the reduction of most of the Chinese to an inferior status within their own country. Missionaries were immune from Chinese law and treated the Chinese as heathen, except, of course, for the converts who also claimed immunity from Chinese law and used the power conferred by their foreign association to intimidate their fellow citizens. Foreign goods were exempted by treaty from internal toll taxes imposed by the Manchu Dynasty to pay for the Taiping rebellion of the mid-19th century, with the result that Western companies destroyed their Chinese competitors in the sale of such products as timber, oil, tobacco and, of course, opium. Each of China's disastrous nineteenth century wars with the West was followed by the levy of a huge indemnity or some further incursion on the economic life of the country.

The first of these wars, the opium war of 1839 to 1842, came

---

[2] John K. Fairbank, "How To Deal With the Chinese Revolution," the *New York Review of Books*, Feb. 17, 1966.

about when the Chinese Government tried to end the traffic in opium. The destructive narcotic was destroying the health and the lives of alarming numbers of Chinese addicts, but it was also a source of great profit to foreign and Chinese opium merchants. British businessmen were the major foreign dealers in opium, but Americans, French, and others also participated; opium became an important factor in the trade balance between some Western countries and China. When the Chinese Government tried to ban the import of opium in 1839, the British refused to pledge their compliance, whereupon a number of incidents occurred culminating in war between China and England. The British won easily and under the Treaty of Nanking of 1842 China was forced to cede Hong Kong to Britain, open five treaty ports for British trade, accept tariffs that could not be changed without Britain's consent, and, in addition, pay an indemnity to compensate the British for lost opium and for expenses incurred in the war.

Following the British example, other powers exacted concessions from China through persuasion and the threat of force. The United States, for example, signed a treaty with China in 1844 under which the United States acquired trading privileges and extraterritoriality for both civil and criminal cases.

The opium war and the Treaty of Nanking exposed China's vulnerability and opened the way to extensive exploitation by foreign powers. In the 1850's the British Prime Minister Lord Palmerston judged that "the time is fast approaching when we shall be obliged to strike another blow in China." In Palmerston's words:

These half-civilized Governments such as those of China, Portugal, Spanish America require a dressing down every eight or ten years to keep them in order.

The Chinese got many a "dressing down" in the years that followed. The British and French fought another war with China in 1856. Under the treaties of Tientain new concessions were granted and old ones enlarged. The European powers acquired new trading ports and additional authority over Chinese tariffs as well as other privileges. The Chinese were required to pay indemnities, and there was also an article guaranteeing the protection of missionaries since, in the words of the treaty:

The Christian religion, as professed by Protestants and Roman Catholics, inculcates the practice of virtue, and teaches man to do as he would be done by.

The Chinese refused to ratify these treaties. Hostilities were renewed and the British burned the Emperor's summer place in Peiping. Under the Peiping Convention of 1860 more ports were opened, more indemnities were paid and the Chinese were compelled to cede Kowloon to England.

The treaties of 1842 and 1844 and of 1858 and 1860, known for fairly obvious reasons as the "unequal treaties," formed the basis of China's relations with the West until the Second World War.

The Chinese also had their difficulties with the Russians. In 1858, while the Chinese were beset with British and French attacks from the sea and the Taiping rebellion in the interior, the Russians presented the Chinese with certain territorial demands. The Chinese were forced thereupon to cede to Russia all of the hitherto Chinese territories north of the Amur River. In 1860 the Russians demanded and received additional territory on the Pacific coast, including the area at which the port of Vladivostok was subsequently established. Under these two treaties Russia deprived China of a territory larger than Texas.

In the last decade of the nineteenth century Japan joined the Western Powers in their depredations against China, Japan attacked China in 1894 and under the treaty of Shimonoseki, which ended that war, Japan exacted large cessions of territory as well as extensive commercial privileges. Pressure by the European powers forced the Japanese to withdraw some of their demands, notably for Port Arthur on the Liaotung Peninsula, but Japan acquired the island of Taiwan and extensive trade privileges, and of course, China was compelled to pay an indemnity.

Having joined with the powers in forcing Japan to return the Liaotung Peninsula to China, Germany now demanded a reward. The Chinese failed to see the equity of this claim, but were brought around when the Germans landed troops. China was thereupon forced to lease the port and Bay of Kiaochow to Germany for ninety-nine years and was also forced to yield commercial privileges on the Shantung Peninsula.

The other powers also sought rewards. Russia demanded and received the lease of Port Arthur and Dairen and the right to build a railroad across Manchuria. France, which had forced China to recognize French authority in Indochina in the 1880's, demanded and received in 1898 an extensive sphere of influence in South China, including the lease of Kwangchow Bay for ninety-nine years. The British, not to be outdone, now demanded and acquired control of the Chinese maritime customs, lease of a naval station at Weihaiwei, and the extension of the lease of Kowloon to ninety-nine years.

China had become a virtual colony with many masters. "Yet," said Sun Yat-sen, then a rising revolutionary, "none of the masters feels responsible for its welfare."

The Society of the Righteous and Harmonious Fists, better known as the Boxers, was a secret organization composed largely of poverty-stricken peasants. Their grievances might well have been directed against the Manchu rulers of China, but government officials had no great difficulty in persuading the Boxers that the foreigns were the cause of the misery of the people. With great savagery, the Boxers fell upon foreigners and their Chinese cohorts in 1900; they were especially merciless toward missionaries and their Chinese converts. The Boxers went on a rampage against the foreigners in Peiping, besieging the foreign legations.

An international rescue force made up of Japanese, Russians, British, Germans, French, and Americans was sent to relieve the legations. The commander of the allied force, Field Marshal Count Von Waldersee, was under instructions from the Kaiser "to give no quarter and to take no prisoners," so that "no Chinese will ever again dare to look askance at a German."

The allies proved the equal of the Boxers in their ferocity. The defeated Chinese were now compelled to sign a new treaty under which the foreign powers received the right to station troops in their legation sites, a new Chinese tariff system was imposed, an indemnity of $333 million was to be paid, and the Chinese were obliged to punish war criminals.

The United States returned a large part of the $25 million which was its share of the Boxer indemnity with the provision that the fund be used to educate Chinese students in the United States. Many Americans have regarded this as an act of extraordinary philanthropy.

The United States thereafter announced its open-door policy

toward China. The open-door policy purported to preserve the territorial integrity of China and to safeguard for all nations equal commercial access to China. Limited and ineffective as it was, the open door policy induced the Chinese to think of the United States as the only major foreign power which might be thought of as their friend and possible protector. The open-door remained the basis of American policy toward China until the Communists came to power in 1949 and closed China's door.

Political history hardly begins to convey the human effects of Western imperialism on the Chinese people. Something of the meaning of life in China under the impact of Western imperialism is conveyed by a Chinese engineer's account of his return to China in 1913 with his Belgian wife and son. He wrote as follows:

In Shanghai it was agony, for there it was only too plain that in my own country I was nothing but an inferior, despised being. There were parks and restaurants and hotels I could not enter, although she could. I had no rights on the soil of a Chinese city which did not belong to the Chinese; she had rights by reason of something called skin.

We boarded the English steamer from Shanghai to Hankow; the first class was for Europeans only, and there was no other steamer. Marguerite leaned her arms on the railings and stared at the river. She was in first class, with our son. I went second class. I had insisted it should be so. "It is too hot for you here below."

Some years earlier as a student in Shanghai the young man had written to his brother about his inability to understand the Europeans. He wrote:

They always bewilder me. At once most ruthless in the pursuit of their interests, caring nothing for the wholesale misery they bring, at the same time their papers are full of verbiage of their nobility, rightness, and the good they do. They become indignant at our public executions, and our cruelty to dogs. Yet the record of their lootings and killings in our country shows no such correct compassion.

The humiliations to which the Chinese were subjected would be difficult for any people to endure. Consider how shocking they must have been to a nation with a far longer and in many ways more illustrious history than that of any nation in the

West, to a people who have always—and not without some justification—regarded their civilization as superior to any other. Before the time of Christ the Chinese had developed the principles and methods which were to hold together their empire until the 20th century. In science and technology as well as government, China was well ahead of Europe by the time Marco Polo visited China in the 13th century. China became the center of civilization in eastern Asia and it became the model for smaller states, such as Korea and Viet-Nam, whose rulers accepted the obligation of tribute to the Chinese Emperor as their suzerain.

When European merchants and missionaries and buccaneers first came to China, they did not come to a land of primitives and pagans. They came upon a rich and ancient civilization, but one which had fallen behind in its technology, especially its military technology, with the result that it was thrown open to exploitation by foreigners whose power vastly exceeded their wisdom. Writes C. P. Fitzgerald, professor of Far Eastern history in the Australian National University:

It is a regrettable fact that the value of a Nation's contribution to civilization, her place in the world, tends to be judged, from age to age, by the strength or weakness of her military power. When China under K'ang Hsi or Ch'ien Lung was manifestly too strong for any European encroachment to succeed, the real and serious weaknesses of the Government and economy were not regarded; the achievements in art and literature were much respected. When China fell behind Europe, her military power becoming negligible, encroachment was continual, and the value of Chinese civilization fell sharply in Western eyes.[3]

The Chinese revolutions of the 20th century were in part spawned by the ravages of the West. Finding themselves militarily inferior to the West, but unshaken in their faith in the superiority of their own civilization, the Chinese undertook, first through the unsuccessful democratic revolution of Sun Yat-sen, then through the successful Communist revolution of Mao Tse-tung, to acquire those Western techniques of science and technology, of political organization and military power, which would make it possible to expel the West from China. It is ironic

[3] C. P. Fitzgerald, "The Chinese View of Their Place in the World" (London: Oxford University Press, 1964), pp. 34–35.

and significant that the Western political doctrine that China finally adopted was the one which the West itself had repudiated.

It is of great importance that we try to learn something more about the strange and fascinating Chinese nation, about its past and its present, about the aims of its leaders and the aspirations of its people. Before we can make wise political—and perhaps military—decisions pertaining to China, there are many questions to be asked and, hopefully, answered: What kind of people are the Chinese? To what extent are they motivated by national feeling? To what extent by ideology? Why are the Chinese Communist leaders so hostile to the United States and why do they advocate violent revolution against most of the world's governments? To what extent is their view of the world distorted by isolation and the memory of ancient grievances? To what extent, and with what effect on their Government, do the Chinese people share with us and with all other peoples what Aldous Huxley has called the simple human preference for life and peace?

We need to ask these questions because China and America may be heading toward war with each other and it is essential that we do all that can be done to prevent that calamity, starting with a concerted effort to understand the Chinese people and their leaders.

The danger of war is real. It is real because China is ruled by ideological dogmatists who will soon have nuclear weapons at their disposal and who, though far more ferocious in words than in actions, nonetheless are intensely hostile to the United States. In the short run the danger of war between China and America is real because an "open-ended" war in Viet-Nam can bring the two great powers into conflict with each other, by accident or by design, at almost any time. Some of our military experts are confident that China will not enter the war in Viet-Nam; their confidence would be more reassuring if it did not bring to mind the predictions of military experts in 1950 that China would not enter the Korean war, as well as more recent predictions about an early victory in Viet-Nam. In fact, it is the view of certain China experts in our Government that the Chinese leaders themselves expect to be at war with the United States within a year, and it is clear that some of our own officials also expect a war with China.

The expectation of war, even though it is not desired, makes war more likely. Writes social psychologist Gordon Allport:

> The crux of the matter lies in the fact that while most people deplore war, they nonetheless expect it to continue. And what people expect determines their behavior. The indispensable condition of war, is that people must expect war and must prepare for war, before, under warminded leadership, they make war. It is in this sense that "wars begin in the minds of men."[4]

The first vital step toward altering the fatal expectancy of war is the acquisition of some understanding of our prospective adversary. Most of us know very little about Communist China, partly for lack of qualified observers in China and partly because there are so few China experts in our own Government and universities. At present, I am told, there are only about six full-time analysts of Chinese affairs in the Department of State. Some of the most knowledgeable "old China hands" were driven out of the State Department by the McCarthy investigations and there are now few if any well-known and influential "sinologists" at the highest level of Government comparable to such Soviet experts as George Kennan and Llewellyn Thompson. There are some highly competent China specialists below the top levels of Government but they are not exerting a major influence on policy. Some of these experts, according to James Reston, do not subscribe to the view that the war in Viet-Nam can be enlarged without drawing China into the conflict—"The New China Experts," *New York Times,* February 16, 1966.

We must acquire knowledge not only of China but of the Chinese. To most of us China is a strange, distant and dangerous nation, not a society made up of 700 million individual human beings but a kind of menacing abstraction. When Chinese soldiers are described, for example, as "hordes of Chinese coolies," it is clear that they are being thought of not as people but as something terrifying and abstract, or as something inanimate like the flow of lava from a volcano.

Both China and America seem to think of each other as abstractions: to the Chinese we are not a society of individual

---

[4] Gordon W. Allport, "The Role of Expectancy," Hadley Cantril, ed., "Tensions That Cause Wars" (Urbana: University of Illinois Press, 1950), pp. 43, 48.

people but the embodiment of an evil idea, the idea of imperialist capitalism, and to most of us China represents not people but an evil and frightening idea, the idea of aggressive communism. Man's capacity for decent behavior seems to vary directly with his perception of others as individual humans with human motives and feelings, whereas his capacity for barbarous behavior seems to increase with his perception of an adversary in abstract terms. This is the only explanation I can think of for the fact that the very same good and decent citizens who would never fail to feed a hungry child or comfort a sick friend or drop a coin in the church collection basket celebrated the dropping of the atomic bomb on Hiroshima and can now contemplate with equanimity, or indeed even advocate, the use of nuclear weapons against the hordes of Chinese coolies.

I feel sure that this apparent insensitivity to the incineration of thousands or millions of our fellow human beings is not the result of feelings of savage inhumanity toward foreigners; it is the result of not thinking of them as humans at all but rather as the embodiment of doctrines that we consider evil such as fascism and communism. Wrote William Graham Sumner:

> If you want war, nourish a doctrine. Doctrines are the most frightful tyrants to which men ever are subject, because doctrines get inside of a man's reason and betray him against himself. Civilized men have done their fiercest fighting for doctrines.[5]

For these reasons it is important that Americans and Chinese come to know each other in human terms. There is no easy way for us to make ourselves known to the Chinese as the decent and honorable people we really are, and it is not likely that the dogmatic men who rule in Peiping will soon remove the blinders of ideology and look at the world in realistic and human terms. This makes it all the more important for Americans to be open-minded and inquisitive, to set aside ideological preconceptions and try to learn all that we can about the Chinese and their behavior and attitudes, and especially to try to find out why exactly the Chinese are so hostile to the West and what, if anything, can be done to eliminate that hostility.

In the hope of making some contribution to a better understanding of China the Committee on Foreign Relations will begin on Tuesday, March 8, a series of public hearings on China and

---

[5] "War" (1903).

on American attitudes toward China. The immediate purpose of the inquiry will be educational rather than political. It seems to me that at this stage the best contribution the committee can make is to provide a forum through which recognized experts and scholars can help increase congressional and public knowledge of China. Whether and in what way the inquiry will influence American foreign policy will depend upon the value of the information provided and the attentiveness and openmindness with which it is received.

Our ultimate objective must, of course, be political: the prevention of war between China and America. At present there appears to be a growing expectation of war in both countries and, as Professor Allport points out, "what people expect determines their behavior." Perhaps a concerted effort to increase our understanding of China and the Chinese would alter that fatal expectancy, and perhaps if our expectations were altered theirs too would change. It is anything but a sure thing but, considering the stakes and considering the alternative, it seems worth a try.

The Chinese today, like Americans a hundred years ago, are in an agitated and abnormal state of mind. It is not only within our means but, as a great and mature Nation, it is our responsibility, as U Thant so wisely pointed out, to try to understand the causes of China's agitation and to try to find some remedy.

On November 14, 1860, Alexander Hamilton Stephens, who subsequently became Vice President of the Southern Confederacy, delivered an address to the Georgia Legislature in which he appealed to his colleagues to delay the secession of Georgia from the Union. He said:

It may be that out of it we may become greater and more prosperous, but I am candid and sincere in telling you that I fear if we yield to passion, and without sufficient cause shall take that step, that instead of becoming greater or more peaceful, prosperous and happy—instead of becoming Gods, we will become demons, and at no distant day commence cutting one another's throats. This is my apprehension. Let us, therefore, whatever we do, meet these difficulties, great as they are, like wise and sensible men, and consider them in the light of all the consequences which may attend our action.[6]

---

[6] Alexander Hamilton Stephens, "Secession," in Modern Eloquence (New York: P. F. Collier & Sons, 1928), vol. II, p. 203.

456 ·   *The Viet-Nam Reader*

What a tragedy it is that the South did not accept Stephens' advice in 1860. What a blessing it would be if, faced with the danger of a war with China, we did accept it today.

ROBERT F. KENNEDY

*Position on Viet-Nam**

This week has been another chapter in a great tradition. For the Senate Chamber still echoes to the distant ringing of the great issues of our past. War and westward growth, civil strife and the rights of man have been argued on its floor; and from those debates have emerged the shaping events and judgments of American history.

The greater the issue, the larger the stakes, the more passionately debate has raged, in the Senate and across the land. Abraham Lincoln was reviled for opposing the war of 1848. The citizens of his own State called Daniel Webster traitor for proposing a compromise to avoid civil war. Those who saw the storm, and tried desperately to prepare the Nation for World War II, were cursed as warmongers, enemies of mankind, subverters of democracy—and worse.

Yet, despite the condemnations and the violent recriminations, there have always been within the Senate enough men of courage and conviction to triumph in the end over those who would stifle free discussion and action. There are hazards in debating American policy in the face of a stern and dangerous enemy. But that hazard is the essence of our democracy. Democracy is no easy form of government. Few nations have been able to sustain it. For it requires that we take the chances of freedom; that the liberating play of reason be brought to bear on events filled with passion; that dissent be allowed to make its appeal for acceptance; that men chance error in their search for the truth.

---

* Statement, February 19, 1966, reprinted in the Congressional Record, March 14, 1966.

"The best test of truth is the power of thought to get itself accepted in the competition of the marketplace," said Justice Holmes. "That at any rate is the theory of our Constitution. It is an experiment, as all life is an experiment. Every year, if not every day, we have to wager our salvation upon some prophecy based on imperfect knowledge. While that experiment is part of our system, I think that we should be eternally vigilant against attempts to check the expression of opinions that we loathe and believe to be fought with depth."

Our Constitution imposes on the Senate the most heavy and grave independent responsibilities. We ourselves owe to the people of fifty States the burden of independent thought and action. Our whole system of government rests on a complex structure of independence and cooperation among the branches; a structure which requires that we make our own judgments about events, giving due weight to the reason and responsibility of others.

Shall we then debate with force and passion the issues of labor relations and housing and trade—while the great issues of peace and war are allowed to pass in silence? Shall we discuss the standard of living of our constituents—while policies which affect their very existence go undiscussed? To do so would be the gravest departure from our duties as representatives of the people of the American States.

Full and informing debate rests upon moderation and mutual indulgence. Men must seek acceptance of their views through reason, and not through intimidation; through argument, and not through accusation. We are all patriots here. We are all defenders of freedom. We are all Americans. To attack the motives of those who express concern about our present course—to challenge their very right to speak freely—is to strike at the foundations of the democratic process which our fellow citizens, even today, are dying in order to protect.

I suggest that the Senate, and this entire Nation, might well adopt for its own guidance the personal creed of Thomas Jefferson. He said:

"I tolerate with the utmost latitude the right of others to differ from me in opinion without imputing to them criminality. I know too well the weakness and uncertainty of human reason to wonder at its different result. Both of our political parties agree conscientiously in the same object—the public good; but they differ essentially in what they deem the means of promoting that good—which is right, time and experience will prove—with whatever opinion the body of the Nation concurs, that must prevail. My anxieties on this subject will never tarry beyond the use of fair and honorable means of truth and reason; nor have they ever lessened my esteem for moral worth, nor alienated my affections from a single friend, who did not first withdraw himself."

The discussions which have been taking place in recent days are therefore worthwhile and important. But we must do all we can to make certain that the exchange of views accomplishes the most for our country—moving our policy toward the goal we all want to achieve. All of us are concerned, as the American people are concerned, about the progress of the struggle in Viet-Nam.

There are several aspects to this concern.

We are concerned at the casualties, the death and suffering, of our young men in South Viet-Nam.

We are concerned over the effect of some of our military action on the people of South Viet-Nam—whether more cannot be done to lessen the death and destruction of the innocent that comes with war. For a military victory at the cost of a completely destroyed South Viet-Nam would be a defeat for our larger purposes.

We are concerned whether the people of South Viet-Nam are being offered something positive to live and fight for—something beyond negative anticommunism. The President's recent initiatives are to be applauded and welcomed; but it is now incumbent on the Government of South Viet-Nam to make good at last on promises which the people of that unhappy country have heard for many years.

We are concerned over our relationship with Communist China—not just concern to avoid a deadly war, but also concern lest the Viet-Nam struggle make any reasonable accommodation with China impossible in the future. The events of the coming decade will determine whether our relations with mainland China will change for the better or for the worse. But they will change and we can influence that change; and the direction of change must receive the earnest attention of the Senate.

And we are concerned about the effect of the war on our domestic efforts to conquer ignorance and disease and unemployment—the problems of the cities—problems which, warned the McCone Commission, could split our society irretrievably. And this concern is heightened by the way in which the war perpetuates discrimination—for the poor and the less fortunate serve in Viet-Nam out of all proportion to their numbers in the United States as a whole.

But the central question before us now—the area of greatest present concern for the Senate, and what we must discuss at all levels of government—is our political strategy in the war in Viet-Nam; not simply how to move, but in what direction we wish to move.

At the outset, it must be realized that negotiations are not an ultimate goal. Negotiations or discussions are only a means by which ultimate goals may be reached. Our arrival at the bargaining table will not make the struggle disappear. Even if we arrive at the bargaining table, the real question is what goals we will seek there. Without clear goals in mind, negotiations are pointless. And without clear goals and realistic objectives, it is doubtful whether the bargaining table will ever be reached.

What, then, are our goals in Viet-Nam?

The Secretary of State and others have stated objectives in general terms. They are the independence of South Viet-Nam —or, at least, its independent right to determine its own future. They are to halt the aggression from the north and to prove to China that a policy of subversion in other lands will not work. These are worthy objectives. All are important. The question remains, however, under what realistic terms and conditions they can be advanced in Viet-Nam.

There are three routes before us: military victory, a peaceful settlement, or withdrawal.

The last is impossible for this country. For the United States to withdraw now, as I said last May, would be a repudiation of commitments undertaken and confirmed by three administrations. It would flatly betray those in Viet-Nam whom we have encouraged by our support to resist the forces of Hanoi and the Viet-Cong. Unilateral withdrawal would injure, perhaps irreparably, the principle of collective security, and undermine the independence of small nations everywhere in the world. And it would offer no hope for a reasonable accommodation with China in the future. There are reasonable and responsible steps which we can take to raise the possibility of improved relations with China in the future. But unilateral withdrawal would only reward aggression and could offer China no inducement to reach accommodation in a peaceful world.

I now turn to the open avenues—military victory or a peaceful settlement.

Military victory requires that we crush both our adversary's strength and his will to continue the battle; that the forces from the north be compelled to withdraw beyond the border; that much of Viet-Nam be destroyed and its people killed; that we continue to occupy South Viet-Nam as long as our presence is required to insure that hostilities, including insurgency, will not be resumed. And this will be a very long time indeed.

I cannot say with certainty that such an outcome is beyond our reach. We do know, however, that it would mean rapidly increasing commitments of American forces. It would mean a growing risk of widening war—with North Viet-Nam, with China, even with the Soviet Union. It would lead, indeed already has led thoughtless people to advocate the use of nuclear weapons. And it would involve all these things—commitment, risk, and spreading destruction—in pursuit of a goal which is at best uncertain, and at worst unattainable.

Despite all these dangers, we may yet come to this course. The intransigence of our adversaries may leave us no alternative. There should be no misunderstanding or miscalculation of this point in either Hanoi or Peking. The American people possess the bravery and the will to follow such a course if others force it upon us. I also believe, however, that given the opportunity by our adversaries, we possess the wisdom and skill to avoid such a grim necessity.

And President Johnson has made clear, on behalf of the United States, in every forum of the world, that this country seeks the other road: the road to negotiated settlement.

In this pursuit we have asked for unconditional discussions. This means simply that we will neither demand nor yield specific formal commitments before bargaining begins. In fact, both sides must come to any discussion with at least one basic condition; one irreducible demand; one point they will not yield.

For the United States it must be that we will not turn South Viet-Nam over to the North. For North Viet-Nam it must be that they will not accept a settlement which leaves in the south a hostile government, dedicated to the final physical destruction of all Communist elements, refusing any economic cooperation with the North, dependent upon the continued presence of American military power.

These conditions, these minimum terms, can be breached only at sword's point; only by driving the adversary's forces from the field. For either side to yield its minimum conditions would be in fact to accept to defeat. If we intend to deny these minimum conditions to our adversaries, then we must defeat them completely. If this is what we intend, we should understand it clearly —and undertake it with resolution.

But if negotiation is our aim, as we have so clearly said it is, we must seek a middle ground. A negotiated settlement means that each side must concede matters that are important in order to preserve positions that are essential.

It may be that negotiation is not possible in this war because our political aims are irreconcilable; because one side, or both sides, are not willing to accept anything less than the fruits of victory. If that is so, then we must reluctantly let slip the hope of reasoned discussion and proceed to the uncertain, uncharted course of war.

I believe there is a middle way, that an end to the fighting and a peaceful settlement can be achieved. It must be said, before all else, that the middle way—the way of negotiation— involves risks. An adversary who lives may perhaps fight another day. And a government which is not continuously sheltered by American military power may be again attacked or subverted or overthrown.

These risks, I believe, we are courageous enough to undertake. They are risks, in fact, which we do take everyday in a hundred countries in every corner of every continent. There are dozens of countries which might be the target of Communist aggression or subversion. If we were unwilling to take any risk that they might be subverted or conquered by the Communists, we might simply have occupied all of them. But clearly, we would rather live with such risks than attempt to occupy these nations. We take these risks because we believe men and nations will not willingly choose to submit to other men from other lands.

If we are wrong in this basic faith, then Viet-Nam will be but a flicker in the conflagration which is to come. But in Indonesia, in Algeria, and in the Central African Republic the Chinese have suffered enormous defeats—not because we are stronger or more skilled than they—not because we defeated them. They were defeated because the people of these lands preferred to run their affairs in their own way—and our faith was justified. This basic faith may not be borne out on every occasion in every land. But in the past when the question has been clearly presented, men have chosen independence and freedom.

With this basic faith in the aspirations of man, what are the elements of a settlement in Viet-Nam?

Whatever the exact status of the National Liberation Front—puppet or partly independent—any negotiated settlement must accept the fact that there are discontented elements in South Viet-Nam, Communist and non-Communist, who desire to change the existing political and economic system of the country. There are three things you can do with such groups: kill or repress them, turn the country over to them, or admit them to a share of power and responsibility. The first two are now possible only through force of arms.

The last—to admit them to a share of power and responsibility—is at the heart of the hope for a negotiated settlement. It is not the easy way or the sure way; nor can the manner or the degree of participation now be described with any precision. It may come about through a single conference or many meetings, or by a slow, undramatic process of gradual accommodation. It will require enormous skill and political wisdom to find the point at which participation does not bring domination or internal conquest. It will take statesmanship willing to exploit the very real differences of ambition and intention and interest between Hanoi and Peking and the Soviet Union. It may mean a compromise government fully acceptable to neither side. It certainly means that we must take considerable risks in the expectation that social and economic success will weaken the appeal of communism—and that sharing the burden and the satisfaction of helping to guide a nation will attract hostile elements toward a solution which will preserve both the independence of their country and their new-found share of power. And we must be willing to face the uncertainties of election, and the possibility of an eventual vote on reunification. We must be prepared to think about what kind of relationship such a reunified country would have to the United States, to Communist China, to the Soviet Union.

If we are willing to accept these uncertainties and run the risks—and if our adversaries are willing to submit their cause to the same arbitration, the same peaceful choice—then a settlement may be possible; and the other hazards, the hazards of widening conflict and devastation, may be ended.

Of course, such a road toward solution must be protected from sudden and violent upheaval. There must be international guarantees to back up agreement, good faith, and mutual self-interest. Foreign forces must be withdrawn, by balanced and verified stages. And we must insist that the political process go forward under the rigorous supervision of a trusted international body.

I would stress that such a settlement would not end our burden or our vigilance in Viet-Nam. President Johnson has made clear that we are ready to help with economic aid for North Viet-Nam. Further, if South Viet-Nam is to remain free to determine its own destiny and to live in harmony with the north, then we must help repair the ravages of twenty years of war. Our reconstruction effort may be nearly as costly, and more demanding of care and intelligence, than is our present military effort. And we must continue to stand guard against any violation of the agreement, which must make clear that the United States would not permit the country or the Government to be seized by an outside power.

There will be many other difficulties and problems. I do not pretend to be able to forecast all the details of a final settlement, or the process by which it may be reached. That is the task of statesmanship, in full command of all the channels of communication. But we must have our terms set firmly in our own minds. And we must reveal enough of our intentions to Hanoi to eliminate any reasonable fear that we ask them to talk only to demand their surrender.

And they must be given to understand as well that their present public demands are in fact a bid for us to surrender a vital national interest—but that, as a far larger and more powerful nation learned in October of 1962, surrender of a vital interest of the United States is an objective which cannot be achieved.

I am aware that the United States cannot proclaim in advance the precise terms of an acceptable political settlement. We cannot show all our cards before we get to the bargaining table. Nor can we make all our concessions before receiving concessions from the other side. To so commit ourselves would be to show a weakness which could not serve the cause of justice or the cause of peace.

But we ourselves must look at our own cards. And we must show enough of them to persuade our adversaries that a settlement is in their interests as well as our own.

The Senate could serve no higher function than to discuss— for the benefit of our own people, for our adversaries, and for the people of the world—a framework within which a settlement would be acceptable.

That is why discussion and debate in the Senate are now so important. We stand at the doorway of great decisions and fateful action. To decide in ignorance is to risk disaster. But if we now can clearly define our ends in South Viet-Nam, if we can at least begin discussing what our future relations with mainland China are to be, if we can adapt our means to those ends, and, most important, if we can use only that force—and no more— that is needed to accomplish these objectives, then there is hope that they may be achieved without prohibitive cost to ourselves, to the people of Viet-Nam, or to the peace of the world.

And if this debate can reach such a definition, we will know at least that we have followed the path of reason and realism as far as it now can lead.

And we will have worked to meet our responsibilities to our posterity—to walk the final mile toward peace, not so much for ourselves, as for those who will come after.

Diplomatic Alternative to
U. S. Policy

Editors' Amended Proposals*

During the eighteen months since these proposals were initially prepared by the Editors in September 1965, the lack of serious diplomatic initiatives on both sides and the quantum jump in military activities in Southeast Asia have confirmed our worst fears and destroyed whatever cautious long-term optimism we expressed then.

However, rather than reaffirm the need for decisive diplomatic action that would limit and finally end the war, we find it imperative, in view of the past political failures of the nations immediately concerned and the seeming incapacity of the United Nations, to insist once more that the steps toward a truly meaningful diplomatic initiative be undertaken at last. We do not believe that the steps outlined below are the only ones that could lead to a settlement of the Viet-Nam problem. In fact, we do not even believe that they constitute the "best" solution to the problem. In our opinion, however, they have the merit of being feasible since some of them can even be implemented unilaterally up to a certain stage.

But above all they have the merit of offering alternatives to the trend of events which, we fear, seem likely to lead to a conflict that will bury all sides in radioactive debris.

---

* From *New York Review of Books*, September 17, 1965. © 1965 by Bernard B. Fall and Marcus G. Raskin.

As we stated in the Introduction to this volume, the Editors are pragmatists. In this stage of the Viet-Nam crisis and the Second Indochina War, it is not enough to deplore what has taken place and the fact that the war has cost the lives, conservatively, of over 500,000 Vietnamese of all age groups and political persuasions (or even none at all) in the last seven years and that it is likely to cost, before it ends, the lives of many thousands of young Americans as well.* It is also not enough to consider in the philosophical sense the political failure of our position— though we ignore such a procedure at our peril.

What can—and, in the view of the Editors, must—be done is to provide the diplomatic alternatives which will end the war in Viet-Nam with due regard to the interests of the Great Powers and the people who are suffering in that unhappy land.

As a first step, we must limit the damage present military operations are inflicting on innocent people; second, we must "de-escalate" the war itself for the sake of meaningful contacts, discussions, and negotiations with the other side; and third, join with others in planning ahead for the restoration of a Viet-Nam that will not be a menace to itself, to its region, or to world peace. More generally, what we must attempt to do is end the present Viet-Nam war, and build from the diplomatic settlement a more rational American foreign policy, one that is not isolated from the rhythm of world change or opinion.

1. Now that American units are actively engaged in combat in Viet-Nam, it is specious and immoral to argue that this is not "their" war and that they are not responsible for the indiscriminate killing or maiming of civilians through the overuse of area-destruction weapons (fragmentation bombs, napalm, plant-killing and incapacitating gases and chemicals) on ill-defined nonmilitary targets. This applies equally to the use of torture and other forceful means of interrogation, and the deliberate killing of captured combatants, who should instead

---

* In a study by S. J. Deitchman, a staff member of the Institute for Defense Analyses (the "think factory" of the Joint Chiefs of Staff), based on current American and Communist "input" figures, the author estimated American casualties at 100,000 dead and 500,000 wounded in six years, on a rotating basis of 675,000 troops. (Cf. S. J. Deitchman, "The Impossible Choices in Viet-Nam," Washington *Post,* May 22, 1966.) These figures presuppose no widening of the war theater to China or Thailand; nor do they include the introduction of nuclear weapons.

have been treated as prisoners-of-war. Impressive photographic and documentary evidence has been amassed by highly responsible Western observers indicating that these acts occur in the presence of American military officials in Viet-Nam. It is now time for the United States as a civilized country, as a signatory to most of the treaties and conventions covering such acts, and as a prosecuting power at the Nuremberg War Crimes Trials, to assume its full responsibilities in the following manner:

(a) All American servicemen in Viet-Nam are to be fully and clearly apprised that, *as a minimum,* the Hague and Geneva Conventions on land warfare and on the treatment of prisoners of war and war victims fully apply in combat operations in Viet-Nam. They will be specifically informed that the Geneva Convention of 1949 extends most of the P.O.W. coverages also to "conflicts not of an international nature" (i.e., civil wars). That Convention, by the way, was ratified or officially adhered to by South Viet-Nam (1953), the United States (1955), and North Viet-Nam (1957).*

(b) Both South Vietnamese and American troops in Viet-Nam will be apprised that nonobservance of those rules by the enemy does *not* absolve the South Vietnamese and Americans from their own responsibility to observe them. The Nuremberg War Crimes Tribunal explicitly affirmed that observance of the rules of war even against a nonsignatory was "binding as declaratory of international law." There is another point to the sadism and torture. Bureaucracies may involve themselves in such matters almost antiseptically. That is a dangerous trend in government. An independent investigation of the activities and directives of American personnel and policy in regard to the conduct of the war would do much to restore responsibility in statecraft.

(c) The Liberation Front Red Cross will be recognized as a humanitarian organization for the purposes of mitigating the suffering of NLF prisoners in our hands (or in those of the South

* Although Secretary of State Dean Rusk informed the International Red Cross on August 12, 1965, that the provisions of the Geneva Conventions would now be applied in Viet-Nam, one of the editors, who traveled extensively in the combat zones of Viet-Nam in August and September, saw from first hand that the rules were by and large violated and that little actual effort had been made to advise American personnel of its obligations under the rules.

Vietnamese) and for that of alleviating the fate of American and South Vietnamese P.O.W.'s in Viet-Cong hands, for whom apparently nothing is being done and whose fate is being hushed up. In both the Indochina and Algerian wars, the French Army granted Red Cross privileges to the other side, without further implication of political recognition.* Inspection of P.O.W. camps on both sides through Red Cross representatives should become mandatory. The reputation of the United States and of South Viet-Nam could only gain, even if the implementation were to remain unilateral.

Last year we noted at this point that the Department of State was in the process of "investigating this proposal." Nothing effective was done over the following year despite the mounting evidence that Communist prisoners were being mistreated and that American prisoners in Communist hands both in North and South Viet-Nam would be the first victims of that dereliction.

With the emerging threat of war crimes trials in Hanoi, the United States began to assume her legal responsibilities as a co-belligerent in the Viet-Nam war, now that the "antiseptic" approach had failed. Whether in fact she will assume her responsibilities in full, remains to be seen. Had the above suggestions been heeded by the Administration when they were put forward in 1965 (as American combat troops began to arrive), much grief could have been avoided to many American families and to the reputation of the United States.

2. A "de-escalation scenario" could include, as a start, the introduction of the United Nations into the Viet-Nam problem. For too long, the U.N. has been kept out of Viet-Nam by all parties to the conflict for a variety of bad reasons. The friends of the United States have no particular interest in seeing her have to explain a position which she soundly condemned when

---

* It was somewhat ironical to hear the American Secretary of Defense, Robert S. McNamara, express the hope in a press conference in August, 1964, that the unrecognized North Vietnamese grant P.O.W. privileges to American pilots shot down over North Viet-Nam (which, in fact, they do) while no one thus far has seen fit to grant similar privileges to North Vietnamese regulars captured in South Viet-Nam. As an obvious result of that policy contradiction, the North Vietnamese announced on September 29, 1965, that they henceforth would treat American pilots as "war criminals." That warning, like all others, apparently went unheeded.

it was held by others in their interventionist adventures. The Soviet Union and her allies, unwilling to jeopardize peaceful coexistence and unable to control the course of events in Peking, Hanoi and (lest one forget) in the NLF; have no stake in a strong U.N. stand. Peking and Hanoi, as well as their friends in and out of the U.N., contest the competence of the organization—the more so as the Communist principals to the conflict are not members. In addition, not one of the vast bloc of uncommitted nations—uncommitted but dependent on foreign aid upon one or all three of the above groups—are prepared to jeopardize their own short-range interests in order to bring the Viet-Nam case to an effective airing before the U.N.

Some U.N. members argue privately that they fear that a demonstration of the U.N.'s impotence in the Viet-Nam case might well destroy the organization. But as the Ethiopian and Spanish cases amply showed in the 1930's, their hushing-up in the League of Nations, far from "saving" the organization, hastened its collapse and contributed to bringing about the Second World War. Still, the U.N. is more than the sum of its component nations. It can on its own call for consultation and negotiations under its auspices which could be accepted by both sides without loss of face and without the ambiguity of "signals." The U.N. accomplished this in the continuing Arab-Israeli conflict.

(a) Greater use should be made of the conventional apparatuses for contacting an adversary, such as neutral emissaries, mediators, etc., to do away with the various obscure "contacts" and "signals" that have been used in the Vietnamese situation. U.N. mediators have in the past worked well where national mediators have failed. The experience could be tried again.

(b) A military evidence of good will would be the de-escalation of air operations. If the massive bombardment of North Vietnamese military and industrial targets, including those of the Hanoi and Haiphong area, was intended to break North Vietnamese morale, it already had failed by late 1965. In addition, it had failed strategically as well, since Secretary of Defense McNamara, on June 29, 1966, in order to justify the bombing of targets near Hanoi and Haiphong, stated that the daily North Vietnamese influx of supplies to South Viet-Nam had increased by 150 per cent, and that of troops by 120 per cent since June

1965. If it had been intended to boost South Vietnamese morale, South Vietnamese Army desertion figures (93,000 in 1965 and over 130,000 in 1966) and political upheavals in Saigon and other major cities, show that the policy had failed on that score as well.*

Hence, the permanent cessation of bombing North Viet-Nam would hardly change strategic realities. It would, however, diminish the chances of dragging China, or even Russia, into the war. Hardly two years ago, in April 1964, Adlai Stevenson, as American Ambassador to the United Nations, condemned a *single* British attack on a border fort in Yemen in retaliation for an attack by Yemen guerrillas against British soldiers by saying that "both attacks and reprisals (are) incompatible with the purposes of the United Nations."† There is no reason to believe that a different system of international law prevails in Viet-Nam and in Yemen.

(c) A U.N. "Presence" would immediately be established at the seats of the International Control Commission (I.C.C.) missions both in Hanoi and Saigon, as a permanent channel for diplomatic communications. The liaison missions of the opposite sides (i.e., a South Vietnamese Army team in Hanoi and a North Vietnamese Army team in Saigon), unilaterally abolished by Ngo Dinh Diem in 1957, would be reactivated. The southern team in the North could include an American section, since Americans are now co-combatants in Viet-Nam. The northern team in the South would include Viet-Congs, since they are the main combatants in the war. (It should be remembered here that in Cyprus the government of Archbishop Makarios deals with the Turkish minority rebels under U.N. auspices; and in repeated negotiations in Malaya, staunchly anti-Communist Prime Minister Tungku Abdul Rahman did not hesitate to meet with Chin Peng, the Chinese Communist guerrilla leader.)

---

* With regard to "bombing pauses" such as the five-day pause of April 1965 and the thirty-seven-day pause of January–February, 1966, the North Vietnamese argue that they should not be expected to make concessions in return for end to an overt act of war on their territory. As a Canadian emissary to Hanoi, Chester Ronning, pointed out in June, 1966, North Viet-Nam's pre-condition to even considering diplomatic contacts with the U.S. is an unconditional and permanent end to the bombing. She yielded on her other pre-condition: prior removal of American ground troops from South Viet-Nam.

† *Yearbook of the United Nations.* New York: United Nations, 1965, p. 184.

(d) The establishment of a demilitarized negotiating area on the 17th Parallel along the lines of Pan Mun Jom in Korea could also serve to stabilize the situation between the two Viet-Nams. It would be patrolled by a reinforced I.C.C. under U.N. sponsorship.*

The above steps are but a few of those which come to mind when one contemplates the various possibilities of a "de-escalation scenario." They are simply meant to underline the fact that there is more to the ending of a conflict than the total surrender of one party, and that the intermediate steps leading to a cease-fire can be as gradual as the local or international situation warrants. But above all they are designed to increase the areas of contact so that the Vietnamese crisis can be seen politically rather than as a wholly military exercise.

3. There seems to be surprisingly little disagreement as to the type of negotiation to be undertaken. Both sides, in various statements, have referred to a Geneva-style conference, either of the 1954 or the 1962 type. Both sides also have agreed that both zones of Viet-Nam would continue to operate as separate states for a fairly long period after a cease-fire, and that both would be free of foreign troops and bases.

(a) Under the British and Russian co-chairmen, what the 1954 and 1962 truce supervisory organizations appear to lack, however, is the "teeth" that were available to other such organizations (i.e., the U.N. Truce Supervisory Organization in Palestine), that is, recourse to an effective higher political authority. The U.N. Security Council or a special U.N. supervisory committee could well fulfill that role.

(b) The reactivated control machinery can be of the I.C.C. type, expanded to include perhaps a wider range of members and a greater number of control detachments, with an actual "Peace Force" patrolling the small demilitarized zone at the 17th Parallel. The full machinery should also include (as mentioned previously, it had existed but was abolished by the South Vietnamese) joint cease-fire teams. The effectiveness of such

---

* How desirable such U.N. control of the demilitarized zone in Viet-Nam would be is best illustrated by the fact that U.S. aircraft in September, 1965, *twice* bombed by error the international bridge between the two zones of Viet-Nam and in the process wiped out the South Vietnamese police barracks located nearby. In June, 1966, also, the North Vietnamese 324–B Infantry Division was said to have crossed directly into South Viet-Nam via a sparsely-controlled part of the Demilitarized Zone.

472 • *The Viet-Nam Reader*

teams has been proven by almost twenty years of operations along the Israeli-Arab borders. The joint teams in turn would operate under the supervision of the I.C.C. and the U.N.

4. But the core problem is the relationship of the National Liberation Front and various rebel forces in the Viet-Cong to a settlement of the Viet-Nam war. The hard and stubborn fact remains that once fighting stops, the Viet-Cong—both its Communist and non-Communist elements—will be in a dominant position in South Viet-Nam because it has control of large areas of the countryside and the villages and has developed in the course of twenty-five years a gigantic and politically effective network throughout South Viet-Nam. That the Viet-Cong is a factor in Viet-Nam is a hard reality, whether the war continues, intensifies, and escalates—or is stopped.

As has been seen earlier, the NLF program does not, at least *formally,* clash with basic United States objectives. The key problem will of course be to create the proper machinery for integration of the NLF as a legal political force into South Vietnamese life.

(a) As a first stage in the de-escalation process the United States, through the good offices of the U.N. or another third party, with the U.N. acting as the guarantor, will undertake to withdraw all American troops ordered into South Viet-Nam after February 7, 1965. Under the supervision of the I.C.C. the North Vietnamese will withdraw forces that entered South Viet-Nam after February 7, 1965. The purpose of this move is to restore the military side of the Vietnamese problem to politically manageable proportions. That is, the greater number of military forces engaged, the greater the possibility for a major war.

(b) During this first stage of withdrawal a political convention of South Vietnamese should be arranged. But first the U.S., the NLF and the South and North Vietnamese governments should formally recognize an amnesty for all political forces in North and South Viet-Nam. The convention would include representatives from all factions and regions of South Viet-Nam: representatives of the NLF, other groups in the Viet-Cong, the armed forces, the Buddhists, Catholics, and other religious sects. The convention would be charged with the responsibility for working out a government which would speak for the Republic of South Viet-Nam at an international conference similar to the one held at Geneva in 1954. This time, however, it would be held under the auspices of the U.N.

5. The U.N. Geneva conference would undertake to set up political and diplomatic machinery to deal with the following problems:

(a) Withdrawal of remaining non-South Vietnamese armed forces from South Viet-Nam within a specified period.

(b) Reactivation of a reinforced and enlarged joint commission and international control commission which would have the power to investigate complaints, act as a police force under certain agreed-upon conditions, and make continuous reports to the U.N. about border difficulties and any other incidents. Its task would include supervision of the withdrawal of remaining non-South Vietnamese troops, guaranteeing of amnesty to all participants in the South Vietnamese war and controlling the release of war prisoners.

(c) The responsibility for serving on the I.C.C. should rotate among members of the U.N., the majority to be from non-Western states. Payment for this activity should come from the Great Powers.

(d) As part of the treaty the nations of Southeast Asia would be required to settle differences by legal means. Cambodia, Laos, Thailand, and North and South Viet-Nam should accept the compulsory jurisdiction of the International Court of Justice to solve border disputes and other difficulties that could be designated as legal. Other means should be explored as well through the office of the Secretary General for the use of international mediation machinery to solve seemingly "intractable" regional political problems. Such international responsibility for keeping peace will do much to stem adverse trends that have now blossomed in Southeast Asia as a result of unilateral intervention and incipient colonialism.

6. A State Treaty under U.N. guarantee would be signed by all major interested powers for the establishment of an independent and democratic South Viet-Nam.

(a) Such a treaty would include provisos on independence, human rights, and democratic institutions similar in intent to Articles 1 through 8 of the Austrian State Treaty of 1955. It will be recalled that the Austrian State Treaty, signed by the U.K.,

U.S., U.S.S.R. and France, has for the past decade satisfactorily governed the relations of Austria with both power blocs and ensured the political stability of Central Europe. The new Viet-Nam State Treaty would provide for free elections in both South and North Viet-Nam, to choose a unified government. It would be mandatory, further, to hold such elections at a specified time from the date of signing of the "Geneva" agreement. Once such elections were held, the terms that are spelled out in Article 6 and Article 8 of the Austrian State Treaty would continue to apply, but now for all of Viet-Nam.

Pending the election of a national government for all of Viet-Nam, normal trade, cultural, postal, and diplomatic relations should be instituted or restored between South and North Viet-Nam. Where any disputes occur, either within South or North Viet-Nam or between them, the issue should be referred to the diplomatic section of the I.C.C. Where the issue is judged by a majority of the I.C.C. members—and we would contemplate an enlarged I.C.C.—the issue would be brought to the U.N. Security Council for debate and action under Article 39 *et seq.* of the U.N. Charter as a threat to the peace.

(b) Agreement by the major powers that South and North Viet-Nam will not join a military security arrangement. In exchange for this neutrality, their security and borders will be protected by the U.N. either through the Security Council or the Uniting for Peace Resolution of the General Assembly.

(c) Pending unification of South and North Viet-Nam, the two countries should be admitted as members of the United Nations.

7. Armed Forces of both Vietnamese states would be strictly limited both in numbers of men in regular and paramilitary formations; and in the quantity and quality of military equipment at their disposal. Any foreign military advisers for such forces will, when required, be supplied under the authority of the Military Staff Committee of the U.N. Security Council under Article 47, their expenses to be borne by the host country.

8. The United States, through the U.N. Special Fund, should offer aid to Laos, South Viet-Nam, North Viet-Nam, Cambodia, and Thailand to fashion a common market among themselves. This may include a customs and payments union, emergency funds to finance special quick-payoff projects (U.S. and U.N.

files are bulging with such projects), and, as already suggested by President Johnson, a long-term economic development plan such as a Tennessee Valley Authority (T.V.A.) for the Mekong River project. This is a striking plan for land and water development, which already has united Cambodia, Laos, Thailand, and South Viet-Nam in this development activity. It is even said by those involved in the project that the Pathet-Lao support the Mekong project and that the North Vietnamese also would if it were extended into their area.*

9. Correlatively, a "planning bank" whose directors would be Cambodia, North Viet-Nam, Laos, Thailand, South Viet-Nam, the United States, France, Great Britain, and the Soviet Union, could direct the expenditure and planning of short-term projects in South and North Viet-Nam and the Mekong project in Southeast Asia. The planning bank could be funded by these powers under authority of the United Nations using the Economic Commission for Asia in the Far East (ECAFE) as its "parent." The organizational structure of the planning bank would allow for inclusion of both donors and recipients as board directors. The People's Republic of China would be invited to join in one of these capacities.

Barring the inability of the United States to control its present tendency toward military involvement, we can find some reasons for some cautious optimism. There are two strong political currents in Southeast Asia. One is nationalism; the other, fear of Chinese domination. The direction of North Vietnamese and of any future South Vietnamese leadership, assuming it is to have any sort of indigenous mass support, will be to achieve national political identity for their nations. This means that the local political and military leaderships will work to lessen the influence of the Great Powers (United States, France, China, and the Soviet Union) in Southeast Asia. They are aware that they cannot successfully maintain themselves by having outside troops prop up their regimes or by being wholly dependent upon outside forces politically, diplomatically, or economically.

---

* An interesting aspect of the esteem for such projects even among the VC was shown in May, 1965: the VC released a South Vietnamese official and five Japanese technicians who had been captured, when it turned out that they were engaged in surveys dealing with the Mekong project.

No doubt this restriction on outside interference will cause the Great Powers some consternation, since historically they have used the Southeast Asian region as a pawn in their game of power politics. However, that era in international politics is over, despite temporary appearances, and it is not a period which the United States should attempt to revive. If the United States is able to control her new-found penchant for global military intervention, Communist China may agree not to interfere in the politics of the smaller Asian nations. Or conversely, the increasingly-widening Viet-Nam war may cause the Chinese to abandon all restraints as they are faced with what they view as an ever tighter American encirclement.

And while American military force may succeed in bombing Communist Asia "back to the Stone Age," as General Curtis Le May the former U.S. Air Force Chief of Staff, once put it; and therefore may cow China into abandoning North Viet-Nam to its fate (a central assumption, incidentally, to the administration's present Viet-Nam policy), the political realities inside Viet-Nam will not have changed: an unrepresentative* and unreformed government in the South, still faced with continued guerrilla resistance; and a desolate North Viet-Nam whose starving peasants will forever bear witness to the relentless brutality, as well as political futility, of American power. The net result of all this will mean an even deeper alienation of China from the United States, and an intensified distrust of the United States even among those whom she now counts as her closest friends.

St. Augustine lived a debauched life before his conversion. If debauchery is a necessary prerequisite to redemption, then the situation in Viet-Nam is ripe for the next step. We may be sure that no policy a government follows is holy. However, at least the policies outlined above would be most clearly consistent with the American national interest and the role that the United States should play in the world of this generation.

---

* The September 11, 1966 elections for a constituent assembly were so tainted as to be almost meaningless: no neutralists (let alone oppositionists) were allowed to run, and of the 117 members "elected," all but forty-four were *North* Vietnamese refugees.

Chronology of Events in Viet-Nam and Southeast Asia

1945

September 2.   Proclamation by Ho Chi Minh of the Democratic Republic of Viet-Nam.

1946

March 6.   France recognizes the Democratic Republic of Viet-Nam as a "free state within the French Union." French troops return to North Viet-Nam.

September 14.   *Modus vivendi* signed in Paris between Ho Chi Minh and French Overseas Affairs Minister Marius Moutet.

November 23.   At Hai Phong French troops open fire on civilian population, kill 6,000.

December 19.   Viet-Minh forces throughout Indochina attack French troops. The French-Indochina War begins.

1947

March.   Last attempts at negotiation between French and Viet-Minh fail.

1948

June 5.   Bao Dai, French High Commissioner Émile Bollert, and General Nguyen Van Xuan sign the Baie d'Along Agreement to establish State of Viet-Nam with Bao Dai as chief of state within the French Union.

1949

March 8.

The Elysée Agreement, in the form of an exchange of letters between Bao Dai and President Auriol of France, outlines the general principles affecting French–Viet-Nam relations.

July 1.

Bao Dai decrees formally establish State of Viet-Nam and provide a basis for its organization on a constitutional framework.

1950

February 7.

Great Britain and the United States extend *de jure* recognition to Viet-Nam.

February 19.

U.S. Consulate General in Saigon is raised to Legation, and Minister accredited to Viet-Nam, Cambodia, and Laos.

December 23.

United States signs Mutual Defense Assistance Agreement with France, Viet-Nam, Cambodia, and Laos for indirect U.S. military aid to Viet-Nam, Cambodia, and Laos.

1951

September 7.

United States signs agreement with Viet-Nam for direct economic assistance.

September 8.

Delegates from Viet-Nam, Cambodia, and Laos participate in the signing of the Japanese Peace Treaty at San Francisco.

1952

July.

U.S. Legation in Saigon is raised to Embassy status. U.S. Ambassador presents credentials to Bao Dai. Vietnamese Embassy is established in Washington, D.C.

October 12.

The 200th U.S. ship carrying military aid arrives in Saigon.

1954

May 8.   Fall of Dien Bien Phu.

May 8–July 21.   Geneva Conference on Indochina. The dele-
                    gates are from Great Britain and the U.S.S.R.
                    (Joint chairmen), France, the United States,
                    Communist China, Cambodia, Laos, and
                    Viet-Nam and the Viet-Minh regime. Agree-
                    ments are signed on July 20 and 21 and the
                    main provisions concerning Viet-Nam are
                    that (1) Viet-Nam is to be partitioned along
                    the 17th Parallel into North and South Viet-
                    Nam, (2) regulations are imposed on foreign
                    military bases and personnel and on increased
                    armaments, (3) country-wide elections, lead-
                    ing to the reunification of North and South
                    Viet-Nam, are to be held by July 20, 1956,
                    and (4) an International Control Commis-
                    sion (I.C.C.) is to be established to super-
                    vise the implementation of the agreements.
                    The United States and Viet-Nam are not sig-
                    natories to the agreements. The United States
                    issues a unilateral declaration stating that it
                    (1) "will refrain from the threat or the use
                    of force to disturb" the Geneva Agreements,
                    (2) "would view any renewal of the aggres-
                    sion in violation of the aforesaid agreements
                    with grave concern and as seriously threaten-
                    ing international peace and security," and
                    (3) "shall continue to seek to achieve unity
                    through free elections, supervised by the
                    U.N. to insure that they are conducted fairly."

July 7.   Head of State and former Emperor Bao Dai
                    appoints Ngo Dinh Diem Premier of Viet-
                    Nam.

October 24.   President Eisenhower sends a letter to Pre-
                    mier Diem of South Viet-Nam stating that
                    American assistance will be given directly
                    to the government of South Viet-Nam. The
                    letter also states that the U.S. government

"expects this aid will be met by . . . undertaking needed reforms."

December 29.   Conference of France and the Associated
States (Cambodia, etc.) terminates the economic and customs union between the Associated States and France.

1955

January 1.   United States begins to render direct assistance to Viet-Nam.

February 12.   The U.S. Military Assistance Advisory Group
(M.A.A.G.) takes over the training of the
South Vietnamese Army.

February 19.   Southeast Asia Collective Defense Treaty
(SEATO)—with its protocol covering Viet-
Nam, Cambodia, and Laos—comes into
force.

April 23.   Chou En-lai and the North Vietnamese Foreign Minister give assurances of "noninter-
ference" to ex-King Sihanouk of Cambodia.

May 10.   Premier Diem forms a new Cabinet composed
largely of his own followers.

July 20.   Talks were scheduled to begin (according to
Geneva Agreement) for the preparation of
all-Viet-Nam elections to be held on July 20,
1956, to reunite the country. The government
of South Viet-Nam rejects the North Vietnamese government's invitation to discuss
the elections, on the grounds that in North
Viet-Nam the people would not be able to
express their will freely and that falsified
votes in North Viet-Nam could overrule the
votes in South Viet-Nam.

October 23.   A national referendum deposes Bao Dai, former Emperor and, since March 7, 1949,
head of State of Viet-Nam. Ninety-eight per
cent of the votes express preference for Premier Diem.

October 26.   A Republic is proclaimed by Ngo Dinh Diem

who becomes the first President of South
Viet-Nam.

December 12.   U.S. Consulate in Hanoi is closed.

1956

January.   South Vietnamese Army units occupy Tay
Ninh, principal Cao-Dai political center, leading to breakup of the organized Cao Dai
armed sect.

February 12.   Tran Van Soai, leader of an important Hoa-
Hao faction, surrenders. Ba Cut, another
principal Hoa-Hao leader, is captured on
April 13. Hoa-Hao armed insurgency continues.

March 4.   General elections for South Viet-Nam's first
National Constituent Assembly, which is to
have 123 members, results in the victory of
the National Revolutionary Movement and
other political parties supporting President
Diem.

April 6.   Viet-Nam government announces it will continue to co-operate with the I.C.C. and reiterates its position of supporting Viet-Nam-wide
elections at such time as conditions in Communist North Viet-Nam permit genuinely free
voting.

April 26.   French High Command in Indochina dissolved.

July 20.   All-Vietnamese election, as provided in 1954
Geneva declaration, fails to take place.

July 30.   Vietnamese liaison mission to the I.C.C. is
established preparatory to the transfer of
functions from the French liaison mission.

October 26.   South Viet-Nam's first constitution is promulgated and the National Constituent Assembly
is officially transferred into a National Assembly.

1957

January 3.   International Control Commission reports
that between December, 1955, and August,

1956, neither North Viet-Nam nor South Viet-Nam has been fulfilling its obligations under the 1954 armistice agreement.

May 5–19. President Diem visits the United States. He addresses on May 9 a joint session of Congress. In a joint communiqué (issued May 11), President Eisenhower and President Diem declare that both countries will work toward a "peaceful unification" of Viet-Nam.

June 30. French naval and air force training mission withdrawn at South Vietnamese request.

October 22. Bombing of U.S. M.A.A.G. and U.S.I.S. installations in Saigon; U.S. personnel injured.

1958

January 4. Large Communist guerrilla band attacks plantation north of Saigon, reflecting steady increase in Communist armed activity in South Viet-Nam since mid-1957.

May 17. North Vietnamese liaison mission to the I.C.C. withdrawn from Saigon at request of South Viet-Nam.

September 10. France and South Viet-Nam sign agreement under which France provides aid for the Viet-Nam government's agrarian reform program —1,490 million francs.

1959

August 30. Second national elections give the National Revolutionary Movement and other pro-Government political parties all seats in the National Assembly in South Viet-Nam. No opposition candidates are allowed to take their seats.

1960

April 17. North Viet-Nam protests to the chairmen of the 1954 Geneva Conference (Britain and the U.S.S.R.) against a "formidable" increase of personnel in the American Military Assist-

	ance and Advisory Group in South Viet-Nam.
April 30.	An opposition group of 18, calling themselves the Committee for Progress and Liberty, sends letter to President Diem demanding drastic economic, administrative, and military reforms.
May 5.	United States announces that at the request of the government of South Viet-Nam, the U.S. Military Assistance and Advisory Group will be increased by the end of the year from 327 to 685 members.
November 10.	South Viet-Nam government sends letter to the I.C.C. charging that Communist attacks in the Kontum-Pleiku area in October (1) involved regular army forces from Communist North Viet-Nam through Laos, (2) constituted open aggression which was well prepared, commanded by high-ranking officers, and conducted by regular forces trained in North Viet-Nam, and (3) employed weapons made in North Viet-Nam and other Communist countries.
November 11.	Military coup attempt against President Diem's regime. Rebel Col. Thi declares that President Diem is guilty of autocratic rule and nepotism and has "shown himself incapable of saving the country from communism and protecting national unity."
November 12.	Loyalist troops enter the capital and subdue the rebels.
November 13.	U.S. State Department expresses satisfaction at the failure of the coup against President Diem and also hopes that "his powers will be established on a wider basis with rapid implementation of radical reforms and energetic action against corruption-suspected elements."
December 20.	Foundation of National Liberation Front of South Viet-Nam.

1961

January 29.   Radio Hanoi praises establishment of the "National Front for the Liberation of South Viet-Nam (NLFSV)."

April 3.   United States–Vietnamese Treaty of Amity and Economic Relations signed in Saigon. National Assembly ratifies treaty on June 14.

April 4.   President Diem appeals to the I.C.C. to make an "immediate and energetic investigation" of growing Communist terrorism and subversion throughout South Viet-Nam.

April 9.   President Diem and Vice President Tho are elected by an overwhelming majority in Viet-Nam's Presidential elections.

May 5.   President Kennedy declares at a press conference that consideration is being given to the use of U.S. forces, if necessary, to help South Viet-Nam resist Communist pressures. He declares that this will be one of the subjects discussed during the forthcoming visit of Vice President Johnson in South Viet-Nam.

May 11–13.   U.S. Vice President Johnson in South Viet-Nam. Joint communiqué on May 13 declares that additional U.S. military and economic aid will be given to help South Viet-Nam in its fight against Communist guerrilla forces.

May 16.   Fourteen-nation conference on Laos convened in Geneva.

June 12.   Communist Chinese Premier Chou En-lai and North Vietnamese Premier Phan Van Dong (in Peking on a visit) accuse the United States of aggression and intervention in South Viet-Nam.

August 2.   President Kennedy declares that the United States will do all it can to save South Viet-Nam from communism.

September 1–4.   Series of attacks by 1,000 Communist guerrillas in Kontum Province. Army Command communiqué states that during the month of August there were 41 engagements between Government forces and Communist rebels in South Viet-Nam.

September 17. British advisory mission on administrative and policy matters, headed by R. K. G. Thompson (former Permanent Defense Secretary in Malaya), leaves for South Viet-Nam.

September 18. Communist forces estimated at 1,500 men attack and seize the capital of Phuoc Thunh Province, only 60 miles from Saigon.

September 25. President Kennedy, addressing the U.N. General Assembly in New York, declares that a threat to peace is "the smoldering coals of war in Southeast Asia."

October 1. Military experts of SEATO meet in Bangkok, Thailand, to consider the increasing Communist menace to South Viet-Nam. Adm. Harry D. Felt, U.S. Navy Commander in Chief in the Pacific, declares that there is no immediate prospect of using U.S. troops to stop the Communist advance in Southeast Asia, but he indicates that among the plans evolved for "every eventuality" some do call for the use of American troops.

October 2. President Diem declares at the opening of the National Assembly's budgetary session: "It is no longer a guerrilla war . . . It is a war waged by an enemy who attacks us with regular units fully and heavily equipped and who seeks a strategic decision in Southeast Asia in conformity with the orders of the Communist International." The President also says that the U.S. committee headed by Dr. Eugene Staley recommended an increase in aid both for military measures and for economic and social development.

October 11. President Kennedy announces at his news conference that he is sending General Maxwell D. Taylor, his military adviser, to South Viet-Nam to investigate there the military situation and to report on it to him personally.

October 18. State of emergency is proclaimed in South Viet-Nam by President Diem.

November 16. Following closely the recommendations in General Taylor's report, President Kennedy decides to bolster South Viet-Nam's military strength, but not to commit U.S. combat forces at this time.

December 8. U.S. State Department publishes White Paper that South Viet-Nam is threatened by "clear and present danger" of Communist conquest.

December 14. U.S. President Kennedy pledges increased aid to South Viet-Nam.

1962

January 4. A joint United States–South Vietnamese communiqué announces "broad economic and social program [to raise living standards] ... Measures to strengthen South Viet-Nam's defense in the military field are being taken simultaneously."

February 7. Two U.S. Army air-support companies totaling 300 men arrive in Saigon, increasing the total of U.S. military personnel in South Viet-Nam to 4,000.

February 8. United States reorganizes its South Viet-Nam military command, establishes new "U.S. Military Assistance Command, Viet-Nam" (M.A.C.V.) under four-star General Paul D. Harkins.

February 24. In a Peking Radio broadcast, Communist China declares her security seriously threatened by an "undeclared war" being waged by the United States in South Viet-Nam. The broadcast demands the withdrawal of U.S. personnel and equipment.

February 27.	Two South Viet-Nam Air Force fighter planes bomb and strafe Presidential palace in Saigon. Mme. Ngo Dinh Nhu slightly injured.
March 17.	Tass Soviet news agency publishes Soviet Ministry note to the signatories of the 1954 Geneva Agreements. The note charges the United States with creating "a serious danger to peace" by its "interference" in South Viet-Nam, in contravention of the Geneva Agreements, and demands immediate withdrawal of U.S. troops.
March 22.	"Operation Sunrise," a comprehensive plan to eliminate the Viet-Cong guerrillas in South Viet-Nam, begins with a mopping-up operation of rebels in Binh Duong Province.
April 20.	National Assembly pledges full support to President Diem's plan to establish thousands of "strategic hamlets" in the Communist-infested Mekong Delta during the current year.
June 2.	Canadian and Indian members of the I.C.C. find North Viet-Nam guilty of subversion and covert aggression against South Viet-Nam. The Polish delegation to the Commission rejects the charge.
June 26.	South Viet-Nam's National Assembly votes to extend its term of office by one year, to August, 1963. The explanation given is that it is impossible to hold elections now, because it would tie down troops needed against the Communist guerrillas.
July 6.	U.S. Secretary of Defense Robert McNamara declares that, while a final victory over the Communists in South Viet-Nam is years away, he is encouraged by the increased effectiveness of U.S. aid to the South Vietnamese forces.
August 20.	Sihanouk asks President Kennedy for an international conference to guarantee Cambodia's neutrality—threatens to ask for Chi-

nese Communist protection in the absence of guarantees.

October 26.　National Assembly extends by one year President Diem's emergency powers to rule by decree.

November 8.　South Viet-Nam withdraws its Ambassador to Laos as a result of Laos' establishment of diplomatic relations with North Viet-Nam.

December 6.　South Vietnamese government protests to the I.C.C. against the introduction of Chinese-made weapons and ammunition.

December 29.　Government in Saigon announces that 4,077 strategic hamlets have been completed (of a total of 11,182 to be built) and that 39 per cent of South Viet-Nam's population is now living in these communities.

1963

January 2.　At the village of Ap-Bac, in the Mekong Delta, 200 VC soldiers hold their ground against 2,000 A.R.V.N. troops supported by helicopters, airplanes, and armor (shoot down 5 helicopters, kill 3 Americans). This is the first "stand-and-fight" battle of the Second Indochina war.

January 9–11.　Adm. Harry D. Felt, Commander in Chief of U.S. forces in the Pacific, confers with Gen. Paul D. Harkins and declares, before his departure, that the Viet-Cong guerrillas face "inevitable" defeat, and he says: "I am confident the Vietnamese are going to win the war."

January 30.　Admiral Felt, Commander in Chief, Pacific, states that "the South Vietnamese should achieve victory in three years."

April 17.　President Diem proclaims an "open arms" campaign to induce Viet-Cong guerrillas to give up their weapons and return to the side of South Viet-Nam.

April 22.　U.S. Secretary of State Dean Rusk calls the

situation in South Viet-Nam "difficult and dangerous," and says that the United States "cannot promise or expect a quick victory" and that its role is "limited and supporting."

March 5. Gen. Paul D. Harkins, Commander of Military Assistance Command, Viet-Nam (M.A.C.V.) affirms that "the South Vietnamese Armed Forces have now attained the experience, training, and necessary equipment required for victory."

May 8. Riot erupts in northern city of Hué, former imperial capital, 400 miles north of Saigon. Involves Buddhist celebration of the anniversary of Buddha's birth and the flying of flags on the special day—12 persons are killed, including some children. Buddhist leaders charge that government troops fired into the crowd, while government officials say that Communists were responsible for the explosion.

June 3. Buddhist demonstrations break out in Hué. Martial law is swiftly imposed.

June 11. Buddhist monk (Thich Quang Duc) commits suicide by burning himself to death with gasoline in front of the Cambodian legation. Further aggravates religious crisis involving South Vietnamese Buddhists.

June 16. Government troops use force to suppress riots in Saigon which follow an agreement between Buddhist leaders and the government.

June 27. President Kennedy announces the appointment of Henry Cabot Lodge as the next American Ambassador to South Viet-Nam.

July 11. U.S. Ambassador Nolting returns to South Viet-Nam after consultations in Washington and issues a statement assuring continued U.S. support to President Diem and warning that "unity of purpose and purpose in action" must not be weakened by "internal dissension."

August 21.   Martial law is proclaimed throughout South Viet-Nam by President Diem after hundreds of armed police and government troops raided the main Buddhist Xa Loi pagoda in Saigon.

August 22.   Foreign Minister Vu Van Mau (a Buddhist) submits his resignation to President Diem. Also on the same day, South Viet-Nam's Ambassador to the United States Tran Van Chuong (father of Mme. Ngo Dinh Nhu) resigns. Both resign in disapproval of government policies toward Buddhists. Department of State issues statement deploring action against Buddhist pagodas.

August 26.   U.S. Ambassador Henry Cabot Lodge presents his credentials to President Diem.

August 27.   Cambodia breaks off diplomatic relations with South Viet-Nam.

August 28.   A senior M.A.C.V. officer is quoted in the New York *Herald Tribune* as saying that "there has been no evidence of any increase in the number of Viet-Cong units in the Mekong Delta even though we expected there would be because our strategy is to sweep them steadily southward and finally corner them. The delta area under our control is increasing, not spectacularly, but steadily."

August 29.   French President de Gaulle issues policy statement on South Viet-Nam. He declares that France is able "to appreciate the role this people would be capable of playing in the current situation of Asia for its own progress and for the benefit of international understanding once it was able to exercise its activity in independence from foreign influence, in internal peace and unity, and in concord with its neighbors. Today, more than ever, this is what France wishes for all of Viet-Nam."

September 2.   *Times of Vietnam* charges that U.S. Central Intelligence Agency agents had planned a *coup d'état* for August 28 to overthrow President Diem. On the same day, U.S. President Kennedy declares that the United States is prepared to continue to assist South Viet-Nam "but I don't think that the war can be won unless the people support the effort and, in my opinion, in the last 2 months, the government has gotten out of touch with the people."

September 13.   Marquis Childs is quoted in the Washington *Post* as stating that "confidential reports from high American authorities in Saigon say that the war can be won in 9 months. They say that the border with North Viet-Nam has been 95 per cent closed. The Viet-Cong guerrillas are being starved out."

September 14.   Decree announces end of martial law in Viet-Nam on September 16.

September 21.   President Kennedy orders Secretary of Defense Robert S. McNamara and Gen. Maxwell D. Taylor, Chairman of the Joint Chiefs of Staff, to go to South Viet-Nam to review the military efforts against the Communist Viet-Cong. McNamara and Taylor in South Viet-Nam from September 24 to October 1.

September 27.   Elections are held for the 123-member National Assembly. All candidates were approved in advance by the government; many were unopposed, including President Diem's brother, Ngo Dinh Nhu, and his wife, Mme. Nhu.

October 2.   In a statement released by the White House, Secretary McNamara and General Taylor reported their judgment that "the major part of the United States military task [Viet-Nam] can be completed by the end of 1965." They reported that by the end of this year the United States program for training Vietnamese should have progressed to the point where 1,000 U.S. military personnel assigned to South Viet-Nam can be withdrawn.

October 8.   U.N. General Assembly agrees to send a fact-finding mission to South Viet-Nam to investigate charges of government oppression of Buddhists. The Diem government on October 4 had invited the U.N. to send such a mission.

November 1.   "Victory in the sense it would apply to this kind of war is just months away and the reduction of American advisers can begin any time now," says Gen. Harkins in *The Stars & Stripes,* Tokyo.

November 1.   Military coup (organized by the key generals of the armed forces) against the Diem regime. Rebels lay siege to the presidential palace in Saigon, which is captured by the following morning. President Diem and his brother, Ngo Dinh Nhu, escape from the palace, but a few hours later are taken by the rebels, and while being transported in an armored carrier to rebel headquarters they are assassinated.

November 2.   Military leaders in South Viet-Nam set up a provisional Government headed by former Vice President Nguyen Ngoc Tho (a Buddhist) as Premier. The Constitution is suspended and the National Assembly dissolved. Buddhists, students, and other political prisoners arrested by the former regime are released.

November 4.   Premier Nguyen Ngoc Tho of South Viet-Nam announces formation of a mixed military-civilian Cabinet which has been approved by the military leaders. United States recognizes the new provisional government of South Viet-Nam. U.S. Secretary of State Dean Rusk rejects, during a press conference, French President de Gaulle's proposals for a neutral, independent Viet-Nam, stating that the result would be a Communist Viet-Nam.

November 15. U.S. military spokesman in Saigon reports that 1,000 U.S. servicemen will be withdrawn from South Viet-Nam, beginning December 3.

November 20. U.S. Defense Secretary Robert S. McNamara and Secretary of State Dean Rusk confer in Honolulu, Hawaii, with U.S. Ambassador to South Viet-Nam, Henry Cabot Lodge and Gen. Paul D. Harkins.

November 22. President John F. Kennedy is assassinated in Dallas, Texas. His successor Lyndon B. Johnson affirms on November 24 the U.S. intention to continue its military and economic support of South Viet-Nam's struggle against the Communist Viet-Cong.

December 19–20. U.S. Defense Secretary McNamara and Director of C.I.A. John A. McCone in Saigon to evaluate the new government's war efforts against the Viet-Cong.

1964

January 2. Secretary Rusk announces in news conference that "A Vietnamese Army group seized in the delta area of Viet-Nam some 300,000 rounds of small arms ammunition, weapons like mortars, recoilless ammunition, made in China" and that almost certainly Hanoi was primarily responsible for their infiltration into South Viet-Nam.

January 17. The joint Vietnamese-American survey of the strategic hamlet program shows serious flaws and less than 20 per cent of the 8,000 villages as viable. Gen. Nguyen Khanh was to say in April, 1964, that VC controlled close to 7 million (about 57 per cent of South Viet-Nam's rural population).

January 27.	Secretary McNamara testifies before the House Armed Services Committee: "Viet-Cong activities were already increasing in September [1963] and continued to increase at an accelerated rate in October and November, particularly in the [Mekong] Delta area."
January 27.	U.S. Secretary of Defense McNamara in a speech before the House Armed Services Committee states that the situation in South Viet-Nam "continues grave," but that "the survival of an independent government in South Viet-Nam is so important to the security of Southeast Asia and to the free world that I can conceive of no alternative other than to take all necessary measures within our capability to prevent a Communist victory." France establishes diplomatic relations with Communist China.
January 30.	Military coup, organized by Maj. Gen. Nguyen Khanh, ousts government of Maj. Gen. Duong Van Minh from power in South Viet-Nam.
February 7.	When asked at a press conference about certain neutralization proposals regarding South Viet-Nam, Secretary Rusk reiterates U.S. policy that, "If the agreements which have already been reached and which have been signed by those in the north would be fulfilled, there could be peace in Southeast Asia."
February 18.	Secretary McNamara testifies before Congress that the "bulk" of the United States forces in Viet-Nam can still be expected to leave by 1965.
March 7.	General Khanh announces a one-year reform program to rebuild South Viet-Nam's political and administrative structure and raise standard of living.
March 8–12.	McNamara and Taylor in Saigon.

March 26.   In a major policy speech, Secretary McNa-mara announces that an additional 50 million dollars would be requested for Viet-Nam, that 50 thousand more troops would be levied in South Viet-Nam, and that the war there might not be finished "in the first thousand days of the Johnson Administration."

April 27.   VC regular strength is now estimated at 45 battalions.

May 2.   Explosion in Saigon Harbor sinks U.S. aircraft transport ship.

May 12.   Secretary Rusk asks NATO members to give greater support to South Viet-Nam.

May 12–13.   Secretary McNamara and General Taylor make fifth on-the-spot review of South Viet-Nam.

May 18.   The White House requests an additional 125 million dollars for economic and military aid to Viet-Nam.

May 20.   France proposes reconvening of 14-nation conference on Laos in Geneva. This proposal is rejected by the United States and United Kingdom and endorsed by the Soviet Union, Poland, Cambodia, India, and Communist China.

May 22.   Secretary Rusk, stating the choices in Viet-Nam, says: "A third choice would be to expand the war. This can be the result if the Communists persist in their course of aggression."

June 12.   President de Gaulle calls for an end to all foreign intervention in South Viet-Nam.

June 23.   President Johnson announces appointment of Gen. Taylor to be U.S. Ambassador to South Viet-Nam and Alexis Johnson as Deputy Ambassador.

July 4–9.   Three Special Forces camps are attacked on the Highlands.

July 28.   An additional 5,000 U.S. troops will be sent

to Viet-Nam, raising total U.S. forces there to 25,000.

July 30.
A South Vietnamese naval force strikes at North Vietnamese radar and naval installations at Hon Mat and Hon Ngu islands. Units of the U.S. 7th Fleet apparently were not informed of the strike.

August 2.
A U.S. Navy destroyer on patrol in the Gulf of Tonkin is pursued by North Vietnamese patrol torpedo boats. They are driven off by gun fire and air attacks.

August 4.
U.S. destroyers *Maddox* and *C. Turner Joy* report torpedo attack. Two North Vietnamese PT boats sunk.

August 5.
United States sends reinforcements to Tonkin Bay area.

August 5.
President Johnson's message to Congress; joint resolution is introduced "To promote the maintenance of international peace and security in Southeast Asia."

August 7.
U.S. Congress approves Southeast Asia resolution (Senate vote, 88–2; House vote, 416–0). Gen. Khanh declares state of emergency in Viet-Nam.

August 11.
President Johnson signs Southeast Asia resolution into law (Public Law 88–408).

August 16.
Gen. Khanh, elected Vietnamese President by "Military Revolutionary Council," ousts Duong Van Minh as chief of state and proclaims new "constitution."

August 25.
Gen. Khanh promises liberalization of regime after repeated protests by Vietnamese.

August 27.
New Viet-Nam Constitution is withdrawn; Revolutionary Council disbands; Gen. Khanh, Duong Van Minh, and Tran Thien Khiem are named provisional leaders.

August 29.
Nguyen Xuan Oanh is named acting premier of Viet-Nam to head caretaker government. He states Gen. Khanh has suffered "mental and physical breakdown."

September 3.	Gen. Khanh resumes premiership; Taylor sees him "rested and recovered." Duong Van Minh restored to position of chief of state.
September 13.	Bloodless coup by Brig. Gen. Lam Van Phat against Gen. Khanh in Saigon. It fails.
September 20.	Tribesmen from the Special Forces mutiny against Vietnamese officers and demand autonomy for the mountain areas.
September 26.	Viet-Nam High National Council formally inaugurated and is charged with preparing a new constitution.
October 20.	Revolutionary Council presents new Viet-Nam constitution.
October 21.	United States charges Cambodian troops crossed South Viet-Nam border and seized a U.S. officer.
October 25.	United States charges Cambodians fired on U.S. helicopter in South Viet-Nam searching for missing U.S. officer.
October 26.	Viet-Nam Revolutionary Council elects Phan Khac Suu chief of state.
October 27.	Cambodia claims it shot down U.S. C-123. United States admits plane over Cambodian territory due to "map-reading error."
November 1.	Tran Van Huong named Premier of Viet-Nam.
November 2.	Russia delivers new arms shipment to Cambodia to replace American equipment.
December 4.	South Viet-Nam military leaders announce support of Premier Tran Van Huong's government.
December 20.	Military stage purge; dissolve civilian High National Council (provisional legislature). United States opposes power takeover of military and dissolution of civilian parliament.
December 21.	Gen. Khanh supports power of military versus U.S. appeals; declares Viet-Nam forces would not fight "to carry out the policy of any foreign country."

December 24.　Terrorist bombing in Saigon kills 2 Americans and wounds 52 Americans and 13 Vietnamese.

1965

January 1.　Battle for Binh-Gia. In a stand-and-fight battle, three Communist battalions attack and destroy a larger South Vietnamese force inflicting heavy casualties.

January 4.　In State of the Union message, President Johnson states: "In Asia, communism wears a more aggressive face. We see that in Viet-Nam.

"Why are we there?

"We are there, first, because a friendly nation has asked us for help against Communist aggression. Ten years ago we pledged our help. Three Presidents have supported that pledge. We will not break it.

"Second, our own security is tied to the peace of Asia. Twice in one generation we have had to fight against aggression in the Far East. To ignore aggression would only increase the danger of a larger war.

"Our goal is peace in Southeast Asia. That will come only when aggressors leave their neighbors in peace.

"What is at stake is the cause of freedom. In that cause we shall never be found wanting."

January 14.　U.S. Army reports that between January 1, 1962, and November 30, 1964, a total of 28 army helicopters were lost in battle and 58 in accidents.

February 2.　Presidential Assistant McGeorge Bundy flies to Viet-Nam for on-the-spot evaluation.

February 7.　8 American servicemen were killed and 62 wounded in an attack by 100 VC guerrillas on Pleiku. Several American helicopters were also destroyed.

The President orders "retaliatory" strikes on North Vietnamese targets. The round-the-clock bombardment of North Viet-Nam begins. Russian Prime Minister Kosygin was in Hanoi when raids began.

February 9.   Prime Minister Kosygin in a speech in Hanoi promises increased aid to North Viet-Nam.

South Vietnamese air force planes also hit North Viet-Nam.

February 11.   Viet-Cong blow up U.S. barracks at Qui-Nhon. Kill 19 U.S. troops and injure 13.

February 12.   160 U.S. and Vietnamese aircraft attack North Viet-Nam.

February 15.   North Viet-Nam asks the withdrawal of International Control Commission Field Teams.

February 16.   Peking urges "concrete action" against the U.S. American dependents are being evacuated from South Viet-Nam.

February 17.   According to a Gallup poll 60 per cent of those questioned are in favor of a United Nations force to deal with the problem of Southeast Asia and Viet-Nam. 20 per cent disapprove and 20 per cent have no opinion.

February 18.   Secretary of Defense McNamara in his annual defense review before Congress states that the U.S. has no alternative but to continue the struggle in South Viet-Nam.

February 20.   India Prime Minister Shastri outlines a proposal for the neutrality and independence of both Viet-Nams.

February 21.   It is reported that major Communist supplies enter South Viet-Nam via the sea rather than via the "Ho Chi Minh" trail.

February 24.   U.S. jet bombers are used inside South Viet-Nam for air strikes against Viet-Cong targets.

February 27.   The State Department publishes a second White Book on Viet-Nam.

March 7.   A Marine force of 3,500 men is being sent to Da Nang. This brings the total of U.S. troops in Viet-Nam to 27,000.

March 24. Secretary of State Dean Rusk explains in a press conference that the use of "police type" gases in South Viet-Nam does not constitute "gas warfare."

March 30. Viet-Cong saboteurs blow up U.S. Embassy in Saigon, kill 20 and injure 175.

April 7. President Johnson, at Baltimore, offers "unconditional" discussions to North Viet-Nam and a regional 1-billion-dollar aid program to Southeast Asia.

April 14. In a joint statement issued by Soviet Premier Kosygin and North Vietnamese Premier Pham Van Dong, a four-point program for negotiations is outlined involving withdrawal of foreign bases and troops from both Viet-Nams and reunification of both Viet-Nams at a later date through free elections.

May 4. President Johnson bids Congress for another special appropriation of 700 million dollars for Viet-Nam.

June 9. American ground combat troops are now openly committed to operations in Viet-Nam. The White House denies that this constitutes a change in U.S. policies.

June 10. There are now in Viet-Nam 54,000 U.S. troops, including 24,500 Army men, 16,500 Marines, 9,500 Air Force and 3,500 Navy men.

June 17. American B-52 heavy jet bombers attack Viet-Cong installations inside South Viet-Nam with conventional explosive bombs. By October, 1965, close to 15,000 tons of bombs were dropped by the B-52's.

June 24. The Soviet Union refuses to receive a Commonwealth mission, composed of representatives of Britain, Nigeria, Trinidad-Tobago, and Ghana; seeking to promote Viet-Nam peace talks.

The new South Vietnamese military regime of Brig. Gen. Nguyen Cao Ky breaks diplomatic relations with France.

June 25.	Red China and North Viet-Nam refuse to receive the Commonwealth peace mission.
July 8.	General Maxwell D. Taylor resigns as U.S. Ambassador to South Viet-Nam and is replaced by Henry Cabot Lodge.
July 10.	At a press conference, the President declares that in Viet-Nam "we committed our power and our national honor and that has been reaffirmed by three presidents."
July 11.	Secretary of State Dean Rusk, referring to U.S. air attacks on North Viet-Nam, states that "the idea of the sanctuary is dead."
July 15.	"Voluntary censorship" of news requested of journalists by U.S. Military Assistance Command, Viet-Nam.
	In Moscow, roving Ambassador W. Averell Harriman begins informal Viet-Nam talks with Soviet Premier Alexey Kosygin.
July 16.	Secretary of Defense McNamara, on another visit to Saigon, is met with requests for additional U.S. troops. Upon leaving Viet-Nam on July 20 he declares that "in many respects there has been a deterioration" in the Viet-Nam war since his last visit fourteen months earlier.
July 25.	Soviet surface-to-air (SAM) missiles positioned in the Hanoi area shoot down a U.S. Air Force jet fighter-bomber operating over North Viet-Nam.
July 28.	United States retaliates by bombing some of the SAM sites. In his press conference of the same day, President Johnson states that "we must not let this mask the central fact that this is really war."
July 29.	A brigade task force of the 101st Airborne Division lands in Viet-Nam, reinforcing the 173d Airborne Brigade and the 3d Marine Division already there. Fifty thousand more U.S. troops are ordered to Viet-Nam.
August 13.	The United States formally reaffirms its ad-

herence to the 1949 Geneva Conventions on the treatment of prisoners and war victims.

August 14.   The 7th Regimental Landing Team, 1st Marine Division, lands in Viet-Nam.

August 18.   The Senate approves a $1.7 billion supplementary appropriation for military operations in Viet-Nam. The presence of the North Vietnamese 325th Division (18th, 95th, and 101st Regiments) inside South Viet-Nam is reported.

September 12.   With the arrival of the 1st Cavalry Division (Airmobile), in Viet-Nam, U.S. servicemen there now number 128,500.

September 21.   The Pentagon recommends the increase of U.S. forces in Viet-Nam to the 200,000-man level.

September 23.   Ambassador Goldberg tells the United Nations that the U.S. seeks "only to insure the independence of South Viet-Nam . . . and opportunity for its people to determine their own future . . ."

October 1.   Air Vice-Marshal Nguyen Cao Ky, in a speech, states that "During the next 1,000 days this land will have to be completely controlled by free men."

October 18.   Beginning of the siege of the Special Forces camp of Plei-Mé, which inaugurates the Battle for the Highlands, in which American ground forces are for the first time committed massively.

November 4.   There are now in South Viet-Nam a total of 39 American generals and admirals, as against the South Vietnamese Army's 36, for a total American force of 154,000, as against South Viet-Nam's 550,000.

November 13.   Beginning of the Battle of Ia-Drang, pitting elements of the 1st Cavalry Division (Airmobile) against the 66th Regiment of the 325th Infantry Division, People's Army of Viet-Nam (PAVN). There are heavy losses on both sides. The battle ends on November 21.

November 30. Two American servicemen, held captive by the NLF for two years, are released to Cambodia. Military authorities in Saigon inform American troops in Viet-Nam that "mistreatment of any captive is a criminal offense."

December 7. The NLF offers a 12-hour truce for Christmas Day.

December 8. The ruling military junta in Saigon decides to set up a constitution-drafting committee of 70 to 80 members by January 1966.

December 10. Hanoi declares American peace offers "a maneuver to pave the way for further escalation of their war of aggression."

December 16. The Administration authorizes U.S. troops "to carry the war . . . into neighboring Cambodia and Laos if their personal safety is at stake."

December 19. Pope Paul VI calls for the acceptance of a Christmas truce in Viet-Nam.

December 22. The United States and South Viet-Nam decide to observe the Christmas ceasefire proposed by the NLF and propose its extension to 30 hours. The International Red Cross for the first time inspects a camp for captured Viet-Cong guerrillas in South Viet-Nam.

December 24. The Christmas truce goes into effect in South Viet-Nam. The United States begins a bombing pause over North Viet-Nam which finally is to last 37 days.

1966

January 1. Pope Paul VI appeals to all nations involved in Viet-Nam to extend the truce and a beginning of negotiations.

January 7. A report by a fact-finding team under Senator Mike Mansfield expresses fear of an escalation toward "general war on the Asian mainland" if peace efforts fail. American peace emissaries visit nineteen capitals. The Department of State issues a 14-point "Official Position" on Viet-Nam.

January 24.   A 78-hour truce for the Vietnamese Lunar New Year ends as ground operations resume.

January 31.   The bombing of North Viet-Nam resumes. President Johnson announces that the United States would present the Viet-Nam situation to the U.N. Security Council. The decision to debate Viet-Nam at a later date passes by a vote of 9–2, with 4 abstentions.

February 4.   Senator Fulbright's Foreign Relations Committee begins hearings on Viet-Nam.

February 6.   President Johnson meets with Air Vice-Marshal Ky, and the South Vietnamese Chief of State Gen. Nguyen Van Thieu in a surprise conference at Honolulu. A Honolulu Charter is signed later to embody both countries' intentions with regard to socio-economic development. Ky refuses to join in promises to negotiate with Hanoi or the Viet-Cong.

February 11.   Vice-President Humphrey visits South Viet-Nam.

February 27.   Vice-President Humphrey states that the Viet-Cong is unfit to be "part of any government."

March 2.   Columnist Joseph Alsop states that "Hanoi's current reinforcement of the VC is . . . clearly a one-shot proposition—a last high raise in the game, in fact."

March 10.   A Pentagon survey shows that 14.8 per cent of U.S. troops in Viet-Nam were Negroes at the end of 1965, while the Negro death rate in Viet-Nam for 1961–65 was 18.3 per cent. Premier Ky ousts General Nguyen Chanh Thi, the commander of the Buddhist-dominated I Corps, setting off a two-month long mutiny centered around Hué and Danang.

March 25.	Premier Ky announces that South Viet-Nam would be given a constitution within two months. (See December 8, above.)
April 14.	For the first time, American battle losses (95 killed, 501 wounded, 4 missing, in one week) exceed those of the Vietnamese and other forces (67 killed, 211 wounded).
April 26.	An aerial dogfight takes place between two American F-4C Phantom fighters and a Mig-21 fighter. The U.S. denies a Chinese assertion that the plane was shot down over Chinese territory. This is, however, confirmed by Western sources a week later. A State Department spokesman confirms that the U.S. pursues a "no sanctuary" policy in Viet-Nam.
May 3.	The Chinese Foreign Ministry announces that during 1965 a total of 43,000 tons of Soviet military equipment transited via China to North Viet-Nam.
May 7.	Premier Ky announces his intention of staying in power "at least another year." (see March 25, above.)
May 14.	Premier Ky begins the reconquest of the mutinous Danang-Hué area. Heavy fighting in Danang.
May 16.	Premier Ky selects September 11 as a tentative date for the election of a Constituent (constitution-writing but without legislative powers) Assembly.
May 24.	Last Buddhist stronghold falls in Danang.
May 27.	The State Department chooses "not to challenge" a Chinese report of May 12 that five American aircraft crossed the Chinese border and shot down a Chinese Mig-17 trainer.
June 10.	Hué is occupied by Ky forces. Buddhist rebels refuse cooperation with Viet-Cong. Buddhist military and religious leaders are detained and brought to Saigon.
June 12.	American troop level in Viet-Nam rises to 285,000.

June 29. American bombers from bases in Takhli, Thailand, attack North Vietnamese oil storage depots in Hanoi and Haiphong. Explaining the action, Secretary of Defense McNamara states that "the daily tonnage of supplies from North Viet-Nam into South Viet-Nam has increased by 150 per cent in the past year and the infiltration [of troops] has increased about 120 per cent during the same period." Vice-President Humphrey states that the raids were carried out with "amazing precision and no civilian casualties resulted." Beginning of a 'round-the-clock air offensive against North Viet-Nam.

July 8. At the conclusion of a meeting of the Warsaw Pact Powers (Soviet Union and East European bloc except Albania) in Bucarest, the sending of "volunteers" to Viet-Nam is threatened.

July 13. Premier Ky brings civilians in to his cabinet. Concern is expressed over possibility of war crimes trials of U.S. pilots in North Viet-Nam.

July 18. In a Jenmin Jih Pao editorial China formally offers its territory as a rear area for Vietnamese Communist use.

July 25. Premier Nguyen Cao Ky calls for armed confrontation with Communist China now rather than later. He urges allied forces to invade North Viet-Nam even at the risk of bringing China into the war. Cites China as the 'real enemy' in Southeast Asia, which must be faced eventually, and is adamant against the possibility of talks with the National Liberation Front.

July 26. Senator Mike Mansfield, backed by Senators Aiken, Javits, Kuchel and Saltonstall, calls on the Administration to disassociate itself 'completely and at once' from proposals for an invasion of North Viet-Nam and armed confrontation with China.

July 30.   44 Democrat and 3 Republican Representatives urge the Administration to disassociate itself from the 'spirit of escalation' being advocated by Nguyen Cao Ky, and urge new initiatives to reach a negotiated settlement. U.S. planes bomb the demilitarized zone for the first time. U.S. military spokesman says attack was ordered to counter infiltration by North Vietnamese troops and their use of the zone as a sanctuary. The International Control Commission says it will act to enforce the 1954 Geneva pact measures which specify that the zone is to be kept free of troops and materiel.

August 6.   The Polish Government confirms Cambodian charges that U.S. planes attacked the village of Thlok Trach near the Viet-Nam border and says that this endangered ICC members there. The U.S. remains silent. Members of the Americans Want To Know—a fact finding group which had visited Cambodia—describe in Tokyo the death and destruction inflicted on Thlok Trach by U.S. bombings, and say they found no evidence of Viet-Cong military activity in the area.

August 31.   French President de Gaulle holds that the U.S. must withdraw its forces from Viet-Nam before a negotiated settlement would be possible. He asks for a withdrawal timetable.

September 2.   In Cambodia President de Gaulle and Prince Sihanouk issue a communique calling on world powers to join in a pledge of non-interference in internal affairs in Viet-Nam.

September 5.   President Johnson tells 'all whom it may concern' that his timetable for a military withdrawal will be offered as soon as he sees a Communist timetable for a comparable retreat.

September 11.   117 deputies are elected to the Constituent Assembly in South Viet-Nam. Of the 5,288,-

512 people registered 80.8% turned out to vote. Elections considered a great victory against the Communists in the South and interpreted in this country as an endorsement of U.S. policy, although no Communists or neutralists were allowed to run.

September 18. In his annual report to the United Nations, Secretary General U Thant decries the idea that the war is an ideological 'holy war' whose settlement depends mainly on power politics and says that the real issue is the survival of the Vietnamese. Appeals for further efforts toward peace negotiations.

September 19. Pope Paul appeals to world leaders to end the war. He says, 'We cry to them in God's name to stop,' urges a peace settlement now 'even at the expense of some inconvenience or loss,' and warns of greater calamity. He asks that October 4th be designated as a peace prayer day—the anniversary of his appeal before the U.N.

September 21. Philippine President Marcos, in behalf of the Southeast Asian Association members, appeals to the U.S.S.R. and all Asian nations to take bold initiatives to end the war.

September 22. U.S. Ambassador to the U.N., Arthur Goldberg proposes a step-by-step de-escalation of the war by both sides, starting with a halt in U.S. bombing of North Viet-Nam. He says that the bombing will stop the moment the U.S. is assured that North Viet-Nam will make a corresponding appropriate cut in its war effort.

September 23. Soviet Foreign Minister Andrei Gromyko rebuffs the U.S. peace move, saying that he sees no serious intent on the part of the U.S. to look for a settlement and to 'stop aggression.'

September 24. The United States has 314,000 troops in South Viet-Nam.

October 8–14. Defense Secretary McNamara and newly appointed Under Secretary of State Katzenbach make a fact-finding trip to South Viet-Nam. McNamara is cautiously optimistic upon his return, telling newsmen that 'military progress in the past 12 months has exceeded our expectations.' In reply to a question regarding plans for large scale operations in the Mekong Delta, Mr. McNamara says that one battalion of the 25th Infantry Division is operating in Long An Province, which is a Delta Province, but that this does not represent any change in our military operations.

October 15. At the Moscow Conference Soviet and Eastern European Communist leaders discuss the war. Soviet First Secretary Leonid Brezhnev demands that the U.S. stop bombing North Viet-Nam and end its 'aggression' before U.S.—U.S.S.R. bloc ties can be improved.

October 24–25. The Manila Summit Conference is attended by Prime Minister Harold Holt of Australia, President Chung Hee Park of the Republic of Korea, Prime Minister Keith Holyoake of New Zealand, President Ferdinand E. Marcos of the Philippines, Prime Minister Thanom Kittikachorn of Thailand, President Lyndon B. Johnson of the United States of America, and Chairman Nguyen Van Thieu and Prime Minister Nguyen Cao Ky of the Republic of Viet-Nam. The participants agree that 'allied forces . . . shall be withdrawn, after close consultation, as the other side withdraws its forces to the North, ceases infiltration, and the level of violence subsides.' And South Viet-Nam pledges to spur its rural pacification program and provide the large share of forces needed for a 'clear and hold' action.

At the U.N. many delegates hold that an end to the bombing of North Viet-Nam would have been a more effective road to peace. Soviet Ambassador Fedorenko assails the Manila Conference.

Soviet news agency TASS charges that the conference shows that the allies aim to continue and broaden 'aggression.' Hong Kong observers hold that the communique does little to narrow the gap between the U.S. and North Viet-Nam on peace terms, noting the omission of the issues of bombing North Viet-Nam and of talking with the NLF.

North Vietnamese Premier Pham Van Dong says that the way to peace and freedom of the Vietnamese is the 'way of struggle until victory.'

China joins North Viet-Nam in rejecting the Manila proposals.

India registers disappointment in the Manila Conference. U.S.S.R. President Podgorny reiterates Soviet opposition to U.S. policy.

The Soviet bloc nations offer new aid to North Viet-Nam.

November 1. U.S. miiltary planners in Saigon urge a possible build-up of men up to 500,000 by the end of '67, and to nearly 600,000 by spring '68, and they propose partial shift in tactics to use the increased number of men in taking and holding territory to enable the South Vietnamese to make more progress in their pacification program. Pentagon leaders resist the proposals.

November 4. U.S. troop strength in South Viet-Nam at 345,000.

November 20. First reports that U.S. forces are ferrying Thai troops in helicopters against guerrillas. Number of U.S. troops in Thailand is classified, although thought to be about 35,000.

December 3. Mekong Delta reported under South Vietnamese Army control; area to be shifted to U.S. control during this month.

December 8. The U.S. has 362,000 troops in South Viet-Nam.

Selected Bibliography

NOTE: This bibliography is merely indicative of the increasingly vast body of literature available on Viet-Nam, but it groups some of the most important recent books on the subject and is representative of the diverse viewpoints now prevailing.

Aptheker, Herbert. *Mission to Hanoi.* New York: International Publishers, 1966. [Very superficial view of North Viet-Nam.]

Bator, Victor. *Viet-Nam: A Diplomatic Tragedy.* Dobbs Ferry, N. Y.: Oceana Publications, 1965. [Documented account of what author, a former Hungarian diplomat, considers U.S. diplomatic errors in Viet-Nam since 1953.]

Bouscaren, Anthony D. *The Last of the Mandarins: Diem of Viet-Nam.* Pittsburgh: Duquesne University Press, 1965. [Thoroughly uncritical, right-wing account of Diem's rule in Viet-Nam.]

Browne, Malcolm W. *The New Face of War.* New York: Bobbs-Merrill, 1965. [Report, with grimly realistic detail, of present situation in South Viet-Nam by Pulitzer Prize-winning A.P. reporter.]

Burchett, Wilfred G. *Viet-Nam: Inside Story of the Guerrilla War.* New York: International Publishers, 1965. [Communist view of South Viet-Nam war, particularly valuable on Liberation Front.]

Burling, Robbins. *Hill Farms and Padi Fields.* Englewood Cliffs: Prentice Hall, 1965. [Scholarly account of life in Southeast Asia's hinterlands.]

Cameron, James. *Here is Your Enemy.* New York: Holt, Rinehart & Winston, 1966. [Good first-hand view on North Viet-Nam today.]

Chaffard, Georges. *Indochine—dix ans d'indépendance.* Paris: Calmann-Lévy, 1964. [On-the-spot survey by one of France's best reporters, of all four Indochina states, including North Viet-Nam.]

Clubb, Oliver E., Jr. *The United States and the Sino-Soviet Bloc in Southeast Asia.* Washington, D.C.: The Brookings Institution, 1963. [Objective account of power-bloc competition in Southeast Asia.]

Crozier, Brian. *Southeast Asia in Turmoil*. London: Penguin Books, 1965. [British view, along U.S. official lines, of situation.]

Fall, Bernard B. *Street Without Joy: From the Indochina War to the War in Viet-Nam*. 4th rev. ed., Harrisburg: The Stackpole Co., 1964. [Military operations from 1946 through 1964. The author feels that same mistakes are being repeated.]

————. *The Two Viet-Nams: A Political and Military History*. 5th rev. ed., New York: Praeger, 1965. [Particularly valuable on background of North and South Vietnamese leaders and on rise of the present insurgency.]

————. *Viet-Nam Witness*. New York: Praeger, 1966. [A collection of the author's major articles over a fourteen-year period.]

Gettleman, Marvin E. (ed.) *Viet-Nam: History, Documents, and Opinions on a Major World Crisis*. New York: Fawcett Publications, 1965. [Emphasis on early background of the Viet-Nam problem.]

Gigon, Fernand. *Les Américains face au Viet-Cong*. Paris: Flammarion, 1966. [A Swiss view of the Viet-Nam war.]

Halberstam, David. *The Making of a Quagmire*. New York: Random House, 1965. [Account of 1963–64 events in South Viet-Nam by Pulitzer Prize-winning reporter of the *New York Times*. Particularly valuable on 1963 crisis.]

Hickey, Gerald C. *Village in Viet-Nam*. New Haven: Yale University Press, 1964. [The best American study on village life.]

Kahin, George McT. (ed.). *Governments and Politics of Southeast Asia*. Ithaca: Cornell University Press, 1964. [Good background on formal government structure and administrative problems.]

Kastenmeier, Robert W. *Voices from the Grass Roots*. Watertown, Wis.: Artcraft Press, 1965. [Informal hearings held by a Member of Congress in his Wisconsin district.]

Lacouture, Jean. *Viet-Nam: Between Two Truces*. New York: Random House, 1966. [Review of recent events by noted French journalist.]

Lartéguy, Jean. *Un million de dollars le Viet*. Paris: Raoul Solar, 1966. [First-hand view of American build-up through the eyes of a veteran French reporter.]

Mecklin, John. *Mission in Torment*. New York: Doubleday, 1965. [Excellent "inside" report on why U.S. erred in Viet-Nam policy estimates, by former U.S. senior diplomat in Saigon.]

Nguyen Kien. *Le Sud Viet-Nam depuis Dien Bien Phu*. Paris: François Maspéro, 1963. [Documented Communist viewpoint on South Viet-Nam since 1954.]

Nguyen Qui Hung. *Neuf ans de dictature au Sud Viet-Nam*. Saigon: n.p., 1964. [Anti-communist account of shortcomings of Diem regime.]

Ruehl, Lothat. *Viet-Nam: Brandherd eines Weltkonflikts?* Frankfurt: Ullstein Verlag, 1966. [A West German first-hand view of South Viet-Nam in 1964–65.]

Schurmann, Franz, et al. *The Politics of Escalation*. St. Louis: (private prtg.), 1966. [An analysis of American escalation and diplomatic rhetoric related to it.]

United States, Department of Defense. *Viet-Nam: The Struggle for Freedom*. Washington, D.C.: Government Printing Office, 1964. [Q's and A's about the Viet-Nam problem.]

———. *Aggression from the North: The Record of North Viet-Nam's Campaign to Conquer South Viet-Nam*. Washington, D.C.: Government Printing Office, 1965. [Evidence of North Vietnamese interference in guerilla war. Poorly documented.]

The Viet-Nam Hearings. New York: Random House, 1966. [Full text of the 1966 Fulbright Hearings on Viet-Nam.]

Viet-Nam (North). *Documents relatifs à l'exécution des Accords de Genève concernant le Viet-Nam*. Hanoi: Ministry of Foreign Affairs, 1956. [Fully documented account of refusal of South Viet-Nam to execute Geneva Accords.]

Viet-Nam (South). *La politique agressive des Viet-Minh communistes et al guerre subversive communiste au Sud Viet-Nam*. Saigon: 1962. [Fully documented account of guerrilla operations inside South Viet-Nam, 1961–62.]

———. *Communist Aggression Against the Republic of Viet-Nam*. Saigon: 1964. [A follow-up on preceding volume.]

Warner, Denis. *The Last Confucian*. London: Penguin Books, 1964. [Australian view, along U.S. official lines mostly, of events in Southeast Asia in 1960–63. Valuable insights on early Buddhist tensions.]

Contributors

Dean Acheson, former Secretary of State, is an adviser to the President of the United States.

Richard J. Barnet is Co-Director of the Institute for Policy Studies and former member of the Department of State.

McGeorge Bundy was Special Assistant to the President for National Security Affairs and is now with the Ford Foundation.

Thomas J. Dodd is a Democratic Senator from Connecticut and member of the Senate Foreign Relations Committee.

Bernard B. Fall was Professor of International Relations at Howard University and author of numerous books on Viet-Nam.

Thomas Hayden is head of an anti-poverty project in Newark, New Jersey.

Warren Hinckle is an editor of *Ramparts*.

Lyndon B. Johnson is President of the United States.

George McT. Kahin is a Professor of Political Science at Cornell University.

Robert F. Kennedy is U.S. Senator from New York.

Joseph Kraft is a journalist and syndicated columnist.

George F. Kennan is a Fellow of the Institute for Advanced Studies and former Ambassador to the Soviet Union and Yugoslavia.

Arthur Larson is the Director of the Rule of Law Center at Duke University, and was Director of U.S. Information Agency under President Eisenhower.

Don R. Larson was a professor of political science who served as the first head of the Department of Public Administration at the University of Punjab, Lahore, West Pakistan.

Russell Long is a Democratic Senator from Louisiana and Majority Whip of the U.S. Senate.

Staughton Lynd is Assistant Professor of History at Yale University.

Mao Tse-tung is Chairman of the Central Committee of the Chinese Communist Party.

Hans J. Morgenthau is Michelson Distinguished Service Professor of Political Science and Modern History at the University of Chicago and Consultant to the Department of Defense and Department of State.

Robert S. McNamara is Secretary of Defense, formerly President of the Ford Motor Company.

Wayne Morse is a Democratic Senator from Oregon and member of the Senate Foreign Relations Committee.

Nguyen Huu Tho is President of the South Viet-Nam National Liberation Front Central Committee.

Eric Norden is a free-lance reporter.

Pham Van Dong is Prime Minister of the Democratic Republic of Viet-Nam.

Gary Porter is a graduate student at the Institute for Policy Studies.

Marcus G. Raskin is Co-Director of the Institute for Policy Studies and a former member of the special staff of the National Security Council at the White House.

Matthew B. Ridgway is former Chief of Staff of the U.S. Army.

Chalmers M. Roberts is a columnist on foreign affairs with the Washington *Post*.

Walt W. Rostow is a Counselor of the Department of State, and former Deputy Special Assistant for National Security Affairs to President Kennedy.

Robert A. Scalapino is a Professor of Political Science at the University of California, Berkeley.

Robert Scheer is a journalist and member of the staff of the Center for the Study of Democratic Institutions.

Prince Norodom Sihanouk is Chief of State of Cambodia.

Edgar Snow has reported, often at first-hand, on the Chinese Communists before and since their conquest of the mainland.

I. F. Stone is a journalist in Washington, D.C. and editor of *I. F. Stone's Weekly* newsletter.

U Thant is Secretary General of the United Nations.

Gilbert F. White is Professor of Geography at the University of Chicago and former President of Haverford College.

Quincy Wright is a Professor of International Relations at the University of Virginia and former President of the American Society of International Law and American Political Science Association.

Index